遇见阿尔卑斯
Encountering the Alps

蒋静贤 著

Billson International Ltd.

Published by
Billson International Ltd
27 Old Gloucester Street
London
WC1N 3AX
Tel:(852)95619525

Website:www.billson.cn
E-mail address:cs@billson.cn

First published 2024

ISBN 978-1-80377-071-0

©Hebei Zhongban Culture Development Co.,Ltd All rights reserved.

The original content within this product remains the property of Hebei Zhongban Culture Development Co.,Ltd, and cannot be reproduced without prior permission. Updates and derivative works of the original content remain the property of Hebei Zhongban. and are provided by Hebei Zhongban Culture Development Co.,Ltd.

The authors and publisher have made every attempt to ensure that the information contained in this book is complete, accurate and true at the time of printing. You are invited to provide feedback of any errors, omissions and suggestions for improvement.

Every attempt has been made to acknowledge copyright. However, should any infringement have occurred, the publisher invites copyright owners to contact the address below.

Hebei Zhongban Culture Development Co.,Ltd
Wanda Office Building B, 215 Jianhua South Street, Yuhua District, Shijiazhuang City, Hebei province, 2207

前言 / 003
Preface / 165

第一章：淳朴的童年与少年 / 005
Chapter 1: Simple childhood and youth / 167

第二章：面对选择 / 010
Chapter 2: Face the choice / 172

第三章：退学 / 020
Chapter 3: Dropping out / 183

第四章：亲人的劝阻与关怀 / 027
Chapter 4: Dissuasion and concern of relatives / 190

第五章：签证之行 / 032
Chapter 5: Visa Trip / 195

第六章：神秘的来信 / 037
Chapter 6: The Mysterious Letter / 200

第七章：离别 / 049
Chapter 7: Parting / 212

第八章：到达异国　　/ 054
Chapter 8: Arriving in a Foreign country　　/ 217

第九章：阿尔卑斯山脚下的寄宿制学校　　/ 061
Chapter 9: The boarding school at the foot of the Alps　　/ 224

第十章：半夜的警报声　　/ 091
Chapter 10: The Siren at Midnight　　/ 255

第十一章：绘画课　　/ 093
Chapter 11: Painting Lesson　　/ 257

第十二章：体验德国家庭的生活　　/ 095
Chapter 12: Experience the life of a German family　　/ 259

第十三章　在德语课上交到的第一个朋友　　/ 103
Chapter 13: The First friend she made in German class　　/ 267

第十四章：勤奋学习　　/ 114
Chapter 14: Study hard　　/ 278

第十五章：Candle light dinner（烛光晚餐）　　/ 118
Chapter 15: Candle light dinner　　/ 282

第十六章：学校里的 disco party　　/ 129
Chapter 16: disco party at School　　/ 293

第十七章：柏林之行　　/ 134
Chapter 17: The Journey to Berlin　　/ 298

第十八章：与阿尔卑斯山的对话　　/ 160
Chapter 18: Dialogue with the Alps　　/ 324

遇见阿尔卑斯

前　言

　　教育在一个人的整个生命历程中占到非常重要的位置。每个人出生的时候，都如同小天使，是那样的纯洁无瑕，单纯而美好，可塑性极强。但由于受到后天因素的影响，例如家庭环境以及学校的教育环境，每个人的成长轨迹又变得截然不同。有的人通过家庭与学校的优良教育会最终在以后的学业、生活或工作中取得杰出的成绩，成为社会的栋梁之材；而反之，如果家庭教育十分失败，学校教育也落后或愚昧，这样的人有可能会自暴自弃，在以后漫长的人生道路中坎坷重重，困难而艰辛，变得十分脆弱与敏感，甚至悲观厌世。但也有些人会在恶劣而磨难的外部环境中依然不放弃自我，越战越勇，变得独立，坚强而勇敢。教育是一个很深刻而复杂的话题，不是用三言两语可以解释得清楚的。

　　现如今，国内的教育环境非常内卷，竞争激烈，由于社会资源的限制以及人口的众多，很多家长为了让孩子拥有一个更好的未来，使出浑身解数，给孩子报各种兴趣班，或是买价格贵得离谱的学区房，只为给孩子创造优良的升学条件，不输在起跑线上。即使争取到了上重点小学或初中的名额，家长和孩子们也会变得更为焦虑或紧张。还有些家长为了避免这样的过度竞争，让孩子拥有更自由而舒服的学习生活，选择了让孩子在年幼的时候出国留学，避免了千军万马过独木桥。但出国这条路是不是最优的解决方案呢？每个孩子真的都适合吗？如果没有父母的陪伴，而是靠自己一个人在海外求学与生活，孩子真的会适应异国的生活，真的可以忍受孤独与寂寞吗？国外的学习生活真的容易吗？显然，对不同的孩子，结果肯定不是都一样的，这取决于每个孩子的性格、处事态度、抗压和抗挫能力以及对新环境的适应力。

教育是一个漫长的过程，如果长期处于这种高压状态下，对孩子的成长是否真的有利呢？竞争固然重要，但过度竞争导致的负面效果是不是会更大呢？孩子的成长是一个循序渐进的过程，而不是一个只追求快、追求超越的过程。

本小说主要讲述了一个名叫简心的女孩，在16岁远离家乡，远离父母，在异国他乡（德国）求学的故事。在新的国度，她需要面对的不仅是孤独与寂寞，还有巨大的学习压力以及西方文化的冲击。但在她求学的道路上，她也遇到了很多善良的人，也不乏带有种族偏见的超市收银员，或是高傲而不可一世的学生。新学校里的各种活动极大地开阔了她的眼界，颠覆了她传统的认知。面对挑战与压力，她是选择妥协还是抗争呢？接下去，请跟随我一起走进简心的故事，希望在各位读者读完这本小说后，能给大家带来心灵的启迪与激荡。在教育这个话题上，获得更多的见解与想法。

感恩一切，感恩各位读者的信任。

作者：蒋静贤

2022年10月10日

第一章：淳朴的童年与少年

简心是一个单纯善良而又懂事的江南乡村女孩。她从小跟着爷爷奶奶、父母和弟弟生活在一个传统的大家庭中。在她的记忆深处，父母工作很忙，做事勤勤恳恳，照顾她生活起居的是女性长辈，妈妈或奶奶。从她懂事起，她感觉父亲经常不在家，因为他很忙碌，为了让家里人生活的宽裕点，或者也为了他自己的野心——实现个人的自我价值。但在那个年代（70—80年代），她的父亲估计不清楚，什么是个人价值。他所面对的，是每天努力工作，养家糊口。那个年代的人过得很苦，物质生活极其匮乏，哪还会关注那么多的精神需求。如果连吃饱饭都成了问题，人们生活的重心更多是拼尽全力，努力工作赚钱，让家里的每个人吃饱饭。所以在简心的童年时光，见到她父亲的时间很少，因为她父亲把大部分的精力和时间都放在了工作中，根本没有很多空闲的时间陪伴孩子，陪伴家人。小时候，简心每次看到她父亲出差回家，不知道和爸爸说啥，有点陌生感，又怕说错话，显得有点木讷的样子。父亲看她的眼神是慈爱、温暖与包容的，虽然他在家的话不多。那个年代出生的孩子多少有这种感觉，就是很想和父母说说话，聊聊家常，但父母忙里忙外，根本没空，所以时间长了，孩子们就不知道如何和父母无所顾忌地敞开心扉了。

在生活中缺少了父母高质量的陪伴与交流，简心会把自己的很多心里话跟小伙伴倾诉，可能因为她和小伙伴生活在同一个年代，很多想法会产生共鸣，彼此可以慰藉小小的心灵。在她小的时候，有很多无话不说的好朋友，大家一起玩耍，谈天说地，好不热闹。在和同龄人的相处中，她收获了自信、大方以及无所畏惧。更重要的一点是因为她成绩优异，是老师经常夸赞的对象，而这些都源于她努力、上进、自律、坚持与不甘平庸的性格。当然她也有软弱的一面，喜欢和每个人和平相处，不喜欢撕破脸弄得不开心。在学校当班干部的时候，老师让她管纪律，她总是不敢按原则办事去惩罚调皮捣乱的学生，不敢太威风凛凛，因为怕和同学的关系弄僵，而是像个和平天使一样维护班级的纪律，对那些捣乱的学生睁只眼闭只眼，或只是苦口婆心好好劝慰。所以她和班里的同学相处得都不错，因为她的这份"软弱"，也由于她所追求的平衡感，虽然在她的那个年纪，她还不懂什么是平衡感或中庸之道。她的这种"软弱"的性格有个人的因素也有家庭教育方式的因素，她的父母为人处世十分宽宏大量，不喜欢因为一点小事就和人家开战或弄得不开心，所以在简心的成长过程中，经常会听到父母念叨：为人要心胸开阔，不能斤斤计较，不然累的是自己，何必呢。这样的成长环境会告诉小孩如何做人，如何做事，孩子也会潜移默化地学习父母的行为举止。父母是孩子的第一任老师，好的家庭教育是所有成功教育的前提。

对小孩而言，日子过得很慢；可对成人而言，日子过得飞快，如白驹过隙。在简心小的时候，虽然很盼望暑假的到来，因为可以不用那么辛苦上学了，可以懒洋洋地过两个月的时间了。但这漫长的两个月，她真不知道怎么打发，因为在80年代或90年代的农村，没有什么先进便利的基础设施，只有一两个设施简陋的小卖部，可以买根冰棍吃，但也不能天天买，因为没那么多零花钱，要省着点用。父母经常教导："要节约一点，不要太浪费，如果不是很必要的东西，就不要买，乱买钱一下子就花完了，挣钱不容易。"所以简心在这样的家庭环境中长大，没有养成奢侈的习惯，即便以后家庭越来越富裕了。暑假里，简心经常和姑姑家的表妹一起玩耍或聊天，有时也会看些电视节目。那时候电视的频道少得可怜，电视节目的品种屈指可数，她们最爱看的是港剧《新白娘子传奇》《射雕英雄传》，还有后来的国产剧《还珠格格》，电视剧里的情节引人入胜，扣人心弦，演员塑造的人物形象个性鲜明。她们乐在其中，经常会讨论电视剧里面的剧情或是评价人物之间的关系。在那个年代，乡村很闭塞，没有很多新鲜的事物，碰到的人永远那么几个，能在电视剧里看到另外一个不一样的世界或不一样的朝代，对小孩而言具有莫大的吸引力，所以简心有时喜欢模仿电视剧里的人物玩过家家。那个年代物质生活虽然贫乏，但人心却很质朴善良，因为大家过的日子都差不多，没有很多贫富差异，并且经常会出现这样的现象：在整体的经济条件落后的情况下，人与人之间的心理距离会更近，当物质水平提高了，大家变得越来越富裕了，人与人之间的距离感反而会加大。这可能是因为每个人的价值观、世界观与人生观在发生改变，在不同的环境中，在不同的年代里。简心有时会很怀念那个淳朴的年代，在她长大以后。因为在那个年代每个人都显得那么单纯与质朴，没有过多的虚荣心与攀比心，也没有太多焦虑不安的情绪。其实简单而平静的生活原本就是一种美好的状态，如何把普通的日子过得如诗如画，过得那样意义非凡，关键还是取决于人的内心世界，取决于人们看待问题的角度与思维方式。

　　简心和她的亲弟弟差3岁，和很多兄弟姐妹一样，他们两个是在打打闹闹中长大的。80年代的中国实行了史无前例的计划生育，一个家庭只允许生养一个孩子。可能当时的领导人感觉中国人口实在太多了，资源分配到每个人头上少得可怜，庞大的人口会阻碍经济的发展，所以中央政府就开始推行计划生育，但传统的中国家庭都喜欢多子多孙，儿孙满堂，所以在当时那个年代计划生育的政策很多家庭都接受不了。在政府机关或城市，计划生育推行得更严格；在乡村，相比较而言，会宽松一点。简心的父母生了一个女儿以后，还想要一个男孩，觉得一个孩子太孤单了，并且他们也有典型的传宗接代的思想。所以历经万般阻碍，简心的弟弟简阳在另一个江南城市出生了。为了不让村里人发现这件事情，简心不能跟着父母躲在另外一个城市，她只能跟着爷爷奶奶留守在家乡。那个时候她才2岁半，应该是很想念母亲，所以每天傍晚都会在家门口张望，期盼母亲回家的身影。她是多么希望父母能给予她无微不至的关怀与陪伴，但显然这是不可能的，父母有更重要的事情要处理或解决。她等不来父母，便会经常问年迈的奶奶："爸爸妈妈去哪里了，我很想念他们，他们怎么一直不回家？"奶奶为了让她心里好受一点，会善意地哄骗她："爸爸妈妈有工作，一时半会回不了家，等他们忙完手头的工作，就会回来了。孩子，你要乖。爸爸妈妈实在没办法，把你也带在身边。"小小的年纪，简心的内心好希望能每天见到父母，能每天陪伴着她长大，会有多温馨甜蜜，她无法用言语表达出内心的伤心和孤独感，因为她没有办法改变现状。有的时候，人面对的很多事情是无可奈何的，心有余而力不足的，特别是人不够独立的时候，听起来有些伤感，但确实是如此的。人面对浩瀚的宇宙是多么的渺小和微不足道，宇宙、山河可以永恒，万古长存，但每个人的一生是短暂而仅有的一次。

简心的弟弟出生后，家里有了更多的欢声笑语，有儿有女，福气满满。后来简心的父亲的事业越来越顺利，也越做越大，是村里很多人羡慕的对象。吃得苦中苦，方为人上人，想要在人前显贵，一定要付出加倍的努力与勤奋，拥有过人的胆识，再加上天时、地利与人和，才能铸就一番成就。这些因素都缺一不可。

简心成绩优异，就读于市里的重点高中，每天的读书生活很紧张：5：30起床梳洗，5：45就开始第一节课的早读，课程排得满满当当，一直晚自习到晚上9：30，10：00准时熄灯睡觉。她和7个女生同住一个宿舍，平时除了读书，也没多少时间聊天玩耍，大家都很自觉，不会互相打扰对方。有的舍友晚上熄灯后还要打电筒在自己的床上温习功课。简心躺在宿舍的单人床上，经常会看到勤学的舍友的蚊帐中还隐隐约约地亮着手电筒的光。她很佩服这样勤奋好学的舍友，抓住一切空余时间努力学习，但她自己是做不到的。因为每天的学习强度已经很高，她不想把少得可怜的空闲时间全部用于学习，休息也同样重要。学习是讲究效率与方法的，而不是仅仅靠时间磨出来的。这样的高中生活真的是充实而紧张，大家都怀揣着名校的梦想，所以再苦再累，这几年都拼了。读书氛围很浓厚，每个人都不甘落后，因为读这所重点高中的都是曾经各个初中的尖子生，可想而知，竞争有多激烈。简心经常和她的一个最好的朋友文华探讨一些人生的问题，畅想未来，她们两个形影不离，互相安慰鼓励，共同成长进步，学习虽苦，但心里有梦想，有坚定的目标，就觉得人生意义非凡，未来可期。目标就如一座灯塔，可以指引着人前进的方向，如果人生失去目标，就会变得浑浑噩噩，失去生活的激情。在简心的骨子里，有强大的内驱力和上进心，她不愿意做井底之蛙，永远待在一个小地方，她想通过自己的努力，去接触更广阔的世界，设定每个阶段的目标，为此而努力，坚韧不拔地执行，当目标达成，会很有成就感，会为自己的付出与收获感到由衷的自豪。

第二章：面对选择

2001年，简心的父亲随当地的一个商务旅游团去美国和加拿大考察，这是她父亲第一次踏出国门。中国的很多大小城市他已经都跑遍了，为了寻找商机，也为了企业的业务。他虽然是企业的掌舵人，但也是一个销售，因为企业的发展规模还不是很大，很多事情需要他亲力亲为，当时她的父亲虽然还称不上有开阔的眼界与开放的思维，但比起村里很多普通人具有更为前瞻性的视野与敢作敢当、开拓进取的勇气。凭借他的努力、勇敢以及商业敏锐度，他公司的业务也在不断的扩张中。第一次踏出国门，她的父亲对外界的一切都充满着好奇心，他和十几个商业伙伴一起游历了美国与加拿大最著名的几个城市，也参观了一些现代化的工厂。

经过这次出国考察，她父亲的思维彻底打开了，他发现了国内与国外巨大的经济差异，在美国等高度发达的资本主义国家，普通人的生活已经达到了非常高的品质，他们过得悠闲自得，生活环境非常舒适美好。相比而言，当时的中国还很贫困落后。如果不出这趟国，他永远都不会感受到国内外的生活差异居然这么大。简心记得很清楚，父亲从北美回来后，带回来一大沓照片，然后意味深长地说了一句："中国和发达资本主义国家的差异还很大，大概差了100年，假设美国等国家原地不动，经济停滞不前，中国需要拼足马力，花至少100年的时间才能赶上。在加拿大的温哥华，整个城市像一个巨大的花园一样，每家每户，每个街道都鲜花盛开，草坪修剪得平平整整，实在太美了。"简心看着照片中似人间仙境的美景，心里很憧憬和向往，也感觉很陌生，觉得太不可思议了，世界上怎么会有这么美的地方，她长这么大从来没有见识过。五彩缤纷、鲜艳夺目的鲜花，高大挺拔的树木以及如绿毯的草坪，她最多只有在当地的一个公园看过，其他地方都是泥土地或水泥地，人们关注的更多的是填饱肚子，粮食有个大丰收，哪有闲情逸致在自家门口种花。乡村的土地都是用来种小麦或稻子，每家每户门口的地面都被铺成了水泥地，方便每年稻子收割后，用来晾晒稻子。这是第一次，简心隐隐地感觉到世界的多样性与广阔，感受到了自己当时的见识和眼界很狭隘，只停留在自己熟悉的这个江南小乡村。她的内心深处产生了对外面世界的一种向往，她想走出去，去看看外面的世界。因为她从未去过，她对未知的事物有着比常人更为强烈的好奇心。

自从简心的父亲从北美考察归来，他重新制定了企业未来的发展规划，决定不再贪便宜买国内二手的机器，而是通过一个贸易中介机构订购了一台德国的进口机器流水线。在那个年代，对他的小企业而言，这台进口的机器简直是天价。他相信产品质量的保证是一个企业发展最核心的因素之一，所以宁愿花高价购置国外先进的机器设备。经过数月的长途运输，机器流水线终于顺利抵达。但与此同时，企业还必须聘请海外的专业技术员工来安装设备。两个高鼻子、蓝眼睛、高个子的德国蓝领技术员工的到来，引起了全企业员工的热情关注，因为在2000年这对一个小乡村是一件轰动的大事，居然有外国人会来这个小地方。当这两个德国技术工在厂里出现，让所有村里人都兴奋不已，他们在生平头一次见到外国人。

大家很想和这两位外国技术员工交流，但发现鸡同鸭讲，根本听不懂他们说什么。简心的父亲为了克服语言障碍，只能为这两个德国技术工请翻译。晚上他躺在床上，感叹地说了一句："怎么外国的技术工人这么值钱，一个小时的工资可以抵得上这儿普通员工一个月的收入了，外国的人工真贵。那个翻译官的工作也很吃香。"

简心的父亲也是个求知欲很强的人，他想看一下这台设备的使用说明书。看着厚厚的说明书（用德语和英文写的），他突然感叹地自嘲看不懂，看不懂，不知道写的啥。歪歪扭扭的字，密密麻麻的像蚂蚁一样。下意识里，他突然感受到知识的重要性，眼界与格局的重要性，也深切地感受到自己知识的局限性。他很想知道，这些说明书里的操作流程，但觉得自己的文化知识有限，已经学不进这些洋文了。他的重心是如何经营好企业，把公司做得越来越好。

他突然想到了他的希望，他的儿女，脑子里闪过了一个很冒险又大胆的念头："对了，我可以让我的女儿先出国留学，让她接受西方教育，学这些洋文，学先进的现代化的企业管理，让她开阔眼界和格局。"但另一方面，他的内心又有点忐忑不安，自言自语："她如果真的出去了，会适应那边的生活吗？她的年纪还那么小，从来没有一个人出过远门。万一她在外面被欺负了怎么办？她小小年纪，在异国他乡，需要面对很多的困难，她能克服吗？她的心理承受能力强吗？"简心的父亲很不舍得把女儿送到这么远的国度，以后一年也见不到几次面，但也不甘心让他的子女永远待在这个小地方，因为他和天下所有的父母一样希望儿女成才，想为他们创造更好的发展机会。父母的内心对孩子的渴望总是很矛盾，一方面望子成龙，望女成凤，另一方面也希望儿女不要远离父母。长大后不要飞太远，因为他们还不放心，希望儿女平平安安，顺顺利利，儿行千里母担忧，说的就是这个意思。父母的内心总会牵挂着远在他乡的儿女。简心的父亲内心很矛盾，最终他决定先问一下简心自己的想法。

有一天，简心的父亲问她："你愿不愿出国留学，如果要出国，至少要读8年。你想出去吗？"简心沉思了片刻，果断地回答："愿意。"

虽然她的内心突然掠过一丝淡淡的忧愁，但她没有经过深思熟虑就给出了这个回答，显得有些干脆利落，这就是她做事的风格，在大是大非和重大的决策上，她绝不扭扭捏捏、拖泥带水、举棋不定，而是凭借自己的直觉与精准的判断力，立刻做出决定，不论这个决定是不是真的正确或适合，她相信自己，可以迎接挑战，可以克服障碍。当然在她做决定的时候，她从来不会去设想或放大未来会出现的种种问题，而是更多地会去憧憬一个未知而又新鲜的环境。她是一个上进心很强的姑娘，推动她一直往前走的是那颗不服输、不甘心浑浑噩噩过一生的心，她的脑子里已经在畅想一些美好的画面，并且她觉得走出去才能打开认知，有更开阔的视野，这一点和她父亲的性格尤为相似，他们都有一颗勇敢的心，做任何事情之前，不会去太多地瞻前顾后，虽然计划不够缜密，会先尝试去做，路都是人走出来的，事情也是一件件干出来的，人只有去实践、去执行，才能知道可不可行，在脑子设想一百遍一千遍都是纸上谈兵，因为实际情况总是不一定和设想的一模一样，实际的情景会在时刻的变化之中。行动起来才是最好的方法，在不变中应万变，兵来将挡，水来土掩，遇到突发状况可以随机应变，及时调整。简心的脑子里冒出了一句学到的至理名言"实践才能出真理"。是的，她现在要做的就是回答她爸爸我愿意，愿意出国留学。

　　她父亲也只是试探性地问她，出乎意料，女儿回答得那么干脆利落。她的父亲不禁有些惊诧，心里想：女儿的回答这么果断，她年纪还这么小，一个人出国不害怕吗？她是不是觉得新鲜，随便说说的。他有些似信非信，但没有在语言上表露出来。然后他接下去就继续问简心："你有没有想去的国家，你说说看。"简心想了想，直截了当地说："我也不知道，没去过外面的世界，爸爸，你帮我决定吧，选择去哪个国家。"她的父亲沉思片刻，语重心长地说："本来我想让你去美国，但刚刚发生9·11恐怖袭击，感觉美国有点不安全，再说每个人都能持枪，这在他们国家是合法的,并且我猜想,这次恐怖袭击后,美国会控制入境,可能美国留学会比以往更严格了,所以不适合选美国了。后来我想加拿大也很不错,环境优美,人民安居乐业,经济也很发达,但有一点,觉得那里的人太安逸了,缺乏斗志和上进心,大家都只忙着享受生活,可能去那里留学,会缺乏努力的动力。我考虑再三,觉得德国很不错,虽然我没去过欧洲,没去过德国,但德国是世界上闻名的工业强国,德国人做事严谨认真,这是很好的品格,我们公司的机器就是从德国进口的,你看人家产品的品质。再者,我也想,去英国、美国、加拿大或澳大利亚留学,你最多只能学会一门英语,但德国不同,你还可以学会德语,德国离英国不远,假期可以去英国补学英语,你去德国留学,可以学会两门外语,这样对你的未来发展可能更好,因为你有更多的语言优势,有更多的发展的可能性;我看大多数华人都是把小孩送去英美那些讲英文的国家留学的,我们不要随大流,我们走一条与众不同的路,虽然德国现在对中国人留学选择是冷门的。其次,德国在治安方面还是很安全的,这点比美国强。最后一点,出国留学要花费很多钱,据说德国公立的大学学费很低,有好多是免费的,只要成绩足够好,公立大学都能申请,这也能缓减一下我们的经济压力。所以去德国是最好的选择,上面几点是我分析得出来的结果,你觉得怎么样?"

简心自己对去哪个国家去留学比较好,也没什么概念,因为她也从来没去过。她相信父亲帮她选择的不会有错,所以就爽快地回答:"好的,那我就去德国留学。"回答得很干脆利落,从那一刻起,简心内心很明朗。从此以后,她的人生轨迹将发生天翻地覆的变化,这是一个重大的人生转折点,虽然那个时候她才 16 岁,这点她很清楚。

简心的母亲不是很赞同这个决定。她的母亲是一个传统的家庭妇女,她善良、端庄、严格,出生于一个当地干部家庭。因为家庭教育的严苛,使得简心的母亲养成了谨慎细心的性格,在简心小时候的印象中,她的妈妈表情经常很严肃，不经常笑，对孩子的教育也比较严厉。所以简心小的时候，内心有点怕她妈妈，做事尽量小心翼翼，不惹妈妈不开心。长大后，简心慢慢理解了做妈妈的不容易，丈夫常年为了事业出差在外，她一个女人要照顾家庭，照顾两个孩子，还要兼顾工作，生活的辛苦与不易让简心的妈妈变得有些焦虑与情绪波动大，所以才会不苟言笑。小的时候，简心不懂，她不理解，为什么自己的母亲时常一脸严肃、有点凶凶的样子。她的母亲也是很细心会照顾人的，她把两个孩子的生活起居照顾得妥妥当当，孝敬公婆，是一个典型的牺牲自我的贤妻良母。她的母亲有懦弱与内向的一面，她对新观念的接受很保守，不喜欢轻易改变，也惧怕未知，喜欢待在自己熟悉的环境中。简心完全没有遗传到母亲的这种性格，而是和她的父亲一样，喜欢迎接挑战，对未知、不熟悉的事物与环境充满了无限的好奇心。所以当简心的父亲提议，打算送她出国留学，她的母亲很反对，不同意让她出国，说："女儿还小，怕她一个人在异国他乡不适应，被人欺负；再者，也是考虑经济原因，因为有两个孩子，怕经济负担太重，出国费用太大了。简心是女儿，留在父母身边好一点，简阳是男孩，男儿志在四方，如果经济条件有限，让男孩接受高等的教育会更好点。"简心的内心有一丝痛楚，知道了妈妈的想法后，一方面她很理解妈妈的顾虑，担心女儿在外不安全，是每个做父母所操心的事情。但第二点原因是简心坚决不同意也不接受的，她感到了不公平，因为在她的内心深处，她有很强的自尊心与不甘落后于男孩的野心，并且她从来也不觉得"女孩不如男孩，女孩没有男孩优秀"，所以母亲这种传统的观念无法得到她的认可。但在那个年代的中国，很多传统的父母都会有简心母亲的这种思想，这种传统思想是根深蒂固的。

决定权始终掌握在简心的手中，因为她的父亲尊重她的决定，不论她的母亲有多么不赞同。父亲希望她成才，为她提供更好发展平台的机会，无论是男孩还是女孩。她很感恩父亲的开明与宽广的格局。一旦做出这个重大决定，她的父亲就立刻着手办理出国留学的相关事项。他不是内行，还有很多企业的事务需要他处理，所以为了节省精力与时间，她的父亲联系了当地的一个中介机构，全权负责这件事情。简心还是和往常一样，寄宿在那个重点高中，每天认真上课做笔记，日子过得紧张又充实，她的心里没有畅想太多以后的事情，而是专注于当下，专注于眼下应该要做的事情。她也没有把父亲跟她谈的出国读书的想法告诉周围的同学，甚至连最好的朋友也没提过，可能她也不确定，这件事情是不是真的能办成，因为在2001年，出国留学还是很罕见的，特别在他们那样的小地方。

生活没有任何波澜，过得平静而又祥和，简心因为学习压力太大，缺乏身体锻炼，病倒了，她被父母接到学校附近的小医院挂水。她躺在床上，看着输液管里的盐水一滴滴往下流，看着母亲像一只辛勤的小蜜蜂忙里忙外，给她倒温水、切水果，嘴里还时常嘱咐着："学习不要太辛苦了，一定要注意身体，自己照顾好自己，父母不可能永远在你身边，你一定要学会爱护自己的身体，这样妈妈才放心。"简心知道，妈妈很爱她，虽然她不会用言语表达出来，中国人都很含蓄，不愿意赤裸裸地表达"爸爸妈妈爱你，很爱你"诸如此类的话，但简心能感觉到母亲的无微不至，正是关爱她的表现。她的眼角有点湿润，鼻翼一阵酸楚，内心很想对妈妈说：妈妈，我爱你，感谢你对我的养育之恩，但她也说不出口，不知道为什么。她静静地凝视着窗外，听着清脆的鸟叫声，就这么静静地躺着，闭目养神。

挂了一两天盐水，简心感觉到身体明显好多了，就又回到了学校，投入紧张的高中生活中。日子在一天天悄无声息地过去，突然有一天，简心的父亲说："简心，爸爸带你去一个办理出国留学的中介机构，你去选一下学校。"简心满心好奇和遐想，就跟着父母去了。那个中介机构就在本市的一个高中里面，很不起眼，就两间房间，里面有三五个工作人员，虽然小小的，但里面的布置和摆设都很精致，地上还铺着很舒服的灰色地毯。进入室内后，有一位年轻的男子热情地接待了他们，眉飞色舞地介绍留学国家的情况。简心也没怎么仔细听他的介绍，而是一直盯着一个资料架，上面有各种手册与学校资料。她很想阅读一下里面的内容，但又不好意思去拿着看，就默默地听着大人们之间交谈，但事后，她记不起任何谈话的内容。那段时间，她的思绪不知道飞向了何方。过了大约一两个小时，交谈完毕，那位男子递给父母一本学校介绍手册，里面有上百所私立寄宿制学校的介绍书，主要是英国、德国与瑞士的学校。简心大致翻阅了一下，随意看了里面几所学校的简短精练的介绍，就被图中的画面深深吸引了：那里的学生有各种各样的户外运动与兴趣爱好课，有骑马、足球、篮球、帆船等，名目繁多。这和她从小到大接受的传统的中国式教育截然不同。她还发现，国外的这些学校特别注重多国语言的教学，每所学校有 4 到 5 种可供选择的语言，例如英语、德语、西班牙语、法语、拉丁文。其他的语种，简心都听过，她心里想："这个拉丁文是什么东西，还有这种语言，属于哪个国家呢？"她自言自语，而后跟着父母离开了那个中介机构。

　　过了段时日，有一天，简心和其他同学一样，正在教室里认真专心地听老师上课，突然窗口出现两张熟悉的脸孔，一开始她不敢往窗外张望，怕老师发现她上课不专注指责她，后来才听到有些同学在窃窃私语，她转去往窗外一看，才知道她的父母来了，这是第一次她看到父母出现在她的学校。教室的同学带着惊讶的表情，都在猜测，会发生什么事情。紧张的高中生活，使得学生对窗外的一丁点风吹草动都显得格外感兴趣，估计是整天闷头读书，觉得枯燥乏味，了无生趣，非常渴望外面的世界。简心跟老师请了假，跟着父母一起去了校长办公室。父母轻轻地敲了校长办公室的门，听到一声"请进"，然后简心就跟在父母的身后第一次踏入校长办公室,她没有仔细地观察室内的摆设,而是听大人们在讨论一些事情,只听到父母开门见山地说:"你好,校长,不好意思,我们准备在明年初就把孩子送去德国读书了,现在是来办理一下退学手续的。"校长听后,沉思了片刻,查了一下简心的学习档案,彬彬有礼地说:"你家女儿的学习成绩很不错,她又在外语特招班,我们学校是这儿最好的高中,她考一个国内的名校,应该不成问题。如果高考发挥失误,到时候读完高中,你们再送她出国也不晚。"简心的父亲礼貌地说:"谢谢校长的建议,我们还是决定让她现在出国了,在德国重新开始读高中,参加那边的大学入学考试。"

这是简心他们家庭内部一致达成的决定,如果学生要退学,校长也不好反对,只是他觉得有些可惜,再苦一年半就可以参加国内的高考了。就这样,简心的父母帮她办理了退学手续。她回到教室,一颗心再也按捺不住了,老师说的什么话,她也听不进去了,只看到老师的嘴唇在一动一动,她的心思早就飞到窗外去了,有点遐想联翩,至于她究竟具体想了些什么,她自己也不清楚。简心的内心既有即将探索未知与新鲜事物的喜悦之感,也有些许伤感,因为她知道,在不久的将来,她便要离开这个熟悉的环境,离开父母亲人与好友,去一个完全陌生的国度,没有一个认识的人,并且会有很大的沟通障碍,她一个人如何克服所有的困难,她的内心没有任何答案。她只是坚信一点:我要走出去,去看看外面的世界,不论将来会发生什么,不论有多困难,我都不会害怕,也不会过多地去想象未来可能会出现的问题。这是她与生俱来的勇气,她的母亲经常说她有个粗大胆,可能就是指的这方面,简心不会去细致地猜测未来会出现的各类困难或问题,而是通过自己的直觉与全局的判断力,选择一个大方向,然后勇往直前,冲锋陷阵,至于会出现什么特殊状况,实际出现的时候再一一解决。因为世间的万事万物是在不断地发展与变化之中的,人不可能精准地预测未来出现的所有可能性,患得患失、瞻前顾后，还不如确定好大方向，先去做了再说，之后根据具体状况再做出不断调整或修正，这样是最省时省力的，也不会容易把好的机会白白错过，因为考虑的时间太长久。

  一切如常，简心在学校里，最喜欢的课是体育自由活动课，因为终于不用紧绷神经，可以自己放松一下了，她有时会和好友在操场散步，走几圈，畅谈一些对未来的想法或八卦一下周围的人和事，有时也会自己一个人躲在宿舍，煮泡面吃，虽然她知道泡面没有营养，但还是忍不住泡面的美味，Q弹Q弹的，很爽口，省时又不费力，高中紧张的学习生活让她懂得了时间规划的重要性。一个人吃着香喷喷的泡面，觉得好幸福，虽然那种幸福是那么渺小，但对她而言，那个时刻能得到片刻的休息，已经是很满足了。在越小的年纪，物质越匮乏的年代，人的欲望越容易得到满足，人貌似越会有幸福感。当经济快速发展，人获得很多物质上的满足，人却越来越缺乏满足感了，因为欲望难填，得到了越多，要求越高，可能幸福感会越低。她是一个花季的少女，对未来的生活充满了无尽的憧憬与希望，就算眼前的读书生活再苦再累，她也觉得值得，因为她的眼里充满了希望的曙光，因为她觉得每天的努力会让自己越来越进步，达到一个一个自己设定的人生目标，而这所有努力的过程都是值得的。

第三章：退学

　　冬天到了，万籁俱寂，窗外很安静，班主任老师如往常一样在上着政治课，教室里的同学都很安静又认真专注地在听讲，边听边做笔记，一堂课结束之前，老师宣布："同学们，高二第一学期的期末考试在3周后举行，希望同学们在剩下的几周时间里好好复习，争取大家都考个满意的成绩，开开心心回家过年。现在你们已经是高二了，这次期末考试以后，离高三的时间越来越近了，大家一定要抓住这宝贵的一年半的时间，努力学习，为自己的将来打下厚实的基础。另外，在下课前，我想向亲爱的同学们公布一个消息，我们班的简心同学将不参加这次期末考试，因为她马上要离开我们，离开学校，去德国读书了，大家在最后的几天，和简心同学告别一下，希望她以后在德国的日子一切顺利，在德国学业有成。好了，今天就到这里，下课了。"当班主任老师的话音一落，安静的教室里顿然炸开了锅，大家七嘴八舌，觉得这个消息实在是出乎人的意料之外，在当时那个年代（2001年），在他们那样一个普通偏远的小镇，是很罕见的大事，几乎没有人会出国，就别说出国读书了，连坐飞机去别的城市旅游都是极其稀少的事情，那个年代的人哪有这么充裕的物质基础，很多人还都活在贫困的边缘，所以那个年代的学生读书普遍努力认真，因为很多人都相信或者说认为，考到好的大学可以更好地改变一个人往后一生的命运。

　　大家都向简心投去了各种各样的目光，目光中充满了深深的祝福，也充满了羡慕与不解，更充满了惊诧。大家都显得很骚动，此时，老师刚宣布的期末考试临近的事情随即抛掷脑后，变得微乎其微，大家更在意或关注的点是"咱们班的简心同学要出国了，去德国"，这可真是一个闻所未闻的大事件，不止在这一个班级里是大事件，对整个学校也是"轰动的事件"。2001年，几乎没有人出国读书，在那个小地方。简心听完班主任老师的宣布，脸颊绯红，她有点不知所措，因为这件事情，把她一下子推到了全班同学关注的中心点，她觉得自己一个人仿佛登上了舞台，暴露在了万众瞩目的聚光灯下，突然变得羞涩与不自在，但也有一点暗自窃喜，不用再像其他同学一样准备紧张的期末考试了，顷刻间，她仿佛获得一个特权或一个赦免，几乎变成了所有同学羡慕的对象。没有哪个学生会喜欢紧张备考，居然班里有个同学可以不用期末考试，可以不用再辛苦地准备国内的高考，这岂不是每个学生羡慕的事情了吗？

上完当天的晚自习，简心和其他舍友一样准时回到了宿舍，大家七嘴八舌，叽叽喳喳，开始讨论这件事情，好不热闹，给平静单调的学习生活增添了很特别的色彩。舍友小红问简心："怎么从来都没有听你提起过这件事情，你这保密工作做得太厉害了。你要去德国，德国应该是世界是很强的工业国，我只知道德国的首都是柏林，你是去柏林吗？"简心答："我也不确定这个出国留学能不能办成功，也不知道是不是我父母跟我开玩笑的，或许不是真的，所以就没说。万一说了，没弄成，岂不是笑话。再说我的重心一直在学习上，每天学习这么紧张，哪有心思关心这件事情的进度。我爸爸应该是委托给一个中介机构办理的，他们也是试试看的。从没去过德国，感觉很遥远的地方。不知道呀，是不是去柏林，没听我爸爸说。也搞不清楚学校具体在哪里。"简心话音刚落，另一个舍友就迫不及待而又充满好奇心地打探："简心，原来你们家实力这么雄厚呀，你父母能把你送出国留学，我看你平时打扮得这么朴素，完全看不出来，真的是真人不露相，太厉害了。"简心听完后，不好意思地回答:"我也不知道,我爸爸怎么突然问我要不要出国,事先没有任何预兆,也没有任何周密详尽的规划,是我爸爸今年暑假去了一趟美国和加拿大,然后就问我有没有想出国的意向。我就很爽快地答应了。"那个晚上,大家聊得很晚才入睡,但看得出来,每个人都真诚地祝福也羡慕简心,可以走出去,寻求更好的发展,去一个更广阔的地方。那一夜,简心躺在床上,睡得很浅,她在想些什么,只有她自己最清楚,或许她什么都没想,只是睡得模模糊糊的。

5:30,听到早起的铃声,简心一跃而起,和其他舍友一样,开始了平常而又特别的一天。快速叠好被子,就去了洗漱间,10分钟就已经整理完毕,然后一路小跑出了宿舍大楼,和很多学子一样急匆匆地奔向教室。5:40,冬日的清晨天空还是黑漆漆一片,学子们已经伴着铃声开启了新的一天的学习,在去教室的路上碰到熟人或朋友,有时大家还要互相寒暄几句或是小聊一会。5:45,准时就到了教室里,座无空席,开始了一天的学习。简心在这个重点高中的学习生活很军事化、制度化,时间都是紧凑地安排好的,一堂课接着一堂课,但学生们已经习惯了这样的学习节奏,所以也就不会觉得特别辛苦,因为每个学生都是如此,大家心里都怀揣着考上名校的梦想,觉得现在的努力都是值得的。简心知道,今天是她在这个学校的最后一天,所以她格外珍惜,以后要再见到熟悉的同学或是回到这个学校就不再那么容易了。她和往常一样,认真听讲,好好做笔记,虽然她知道,现在做的这些对她以后的读书可能没什么大的益处了,但她不愿意破坏课堂纪律,也不想要影响大家的学习氛围。就这样,到了晚自习,班主任老师突然出现在了讲堂上,郑重其事地宣布:"同学们,今天是简心同学最后一天在我班学习,明天她将离开校园,我们给她办一个欢送晚会,好吗?下面请简心同学上台发言,和大家做一个告别。大家欢迎。"顿时教室里响起了雷鸣般的掌声,简心有点不知所措,但最终还是大大方方走上了讲台,做了一个简短又难忘的告别演讲。她看着一张张熟悉的脸孔，有点不舍地讲道："亲爱的同学们，我很感恩认识你们，今天我要离开你们了，但你们会永远藏在我的内心深处，希望我们一起努力，不论在哪里，都要勇敢地去追逐自己的梦想。付出总有回报，努力不会被白白辜负，我们大家一起加油。谢谢大家。"话音刚落，教室里洋溢一片热血沸腾的气氛，同学们在自己的座位上准备着各种各样温暖人心的祝福卡片以及通信册，想与简心同学保持联系，不论她今后在哪里。在那个年代，先进的通信设备，例如智能手机或手提电脑还没有研发出来或普及使用，人与人之间的连接主要依靠文字的记录与书写，为了与某人保持联系，人们通常会使用书面的地址簿，里面写的主要信息有姓名、电话、家庭住址与祝福语，虽然和现在发达便捷的通信工具相比而言，显得有些原始，但却印证了那个年代的特有记忆，手写的通讯录更带有温度、更具有个性化，因为每个人的笔迹是不同的，那样的记录是记忆最真实的保存。简心看着同学们纯真而质朴的脸庞以及所做的这些事情，心里充满了感激之情，她突然变得很不舍，不舍得离开熟悉的教室，离开熟悉的同窗，虽然学习生涯紧张而辛苦，但这期间也有很多感动，很多难忘而美好的回忆，并且人只有即将离开时，所有难忘的时光会涌上心头，所有即将逝去的时光成为回忆时才会觉得弥足珍贵。失去了才会懂得珍惜，真的是这样的感受。她在同学们的通讯录上写下自己的联系方式以及祝福语，祝福语大致如此"未来可期，我们共同努力；海上生明月，天涯共此时""吃得苦中苦，方为人上人""千里之行，始于足下""永远的挚友"等等，写到后来，她的手都有些麻麻的了。在最后的一刻，同学们准备为简心同学高唱几曲，教室里的灯熄灭了，点起了星星点点的蜡烛，像燎原的星火，也似广袤漆黑夜空的繁星，简心听着同学们时而嘹亮时而深沉的歌喉，深深地沉浸其中，唱的很多歌词她都没有留意，只记得一首周华健的《忘忧草》，她也跟着情不自禁地唱了起来，"让软弱的我们，懂得残忍,狠狠面对人生每次寒冷,依依不舍的爱过的人,往往有缘没有分……美丽的人生,善良的人,心痛心酸心事太微不足道,来来往往的你我与他,相识不如相忘淡淡一笑,忘忧草,忘了就好,梦里知多少……"是的,其实每个人都有烦恼,即使青少年,应该是少年不知愁滋味,但也是有烦恼与压力的。简心虽然没有很多学习的压力,但她知道自己也有个人的烦恼,她是一个青春期的女孩,对外貌尤其在意,从初二开始,她的脸上就长了很多青春痘,原本好好的稚嫩的脸蛋一下子长满了各种痘痘,她虽然嘴上不经常提起,但内心深处还是很介意的,所以额头的痘痘,她都会习惯性地用刘海遮掩,这样会让她更有安全感一点,她也不清楚,为什么同样是父母的孩子,弟弟从来不会有皮肤问题的困扰,即使之后简阳在青春期,也没有像她一样大面积长过很多青春痘,她很羡慕弟弟或其他人白净清爽的皮肤。她不曾一次在内心中疑惑过:"老天爷,为什么你让我长这么多痘痘,为什么我不能像其他人一样拥有清清爽爽的皮肤,什么时候痘痘会消失呀?"她也一遍遍地找各种长痘痘的原因,"是不是我经常吃炸鸡腿,所以才这样?"但别人也吃呀,怎么不长。总而言之,她不知道用什么办法来解决这个"青春的问题"。她的妈妈也一度安慰她:"不要担心,过几年就会好的,等青春期过了,油脂分泌不那么旺盛,就会好起来的,你不要去挤压,不然会留下疤痕。"但她的母亲也不是所有时候面对简心的皮肤问题能镇定自若、稳如泰山,有的时候她也会随口说:"不管皮肤白皙不白皙,只要脸上干干净净,清清爽爽,就好了。长这么多痘痘,总归有些影响的。"简心心里也清楚得很,觉得这些恼人的痘痘实在太影响一个女孩的美观了,所以她开始变得不愿意照镜子,不愿意看到长满痘痘的自己,走路也喜欢低着头,害怕别人注意到她长满痘痘的脸,觉得很不舒服,或没有自信。从初二开始一直到高中,没有停过,一开始的时候她为此难过,也无奈过,但后来慢慢习以为常了,有时实在觉得心里不开心,会写日记疗愈内心。日记是她精神世界诉求的记录，是她的精神领地，是完全属于她一个人的纯粹世界，有什么想不通的或小烦恼，她都会写在日记里，这样她的内心世界的痛楚会得到释放，很多不快会释然。大人总会觉得，小孩子没有任何烦恼，就只要把书读好了，但其实不然，小孩子和青少年也有他们自己的烦恼。那个年代，父母工作都很忙碌，鲜有时间与精力关注孩子们的内心世界，只要吃饱穿暖，一切都在正轨上，就觉得没有任何问题。简心的内心世界多样而敏感，就算最好的朋友，她也不会把所有的心事都倾诉出来。有一片领地，只属于她自己一个人，她不允许别人踏入其内。她永远会留着这一片领地，当她觉得内心很累的时候，她会通过自己的方式去调节，这个阶段主要的方式是写日记，倾诉给自己听。写日记就如同把自己的心事与烦恼告诉一个素未谋面的知己，这个知己在世界上不存在，她绝不会有泄密或嘲弄的可能性，因为这是她自己臆想出来的另外一个自己。通过写日记的方式，她找到了很好的发泄口，有时去阅读自己曾经写过的文章，会觉得那个时候觉得天大的事，或者特别影响她心情的事情，已经变得不再那么重要。那里是她心灵的绿洲，也是她为自己建立的防护墙与安慰剂，她通常会用精美又振奋人心、富有哲理性的名言警句告诫自己，或宽慰自己。所以虽然痘痘长了好几年，对她有影响，但那个影响不足以让她产生深深的自卑感，因为她从很早开始，已经学会了自我调节，不论遇到多么不如意或棘手的问题。还有一点也可能是因为学业上的优秀，让她拥有更多的自信与不服输的精神。她把对外貌的关注点完全转移到了学业上，既然无法控制长痘痘，那过多地关注也无济于事，还不如把精力花在学业上。到了高中，她的脸上依然有痘痘，但她已经不在乎了，不能说不在乎，应该是已经习惯了这种状态，习惯了有痘痘的自己。人就是如此的生物，一旦习惯了，就不会觉得那么挣扎了。

简心唱着忘忧草，感同身受，她觉得这首歌的歌词写得很好，很安慰人心。唱着唱着，看着星星点点的蜡烛光，看着同学们沉浸在歌曲中的样子，她此刻觉得内心很平和淡定，忘忧草，让我们彼此相拥，淡淡一笑，忘记所有的烦恼，只记住美好开心的时刻。她在心里默念着这样的祝福。欢送会最后在一曲忘忧草中接近尾声，大家彼此送上了最诚挚的祝福，这样特别的欢送会在此前绝无仅有，因为这里最关注的是学习，并且也没有哪个学生像简心一样，书读了一年半就离开这样一个省重点高中。

第四章：亲人的劝阻与关怀

回家后，简心觉得有点不可思议，就这么中断了在高中的学业，她曾经和她最好的伙伴探讨过想考哪一所大学。她的首选是北京外国语大学，那所大学应该是很多学子梦寐以求的高等学府，那里人才济济，是中国外语专业的顶级大学。原来在她的内心深处，一直有这种想法，多掌握几门外语总是不会有错的，会拥有更强的竞争力，以后走遍世界都不会怕，天涯海角自由翱翔，和成长在不同的文化的人交流，认识来自不同民族、种族的人，想到这些，她就会觉得那样的生活会很丰富与多样化。她与生俱来就是一个喜欢挑战新鲜事物的人。现在她选择了出国留学，那应当也是一条未知而新鲜的道路，极富挑战性。

在家的日子，简心听到了很多反对与担忧的声音，除了她父亲的赞同与鼓励，其他亲人与朋友都带着或多或少的顾虑。有一次，她父亲的一个生意伙伴受邀参加一次公司的商务聚会，刚好简心也在场，这位好心的叔叔古道热肠地说："简心，听你爸爸说，你马上要去德国留学了，是真的吗？你爸妈怎么舍得把这么小的孩子送出国的，难道不担心吗，让一个小孩孤孤单单地在国外读书生活，万一碰到点紧急情况，没有一个亲人在身边，简心，你真的想去吗？你有没有仔细地考虑清楚利弊。出国后会遇到很多问题，一切都要重新开始，你想过没有。在父母身边多好，风吹不着，雨淋不湿，安全呀。"然后他顺便说了简心的父亲："你真狠心呀，要把这么小的孩子送出国，还一句德语都不会呢，就这么突然决定，她是女孩子，女孩子在外面容易吃亏的。"简心的父亲听了，没有太多的辩解，坚定自己的立场，说了一句"我相信我的女儿，应该不会有问题"。简心也没有太在意旁人的顾虑，她自己一旦打定主意，是不会轻易受旁人影响的，她会更多地听从自己内心的声音。简心的堂哥听说了这消息，也劝慰她干嘛要出国呢？在这不是挺好的吗？你好好努力，一定能考到很好的大学。去了国外，一切都要靠自己，难度系数更大，没有人可以帮到你。你有没有想过会遇到很多困难，一个人在外多不容易，又是女孩子。简心听了堂哥的话，很感激他的关心，但她最后还是回答："哥，你不用担心，我想应该没事的，我既然选择了这条路，就不会害怕以后要面对的各种困难，这些困难我在脑海里真的没想过，我想以后的日子还长，一切会慢慢好起来的，未来的难题让我在未来解决。我已经决定了，谢谢你热心的建议"。简心最亲爱的妈妈、奶奶、外婆其实都很舍不得她即将要离开，满头花白头发的奶奶有一次拽着她的手，温和而慈爱地说："孩子，在外面一定要照顾好自己，奶奶其实很不想你走，但你已经决定了，奶奶也不好说什么了，你一定要照顾好自己。"看着奶奶布满皱纹的慈祥的脸庞，简心鼻子一酸，想到了与奶奶在一起的时光。自从两岁半开始，简心就和奶奶度过的时光比父母还多，和奶奶的感情很深，这一切源于奶奶每一天对她的陪伴和照顾。简心的父母因为工作的繁忙，没有充裕的时间陪伴孩子，奶奶就成了她父母最重要的后盾与帮手。奶奶淳朴善良、认真而严肃，她的脸也时常有笑容。她生养了5个孩子，在那个贫困的年代，没有其他的经济来源，所有的收入都来自双手辛勤艰苦的劳作，没有足够的食物，奶奶经常吃发霉或已经馊了的饭菜，她想把好的东西留给孩子们吃。奶奶的爱是无私而伟大的，没有任何抱怨与不满，虽然嘴里有时会念叨一些不满的话语，经常称孩子是前世的讨债鬼，但她的内心深处充满了对自己孩子无尽的爱与奉献，她把最好的仅有的东西留给孩子们，留给自己永远都是吃剩的或变质的。她不会用温情而华丽的语言来表达对亲人的关心，而会用实际行动来表示她的那份满满的无私的情谊。奶奶走路的步伐尤其快。记得小时候，简心从来都跟不上奶奶的步伐，奶奶似乎急着去赶集一样，其实不然，这就是她独特的风格，做事或走路从来都是风风火火，从不喜欢拖延。父亲或其他的伯父、姑妈可能都遗传了奶奶认真负责、坚韧的性格以及极强上进心，所以奶奶生的孩子们，在当地都很有成就，靠的就是敏锐的生意头脑以及艰苦朴素的品格。奶奶很有福气，是真正的儿孙满堂，她自己生养了五个孩子，四男一女，孩子们每家又生了两个孩子，所以奶奶一共有10个孙儿孙女。家里真的是热闹非凡，俨然一个大家族，每次过年亲人齐聚一堂，幸福满满。有时候，亲戚朋友们会开玩笑地捉弄简心："简心，奶奶不见了，今天奶奶要去照顾其他的孙儿孙女了，不能在你们家住了。"简心总会哭鼻子，然后奶声奶气地说："不会的，奶奶会一直陪着我，她是我的奶奶。"对简心而言，奶奶暂时代替了妈妈的位置，给了她安全感，但完全替代是不可能的，奶奶就是奶奶，妈妈就是妈妈。简心的内心很渴望，妈妈能多陪伴她。可妈妈有工作，还要照顾年幼的弟弟，没有过多的时间给予她，而女孩子的内心敏感又脆弱，对情感的需求很强烈。在幼小的简心的心中，奶奶自然而然成了简心很重要的精神支柱之一。奶奶信佛，她每天都坐在一个小凳子上，默默地念经，一坐就会坐一整天，很有定力。虽然她不识字，但很虔诚，她希望佛祖能保佑家族里的每个人平平安安，健健康康。记得小时候，简心看着奶奶一直在念经，不理解她为什么这么做，究竟有什么意义。但现在的她明白了，奶奶这么做，是多么的爱自己的家人，她希望自己通过信仰和拜佛能为家人带来一生的平安与健康。

　　她马上就要离开奶奶，去很遥远的国度，不知道多久才能再见到奶奶。看着奶奶满头银发，她知道奶奶已经老了，最希望的是儿孙绕膝，陪着她，就这样平平安安地待在她身边。可这次，简心做不到了，因为她也有自己的梦想要追，或者说，不论在哪，奶奶会永远藏在她的心中，默默地保佑着她平平安安。

时光流逝得飞快，不知不觉，快过年了，在中国人的心目中，春节是所有传统节日中最重要最隆重的，这是家人聚在一起的团圆节，无论身在何方，只要是中国人，都会想尽办法赶回家，只为在忙碌了一整年后可以和家人在一起欢声笑语，聚集一堂，应该说在那个年代这种亲情感特别浓烈与淳朴。在如今这个飞速发展的时代，春节的氛围已经变得越来越淡薄了，很多家庭选择以旅游的方式欢度春节，也不再像过去一样，从初一到初十每天都有吃不完的亲戚宴席，现在的春节已经一切从简了，亲朋好友之间的走动也少了很多，大家都彼此重视私人空间，年味自然而然也不如从前了。但在2002年，简心即将离开家乡之时，那个春节还依旧过得如火如荼。除夕夜，每家每户都在为年夜饭忙碌着，贴春联、放烟花、放鞭炮，小孩子们开心地追逐嬉戏，大人们聚在一起，卸下忙碌的工作与生活，谈天说地，聊家常，夸海口。平常的日子里，小村到了夜晚就格外宁静，但在除夕夜，夜空被绚烂烟花的绽放点缀得特别迷人，耳旁时而传来噼噼啪啪的鞭炮声，简心用心感受着这热闹的节日，在心中默默地为家人、为自己祈祷，希望在新的一年一家人平安顺遂，永远开心幸福，也希望她即将开启的新生活一切顺利，心想事成。人生不如意之事十之八九，这是很多人长大后或经历了社会上种种磨难后的感慨，人的一生怎么可能永远平安顺利，无风无浪呢？总会有挫折与困难，但每个人在祈愿的时候总还是会在心中默念一切平安，这是人的愿望。虽然愿望和现实差异很大，但是人类的这种精神慰藉和心理安慰也是弥足珍贵的。简心心里很清楚，以后在异国他乡的生活，她能靠的只有自己了，父母或亲人不可能永远都会在她身边保护她或是为她处理生活中遇到的各种难题。但她不胆怯，这就是成长的过程，每个人都会长大，都要自己去面对未来的一切未知与变故，如果因为不敢独自去承受或面对，这不是真正地长大，也不是真正意义上的独立。她不害怕，因为她对自己有信心，她也不会想太多，因为未来的各种变数她无法预知，现在想太多，是庸人自扰，没有任何意义。

她看着家人坐在一起，热气腾腾地吃着年夜饭，啃着猪头肉上的香喷喷的肉骨头，听着屋外接二连三的烟花爆竹，心里很暖和，也很温馨，每一次过年都给她带来希望与憧憬，也给她带来美好时光的回忆。她的年纪还不大，也不禁会感叹一句"时间过得好快呀，又过年了，新的一年到来了，新的一年，继续努力吧，开开心心的"。

第五章：签证之行

　　过完年后，有一天，简心的父亲出差回来后，就迫不及待地对她说："准备一下，这几天我们要去德国驻上海大使馆签证，你有了学生签证，即将就要动身去德国了。"简心听了，都不知道签证是个什么东西，因为她长这么大，一直在这个小地方待着，最多跟父母和弟弟一起去周边的一两个城市玩过几天，根本没有踏出国门。对她而言，这个词如同来自外太空，她摸不着头脑，究竟需要她干嘛，反正就听着她父亲的安排与指示，他说怎么做就怎么。过了没多久，便等到了大使馆的回复，简心的父母准备带着她去德国驻上海大使馆签证。那一天，她坐在车上，觉得车子开了很久很久，长这么大很少坐这么长时间的汽车，车窗外的建筑群以及成排的树木仿佛长了脚似的，在不停地移动。她虽然知道是车子在动，但坐在位置上，她又感觉车位是静止不动的，动的是窗户外的所有事物，这就是视角的问题。人站在不同的角度，用不同的思维方式对待同样的事物，得出的结果或是做出的选择是截然不同的。不同性格的人看待同样的问题，得出的答案或选择也是差异很大。简心还不理解这么深奥的人生哲理，但她心里清楚，不去过多地担忧未来，只是过好当下的每一天，每一刻，现在的她完全沉浸在当下的情况中。她父亲在途中突然提起："简心，今天和你一起去德国大使馆签证的还有另外两个同学，他们是在市区上学的，也去德国读高中。他们两个是去的同一所寄宿制高中，你一个人去另外一所，你们到时候一起坐飞机也有个伴，这样我们也放心点，因为爸爸妈妈不能亲自送你去德国了。你们好好相处，以后在德国有时间也能聚聚，出门在外一个亲人都没有，老乡就算是亲人了。"简心听了，默默地点了点头，乖巧地回答："知道了，爸爸。"汽车行驶了三个半小时左右，便顺利到达了德国驻中国大使馆的停车场。按照预约的面试时间，简心战战兢兢地一个人排队进入大使馆，她的父母不允许进入馆内，只好在车里耐心地等待。简心第一次去签证，对所有的流程都不熟悉，只看到一个保安拿着电警棍在门口检查申请者的随身箱包以及所带的资料袋，语气严厉，态度不是很友好。简心被告知，不允许带随身的包以及其他物品进入大使馆，只允许带签证的文件资料，她就小心翼翼地把包放在了储藏箱内，然后经过安检，顺利进入了馆内。大使馆内的工作人员示意她，需要取一个号码，轮到她的时候，电子屏幕上会自动出现她所抽取的号码，如果没有出现对应的号码，她就需要耐心等待。她环顾四周，发现申请签证的人很多，整个大厅都塞满了，她心里暗暗地想："原来也有这么多人要出国，我还以为就很少的一部分人，我们那里几乎都没人出国，我的见识真的太少了。"她不愿意人挤人，就在角落里找到一个座位安安静静地坐了下来，耐心地等待着。那个时候，她还不怎么敢主动和陌生人搭话或聊天，有点胆怯，也有点不知所措，不知道如何开场。这一切对她而言新奇而陌生，馆内的申请者都穿得很新潮、时尚又体面，而她瞅了瞅自己的穿着，一点也不洋气，只有浓浓的乡土味，总觉得自己的打扮和这个高级场所格格不入，有些许的不自在，但也没有深究。她心里想："爸爸不是说有两个老乡也来签证的吗，我都不知道他们长什么样，从来没见过，他们在哪里，如果坐在一起，还能一起聊聊天，也不会觉得时间过得这么漫长。算了，我都不认识他们，也不知道他们到底在哪，就耐心地坐着等吧。"眼看着一个个申请者在面试官面前逗留了很久，她也很纳闷到底问了他们什么重要的问题。电子屏幕上的等待号码在频繁地更换，但始终还是没有轮到简心。时间在滴滴答答地悄然流逝，这一等便已经等了5个多小时,依然没有轮到她面试。这时候她已经等得有些心急火燎,十分不耐烦了,肚子也咕噜咕噜地叫了起来,她突然意识到好饿,但大使馆内不允许吃任何东西。她很疑惑,不确定需要等多久才真正轮到她,还要1个小时左右就要闭馆了。她的内心有点急,父母带着她,开了三个半小时才到达的,在馆内又等了这么长时间,几乎一天的时间都耗在上面了,总不能今天轮不到她办理吧?她在心里默默地祈祷:"老天保佑,保佑我能顺利通过签证,保佑我今天能轮到。"在闭馆前的半个小时,终于轮到了她。她整了整衣服,清点一下需要的资料,然后大步流星地走向面试官。面试官也是一脸严肃,不苟言笑,简心恭恭敬敬地坐着,等待着面试官的提问。一开始,她还有些担心,怕会有很多刁钻的问题或会用英文问她一些事情,但这些担心完全是多余的。面试官用中文简短地问了很基础的问题,例如"为什么要去德国留学?""去德国读书的话,住在哪里?"简心不假思索,直截了当地回答了面试官的提问,不加任何修饰。面试官没有说什么,把资料整理了一下,然后就告诉她:"面试结束了,回家等通知,签证会在两个礼拜或一个月左右发出。"简心内心很感激签证官的宽容与不刁难,让她顺利通过了面试这一关,她原本想着这个面试可能会很复杂,结果却出人意料,整个问答的过程简单而轻松。面试结束后,她出了大使馆的大门,父母关切地问:"简心,你肚子饿了吧,等了这么长时间。签证顺利吗?"简心如释重负地回答:"爸爸妈妈,你们放心,签证一切都顺利,虽然我等了很久才轮到,但面试官问的问题很简单,都是用中文问的,我一开始还担心,自己的英文口语不够流利,或怕我听不懂他的提问。一切都好,应该没问题。面试官让我在家耐心等待结果。"父母听了简心肯定的答复,一块石头终于落地了,温和地说:"如果签证没什么问题的话,一切都行驶在正轨上,就可以着手安排接下来的事项了。"

当他们刚准备离开的时候,简心突然看到两个年轻人正朝他们的方向走过来，父亲彬彬有礼地跟他们打招呼。简心仔细地打量了一番这两个年轻人，两个人都打扮得很前卫时尚，男子穿了一件黑色羊绒大衣，显得风度翩翩，而女子穿着时髦而又俏皮的呢绒裙子，显得既有青春活力而又气质非凡。简心在心里嘀咕："这两个年轻人应该也是准备去德国读书的，上次父亲好像提起过。"顿时，有一种羞涩感夹杂着些许的不自信涌上了简心的心头，她感到自己的打扮很老土，跟这两位气宇轩昂、精神抖擞的年轻人根本不在一个层次上。再加上她常年脸部长满青春痘，所以显得格外不自信。她心里悄悄地在跟自己对话："呀，我的脸怎么见人，人家的脸蛋干干净净、清清爽爽的。我的脸长满痘痘。"另一个声音又给她敲响了警钟："简心，你不用介意这么多，人家哪有空来关注你脸上的痘痘，没事的，不要想那么多，你要自信点，不用去揣摩人家会怎么看待你，做好自己就可以了。"两种不同的声音在她的耳畔响起，显得自相矛盾，在一个劲地相互抗衡。原来每个人的性格都有不同的面，每个人的内心深处都有不同的声音，正所谓"一念天堂，一念地狱"，在每个人的青春时代，当人还不够沉稳，会更容易受外界的影响，会更在乎他人与世俗的看法。但值得庆幸的是，最终简心还是被强大的自我心里暗示与调节能力所推动，不再顾及一些消极而胆怯的想法，她大大方方地和这两个年轻人握手聊天，谈了一些自己的近况以及对未来的畅想。他们三个聊得很开心，同龄人之间永远有说不完的话题。简心和那个女生属于外向一点的性格，不怕生，很容易和陌生人聊起来，不会有太多的忌讳或防备心，她们都很热衷于分享。个男子略显得内敛和沉稳，话不多，应该是一个老实可靠而又单纯的人。大人之间也在热闹地交流，他们都有一个共同的目标：把孩子顺利送去德国留学。所以整个谈话的内容就围绕着这个主题，除此之外，没有其他更深入的交流。大人之间的谈话总会更带有边界感与警惕感，而年轻人之间的交流显得开放与有趣。通过聊天，简心得知这两个和她年纪相仿的年轻人都是在市里读重点高中的，其中那个女生是体育特长生，她的文化成绩一般，但体育成绩尤为拔尖，每次跑步比赛都名列前茅。行行出状元，每个人都有自己独一无二的天赋与特长。简心觉得城里的学校和乡村或区里的就是不一样，教学更灵活，更注重个性化培养，因材施教，所以这两位年轻人显得很有气质，充满自信。城市里丰富的文化氛围以及宽松灵活的教育体制滋养了他们的心灵。而相对而言，简心觉得自己接受的教育更传统与僵化，也更淳朴，具有浓浓的乡土气息。这不是一种不自信或自我贬低的看法，而是客观的自我剖析。

第六章：神秘的来信

　　上海签证之行一切顺利，接下来的日子，简心就在家耐心地等待通知，平静地过着每一天。有一天，简心和往常一样，在父母的公司里玩耍，家族企业就是如此，在公司待的时间比家里还要多。父母常年辛苦工作，很多事情都要亲自操心，所以早就把工作场所当成了自己的家，简心和弟弟简阳每次放学回家，也会跟着父母，在公司里面写写作业、看看书，或是玩耍玩耍。她在母亲的办公室里坐着，随意翻看《读者》杂志，一个邮递员急匆匆地进入办公室，大声问道："请问谁叫简心？这封信来自海外，是她的信。"简心听到这个消息，觉得很诧异，他们家在国外没有任何熟人或亲朋好友，有谁会给她写信呢，她也没有任何笔友呀。她心里觉得很纳闷，也很好奇："不管如何，先打开看看再说。"她向那个快递员说了声谢谢，然后接过信，看到信封上真真切切地写着收件人的名字"简心"，然后她快速扫了一下寄件人的名字与信息，只见上面歪歪扭扭地注明两种语言，中文"黄小丹"以及一种不同于英文的外语。简心迫不及待地打开这封信，带着一丝疑惑开始读，信里面写道：

　　亲爱的简心同学，欢迎你即将来 SCHLOSS NEUBEUERN 读书，开始崭新的异国学习生活。我在这个德国私立寄宿制学校已经就读两年了，我来自北京，现在是 11 年级，对这里的一切比较熟悉了。你刚来德国，一定会感到不适应，很陌生，请你千万不要太担心，随着时间的推进，一切会慢慢好起来，这里的学习生活和国内完全不同，如果你来到这个学校，有什么生活或学习上的问题，可以随时来问我，我很乐意帮助你，为你解答。很高兴你的到来，至此希望你一切顺利。

黄小丹
2002年2月

简心读完这封信，觉得心里暖洋洋的，她感受到了一个远方伙伴的真诚与善意，对母亲说："妈妈，你快看这封信，是那个德国寄宿学校的一位中国学生写给我的。她说，以后如果遇到困难，可以去找她，她会帮助我的。"简心的母亲听完后，感到很欣慰，本来她还担心女儿第一次出国，什么都不懂，也不会当地的语言，怕她在外面吃亏或不适应，现在收到这样一封热心的信，她的内心顿时踏实了很多，她由衷地感谢这位北京女孩的热心肠。随后对简心语重心长地说："简心，你到了新学校，有什么不懂，就去问黄小丹，她会帮助你的，不要一个人硬抗，大方一点，有句话说得好，'在家靠父母，出门靠朋友'，多个朋友多条路，一个人的力量毕竟有限，有个自己国家的小伙伴在那个学校，也能好很多，你就不会觉得那么孤独无助了，不懂的事情多去问问她。看她信里写得那么真诚，一定是一个热情又善良的姑娘。妈妈这样放心多了，我和你爸爸也不可能把你送去德国，你一人去德国，本来我很担心，现在收到这样一封信，心里踏实安心多了。你也写一封回信，谢谢人家，不能收了信件不回复人家，这样显得不礼貌。对了，这几天我就抽出时间，去城里为这位北京姑娘挑选一件礼物，你去了学校，就送给她，表达感谢之情。"简心听了母亲的话，很懂事地点点头，回答母亲："知道了，妈妈，我会写一封信回复她的，让我想想怎么写好。"就这样，简心在心里思考着，如何礼貌而周全地回复黄小丹。为了表达感谢之情，也为了让简心以后的路走得顺畅一点，简心的母亲过了几天就去城里为黄小丹挑选礼物了，想买件漂亮的衣服送给她，但是在现实生活中从没有遇见过，所以这显然是不合适的，因为不知道她喜欢什么样的风格，挑来挑去，最后决定买一条雅致而精致的苏州丝绸给黄小丹。每个女孩都会喜欢丝绸，摸上去那么光滑柔顺，图案显示的是江南的雅致与文人墨客的风韵，不是那么花里胡哨。一条丝巾花了大概680块钱，在那个年代，这样的一件礼物已经是非常昂贵了，足见简心父母对这个远方中国女孩的诚意与感谢之情，感谢她给简心一颗小小的定心丸，让她在今后的日子里可以和一个好友相互作伴，不会那么孤独和无助，也感谢黄小丹的热忱之心。其实简心也想拥有这样类似的丝巾，但她清楚地知道，父母挣钱不容易，所以她是绝不好意思开这个口的，这样的一个小心愿只能默默地埋在她的心底，她不愿意让父母为难，也不愿意乱花父母挣的钱。她心想：以后等我有经济能力了再买，现在我不需要这样的丝巾，这么贵，不值当。其实简心内心深处很多隐秘的想法不曾一一告知她父母，其一她觉得父母未必能理解她的想法，其二这是青春期的特征，这个年龄阶段的孩子们喜欢在内心深处拥有一片自己的私人领地，不让任何人进入，因为这是最安全和神秘的。这就是成长的过程。小的时候什么都愿意和知心的小伙伴或亲人倾诉，但随着年龄的增长，这样的分享感变得越来越少，人真是奇妙的高等动物，在成长的不同阶段以及在不同的环境中，思维方式与认知在不同的变化之中，不会永远保持一成不变。

简心和她的母亲去城里采购完后就回家了。她像往常一样，在空闲的时候会经常去找她的表妹一起玩耍、聊天，表妹和她从小一起长大，是她最值得信赖的小伙伴，她们之间总有说不完的话题，聊得实在没什么新鲜事了，就会开始评论电视剧的情节与各种人物。她们两个的关系亲密得犹如亲生姐妹，简心和她的弟弟就没有这么多话题可以聊，很大的一部分原因可能是性别不同，兴趣爱好也不同吧。在表妹那里，经常可以寻找到心灵的慰藉，因为她们互相感同身受，也由于她们的性格中有类似又有不同的方面。相较于简心而言，表妹的心思更为细腻，考虑事情比较周全，但胆量却不如简心，她会更传统与内敛一点，如果事情不是十分有把握或稳妥，她是不会轻易去冒险挑战的。所以简心和她谈起出国读书的选择，表妹呈现出的是担忧居多。她担心简心是不是会适应那边的生活和环境，担心简心一个人在外会不会很孤独等。其实这样的担忧完全是出于对简心的关心与不舍，她不舍得简心就这样离开，这样她们见面的机会变得很难得，但最后表妹还是衷心地祝福简心，希望她以后在异国他乡的日子里顺顺利利，平平安安。"人有悲欢离合，月有阴晴圆缺，此时古难全，但愿人长久，千里共婵娟。"最近这样的诗句总是会萦绕在简心的耳畔，她越来越清晰地感受到世界上的事，不可能所有都称心如意，有得也有失。再好的朋友，再亲密的关系，也有分开的一天，最重要的是珍惜在一起的美好时光，以后如果分开了，脑海里还可以像放电影一样，回首一个个难忘而美好的片段。简心也很舍不得离开她的表妹，但为了追求她向往的未知而新奇的生活，这是无可奈何的事，人不可能拥有所有想要的东西。表妹看着简心，想到她即将远行，眼泪模糊了双眼，她说："姐姐，你一个人在外一定要注意安全，希望你一切都顺顺利利的，我会为你祝福和祈祷。以后我们见面的机会变少了，但我们可以写信联系，一直保持联系，无论以后身在何方。我们好好努力，相信一定会有灿烂的将来。好吗？"简心听了表妹的话，眼睛也湿润了，她很不舍得离开这个亲爱的表妹，对表妹说："不用为我担心，出门在外我会好好地照顾好自己。你也一定要保重，爱惜自己。到了那里，我会经常给你写信，我们保持联系。小妹，我们一起加油，相信自己的潜力，相信自己不会比任何人差，只要肯努力，只要坚持。我们相互鼓励，不论遇到多大的困难。但现在我有一个困惑，就是不知道去了德国，我那个德语老师怎么教我德语，难道他会中文吗？如果不会，那我要怎么学，我的英语也不行，都不能流利地用英语交流。心里真的纳闷，刚开始怎么学德语。"表妹听后，也觉得这是个问题，但为了让简心放宽心，她安慰道："姐姐，这个你别担心，那个德语老师肯定有办法把你教会的。你不要想那么多，办法有很多种，可能他可以通过别的方式教你德语，不需要用中文解释。"听了表妹的话，简心心里释然和明朗了很多，不再过多地思虑未来的事情，未知的难题等出现的时候去解决，现在这些担忧或考虑都是无用的。简心也曾想过，要不在国内先上个德语初级班，这样至少有一点语言基础，不会去了陌生的环境这么茫然或不适应。这个提议是简心的母亲提出的，她担忧女儿一句德语都不会，去了新的学校，很难适应或融入。在国内稍微学点基础的话，可能会好点。但当时在他们那个小地方，像德语这样小语种的外语培训班很少，几乎没有，大家都只热衷学习英文以及应对各门考试，哪有时间或闲情逸致去学第二门外语。只有在上海或北京那样的国际大都市，才会有德语培训班。简心的爸爸表达了他的观点："我觉得简心没必要在国内学德语基础课程，因为这里的德语老师发音可能不标准，这样会误导她。直接去德国学，现在没有一点语言基础也没关系，到了那个语言环境中，应该会很快学起来的。我相信我女儿的学习能力，这样的困难是不会压垮她的。只要勤奋努力，一定就可以。"简心听了她父亲的话，点点头表示赞同，她再也不过多去考虑这些事情了，一切自然会有最好的安排。

　　日子在不知不觉中流逝，在时间的长河中不留下任何的痕迹，仿佛一切都是那么自然或顺理成章，但对每个人而言，时间的流逝将成为过去的记忆，而这些记忆只会留在人的脑海深处，或成为模糊的画面，不再会在现实中重复出现。在家的这些日子里，在等待签证的时光中，简心曾在脑海中不止一次对过往的经历或记忆进行梳理，有时她不禁会惊叹人的大脑的神奇,她不能解释,为什么人的大脑可以存续这么多的信息,不管有用还是没用的,她也无法理解,为什么有些事情或画面会在大脑中留下特别深刻或挥之不去的印象,而有很多发生的零零散散的事件会随着时间的推移变得越来越遥远,只留下很模糊的片段,模糊到她要怀疑,这些事情是真实发生过,还是她自己想象出来的。并且她的性格虽然大大咧咧,但也有极其敏感与细腻的一面,特别是对有些她很介意或在乎的事情,会一而再再而三地在大脑中呈现,然后就会有两个声音在打架,一方面是消极的,另一方面是积极的,但通过她自我意识的控制,最终大多会是积极的方面战胜消极的方面。她一个人待着的时候,遥望远方,不知道看见了什么,其实她关注的不是外界发生的事情,而是大脑会时常空下来思考一些事情,这些事情只有她一个人知道,也只会留给她自己思考。她有时会使劲地去想象自己三岁或四周岁以前所发生的事情,因为她对生命的起点特别好奇,不知道自己是怎么出生的,也不知道自己小时候是什么样子,又发生了哪些事情,那个年代留下的照片太罕见了,屈指可数。她看到的为数不多的几张照片,其中一张是在她一周岁的时候,一个胖嘟嘟的可爱的小女孩骑在木马上,背景很简单朴素。还有一张照片是妈妈抱着一个小婴儿在外婆家院子里。她看着这些照片,觉得既熟悉又陌生,应该说更多的是陌生,她的脑海里完全没有这些记忆。有时她会去质疑生命的起点,她不理解大脑怎么这么奇怪,人在三岁以前所有的记忆都基本不会留在脑海中,而随着年龄越来越大,记忆开始清晰或会在大脑中留下影像,但又会有更令人费解的事情,就算以前很多事情不记得,但如果孩子熟悉一个抚养人的气味或经常被这个抚养人照顾,又会对她有依恋感。她经常会独自感叹,人真是神奇又复杂的动物。

等了将近一个月,有一天,一个邮递员送来了一个来自上海的快递。那个时候,简心正在父母的公司看小说,她看得正津津有味,沉浸在曲折离奇、跌宕起伏的故事情节中，看到这样的一个快递，她心里激动了一下，下意识地已经猜出这个快递是谁的。"妈妈，有个来自上海的快递，我想，这肯定是关于德国签证的。希望一切顺利，没有拒签。"简心的妈妈安慰她，说："肯定没问题，打开看看就知道了。"她从快递员手里接过信件，心扑通扑通地跳，很紧张，打开信件的时候，手与身体不由自主有一丝颤抖，她虽然看不懂信件中德语的意思，但还有英文的注解，上面清清楚楚地写着 "your student visa for Germany is successfully processed（您申请的德国学生签证已成功办理）。"看到这样的答复，她内心有说不出的欣慰与喜悦，她心里的一块石头落地了，学生签证已经顺利签过，本来她还有隐隐约约的担心，怕签证没那么容易通过。如果签不下来，会让她陷入很尴尬的境地，因为她放弃了国内的求学道路，现在真的是破釜沉舟了，只能走出国留学的路了，再也没有退路可言。现在这样的顾虑完全解除了。她感激父母为她的辛勤付出，也感激亲朋好友的鼓励与关怀，感激上天对她的厚待，让她的人生路走得那么顺畅。她在内心默念："感谢一切的一切，感谢佛祖的保佑，谢谢，今后的道路，我会持续努力，不会辜负父母与亲人的期望。"简心的妈妈知道了这个答复，也很欣慰，立刻跟简心说："快去告诉你爸爸，签证顺利通过了。"简心飞奔去她父亲的办公室，看到父亲正在和客户谈事情，不想打扰他工作，刚要说出口的话又被简心咽了回去。等父亲谈完事情后，她郑重其事地说："爸爸，我去德国读书的签证已经顺利通过了，我真开心。"父亲听了以后，同样喜笑颜开，对简心慈爱温和地说："真好，一切顺利，简心，爸爸看一下国际航班，然后和负责你留学的中介机构联系一下，看你什么时候去德国。"简心听了她父亲的话，觉得太不可思议了，她都无法想象，接下去的日子是怎样，德国究竟是怎样的一个国家，一切都那么未知而新鲜。

简心的父亲立刻联系了中介机构，商量简心前往德国的日子，国际航班定于两个礼拜之后，也就是3月4日，从上海浦东国际机场出发。因为简心的父母决定不亲自送她去学校，所以为了安全起见，父亲特意联系好了上次在德国大使馆见面认识的两位同学的父母，他们的孩子也顺利收到了德国留学的签证。如果定同一个航班，一路上可以相互作伴，有个照应，父母们也会安心很多。

简心的母亲这几天显得特别忙碌，她要为女儿准备很多行李，路途这么遥远，以后回一趟家也不容易了，所以需要采购和准备的东西很多。这又是简心长这么大第一次离家，并且还是去那么遥远的国度，人生地不熟，没有一个熟人和亲戚在那边。简心的母亲心里还是很放不下，其实她和奶奶是最舍不得简心离开的，她对这个女儿有太多的不放心，担忧外面的社会复杂，女儿一个人在外会吃很多苦。作为父母，尤其是母亲，是最见不得孩子吃很多苦，但最终她还是执拗不过简心的决定。现在母亲也不愿意去劝阻了，事已如此，她能做的是帮助简心收拾行囊，带上一切用得着的物品。她带着简心去当地的超市买了很多零食、方便面、榨菜等，还添置了四季的衣服。当时简心的父母还很节约，不舍得为自己和孩子买品牌的衣服，买的都是小镇服装店的普通衣服，一家人开销很大，再说公司需要运营的成本也很高，生活方面能节约就节约，赚钱很不容易。但简心的父母，尤其是父亲会给孩子创造好的教育条件，不论有多贵，他都觉得这是值得的。知识和眼界是无价之宝，衣服或这些物质类的东西都会贬值。简心的父母觉得，衣服只要穿得舒适，不用讲究牌子，再说他们都没有这种概念。简心的价值观也受到父母的影响，她对衣服穿着不是很讲究，只要合体舒适就好。在当时，她关注的是个人发展，努力有好的学习成绩。简心的母亲为她添置什么东西，她都觉得可以，没有什么特别讲究的。采购了大半天，基本上已经买好了所需要的物件，离远行的日子还有一段时间。在这段时间里，母亲就为她整理行囊，一个超级大的箱子塞得满满当当，几乎把半个家的用品都带上了，感冒药、围巾、手套等等，所有母亲想得到需要用的，都塞在了这个箱子里。简心看着这么大一个箱子，心想，肯定要超重了。家里时刻都会备着一个称重机，年迈的爷爷虽然已经70多岁了，但手力还是很不错，据说简心的爷爷小时候跟着曾祖父练过武功，有点拳脚功夫，所以体力和手力比一般人强很多。爷爷把大箱子扛到了体重机上，电子秤上立刻显示40公斤，这显然严重超重了。据了解，对国际航班的经济舱客人而言，可以免费携带的行李重量上限是30公斤，如果超过这个指标，超重的部分是需要支付异常昂贵的费用的。简心的母亲说："行李太重了，我们需要精简一下，不然要罚钱的，可贵了。可是第一次出这么远的门，又不能经常回家，需要带的东西很多，怎么办？"后来，经过和简心父亲的讨论，决定不打算精简箱子里的物品，因为她的父母觉得，女儿第一次出远门，在异国他乡刚开始会有很多不熟悉的地方，语言又不通，万一缺了什么，也很不方便，国际快递又贵，再说也麻烦。额外需要出钱就出钱。虽然简心的父母平时省吃俭用，但应该用的钱还是舍得用的，他们一直秉承这样的金钱观：钱要花在刀刃上，一定要花的，就花出去；但可有可无的，也不是很必要的花销，就不要轻易把钱花出去。挣钱比大手大脚花钱难多了，对于教育以及可以开阔眼界，提升认知的，是必不可少的，不需要吝啬投资，尤其对孩子的教育。简心的父母这回舍不得让孩子少带行李，即使要出高昂的行李费，他们一致认为，这样的钱不能省，一个16岁的女孩独自一人出国留学，刚开始会有很多的不方便，他们又不能亲自把女儿送到学校，准备充分总比到时候缺这缺那要强得多。

简心看了母亲为自己准备那么多行李，觉得有些可能用不着，但那是父母的良苦用心，以后一个人在外都要靠自己了，再也不能那么快捷地联系到父母，帮自己解决难题，今后的路更多的要靠自己走好、走稳。简心指着偌大的行李箱，对她的母亲说："妈妈，我需要带那么多东西吗？为什么还要带高中的书籍，都是中文的，用不到了。怎么还带这么多榨菜和方便面，那里也可以买到吃的。还有这么多感冒药。"她的母亲关切地回答："这些都需要带，万一你刚开始吃不惯西餐呢，又不是那么容易吃到家乡的饭菜，带些方便面和榨菜可以应应急。要带些日常的药，万一感冒了呢，一开始又什么都不懂，也不会讲当地的话，有了这些日常药，也可以缓解一下感冒症状。虽然你可能用不上中文的书籍，但或许内容也有类似之处，你德语不懂，可以翻阅一下中文的资料，会容易理解一点，带着总没错。万一你现在不带，以后要用，寄过来又要很长的时间，再说国际快递也不便宜，就先带去吧。你以后一个人在外，一定要注意安全，自己照顾好自己，父母不在你身边，生活和学习完全靠你自己了，简心，你记住了吗？"说完，简心的妈妈眼睛里闪着泪花，儿行千里母担忧。简心的母亲内心有万分不舍，不希望女儿这么早一个人就离家去那么遥远而又陌生的地方求学，还不会当地的语言，也没有任何熟悉的人在那里。她内心其实是不安的，也是很不放心的，但德国留学的签证都已经顺利签过了，航班都已经订好了，一切已成定局，是再也没有回头或反悔的可能了。如果简心一旦反悔，会有很大的损失，不论是经济上，还是她的学业上。在经济方面，签证费、中介费以及保证金，还有私立学校的学费对当时的中国普通家庭是个天价，一般的家庭都无法想象，要花那么多钱送孩子出国。在学业方面，简心已经退学了，放弃了在国内参加高考的可能性，虽然她曾经就读的是本地最好的高中，曾经所在的班级，也是全年级中的尖子班，但这一切就因为这个出国读书的决定而结束了，她再也不可能临时反悔，再回到曾经的校园，选择了另一个方向也就意味着放弃了曾经要走的路。这些顾虑简心其实很明白，自从她决定的那一刻起，她就没有后悔过，决定是她自己做的，未来无论有多难，她都不会再动摇。摇摆不定是大忌讳，她还很年轻，对未来充满了无限的期待，她相信自己的选择。在当时，简心的母亲还没有像她女儿那样坚定的信念，因为做妈妈的总有操不完的心，总是希望能经常见到孩子，在安全的范围之内，这样就会感到很安心。孩子一旦离开了，不在视线范围内，或是经常看不见了，会出现各种猜想或担忧，这就是做妈妈的那份浓厚、伴随一生的爱；相比而言，简心的父亲没有为此显露出过多的担忧与不放心，他对孩子的爱是深沉的，考虑得更长远与开阔。他不愿意把孩子永远拴在自己身边，而是在他的能力范围之内，会为孩子们创造机会、提供机会，让他们飞出去，像鸟儿一样，在广阔的天地自由翱翔，去选择自己喜欢的生活或职业，开阔眼界，因为外面的世界是另一番天地，如果永远待在熟悉的环境中，人的眼界和思维方式会很狭隘，不利于未来的发展。简心的父亲能这样想，也是因为他和小地方普通老百姓不同，常年出差做生意，接触了很多开放和新鲜的思想，尤其是不久前那次北美商务旅行，极大地颠覆了他对这个世界的认知，看到了国内外经济与生活的巨大差异。他才真正想通了，才舍得放开孩子的手，让简心走出去。如果不是那次北美之行，简心的父亲也还是很舍不得把孩子这么小就送出国，因为那毕竟是未知的世界，他也从来没有去过。

　　时间就这样悄无声息地流走了，离出国的日子越来越近。简心从小人缘就很好，有很多小学、初中以及高中的同学和朋友给她寄来了贺卡，上面写满了暖心的祝福语，比如"亲爱的伙伴，愿你在异国他乡顺顺利利，平平安安，每天都开心。"又例如"亲爱的简心，我们永远都是好朋友，愿你学业有成，万事如意。"还有朋友这样写道"亲爱的简心，这是我的邮寄地址，我们保持联系，你去了德国，可不要忘了我这个好友。虽然我们以后隔得很远，但海内存知己，天涯若比邻，我们的友谊万古长青，我会想念你。曾经和你在一起的美好时光会永远留在我的脑海中。你去了德国后，一定要记得给我写信呢。我收到了你的信件，就知道你的地址了。到时候我们就可以书信往来了。"

贺卡数不胜数，简心的内心很感动，被这些真挚的友谊所打动，也被这些暖人肺腑的话语所感动，文字可以这么有魔力，即使不在一起，即使默默无语，看到这温暖人心、质朴善良的一言一语，就会觉得世间很美好，会感到人心的善良。简心收着这些珍贵的贺卡，把她放在了一个随身包里，她要把这些朋友赠送的贺卡一起带去异国他乡，当她感到孤独无助的时候，当她想念国内的亲人和好友的时候，翻出来阅读，重温这份暖暖的情义，这会给她力量以及努力的勇气。简心其实是一个特别懂得自我激励、自我暗示的姑娘。在学业上，每次遇到困难，她都会在本子上写下激励自己鼓励自己的话，例如"相信自己的潜力""不要担忧未来，不要太多地关注结果，只需要每天把该做的事情做好，自然会有好的结果；即使没有，也已经尽力做好了，顺其自然""微笑吧，在每一个清晨，在每一次太阳升起的时刻，从这一刻开始保持微信息，你就会离成功很近，离幸福不远"。这些话就像一个个良师益友，时刻鼓励与安慰着她前行。也许对很多人而言，这样的做法有点傻或是形式主义，但对简心而言，真的很受用。她的内心需要安慰与鼓励，这样她才会面对每一次挫折与困难，重拾信心，继续往前看，义无反顾地往前走。

第七章：离别

  离开前一天，家里来了很多亲戚，显得很热闹。简心的父母是很讲究礼仪的，女儿即将离开家乡，去很遥远的欧洲留学，这在他们家真的是一件轰动全村的大事。为了给女儿饯行，他们邀请了很多亲戚，外婆、外公、舅舅、舅妈，以及伯父、伯母等。几乎在场所有的亲戚都不能理解简心父亲的决定，要把这么小年纪的女儿送出国，也觉得她父亲的这个举动很大胆冒险，不过这是别人家的家事，亲戚们也不能阻挠什么，只能由衷地祝福简心今后的日子一切顺利，没有太多的波折。简心那天吃得不多，她的心也五味杂陈，离别在即，她很舍不得家人，舍不得离开这个生活了16年的温馨的家，虽然父母从小没有花很多时间陪伴她，但她理解他们，在那个年代，是多么不容易，物质生活都没有很多保障，哪来精神生活的重视，哪有那么多时间整天陪着孩子成长。父母不溺爱她，让她变得独立而坚强，也变得不那么胆小怕事，勇于探索，就是这样的一个家庭环境后天铸就了她的性格：她有女子对情感的敏感细腻，但更多的是无所畏惧，敢于挑战以及坚强自信。简心的父亲在这一天，有一点担忧，因为他其实害怕女儿的反悔，害怕她在机场可能又不愿意出国了，前几天他刚听说一个朋友也准备送他孩子出国读书的，人都已经到机场了，在出境的那一刻，那个孩子突然哭着闹着，说不愿意离开家、离开父母。所以最终还是放弃了出国的那条路，还浪费了很多时间和精力。简心的父亲也担心，万一简心也这样子，该怎么办，这样一切不就打水漂了吗？相当于赔了夫人又折兵。在那天晚宴上，他的这种思虑只保留给了自己,他没有去询问简心,有没有彻底想好自己的决定,也没有对她说一句:"女儿,你一定不能反悔,因为你已经做了决定。"简心马上要离开家了,父母亲也还是很舍不得。年迈的奶奶握着简心的手,语重心长地说:"简心,你出门在外一定要照顾好自己,奶奶会每天念经,在佛祖面前保佑你,平平安安,顺顺利利,保佑你学业有成。奶奶会想你的。"说完后,简心看着奶奶布满皱纹的脸,望着奶奶湿了的眼睛,不知道该如何安慰亲爱的奶奶,其实她的内心很是万般不舍,既伤感,又憧憬新的生活。人生有悲欢离合,有聚有散。

时间就这样悄无声息地流逝了,门口开来了一辆商务车,简心一眼就认出来,是她父亲的司机开的,她心里跟明镜似的,时间已经到了,要离开家去上海国际机场了。航班是凌晨00:30,现在是晚上7:00,开去国际机场大约需要三个半小时,一路可能会有交通堵塞。为了让时间充裕一点,不会出现临时错过航班的状况,简心的父母决定提早出发,以免慌慌张张。再说这是简心第一次出国,行李严重超重,可能需要在行李托运方面多花点时间。

简心的父母说:"简心,和亲朋好友道别一下。"简心点点头,和亲人们挥手告别,"再见了,我们下次再见,我一定会好好照顾好自己的,也希望你们过得顺顺利利,等我下次从德国回来后,我们再一起欢聚。"话音刚落,有些亲戚的眼睛也湿润了,他们叮嘱简心说:"孩子,你在外一定要保重,我们为你祝福,再见了。"简心和她的爷爷、父母、舅舅、舅妈以及弟弟上了商务车,司机把行李提上了车,简心的妈妈再次提醒她:"简心,你有没有带好所有重要的东西?特别是护照,护照就像你的身份证一样,每次出门前,一定要好好检查一下。忘了可就麻烦了。"简心爽快地回答:"妈妈,你放心,我已经检查了随身包好几遍了,没有忘记,你看呢,在的。"虽然妈妈唠叨,但藏满了她对孩子的关心和深深的母爱。一切准备就绪，车子发动了起来，一下子就飞驰在马路上，一路往目的地前进。

窗外已经漆黑一片，看不清任何的树木，只能隐隐约约地看见一些房屋里透出的亮光，简心内心突然感到人生的奇妙和不可思议，人生走走停停，一开始的一条路笔直地伸向远方，仿佛人可以清晰地看到不远处的灯塔，那就是她这么多年追寻的目标或是想要到达的地方，但不一会儿出现一个岔路口，如果不转弯，还是继续往前走，可以预测到未来大致会到达哪；但如果转了一个方向，选择了另外一条路，一切都会改变，所有的人生轨迹已经和以往完全不同了。她现在就是这种感受：本来她是想好好走好之前规划好的路，努力读书，在国内考个好大学，在国内找工作等；现在出现了一个岔路口，换了一条崭新的路，以后会怎样，不得而知，会是完全另一番面貌。简心想：这就是人生，人生不是预设好的，而是充满了无限的未知与惊喜。如果稳定与惊喜相比，我更愿意选择惊喜和新奇，虽然不能确定未来一定会如愿以偿，但至少这样的人生更有趣，更有挑战性。我宁愿走少有人走的路，也不愿意那么平庸的墨守成规。人就活一次，出去闯一闯挺好的。简心想完后，不想再思虑太多，闭目养神，她听着耳旁时而有父母和亲戚间的对话，具体说了什么，她也不知道了，此刻，她的内心已经听不见很多外界的声音了，也许她有一点困乏了，也许她大脑在思考着她感兴趣的一些事情，不得而知。

车飞快地奔驰着，大约过了三个半小时，他们顺利抵达了上海国际机场。简心下了车，她第一次看到这么气派的国际机场，里面灯烛辉煌，旅客穿梭其中，穿得很讲究，很有气质，显得都气宇轩昂。简心感到世界的广博，在她们那个小地方，大伙的穿着都很朴素，甚至可以说乡土味十足，在离家200多公里的上海大都市，在这个国际机场，这儿的旅客却有着截然不同的气质与谈吐。这些人都是见过世面的人呐，简心心里暗暗地想。她觉得自己和这个机场里的人群有很大的差异，她上下打量了自己一番，感到也有些土气，与这么气派的地方有些格格不入。司机帮忙从商务车上取下行李箱，从机场门口取了一辆行李车，使出九牛二虎之力把这个笨重的行李箱抬上了机场行李车，然后推着行李车进入了机场。父母、其他亲人与简心一起进入机场。随即映入她眼帘的是在一排电子屏幕上滚动的所有国际航班的行程，出发与到达时间，出发地与目的地。简心仔细地搜索凌晨飞往德国慕尼黑的汉莎航班，找了好一会儿，发现还没出现，然后心里觉得有些纳闷，会不会临时取消？因为这样的事情很常见，特别是突发状况或气候不好的时候。简心的父亲安慰说："简心，不要担心，航班一切顺利，我们可能来得太早了点，所以航班信息还没有在电子屏幕上显现出来。要不我们找一个地方先休息一会，慢慢等待，等航班出现了，再去托运行李。"简心赞同地回答："好的，爸爸。"然后一伙人开始找位置坐下，但找了好久，都没找到，机场的空位都被其他旅客占领了，根本没有空余的位置。最后他们决定就站在电子屏幕附近，等待航班信息。时间滴滴答答地流过，过了大约一个小时，简心终于看到了自己所要乘坐的 MU557 航班，她激动不已地告诉父母："爸妈，航班信息已经出现了，你们快看。"因为第一次出门，其实她也不清楚找到航班后，接下去要干什么。她的父亲对坐飞机是最轻车熟路的，因为他经常一个人出差，所以他最了解坐飞机的流程。他说："我们看是哪个登机口，然后就拉着行李去登机口托运。"

话音刚落，大家就听着简心父亲的指示，匆匆赶往登机口 H。到了登机口，看到那里已经排了很长的队伍。在这种国际机场里，肯定是不能乱插队的，要遵守秩序。简心和父母推着行李车就排在队伍里，其他的亲人站在附近等候，队伍一点点往前挪动，速度真的和蜗牛差不多，等了大约 1 个小时，终于轮到他们 check-in（办理登记手续）。工作人员不带任何表情，像执行公务一样地说："请把托运的行李放在这个滚动带上，国际航班一个人的行李上限是30公斤，超过的公斤数需要补差价。"简心的父母默认地点点头，然后父亲花了很大的力气把她的行李箱抬上了滚动带，电子屏幕上立刻显示"42公斤"。简心的父亲说："超过12公斤，没关系，补差价就补差价。"母亲反对说："超过这么多，要不我们看看，哪些东西可以不用带，我们取出一些。"工作人员说："你们加快一点，后面还有乘客在等待，超过一公斤，每公斤需要补300人民币，12公斤需要补3600。"简心的父亲说："算了，不要取出来了，就这样吧，第一次出门，需要带足够点，不然少了什么，路途这么遥远，会很不方便。贵点就贵点。"简心的母亲最后也赞同了。在当时那个年代2002，3600块钱是很大的一笔钱了，是一个普通家庭一个月的工资都不止了。就这样，补完差价，行李就顺利托运掉了，然后父亲跟简心温和慈爱地说："简心，现在你要过境了，爸爸妈妈不能再陪你一起了。我现在教你，如何过境，需要注意些什么。还要一个多小时，飞机就要起飞了。你进入出入境，然后顺利找到登机口，在那里耐心等待飞机。希望你一路平安。"其他的亲人也一起把简心送到了出入境之处，简心和亲人告别："放心吧，我会照顾好自己的。"母亲的眼泪在眼眶止不住地打转，她万般不舍女儿这么小就离开父母，去那么遥远的地方。父亲叮嘱完，在简心要挥手离开之际，双眼也湿润了，简心长这么大，第一次看到父亲也会流泪，也会那么感性，平时他从来都是笑嘻嘻的。简心也忍不住哭了，其实她也是很舍不得离开父母，离开亲人，毕竟她从小到大都没有真正离开家这么远，她其实还没有完全长大，也还是很留恋亲情。

第八章：到达异国

挥手告别后，简心独自一人进入出入境处，父母的身影已经不见了，她心里不知道是一种什么滋味，有一点空荡荡的，也有一点伤感。从此以后，路要自己一个人走了，她才16岁，是一个花季的年龄，很多这个年龄的女孩对家还是有百般的依赖感，不愿意远行，也不愿意真正独立，可从今天开始，她不能再一直依靠父母了，而是真真正正地要走向独立了。她排着长队，一步步往前挪动，等了许久，工作人员叫她取出护照，检查护照首页以及签证，然后跟她说："填写一张入关卡，在那个长桌上。"简心按指示，向几个人聚集的长桌走去，看到大家都在填写入关卡，她也拿了一张空白卡，开始填写起来，因为是头一次填写，有些地方不是很清楚，所以她会主动问一下其他乘客，她并不是那种特别内向的人，遇到不懂的方面，还是会不拘一格，大大方方地询问的，不会觉得不好意思。填写完毕，后来按次序排队后，过了检查随身行李的关卡，就顺利到达了登机口，她看了看手表，离登机时间约莫还有45分钟，就随便逛了一会，然后坐到登机口的位置继续等待登机。此刻，登机口205已经坐满了旅客，简心想："这么多乘客都要飞往慕尼黑，大约有好几百个人。貌似上次碰到的两位同学也是这个航班，我怎么在机场没有碰见他们。估计人太多了，没注意，现在我来找找看呢。"简心环顾了一下四周，找了一会，看到两张熟悉的面孔，心里一阵高兴："终于找到他们了。"他们三个又见面了，这回没有刚开始的生疏和内敛，父母不在身旁，他们三个又是同龄人加老乡，感觉再次见面很亲切，欢呼雀跃地聊了起来。聊的内容无非就是关于对未来的设想以及新学校会如何如何。简心也不觉得时间过得缓慢了。聊着聊着，就到了登机时间，他们依次排好队，通过检查，上了飞机，找到了自己的位置，把行李放在行李架，就坐在了自己的座位上。简心有一个怪癖，她不喜欢把随身行李放在行李架上，就喜欢把它们放在座位下的脚边，这会让她觉得很安心，因为她害怕自己丢三落四，下飞机时手忙脚乱忘记随身行李。所以在以后的每次坐飞机回家过暑假，或是回德国，她都永远会把随身行李放置座位前，在她的视野范围之内，她可以随时看见的地方。因为在外面，她只能靠自己一个人，没有人再会提醒她需要注意的地方，她得自己小心谨慎了，丢了东西是最麻烦的。

  他们三个没有坐在临近的位置，因为乘客太多了，位置也不是随意可以选择的。但这没关系，11个小时的行程，没有父母亲自陪伴，却可以和认识的小伙伴同一架飞机一起飞往目的地，对简心而言，已经是莫大的幸运与安心，也少了一份孤寂和空落落的感觉。随着时间的流逝，飞机到了起飞时间，飞机上各种安全指南以及准备工作做好以后，这么大的客机平缓地升空了，一步步向更高处飞去。简心闭目养神，经过了一个晚上在机场的折腾，她感觉有些累了，也有些困了。深夜12点是睡觉的时间了，可飞机上闹哄哄的，有很多乘客的说话声，也有飞机发动机的噪音，各种声音混杂在一起，她虽然累了，但无法入睡。座位又是出奇的小，坐时间久了，会觉得腰酸背疼，都无法把四肢舒服地伸展出来，她想坐着入睡，但过一会，又觉得坐着睡不着，然后就取下座位移动板，趴在小桌子上睡觉，但折腾了半天，怎么都睡不着，过了时间点，睡意全无，但身体是真的觉得累了。整个机舱还是灯火通明，经济舱挤满了人，过了大约1个多小时，等飞机在空中飞稳以后，空姐叽里咕噜用英文说了一通什么话，舱内的灯全都熄灭了，每个座位前的电子屏幕也收起了。简心虽然听不懂空姐具体说了什么，因为她当时的英文水平还很有限，口语和听力很薄弱，基本不能在现实中很好地运用这门外语，但她的直觉告诉自己，舱内的灯关闭了，应该是休息时间了。不论她是不是睡得着，还是应该逼迫自己休息，11个多小时的飞行时间真的很漫长，就算睡不着，闭闭眼睛也是好的。当时她没有任何电子产品可以来消遣一下，她连一部手机或一台手提电脑都没有，没有任何现代化的通信工具，真的是发生什么，都无法联系到父母。她不想去设想任何不祥或倒霉的事情，因为这不符合她的性格，并且她觉得去忧虑没有发生的，完全是无用或伤神的，她喜欢往前看，往前走，不习惯从后视镜里去研究自己曾经走过的路，问自己是不是选错了道路或是做错了什么，这就是那个朴素而又潇洒的简心，大踏步地往前走，一切往前看。她有些朦朦胧胧地睡着了，睡得很浅，仿佛听得见周遭的所有动静。小伙伴在飞机上估计也睡着了，他们上了飞机，就没有再说过话，因为隔着好多个位置，聊天不方便，再说已经深夜了，每个人都很累了，都逼迫着自己在狭小的空间中能睡多久就多久。

　　简心第一次感受到时间的漫长，时间过得太慢了，以前都没有这种感觉，蓦然回首，回忆过往发生的事情，或有时候回忆童年的往事，会感到时间流逝如流水，一去不复返，流走得那么悄无声息，不知不觉。但这次，这回11个多小时的飞行时间，流逝得如同一只蜗牛在缓缓向前爬行，如一只老态龙钟的老黄牛走不动路似的。简心是真心觉得这长途飞机的时间难熬，空间又狭小，没有熟人或朋友说说话，就一个人呆呆地坐在小位置上，左右都动弹不得，出来走动是逼不得已，只有上洗手间才会离开位置，不然屁股就仿佛黏在了位置上，就一直这么坐着，等待时间一点点流走。她真的是睡不着，睡得迷迷糊糊的，平时她的睡眠质量很好，属于倒头就睡的那种，完全属于秒睡型，每天醒来的时间很规律，完全不用闹钟，总是深夜无梦，一夜到天明。起床后精神很好，会感到新的一天又开始了，所有的不快或忧虑都会随着新一天的开始烟消云散。所以很多睡眠专家都认为：高质量的睡眠是治愈人最好的良药，一个人如果当天有些想不通的事情或找不到解决方案，那就好好睡上一觉吧，明天又会是崭新的一天，说不定会有新的灵感，或是立刻就会找到解决问题的方法。但如果一个人总是思索，晚上也不能好好入睡，醒来就会觉得一天很难熬，因为精力不济。所以对简心而言，睡眠的确是最好的良药，每次太阳升起，她睡到自然醒，就会觉得美好的一天又开始了，又拥有了新的希望，什么难题都会迎刃而解。也有很多运动专家认为：运动是治愈一切的良药，如果觉得工作学习压力过大，如果感到因为吃多了，怕发福长胖，有心里负罪感，或者是经常感冒发烧小毛病不断，那就规律地运动，特别是有氧运动，因为运动能让人提高机体免疫力，也可以让人保持身材以及提高血清素的浓度，使人变得乐观向上，拥有更强的抗压能力与抗挫折能力，还有最重要的一点：规律的运动可以磨炼人的意志力，让人变得很自律以及更能学会坚持。运动的好处数不胜数，但当时的简心还不知道运动有这么多的益处，因为在她生活的圈子里，无论是她的父母亲人，还是同学圈，都没有养成规律运动的习惯，没有这种健康生活的意识，因为很多人忙于工作赚钱，还没有那种想法，如何真切地提高生活品质，并且他们觉得如果没有物质基础的保证，哪有那个闲情逸致去规律运动；在同学圈里，特别是她曾经就读的重点高中，留给自己的时间少得可怜，学校除了每天早餐后短时间的小跑与做早操，一天的重点任务就是文化课程，上不完的课，做不完的练习，规律运动习惯的培养在学校里根本不可能。所以简心在当时的情况下也没有养成这种健康的运动习惯。但好的睡眠是她从小就培养好了，她的家庭注重日出而落，日落而息的生活方式，在农村，没有大城市的各种娱乐设施，灯红酒绿。一到晚上，小乡村连路灯也没有，漆黑一片，只有夏天白天比较悠长，所以几乎每家每户都会在吃完晚饭后稍微溜达一下，就上楼看一会电视，早早地入睡，没有什么熬夜的习惯。记得小的时候，她每天都会在晚上9：00准时上床睡觉，几秒钟会立刻进入深睡眠状态，然后每天在5：30就会起床，是真正按自然规律休息的。这样的睡眠习惯源于奶奶以及父母的健康的作息时间，所以简心的父亲无论工作多忙，出差多频繁，有时要凌晨4：00起床出差，他的父亲都会在晚上很早入睡，第二天无论有多早，都是信心满满，精力充沛。回想起这些，简心真的觉得，这是人生中头一次，睡得这么浅，时间过得那么漫长，几乎一夜没有真正地睡着，她看了无数次的手表，实在睡不着，就起来翻看飞机上的杂志，看各种广告图片，就这样等啊等啊，到了早上5:30（相当于中国时间12：30，德国与中国的冬令时时差是7个小时），飞机终于将要安全着落在目的地：慕尼黑国际机场。机舱内播出了即将到达的信息，简心喜出望外，心里有说不出的激动，当飞机缓缓降落，最后滑行在飞行跑道上，她的心安定了很多，一个人自言自语地说："终于到达了。"

下飞机的时候和另外两个坐在别的位置的小伙伴打了招呼，虽然是清晨的5：30，一晚都没怎么睡着，但三人都精神振奋，没有丝毫的困倦。他们结伴而行，跟着人群进入了机场内。机场内，主要人群不再是亚洲脸孔，而是高鼻子蓝眼睛或棕色眼睛的欧洲人，只有极少的亚洲脸孔也穿梭其中。他们三人按照指示标记"luggage pick up"（行李领取处）找到了行李提取处，一个个行李箱在滚动带上巡回转动，到达乘客都拿着小型的行李车站在一旁，检查自己的行李箱是不是已经出来。简心也拿了一个行李车，盯着一个个行李从滚动带上经过，就仿佛一个妈妈站在校园外，目不转睛地盯着自己的孩子是不是已经出了校门。等了好长一会，她终于看到了自己熟悉的偌大的棕色行李箱，上面还挂着一把锁，为了便于她识别。她使出浑身力气想从滚动带上取下箱子，但箱子实在太重了，她一个人身单力薄，第一次取没成功。这时身旁有个很高大的德国年轻人立刻帮她了一把，把这个超级重的箱子从滚动带上取了下来，友好地向简心微笑了一下。他说了什么，简心也听不懂，但那个德国人的乐于助人，简心已经理解了，她很礼貌地对这个德国人说了"thank you"，虽然她的英文口语不是很好，但最基本的交流还是有点会的。那个德国人也彬彬有礼地回复"you are welcome"，突然就消失在简心的视线中了。她心里想："这里的人还挺友好的，看到陌生人也会热心帮助。"她觉得心里暖暖的，感受到了人性的善良与温暖。其他两个小伙伴也顺利取到了自己的行李，三个人推着行李车，通过安检，最后到达了机场入境口。

  门口站了一些接机的人，几乎每个人手里都高举着牌子，上面写的反正不是中文，是德语或英文。简心问了一下两个小伙伴："你们看，哪个是接我们的人，我也不认识。"写的是德文，不懂呢。他们两个要去往同一所学校，路上还能有个伴，也能壮壮胆，没一会儿，有个人举着牌子的人就冒出来，叽里咕噜说了几句，这两个小伙伴就跟着接机的人走了。现在就剩下简心一个人了，接机的人越来越少，过了没多久，她仔细看了一眼一个牌子，上面写着"Schloss Neubeuern Internatsschule"，虽然她从没学过一天德语，对德语真的是一窍不通，但她有很强的记忆力，她觉得那几个单词似曾相识，貌似在她曾经浏览的那个介绍国外私立学校的册子上看到过，她觉得那个应该就是她要去的学校的名字，当然她无法精准地验证，因为真的是不懂德语，但直觉告诉她，脑海中模糊的记忆告诉她，这就是那个学校。然后举着那个名字的牌子的一位女士径直走向她，跟她热情地握了握手，叽里咕噜说了一通，说的是英语，但简心就是听不懂，因为觉得语速太快了，她还没反应过来，就跟兔子一样，一溜烟地跑了。她猜想，这个人应该是接她的人，准没错，然后不管三七二十一，对她礼貌地回复了"thank you"，就义无反顾地跟着这位身材瘦弱的女士上了小型商务车。随后这位女士把简心的大箱子放入了后备箱,坐到驾驶位置,干脆利落地发动汽车。刹那间,车子飞驰在高速公路上。

清晨5点多的高速公路,已经有很多络绎不绝的卡车,私家车却很少。简心望着窗外,感觉这里的人口稀少,没有成片的房屋群,一路上是大片的农田,农田被整修得出奇得规整,一个个整整齐齐的干草垛滚落在农田里,她就觉得特别新奇,长这么大,第一次看到这样修整得像一个个圆筒形的干草垛,虽然农田的规模非常大,但却几乎不见一个人影,那些干草垛就像排着队伍一样齐齐整整、孤孤零零地洒落在大片的牧场或农田中。车子飞驰的速度是出奇得快,耳旁传来风呼啸的声音。那个接机的女士全神贯注地开车,其间没有和简心闲聊过一言半语,简心因为语言的限制以及人生地不熟,也不好意思问些什么,就一个人默默地坐在后座,望着窗外的风景,望着疾驰而过的一片片了无人烟的农田与牧场。

第九章：阿尔卑斯山脚下的寄宿制学校

大约过了一个多小时，车子停在了一座貌似古宫殿的门口，女士把简心的行李取了下来，简心小心翼翼地下了车，然后女士关上车门，就开车扬长而去。门口站着一个矮矮胖胖的女人，她长着一头金黄色的头发，看样子年纪已经不小了，估摸有四五十岁的样子。她很热情地欢迎简心的到来，然后就叫了两个身穿 T-shirt 的男孩子帮忙拎行李箱。那是三月的季节，但在这个地方，户外还是积满了皑皑的白雪。简心觉得很好奇，这么冷的天，这两个男孩子只穿了夏天的 T-shirt，难道他们不觉得冷吗？简心也没有想太多，一到达目的地，她自己整个人也如同做梦似的，在经过了一天一夜的折腾与奔波（大概22个小时），完全到达了一个陌生的国度，这里的一切都和她熟悉的家乡截然不同，人也长得完全不一样，几乎没有一个人长得和中国人一样，一眼看过去，户外三三两两地走着几个蓝眼睛、金头发、高鼻子的年轻人。她由衷地感叹：人生太神奇了。简心进入了古宫殿内，被眼前古典的建筑风格所吸引，她说不清楚这是什么风格，她首先爬了十几层楼梯，然后又过了一道门，映入眼帘的是一个宽敞高雅的大厅，中间是长长的木制楼梯。她就跟着这两个帮她提行李箱的年轻人爬了很多很多层楼梯，七拐八拐，经过十几道门，然后爬到了大厦（宫殿）的最高层，那两个年轻人把箱子放在了一个宽敞明亮的卧室里，也没说什么，就离开了。简心猜想，这应该是她住的房间，不然他们也不会把她的行李箱放在这里，虽然她语言不通，但这点直觉还是有的。她仔细地看了一眼房间内的摆设，室内干净整洁，用的都是木制的柜子和床，其他多余的家具也就没有了，里面的东西不是很多，房间挺大的，中间还有几层楼梯，把整个房间巧妙地隔了两部分。几层台阶以上的部分貌似是独立的居住空间，有一张床以及一个衣柜，还有一张书桌；楼梯以下的一小部分又有一张才90厘米宽的很小的单人床，一张书桌和一个衣柜。很显然这是两个人住的卧室，她很好奇，她的舍友长什么样，会是怎样的一个人。现在舍友也不在房间内，简心想舍友可能去上课了。已经早晨7点左右了，在这个时间点，她在以前的高中，学生早就在教室里早自习了。她想，房内台阶下的部分应该是她的空间，这个单人床应该是为她准备的。她就把箱子先晾在了房间里，不急着收拾，想先了解一下周围的环境。走出卧室，听到一个房间里传出吹风机的声音，然后有几个漂亮青春的花季少女在她身旁走过，她们跟简心简单友好地打了招呼，就走开了，噔噔噔地下楼梯。简心还注意到，这个阁楼的部分有一台健身器械，整个空间看起来简约清爽，没有过多的装饰，更多的是实用与整洁。她看到一个房门里有个人影在晃动，吹风机的声音就是从那个房间里传出来的。她很纳闷，是谁在吹头发，莫非早上还有人洗澡吗，那里应该是洗手间。她一个人回到了自己的房间，就坐在书桌前的凳子上，书桌前刚好有一个小窗户，透过窗户，可以看到一点户外的风景，她往窗户外张望，看到楼下有一个很大的花园，草坪修剪得整整齐齐，在草坪的中央有一个古典的欧式喷泉，石柱上有一个雕刻的惟妙惟肖的小天使，双手捧着一个石壶，水流就是从这个石壶倾泻而下，周而复始，生生不息。喷泉四周种满了各种灌木以及花草，因为是下雪天，草坪像披上了一条天然的白毯子，灌木以及花草银装素裹，山脚下是一片片整整齐齐的尖顶房屋，远处便是连绵不断的山脉，这样的景致显得田园又诗意，那样的与世无争，静谧而美好。简心深深地感受到大自然与人类生活的和谐美好。耳畔突然传来了教堂的钟声响，她数了一下，一共敲了8次，原来在古老的年代，教堂的钟声也是用来整点报时的，一直沿用至今，在这样神奇的一片土地上实现了现代与古典的完美融合。简心一个人静静地待着，房间里静得出奇，经过了一天一夜的长途跋涉，她竟然没有很多困意，觉得很纳闷，原来人一天一夜不睡觉，也不会觉得特别累。可能是她还很年轻，体力和身体素质还很好，也有可能是因为这是人生的第一次出国，是她人生路中重要的一个转折点，她对这一切很兴奋期待，同时也夹杂着乡愁，所以暂时忘却了疲倦的滋味。她望着远处的山脉，心里想："这会不会是举世闻名的阿尔卑斯山脉，据说这里与奥地利接壤，那本介绍书上也貌似写了学校就坐落在阿尔卑斯山脚下。"昨天她还在遥远的东方，生活了16年的熟悉的家乡，有父母亲人的庇护，好友的陪伴，今天她却孤身一人来到了西方，一个完全陌生的国度，见到了闻名遐迩的、著名的阿尔卑斯山脉，从这个房间窗户外，可以肉眼清晰地看到，她真正觉得人生太奇妙和不可思议了，一旦踏出去，世界这么多姿广博。对这儿的一切她都感到新奇和陌生，犹如初生的婴儿，显得懵懵懂懂，不知所措。顿然，房门被打开了，一个女孩围着白色的浴袍走了进来，头上也围着一块白色的毛巾。她淡淡地向简心微笑了一下，然后走进了房间内几阶楼梯以上的区域，简心也向她含蓄而又友好地微笑了一下，不知道说什么，显得茫然而陌生。虽然她不知道如何用语言和那个女孩沟通，但她猜测，这应该是她的室友，刚才在那个淋浴房里洗澡的便是她。那个女孩也没有过多热情的欢迎，投给简心一个淡淡的微笑后，就开始吹头发换衣服，梳妆打扮，做自己的事情，她过一会可能要去上课了。简心坐在自己的书桌前，就这样安安静静地坐着，她是在等待着什么吗？她也不得而知，只是她突然觉得自己变得一无所知，对今后的生活，每一天如何安排，怎样开始融入这个新的环境等。突然，她开始变得很想家，很想远在万里之外的父母亲人好友，在她曾经生活学习的地方，有这么多熟悉的人，这么多关心她爱护她，给她温暖关怀的亲人朋友，还有最重要的一点：她可以无所顾忌地说话，和好友聊天玩耍，语言应用自如。可现在，她像一个刚出生的婴儿一样，什么话都不会讲，也不知道如何跟周围的人交朋友或互动。她显得无助而伤感，她真的很想念曾经的家，眼泪情不自禁地在眼眶里打转。人生第一次，她感受到了孤独，可能是因为她舍友的那一个很淡的微笑，她感到了人性的一丝冷漠与距离感，这是她在自己熟悉的家乡从未感受到的。那里的人都很热情质朴，好像每个人都认识对方一样，相处起来没有任何的尴尬与距离感。但她觉得可能自己想得太多了，神经太过敏感纤细，或许因为语言障碍，她们之间无法交流，所以舍友一个淡淡的微笑也不能说明人家的清冷与傲娇。她心里默默地安慰自己："简心，你不要想得太复杂，或许舍友不是那种高傲的人，只是人家无法和你沟通，也不知道该如何欢迎你，所以才会对你只是很淡地微笑一下。再说，你和她非亲非故，人家凭什么一定要对你很热情，每个人都是不同的。"她的内心戏开始变得更丰富了，因为很多心里的猜测也无法用当地的语言表达出来，只能把很多话藏在内心，自己与自己对话。才离开一天父母，她就觉得内心越来越空落落了，看着偌大的一个行李箱，她闲着没事干，就开始把箱子里的东西一件件取出来，放在柜子里。因为柜子的空间有限，所以也不能把箱子里所有的东西都取出来收拾好，有些东西也还是只能躺在箱子里。过了没多久，舍友精心打扮完后，一句话没说，就离开了房间。当简心正在忙着安顿自己的时候，门口突然响起了咚咚咚的敲门声，简心顺口说了一句"请进"。一个中等个子，穿着一件黑色 T-shirt 和蓝色牛仔裤的中国女孩子出现在了简心的面前，她长得不是很漂亮，但却也有几分秀气，脸上写满了自信与独立。简心想：这应该是给她写过信的那个中国女孩黄小丹。女孩滔滔不绝地先做了简短的自我介绍，然后就如同一位威严的老师一样，告诉简心以后需要注意些什么，没有说得很详细，只是轻描淡写地描述了一番。简心很感激有这样一位来自同一国家的学姐给她诚恳的帮助与指导，她突然想起，还有一份礼物要送给黄小丹，然后显得有些胆小而又羞涩地说："谢谢你的来信与帮助，我为你带了一份礼物，希望你喜欢。"之后，她就把那个装有苏州丝绸的礼物递给了黄小丹。黄小丹收到礼物后，简短而精悍地说了句："谢谢。"简心很想跟黄小丹套近乎，但她发现，她对黄小丹的初次印象和她内心想象的截然不同。在她设想之中，黄小丹应该是很热情大方，拥有很好的亲和力，为人纯真而健谈。但眼前的黄小丹，给她的感觉完全不同：她是有距离感的，威严、傲慢、清高得像一个严厉的老师。所以在黄小丹说话的过程中，简心没有问她太多的问题，因为这种距离感让简心觉得陌生，不可亲近。她说不清楚，为什么黄小丹给她会有很远的距离感，可能是她说话的方式，也有可能是她严肃的表情：太一本正经，不苟言笑。简心就安静而耐心地听着黄小丹说话。过了没多久，黄小丹对简心说："走，我们一起去山下，我们的学校建在半山腰，如果要去买点东西，需要去山下的一个小镇，小镇上就只有几家店，有超市、邮局，还有一两个餐馆。我带你去走走，以后你自己就知道怎么去买东西了。"简心谨慎地回答："好的。"然后她们两个出了房间，穿过一道道门，七拐八拐，途中遇到三三两两的德国女孩，长得亭亭玉立、楚楚动人，她们用好奇的眼神看着简心，因为学校里又来了一个新的中国女孩，这是第二个中国女孩，她们在这个学校没怎么见过太多亚洲人。也有些学生很有礼貌，见了简心和黄小丹，很大方地打招呼"hallo"。简心突然觉得每个人的脸都长得差不多，都是高鼻子、大眼睛、小脸蛋、白皮肤，头发颜色有金黄色，也有深棕色，她感到自己脸盲了，都分不清楚人脸的差异。如果是中国人或亚洲人，在她面前晃悠，她能很好地区分开不同点，但面对这一群来来往往的欧洲男孩女孩，她真的搞不清谁是谁，貌似每个人都长得差不多，好像都是一个模子里刻出来似的。在她往楼下走的过程中，她突然发现一个黑皮肤女孩，正和她热情地招手，此刻那个黑人女孩被一群白种女孩围着，在一个有透明玻璃门的小型活动室里边聊天边看电视。黑人女孩特别热情洋溢，看到简心走过，向简心招手微笑。虽然语言不通，但简心的直觉告诉她，这个黑人女孩是热情的，很欢迎她的到来，肢体语言可以很好地诠释这一切。其他的白种女孩只是冷冷地看了一眼简心，没有显露出她们欢迎新生的表情。在人生第一次，她见到了黑种人，她感到这个世界真的太奇妙了，居然还有皮肤黑得如同炭一样的人，牙齿却出奇的白，这个黑人女孩和白种女孩形成了强烈的黑白对比，她黑得真的是无法用言语形容。此刻，简心的审美观还是很狭隘与传统的，她感到黑人真的长得丑，皮肤黑如炭，嘴唇厚得如两条粗粗的香肠，头发像棉花一样，不是一丝丝的，而是一团团地编起来的，像一个个隆起的小疙瘩；相比较而言，白种女孩个个美若天仙，脸庞精致小巧，眼睛炯炯有神，深邃而明亮。但她的这种审美现在今后的留学生涯慢慢改变了，她后来也觉得，黑人也有黑人的美，皮肤紧实细致，嘴唇性感饱满；而白人也有白人的普通与缺陷：嘴唇太薄，身材走形，皮肤粗糙等。但从人种的性格来说，简心感受到了黑人的热情友善，白人的高傲、内敛与清冷。虽然她还不是很了解或者也是误解，但今天她走过学校宫殿里的一道道走廊，碰到了很多学生，从他们的反应，她大致感受到了这种细微之处。当然学校里的工作人员极其友好，看到学校来了位来自遥远东方的新生，会很有礼貌和涵养地微笑打招呼"hallo"。简心也会以同样的方式回应他们的迎客之道，用简短而最实用的"hallo"回复他们，只是表情略显得有些羞涩与内敛，或许是因为人生地不熟，有点缺乏安全感的缘故，所以她性格中坚强果敢以及大方的一面完全被隐藏了起来，她需要小心翼翼地探索这个未知的世界。

过了没多久，她们俩就走出了学校的大门。简心环顾四周，大门外是一片宽阔地铺满小石头的空地，围绕着这座宫殿般的建筑物四周坐落着其他现代化的建筑群，其简约现代的风格与大楼主体有些格格不入，但也无太多的违和感。黄小丹带着简心选择了一条石阶小路往山下走，台阶众多，路旁有茂密的树木，此刻都披上了银装，但隐约还可以看到嫩绿的叶子在白雪的覆盖下显得格外新鲜翠绿。路上有些湿，她们俩小心翼翼地走在台阶上，黄小丹慢条斯理地说："这一条路是最快捷通往山下的，虽然台阶多，但下山不会觉得太费力，而且没有车辆，天气好的时候，风景很不错，有没有看到山下一座座房子，那就是小镇，马上快到了。"简心回答道："我看见房子了。"沿着山路，她们过了十几分钟以后就到达了小镇上。小镇的房子矮矮的，没有摩天大楼，但看上去很雅致与精巧，房子被刷成了好几种颜色，有淡粉色的、白色的、绿色的等，墙体上还画满了精美的壁画。小镇的街道是用大大小小的石块铺砌成的，显得古老而唯美，街道特别干净整洁，没有一丁点的灰尘与杂物，街道上空空荡荡，几乎看不见人影，简心想：可能是下雪天的缘故，大家都躲在室内，不出门。小镇规模真的很小，一眼可以望到头。黄小丹指了指不远处的一个白房子，上面有一个黄色的标记"POST"（邮局）。然后她们一起来到了小镇上唯一的一个超市，超市不大不小，整整齐齐地摆放着各种日用品，但简心发现，超市居然有一半的空间卖的是宠物食物与用品，这和国内的超市截然不同。在2002年，国内的超市几乎还没有任何宠物用品，卖的所有的都是人吃的用的，但在这里，居然有一半是给猫和狗吃的用的。简心暗暗地想："真是神奇，宠物和人类在这里完全平分天下。"她觉得有点纳闷，这儿的人这么喜欢小动物吗？在她们那完全没有这种概念，大家都还生活在贫困的边缘，经济还是很弱，并且她记得从小到大，她没有一个玩具，更别说宠物了。不同的国家和地区，差异还是挺大的，不论是经济方面还是人们的生活方式方面。超市里所有的物品都明码标价，下面是用德语注释的物品名称，她也完全看不懂，和睁眼瞎差不多。超市里人很少，就一个营业员和三三两两几个客人，不像国内，到处都是人，几乎所有场所都塞满了人。简心感叹：这儿的人好少，有点冷清孤单。她习惯了国内熙熙攘攘的人群，习惯了人声鼎沸、人头攒动的氛围，而这里却人烟稀少，安静地可以听到一根针掉落的声音，这巨大的反差让她觉得有很强的孤寂感与不适应感。逛完超市，她们走到了街道上，黄小丹指着另外一个刷成粉颜色的房子，说："你看，那是文具店，如果你以后要买学习用品，就可以去那里。挨着文具店的是杂物店，里面卖各种熏肉奶酪等，这里也有提供邮寄信件的服务。"沿着街道往下走，她们来到了一个小型的中央广场，一座尖顶的古老的教堂巍峨地矗立在那里。简心听到的钟声就是从这个小教堂里传出来的。再往下走便是一个小餐馆，然后就到小镇的尽头了。出了小镇，便是大片的农田。小镇的规模在简心眼里，真的是迷你型的，10分钟就能走完，虽然她觉得空荡荡的街道以及安静得出奇的氛围让她觉得有点孤独感，但小镇整体还是很美，很精致，很宁静。在她后来待了2年以后，她却很好地习惯了那种平静安详、与世无争的生活。

逛完小镇后，黄小丹选择了另外一条人路带着简心回学校，她边走边说："从学校去这个小镇一共有三条路，这是第二条路，一般行人走得比较少，因为有很多车辆经过。"多余的话，她也不多说，也不多问，简心就默默地点点头，也不知道如何跟黄小丹畅谈。人与人之间的缘分真的很奇妙，有些人碰在一起，相互吸引对方，会有说不完的话题，会觉得很容易沟通或交谈。但也有些人相遇了，却觉得尴尬，紧张或不知所措，不知道如何谈天说地。简心和黄小丹之间属于第二种情形，她们之间的磁场有些不对，见了面，没有那种特别亲切的感觉，觉得很生疏。所以沿着这条大道回学校的路上，她们两个默默无语，就这样静静地走着。到了学校的大门口，黄小丹指着第三条路的方向，对简心说："你看，那是第三条下山的路，山下是上艺术课的一座老房子，以及体育馆，到时候你上了课就知道了。如果今后你有什么问题，可以随时来问我。但最好不要用中文问。"简心感激地说："谢谢你，黄小丹。"黄小丹说她还有事情，就匆匆离开了。简心对这里的地理位置大致了解了。她现在没有别的地方可去，一切对她而言是那么陌生，她就只想回自己的宿舍。她脑子里很乱，走了好几趟，还是不记得她住的房间具体在哪里，因为这个宫殿的建筑结构尤为复杂，不像现代化的大楼一样，方方正正，而是七拐八拐，要绕过很多弯弯曲曲的走廊与门廊，才能回到她住的房间。"不管怎样，总要回去吧，不然一个人杵在这里干嘛，别人肯定会觉得莫名其妙或很奇怪。"简心心里想。然后她就凭着记忆力，爬上楼梯，踏着咯吱咯吱的木地板。到了二楼，朝左的方向，沿着长长的走廊穿过一道道门，然后又爬台阶，又穿过好几道门，才终于回到了自己的房间，她的房间是这座大楼最高处的卧室，找到还是有点难度的，她希望下一次不要再迷路了。简心觉得很纳闷，不是很理解自己的记忆力出了什么问题，看到很多学生，也分不清楚谁是谁，就觉得她们都长一个样。找自己的房间，中途也差点迷路，走过好几遍了，居然还不记得，她无法理智地解释这样的状况。回到房间后，她看到舍友已经在房间里，舍友一声不吭，一直在忙自己的事情。简心坐到书桌前，望着窗外的阿尔卑斯山脉，心里有些茫然。她看着看着就发起呆来，她回想了以前在家时发生的事情，有些回忆依旧很清晰，仿佛发生在昨天一样，也有很多记忆已经成了模糊影像，离现实越来越遥远，只留下一些痕迹。此刻的她，思乡情结越来越重，她很想念国内的亲人和朋友，真切地感受到一人在外心灵的孤寂感。她从箱子里翻出相片，把全家福贴在床边的墙壁上，看着笑容灿烂的父母和弟弟、爷爷奶奶，她有说不出的伤感与孤独，离家之前这种感觉还不是很强烈，那时候夹杂的更多的是兴奋、好奇以及对未来生活的憧憬。但现在真的到达了目的地，她突然变得很想家，很怀念以往热闹而温馨的家，在这里是完全不同的氛围，没有了家的温暖，所有的一切对她而言是那么陌生以及冷冷的，天气也是冷冷的。她很想联系父母，但她没有任何通信工具，没有手机，也没有电脑，那时候的通讯还极不方便，只有国际长途。但她的宿舍里根本没有电话机，她很想听到父母熟悉的声音，听到他们的安慰，但无可奈何，这一切暂时都不可能。父母想联系她，也不知道怎么联系。那个年代，远在不同的国家，亲人之间的联系如同像断了线的风筝，风筝越飞越远，不知道飞去哪里了。简心的父母也只知道她去了德国，有没有顺利到达学校真的不得而知了。简心想爸爸妈妈可能会很担心她，不知道她是不是一切顺利，自从她离开上海的出入境，就再也没有联系过。窗外已经漆黑一片，简心觉得这一天过得特别漫长，夜幕降临，已经是晚上 9：30 了，她一个人静静地躺在床上，长途跋涉了几十个小时，现在终于能好好地睡上一觉了，没过几秒钟，就进入了梦乡。梦中她仿佛还是在熟悉的学校里，在父母亲人的身边，仿佛不曾离开过。

简心的父母确实很担心她，尤其是她的母亲，那天送完女儿回到家后，她的心里很不是滋味，躺在床上，翻来覆去就是睡不着。母亲跟简心的父亲对话："女儿怎么样了，她才 16 岁，就孤身一人离开了家，去一个这么遥远的国度，人生地不熟，不会一句德语，万一遇到骗子坏人怎么办？飞机有没有安全抵达？简心到底有没有被接机的人顺利送到学校？"脑子里出现各种各样的问题，她左思右想，实在是难以入眠。做母亲的永远是最关心爱护自己的儿女的，为孩子操碎了心，无论孩子长多大，在父母眼里，永远是长不大的孩子，是父母一生的牵挂。简心的父亲虽然也有点担心女儿，但他自我调节能力很强，他安慰简心的母亲："你不要胡思乱想，瞎操心，简心肯定已经平安抵达了。快点睡吧，忙了一天了。"说完，他就呼呼大睡了。但她的母亲却怎么也睡不着，听了这些安慰的话语，心里安稳了一些，但更多的还是担心与不踏实，她彻夜未眠。早上父亲醒来，看到简心的母亲一个人在偷偷地抹眼泪，她说："我一个晚上怎么都睡不着，你怎么睡得着的，辛辛苦苦养大的女儿，一个人去了这么远的地方，也没法联系，她现在怎么样呀？都怪你，让她这么早出国留学，留在我们身边不好吗？为什么一定要让一个女孩子去那么远的地方，发生些什么事情，我们也帮不了忙。我真的是担心呀，简心现在在哪里呀？我好想念我的女儿呀。"简心的父亲听过后，温和而又耐心地安慰道："老婆，你不要太担心，不要想太多，简心肯定顺利到达了，不要自己吓自己。把自己的生活过好，孩子长大了，总是要飞走的，怎么可能一直在我们身边，这样也会耽误他们的前途。"他们你一言我一语，彼此慰藉着对方，祈祷女儿在异国他乡顺顺利利，也很希望亲爱的女儿能尽快跟他们联系，给他们报一个平安，让父母这颗悬着的操不完的心能安心放心。

经过一个晚上充足的睡眠，她精力充沛，不再那么多愁善感，而是又恢复了以往的自信与果敢。舍友还在梦乡中，简心听着窗外小鸟欢快的叫声，以及远处教堂的深沉的钟声响，从床上一跃而起，进入房间旁的洗手间，刷牙洗脸，淋浴，梳洗打扮。以前她从来都不会在早晨洗澡，因为在国内的时候，一般都是晚上洗澡。国内读书的时光，早晨的时间安排得尤为紧凑，根本没有时间好好地梳洗，只能草率快速地收拾一下，立刻跑向教室，开始一天的早自习，那样的生活节奏跟打仗差不多。现在她学着和当地的学生一样，早晨淋浴，开始新的一天。她发现，早晨洗澡之后，感觉一切很清新，充满了希望，益处多多，所以在今后漫长的留学生涯中，她都保持了这个晨起洗澡的习惯。一切准备完毕，她就沿着之前走过的路线，经过七八道门，途中又遇到了好些学生，有些学生见到她后，很有礼貌地跟她打招呼："HALLO, Guten Morgen（早上好）。"还有一些很腼腆内敛的学生，好奇地盯着她看。简心心里想：在没有了解别人之前，不要擅自评价别人好还是不好，好好地做好自己。这儿大多数人还是很礼貌很有涵养的。新的一天开始了，这是新的起点，我会好好适应这里的生活的。相信自己，你一定可以的，不要怀疑自己的潜力。

不一会儿，她就到了食堂。这儿的食堂和以前国内的食堂截然不同。记得以前的食堂挤满了学生，设施陈旧落后，每个人都要排队去取菜打饭，几乎每天队伍排得跟一条条长龙差不多。食堂里人声鼎沸，每个人都需要扯着嗓子大声说话，怕对方听不见自己的说话声。取了饭菜以后，就随便找一个空位坐下，和几个要好的同学一起吃饭。简心属于活泼外向型的，每次吃饭的时候，别的好友都专注着吃饭，她却喜欢滔滔不绝地聊天，聊很多学校里发生的事情或一些八卦，有时聊着聊着，饭菜还一口都没动，别人已经吃完了，然后朋友们总会说："简心，快吃呀，你的饭还没动呢。你是聊天大王，聊天会上瘾，饭也不吃了。"简心看大家都吃完了，就立刻狼吞虎咽地吃起来，然后跟好友手挽着手，还要去零食铺买点零食，满足一下她嘴馋的欲望。这儿的食堂，确切地应该不能用"食堂"这两个字来形容这个场所，当她推开门，见整个室内空间分成了三个宽敞的大厅，里面巧妙地摆放了几十张大圆桌，大圆桌上都铺上了白色的桌垫，大厅的墙面上是充满艺术气息的精美绝伦的欧洲壁画，壁画上的人物惟妙惟肖，生动而有趣，风景画如痴如醉，宁静而美好。大厅的主色调是暖黄色，地板也是高雅而又耐用的深棕色的木质地板。只有最里面的一个大厅的主色调是淡绿色，墙上的壁画显得更夺人眼球，壁画依照顺序整个浏览一遍，貌似是一个完整宗教故事的情节展现。绿色的大厅显得清新而雅致，大厅里的主灯都是欧式水晶吊灯，奢华而精美，一扇大大的弧形的窗户镶嵌其中，透过窗外，便是生机勃勃、妙趣横生、典雅美观的南花园。简心惊叹："好美的餐厅，果不其然像宫殿一般金碧辉煌，精美绝伦。"原来，简心就读的学校曾经是一个公爵的府邸，后来公爵去世后，便改建成了巴伐利亚州著名的私立学校，从5年级一直到13年级（相当于国内教育的小学5年级，初中到高中）。这是一所男女混合的私立学校，学费高昂，不是一般的家庭可以承受的。相传这里出过很多有名的校友，后来校友在社会上取得事业上的成功后，会回报母校，做慈善捐款。简心被这个高雅的 dining hall（食堂）深深地吸引了，她由衷地感叹："太美了，真的太美了。"

当她正沉浸其中，一位五十多岁的老太太向她迎面走来，她围着一个白色的围裙，笑容可掬地问她"WILLST DU FRUSTUCKEN?"（你想要吃早饭了吗？）简心不知道她叽里咕噜说什么，就很纳闷，然后就用手势比划，说她肚子饿了，想吃早饭了。老太太很聪明，看懂了她的意思，然后就带着简心来到了厨房。厨房里井然有序，十分干净整洁，与旁边的餐厅风格截然不同，用的都是品质卓越的现代化厨房器具。老太太温和而又礼貌地用手势比划，问简心想吃什么？简心看了厨房里摆放的热气腾腾的刚出炉的面包以及黄油，就指了指面包和黄油。老太太读懂了她的意思，耐心地把面包黄油放在一个精致的碟子中，然后给了简心一副刀叉，嘴里一边说德语，一边带简心来到了餐厅，找了一个位置坐下，让简心享用早餐。此刻，简心感到很温暖，心里没有那么空落落了，碰到善良而热心的人，会给她带来莫大的安慰与鼓励，虽然她听不懂老太太说什么，但是厨房老太太的热情与友好让简心觉得世间的美好，人性的美好，即使是陌生人，但人心善良起来，人与人之间的距离是那么近。

简心在出国以前，从来没有吃过西餐，所以她也不知道怎么使用刀叉，到底是左手拿刀还是右手拿刀，根本搞不清楚。她觉得有些尴尬，怕别人看到笑话她，刚好现在还很早，还没有其他人来餐厅吃饭，所以不管三七二十一，她就按自己舒服的方式，或是她自认为对的方式用刀叉。她也搞不清楚奶酪与黄油的区别，以为老太太给她的是奶酪，奶酪应该是硬乎乎的，可以单独吃的。然后她就把整个一块黄油当作奶酪往嘴巴里塞，发现居然什么味道都没有，嘴巴里只留下油腻腻的感觉。老太太进来看了她一眼，发现她吃错了，用一把刀刮了些黄油，抹在松软的面包上，让她尝尝。简心尝了一口，感觉真是人间美味，面包涂了黄

第九章：阿尔卑斯山脚下的寄宿制学校

油后，吃起来又香又润，像涂了淡味的冰激凌一样，入口即化。简心第一次感受到西餐的魅力，这只是很普通的面包加黄油，她第一次尝试后就爱上了。简心的母亲担心她刚开始吃不惯西餐，还为她在行李箱里准备了大量榨菜和方便面。但出乎意料的是，简心却没有一丁半点不适应西餐，她对新鲜的事物以及从未尝试过的料理有着极大的兴趣和探索欲，再者西餐真的是符合她的口味。所以那些榨菜与方便面完全没有发挥它们应急的作用，而是默默不语地一直躺在箱子里。简心吃得很开心与满足，不一会，陆陆续续几个其他的住宿生也来餐厅吃饭了。他们看到餐厅里有一个来自东方的新学生，盯着看了一会，然后远远地打了招呼，就去取自己的早餐了。简心吃完以后，便回了自己的房间。

  舍友已经起床了，在隔壁的洗手间梳洗。简心懵懵懂懂，不知道这一天怎么安排，没有一个人告诉她每一天的课程表是怎样的。她就像一个傻里傻气的孩子一样，对接下去的学习生活一无所知。过了没多久，她觉得在房间待着实在无趣，就下楼去看看能不能摸到一点头绪。走出这座主楼的大门，看到一群学生正朝主楼左侧的一座建筑物里走去。他们个子高大挺拔，每个人手里都拿着文件夹，有的学生背着书包，简心也想跟着他们去看看。坐到教室里，教室里变得很活跃，因为一个新学生的到来。大家都目不转睛地盯着简心看，带着好奇的眼光，七嘴八舌地讨论着什么，简心一个字也听不懂。教室的墙上挂着一个钟，当时钟指到 8：10 分，有一个满脸络腮胡子的老师走上了讲台，叽里咕噜地开始讲课。简心像进入了一个外太空一样，对所有的人，所有发生的事以及他们所叙述的，一概不知，完全听不懂在说什么。她只是看到这个教室有一排操作台，上面摆着各种烧杯器皿，以及做实验的小装置，如果她猜得没错的话，这节课应该是化学课，走进来的应该是化学老师。这位老师头发已经花白，有五十多岁的样子，虽然长满了络腮胡子，但很有亲和力，语调平缓。他讲课的时候，台下还有学生窃窃私语，有些调皮捣蛋的学生一个劲地想跟简心套近乎，挤眉弄眼的，很好奇怎么教室里突然莫名其妙地出现了一个新学生，还是来自遥远的东方。课程讲了一小半，这位和蔼可亲的化学老师也注意到了简心，然后走下了讲台，径直朝简心的座位走过来，先说了几句的德语。简心一个劲地摇头，最后蹦出来"English please"（请说英语）两个单词，然后老师领悟这位新学生不懂德语，他用娴熟的英文问"May I help you（有什么可以帮你的吗）?"简心听懂了老师的话，但接下去她不知道怎么用英文表述她想干嘛，其实她是真心不知道她要做什么，是一个人在房间待着无聊，又没有人告诉她课程安排，她就下楼想自己探究以下情形的。

化学老师见这个学生什么都答不上来，然后就对她说"Are you searching for Herr May? Follow me, I will bring you to Herr May's office（你是要找 Herr May 吗？跟我来，我带你去他的办公室）。"简心也不确定她是不是真的要去找什么 Herr May，就点点头。然后化学老师就带着简心回到了主楼，一路往楼上奔去。到了二楼，问了路过的一些其他人 Herr May 的办公室在哪。突然出现一个高个子的黑人，穿着笔挺气派的西装，化学老师看到了他，就跟他礼貌地寒暄了几句，说了一通话，然后就和简心挥手再见了。这个黑人就带着简心来到一个宽敞而现代化的办公室。办公室里有一块很大的白板以及几张课桌椅。另外一部分是办公区域，有一张办公桌，上面整整齐齐地摆放着一堆文件，一台电脑，办公桌后是一排书柜。这个高个子的黑人长着一双很大的眼睛，鼻翼宽大，嘴唇厚厚的，头发剃得很短，他微笑着说"I am your German teacher Herr May. You are the new student from China, right（我是你的德语老师，你是来自中国的新学生吗）?"他说话的语速很慢，发音很清晰，简心听懂了，这是她的德语老师。简心很纳闷，心里想：怎么一个黑人做他的德语老师，他是不是纯正的德国人呢，是不是也是外国人，外国人教外国人德语，这样也可以吗？不过她也没想太多，就觉得出乎她的意料之外，今后教她德语，领她入门的是一位高高大大的黑人老师。这是学校的安排，肯定有它的合理之处。后来简心才了解到，这位德语老师也来头不小，虽然他不是纯正的德国人，但他很有语言天分，会好几种语言，法语是他的母语，他大学主修的专业是德语系，是一位语言系博士。这位 Herr May 是学校国际部的主任兼德语老师，负责就读于这所私立学校所有国际学生的德语课程。

简心从此以后就开始跟着 Herr May 学德语了，正常年级的课她暂时上不了，因为首先要把语言基础打好，不然所有的高中课程都没法学。第一节德语课，她学的是一头雾水，云里雾里的。Herr May 当然是不会中文的，所以对于简心这个德语初学者而言，他需要用一点创新思维来教学。虽然简心的英语基础不是很牢固，仅限于哑巴英语，会看英语短文，但听说很薄弱，因为那时候在国内学英语，没有好的外语环境，平时大家几乎都用不着用英语交流，纯属是为了应试的目的。但不管如何，简心已经有了一些英语的基础。自然而言，Herr May 就通过英语作为语言媒介开始教导简心德语。他尽量用最短最慢的语速教导与解释。第一节课，他在白板上写下了德语的基础字母，然后一个一个地教简心每个字母的发音，德语的字母比 26 个英文字母还多出好几个特殊字母。他写的字比较潦草，所以当简心在笔记本上抄写课堂内容时，经常搞不清楚，到底是什么字母，具体怎样写，跟国内英语老师端端正正地写的外语完全不同。教完了德语字母的写法与读法，Herr May 便开始教最常用的词，例如 Lehrer（老师）、dieFrau（女士）等，简心聚精会神地听着老师的发音，然后记好课堂笔记。第一节课，对她而言，既新奇而陌生，内容虽然是最初级的，但对她这个零基础的学生来说，还是觉得很不适应，跟不上德语老师的节奏。但唯一让她感到欣慰至极的是，Herr May 是个具有亲和力的老师，会经常鼓励学生，不像国内很多老师都很严肃，不苟言笑。这样她的内心踏实了很多，在这个人生地不熟的地方，她需要别人的鼓励与耐心的教导，这会让她的求学生涯顺畅很多，也可以稍微弥补一点内心孤独与迷茫的感受，但想念亲人朋友的问题是无法在短时间内彻底解决的，她还只有 16 岁呢。

下课后，简心一路跑回了自己的房间。经过好几次来来回回，她已经可以很准确地找到自己的卧室了。虽然她需要和一个德国女孩共同享有这个房间，但这里是她栖身的小小天地，除了这个卧室，她没有其他地方可去，或者可以精准地理解为，她在没有掌握当地语言之前，是没有足够的勇气出去探索其他的地方，因为怕迷路，怕自己无法掌控未知的状况突然出现。她这才感到了自己的渺小与无助感，所以心里充满了无限的渴望与动力，她对自己默默地说："不论多困难，我一定要适应这里，适应这里最首要的任务，是需要很好地掌握这门生疏难懂的德语。"所以她回到了自己的小天地后，就立刻一头扎进了复习第一堂德语课的内容中。她对有些词汇的正确是否感觉很模棱两可，因为老师潦草的笔迹，真的是勉强记下来的。她闷着头，很使劲地回忆老师课堂教她的字母发音以及词汇发音，但是头脑里还是模糊一片。对她而言，这第一堂课真的是上得糊里糊涂，她还没有进入学习德语的状态，也可能没有适应 Herr May 的授课方式，还有一点是她没有录音机，可以反复听学过的单词与字母，所以仅凭脑袋存储的记忆，她就这么一个一个读着奇特发音的德语字母以及一些词汇，也实在是要质疑自己，现在复习时发的音是不是准确。她心想："如果是在语言学校，至少会有一起学德语的外国学生，大家可以相互交流，不懂的可以一起探讨，可这里所有的学生基本都是本国人，德语是人家的母语，别人怎么可能会跟我探讨这发音的问题呢。再说，我都不知道如何用德语或英语问他们，这个音怎么发。"她很努力地读着读着，望着窗外优美的风景以及高高耸立的阿尔卑斯山脉，显得那样的平静与悄无声息，她没有别的办法，她现在想做的就是每天好好地把课堂所有的内容复习好，不论是不是发音正

第九章：阿尔卑斯山脚下的寄宿制学校

确，随着时间应该会越来越顺畅和习惯。现在只是刚开始，万事开头难，等适应了学习节奏，一切会慢慢好起来的。不要想太多了，好好努力吧。然后她就继续读课堂笔记。这时候，她的舍友回到了房间，跟她淡淡的打了一个招呼，就去忙自己的事情了。她们两个之间几乎没有任何的对话，对简心而言，这个舍友显得很有距离感以及神秘感，虽然同处一室，但她只忙自己的事情，对新来的舍友毫不在意、漠不关心。她听到简心在读德语字母以及一些简单日常的词汇，也不加任何点评，是对是错，什么都不说，过了没多久，就离开了房间。简心就一个人默默地坐在书桌前，读呀读呀……

起初，简心对学校的课程计划以及饮食起居时间表真的是丈二和尚摸不着头脑。下午 1:00 是午餐时间，她便跟着其他学生一起去了那个高贵典雅的餐厅，只见一张张铺着白色桌垫的圆形桌子优雅而富有艺术感地摆在餐厅里，如一朵朵洁白的莲花。在两个大厅的连接处，摆放着一条几乎有 3 米长的长桌，桌面上也铺着洁白无瑕的白桌布，各种各样的美味食物摆放在这个长桌上。有蔬菜沙拉，主食牛排，或是意大利面，饭后甜点蛋糕或布丁，以及各色水果等。简心看到这些美食，肚子咕噜噜叫个不停，她很想立刻就去取餐，尽情大吃一顿。但是学校有学校的规矩，到了餐厅，学生不可以立刻随意去取餐，是要严格遵守这个私立学校的用餐礼仪的。每个学生找到自己的座位后，不准马上坐在椅子上，而是需要端端正正地站在自己的座位旁，不允许喧哗吵闹，等餐厅里鸦雀无声后，有一个学生代表宣布：Guten Appetite（祝好胃口），然后才可以开始用餐。当大家听到了"Guten Appetite"后，就如水电站的阀门一打开，汹涌澎湃的水流涌出来一样，整个餐厅也变得热闹非凡。聊天声、刀叉声以及意大利厨师与他的助手踏在木质地板上的脚步声汇成一首最自然和谐的交响乐。简心也模仿着其他学生，一开始站立在自己的位置旁，等到学生代表宣布结束后，看到其他人都可以坐到位置上了，她也坐在了自己的位置上。她不敢出错，因为怕闹洋相，再说对西餐的用餐礼仪，脑子里几乎是一片空白，到底是哪只手拿刀叉，她也搞不清楚。所以只能依葫芦画瓢，仔细观察模仿其他人的用餐举止和习惯。不一会儿，有个厨师送来了今天的主食牛排，八到九块牛排整整齐齐地躺在一个长方形的不锈钢容器中，大家看到主食已经上桌了，每个人井然有序地夹了块牛排放在自己的碟子里，然后娴熟地把棕色浓稠的肉汤汁浇在牛排上。刚开始，简心还有些疑惑：这个不锈钢小壶是干什么用的，怎么长得像阿拉丁神灯一样，造型精巧别致。现在她才恍然大悟，原来是用来盛放牛排汤汁的。她心里暗叹：西餐真的考究，每一种餐具都有它独特的用处，并且还考虑得这么周全细致，这和她以前在国内学校用餐的情景截然不同。一桌大概8到9个学生，大家都取完牛排后，就剩下简心还没拿，她虽然肚子很饿了，但很小心谨慎，想等大家都取完后，自己再拿。有一个德国女孩，长得皮肤白皙，大大的眼睛，鼻子特别高挺，看上去长得有点像古典美的蒙娜丽莎，看到简心盘子里还空空的，就好心地帮简心夹了一块很大的牛排。简心忙不迭地对这个女孩说了"thanks"，也学着其他人一样，浇了些汤汁在牛排上，生疏地使用着刀叉，低着头默默地吃了起来。牛排烤得恰到好处，淋上汤汁，鲜美香醇，真的是人间美味。简心小心翼翼地吃着，不发出太大的咀嚼声，就怕自己出洋相，让别人笑话。其间，她也会时常观察一下周围学生的脸部表情，发现有些学生会向她投来友好和善的眼光，而有些学生面无表情地瞅了她几眼，和旁边的学生叽里咕噜地说着什么，也不知道是聊的别的话题还是在评价她。她觉得自己就是一个异类，她能说的话只有她自己一个人懂，这一群人说的话，她完全一窍不通。她心里想不是已经上过一节课了吗，怎么什么都听不懂，一个熟悉的用词都捕抓不到。他们聊得滔滔不绝，语速超快，对她而言，真的如同天书。还是好好吃饭吧。简心津津有味地吃着，不一会儿，一块牛排就吃完了。之后，她学着其他学生那样，去那个摆满各色食物的长桌上取其他的东西吃。她对沙拉不感兴趣，都是生的，也不知道吃了会不会肠胃不舒服。甜点是她的最爱，西式甜点做得非常精致，看了让人垂涎欲滴。她胃口很好，一下取了好几块不同种类的，有黑森林蛋糕、苹果派以及梨子派。然后回到了自己的位置上，把蛋糕往嘴里塞。其他人看她吃东西的表情，她也无暇顾及了。此时此刻，她正被美食吸引着，这是她初到这个学校最享受的方面，因为她真的很喜欢西式餐饮，完全不需要适应，仿佛是与生俱来的热爱。所以即使刚开始在这个新学校的生活对她而言陌生又新奇，她会时常感到孤寂与无助感，但学校的食物给了她最好的味蕾满足与心灵慰藉，每当学习压力很大，或是思乡情结很重的时候，她会通过美食来调剂自己，寻找到生活中的快乐。很多学生不像简心那样吃得那么满足、意犹未尽，她们吃了几口就不再吃了，她们仿佛对聊天更感兴趣。这些学生都是德国上层阶级的子女，父母不是医生，就是律师，或者有自己的公司。因此他们的嘴巴肯定是比较挑剔的，什么西式菜品都已经品尝过了，学校的这些菜对他们而言是很稀松平常的食物，谈不上特别出众。有很多学生的盘子里总会剩下些许菜或丢弃的面包，他们习惯了优越的物质生活，全然不会感受到这是对食物的浪费。简心这么喜欢这些菜品，是不舍得扔掉的。很多中国父母都会教育孩子"谁知盘中餐，粒粒皆辛苦"，因而她没有剩菜或丢弃食物的习惯。

　　午餐持续了大概一个半小时，那个英俊潇洒、高高大大的学生代表又出来叽里咕噜地演讲了大概5分钟左右，然后就结束了。相比国内学校的就餐环境与形式，这里的餐饮更注重仪式感与次序感，完全是一种别样的体验，简心觉得非常特别与新鲜，虽然这个陌生的环境以及语言的障碍给她带来了重重困难，但也给她带来了很多探索新鲜事物与其他文化的机会。学生和老师们陆陆续续地离开高雅如古典宫殿般的餐厅，还有一些学生还没吃完，就留在那里继续享用美食，有一些学生还沉浸在聊天的氛围中。简心在离开餐厅时，无意识地发现这里的学生很开放，在公众场合互相接吻或拥抱，还有的女朋友竟然会坐在男朋友的大腿上，双臂挽着男朋友，亲热地聊着什么或在打情骂俏，周围的人看到了不会感到很惊奇，而是欣然接受学生这样公开的恋爱关系，或是至少大家不会用异样的眼光去瞅这些情侣，只会觉得这是再正常不过的事情了。简心此刻觉得实在是太不可思议了，在这里早恋竟然是被包容和鼓励的，年轻男女之间的爱恋可以毫不掩饰地公之于众，毫不顾忌地在任何场合谈恋爱，这可是一所从5年级到13年级（横跨小学后半部分，初中与高中学年）的文理寄宿制学校。如果在中国的学校里，早恋几乎是被禁止的，就算有这种现象，也只能偷偷摸摸的，在公众场合尤其在学校中，是绝对不可能看到互生爱慕的男学生女学生抱在一起，热情地接吻等。简心简直像发现了新大陆一样，惊掉了下巴，在国内的高中，每个学生都规规矩矩的，都像受过军训的士兵一样严格地执行或遵守学校的所有课程安排，别说谈恋爱了。寄宿生不和校领导申请出门许可，出校门都是禁止的，完全是封闭式管理，并且没有自由的个人时间安排，大家都一个劲地蒙着头读书，夜以继日地勤奋读书，考上名校是人生中最重要的事情，其他的和学习无关都放在了次要位置。除了上课、做题以及自习课，还有早起晨跑，几乎没有任何其他的课外活动。可这里的学校是一种截然不同的课程安排，虽然也是寄宿制学校，但下午3：30课程结束后，学生有充分的自由安排自己的业余时间，可以去山下的小镇买些日常用品，或是参加各种兴趣课，例如画画、羽毛球、攀岩、乐器课、舞蹈课等，或是和三五好友去咖啡馆聊天，也可以一个人独处，做自己想做的事情等。简心觉得，这个新学校的自由空间大了很多，虽然她会有些想家，不能和周围的学生交流，但这样充满着自由气息的学习氛围是她所喜欢的，因为她其实是一个不喜欢通过外界逼迫而学习的人，是喜欢按自己舒服的节奏安排学习与生活的，而新学校这点开放而人性化的氛围是她很推崇的。并且随着时间的流逝，她越来越了解，新学校不是光把学习成绩放在首位，而不顾及学生其他方面的发展，新学校注重的是个性化教学与全人教育，所以这里的学生更活泼调皮，更喜欢搞恶作剧，没有那么循规蹈矩，十五六岁的花季少男少女谈恋爱也是完全被允许的，是绝对不会被扣上早恋的帽子，或是被家长、老师或周围的人指指点点的。这里更注重个性的施展与自尊的保护。简心觉得实在太不可思议了，中西方文化竟然差异如此之大，东方文化显得含蓄、保守以及传统，西方文化显得自由、开放以及注重个性化发展以及个人空间。她深深地感叹：世界之大，无奇不有，这回我是真的开眼界了，早恋竟然是被鼓励或允许的，男女朋友可以在学校各处随便秀甜蜜幸福，实在是不可思议。因为简心受到了很多东方思想的影响，所以对她而言，这样大胆的谈恋爱就像发现了一个大新闻一样。

因为语言的缘故，她还不能像其他学生一样，按一个年级的正常的课程表上课，因为就算插班去上，也是和听天书一样，没有任何效果。所以她的课程主要是国际部的德语课。Herr May 还有很多来自其他欧洲国家的国际生，只是像简心这样德语零基础的学生，仅此一个，别的国际生或多或少已经在他们暑期夏令营或是语言学校学了初级或中级课程，所以他们已经可以毫无障碍地进行简单的日常交流。简心确实是一个特殊的存在，德语零基础，来自遥远的东方（整个学校除了黄小丹来自中国，她便是第二个），还有一点尤为不同：她在来到德国这个寄宿制学校之前，几乎没有去过其他任何国家或任何中国的城市，而只是在她出生的那个小村镇勤奋努力地读书，也就是说她没有开阔的眼界与国际化的认知，而是一个土里土气，行为举止很谨慎规矩的学生；相比而言，这里的学生（包括国际学生）均来自家境优渥的上层社会，出生在高度发达的资本主义国家，从小跟着父母就游历了很多国家，见识了广阔的天地，见识了多样化的文明，所以这儿的学生是自信、活泼且优越感十足的。简心面对他们，会有些许的不自信，因为觉得和他们所经历的差异太大了，她对很多东西都不懂也没有见识过，所以她像刺猬一样，喜欢把自己的身体蜷缩在一起，藏起来，保护自己，而同时面对别人的负面评价或语言攻击，她又会像刺猬一样，全身长满了刺，如果有敌人伤害她，准备随时打开防御机制，驱除或反攻挑衅者。午餐过后，她又去了德语老师 Herr May 的教室上课。Herr May 热情而友好地用英文问候她："hi, how are you? everything is fine（怎么样？一切都好吗）?"简心也礼貌地回复"I am fine, thanks（我很好，谢谢）。"前一节课，Herr May 已经问过她的姓名，但这节课，他又忘了简心的名字怎么发音，Herr May 显得有些不好意思，问："Do you have a English name? your Chinese name is really difficult for me to remember and pronounce（你有英语名字吗？你的中文名字对我而言很难去记忆与发音）。"虽然简心的英语口语薄弱，但 Herr May 放缓语速问的这个简短的问题她还是听得懂的。然后她就对德语老师说："You can call me Nancy。Nancy is my English name（你可以叫我南希，南希是我的英语名字）。"Herr May 听了，喜出望外，终于不用那么拗口地说简心的中文名字了，他干脆利落地回答"Great。I will call you Nancy from now on（好的。从今以后，我会叫那你南希）。"简心默认地点点头，表示赞同。对外国人而言，准确地发出中国人的姓名（用拼音写出）貌似是很难的事情，那是因为他们对汉语这个语言体系不了解。对简心而言，也是同理，因为她对德语体系几乎一窍不通，所以看到德国人的名字，就觉得名字特别长，看一眼，不知道究竟怎么读，完全是门外汉。其实在国内的时候简心根本不用她的英文名，因为大家习惯称呼中文名字，简心曾经所出生以及生活学习的地方还是非常淳朴与闭塞的，没有那么多新潮的思想，哪会有人动不动就用英文名。她的英文名也不是自己精心挑选或自己想到的，而是在初二的时候时髦的英语老师给了全班同学一张英语名字的单子，让学生自己挑选中意的英文名。大家都挑选得差不多了,还剩下几个没人要的英语名,然后简心便挑了 Nancy 这个名字,可能是读起来有点朗朗上口,也有可能是没有太多其他的选择。总而言之,这一切都是出于缘分,其实一个人与自己的名字也有着千丝万缕的内在联系,名字就如同一个人在社会上的符号,有了这个符号就可以更好地识别这个人,与其他人建立起更有效的连接。至于名字究竟会不会给人带来吉祥或是厄运,这就不得而知了。一般情况下,长辈都会选择吉利的字眼来称呼自己新出生的孩子,希望他一生平安、幸福健康、顺顺利利。由此可见父母与亲人的良苦用心,在出生时便已经给予了孩子无限的期望与祝福。中国的父母尤其伟大,苦自己也不能苦孩子,一生都在为孩子的前途与将来奔波忙碌,自己宁愿吃再多苦,只要想到可以给孩子更好的未来,创造更高的平台,这些苦这些累都是值得的。父母对孩子的爱是多么的无私与伟大,不计回报,只希望孩子能够茁壮成长,成了一个有道德有素养,对社会有用的人才。简心的父母也是如此,宁愿自己勒紧裤腰带,承受运营企业的巨大压力与风险,也希望尽自己最大的努力,把孩子培养成才,成为栋梁。简心深知父母的良苦用心,也体会父母生活与工作的不易,所以她非常懂事,在学业与生活上从来不用父母为她操心,因为她不想辜负父母与亲人,也因为她是一个懂得感恩、内心温纯善良的女孩。她不忍心父母的付出白白打水漂,所以不论这条路多辛苦,她都会心无旁骛、勇敢而坚定地走下去,为了父母,更为了自己。

今天下午的课程已经是第二次了,简心感觉没有第一节课那么不知所措了。Herr May 耐心地继续讲学,他给简心准备了初级的德语教材,里面有很多绘图以及生词、对话。Herr May 自己先读一遍语句或单词,然后让简心重复,中间如果有发音不正确的,老师再及时纠正。读完对话以后,老师再用英文或肢体语言解释词汇的意思,简心对有的词心领神会,有的还不确定是什么意思,因为这教材没有中文或英文解释,全是德语。教完书面课程后，Herr May 会给简心播放录音带，让她再多听几遍，真正感受到这门语言的独特魅力。多听录音，会了解实际场景中人们如何交谈，人物的语调与发音。简心听得聚精会神，非常专注，老师讲得每句话，她都很认真地记在心里。Herr May 告诉她学过的日常用语要大胆地在实际生活中应用，不要怕说错，关键是要多说多练习，如果说错了，别人会帮忙纠正，人家是不会笑话她的。一定要多练习，语言环境这么得天独厚，只要努力，慢慢会越来越适应这里的一切的。如果有什么不懂，可以随时问。简心很感激这位德语老师带她入门，也很感激他用耐心而友善的语言鼓励安慰她。今后的每次课堂，即使只有很小的进步，Herr May 都会毫不吝啬地夸赞她，让她越来越充满信心，相信靠自己的努力与勤奋一定可以冲破重重障碍。Herr May 在上课结尾，会一再强调，不要经常把德语翻译成中文来思考问题，而是直接应用德语，把德语当母语那般来学。所以后来，他给简心推荐了一本非常实用有效的朗文字典（德语－德语字典），每个新的词汇都没有用其他语言，例如英语或中文来注解，而是用完整而准确的德语长句来解释这个新词汇。

　　上完课后，她像往常一样和 Herr May 礼貌地道别，然后一路奔回自己的房间，坐在书桌旁，远眺一下窗外宁静而美丽的风景以及远处绵延不断的阿尔卑斯山脉后，又全身心地投入复习功课中。她的室友貌似经常不在房间，不是上课还没回来，就有可能逗留在她朋友的房间中，或者也有可能去小镇上和朋友欢聚聊天，或参加其他的兴趣活动。她也不得而知室友的去向，室友也不会主动跟她谈起任何事情。她们俩碰头见面了，也是点头微笑一下，没有任何交流。所以，简心几乎整天是一个人待在这个卧室里，因为她的课程没有其他学生那么紧凑，只有德语课，所以空下来的时间，她就自己一个人在房间里待着，复习德语功课。她真的一个说话的人都没有，虽然学校里的年轻面孔很多，学生叽叽喳喧，都很活泼热闹，但她没有一个朋友，没有一个可以交流的同龄人。她的内心深处是很孤独的，她经常也会想起在国内的时候有疼她的亲人以及很多热心的朋友，可在这里真的是举目无亲，没有任何朋友。她好希望找到一个好朋友，就不会那么孤单无助，也不会总是那么想家了，在异国他乡的日子也不会觉得过得那么慢了。来新学校才3到5天，可她觉得时间怎么突然变得这么漫长，仿佛已经过了一个多月似的。看到墙上贴的全家福，她自言自语地说："爸爸妈妈，爷爷奶奶，我好想你们。你们好吗？"正如前文所说，那个年代才2002年，国际通讯还很不发达，没有智能手机，简心出国留学的时候连一部手机和手提电脑都没有，所以她是没法联系家人的。她感觉自己完全和家人断联了，就像断了线的风筝一样，越飘越远。想着想着，她会感到莫名的伤感，她觉得自己和这个新的环境还是很格格不入，虽然新学校很美，老师也挺友好的，对她从来没有一次高声呵斥过，但她就是有点开心不起来。她总是觉得缺少了什么，具体是什么，她也说不清楚，可能是内心深处的那份温暖与感动，在这里，她始终觉得整个氛围有点冷冷的感觉，正如大多学生对她的态度。她现在唯一能做的便是尽自己最大的努力，以最快的速度掌握这门语言，不然其他的一切都不可能正常化。如果想要交朋友，填补内心的孤寂感，不会语言，简直是天方夜谭。可德语零基础的人，要立刻掌握是需要时间的，不是一两天可以解决的问题。简心知道多想也没用，还不如行动起来，欲速则不达，每天努力好好学习，把老师教的德语课好好复习好，其他的事情都不去想了，找不到朋友就找不到，这也不是我能控制的。不要纠结找朋友了，顺其自然吧。想完后，她就立刻高声朗读课堂上学的新的词汇与对话，但是她对有些德语发音有些模糊，不清楚是不是准确，旁边又没有其他的同学可以问。就这样她埋头苦读，每天花在语言学习上的时间很长很长。

过了大概一个礼拜，有一天，有一个同学告诉她，快去学校秘书处接听国际长途。她立刻飞奔到秘书办公室，当她接到电话，听到了父母熟悉的声音，电话那头她的父亲温和而亲切地问："简心，简心，是你吗？你在新学校一切都好吗？是不是一切都顺利？"听到了电话里父母关切的问候，简心终于忍不住大哭了起来。她本来不想哭的，但是憋了好几天的眼泪像决堤的洪水一样奔涌而出，她本来以为自己很坚强，离开了父母与朋友，可以很快地适应新的环境，适应这里的一切，可实际中却不是这样的。离开了才懂得珍惜，记得曾经出国以前，母亲经常会唠叨她，她还会嫌弃母亲对她的挑剔与唠叨，可现在的她，耳旁再也听不到母亲的唠叨以及父亲的鼓励。今天，终于在电话中又一次听到父母关切而又担心的话语，她真的再也无法控制自己的情绪了。她哭着回答父母："爸妈，我一切都好。你们放心。"然后听到了妈妈熟悉而关切的声音："简心，那天你离开家里后，我一夜都没合眼，不知道女儿是不是安全抵达，我很担心，这么遥远的路途，一个人就这样离开了。早晨，我坐在床边，眼泪又不自觉地流了下来。父母希望你在那里一切都好，家里一切都好，你不要挂念。"简心听了后，已经泣不成声了。她真的很想念父母，很想念自己的家乡，虽然家乡还很穷，很多设施还很简陋粗糙，但那里毕竟是她生活了16年的熟悉的家乡，有很多温暖的美好的回忆，也有她挂念的家人和朋友……最后电话那头，又听到了她父亲的声音："简心，好好努力，天天向上，爸爸相信你一定可以的。"简心含泪，坚定地回答父亲："爸爸，你放心，我会努力的。既然已经选择了这条路，我就好好地走下去。"之后，简心的父母说："我们不多说了，国际长途电话非常贵，刚才已经说了好几分钟了，今天先聊到这里，知道你一切顺利，我们也放心了。你好好照顾好自己，下次我们再打电话给你。"简心舍不得跟父母在电话里就这样说"再见"，但她懂得，国际长途太贵了，只能长话短说，让她读这所私立学校，父母已经支付了很高昂的学费，她再不能乱花钱了。通话结束了，电话那头父母的声音已经消失了。就这样，这是简心来到学校几天后和父母通的第一个电话，整个电话就持续了几分钟。简心的泪水止不住外流，秘书办公室的一位女士看到简心这么伤心难过的样子，很想安慰她，但不知道怎么和她说话，突然秘书处又出现了另外一个老师，看到简心泪流满面，他很富有同理心，真切地能感受到一个 16 岁的女孩离开自己的国家，离开父母，来到这么遥远的西方求学，内心会有怎样的孤独与不适应，然后就很真诚地安慰简心："Are you ok? I understand you are very sad because you can't see your parents and you miss them very much. Come on, You will get used to the life with time. Be strong（你还好吗？我理解你很伤心，因为你不能见到父母，你非常想念他们。加油，随着时间你会慢慢适应这里的生活。要坚强）。"简心听得似懂非懂，但那个老师拍了拍简心的肩膀，然后拥抱了一下她。她知道老师是想安慰她，简心很感激，随后她谢过了那位热心的老师以及秘书，离开了那个秘书办公室。像往常一样，她又孤孤单单地回到了自己的卧室，擦干眼泪，望着远方，耳旁再一次传来父亲鼓励的话语"好好学习，天天向上。"她再一次地安慰和鼓励自己："简心，不要再哭了，哭也解决不了任何问题。亲爱的爸妈，你们放心，我一定会好好努力的，不会让你们失望，也不会让你们对我教育的投资打水漂。我会坚强的，不论遇到多大的困难，我相信这些都只是暂时的，一切都会慢慢好起来的。"

　　随后，简心记得父亲送给她了一幅字画，那字画还在箱子里躺着呢。她立刻从箱子里取了出来，把它打开，上面写着"千里之行，始于足下"，字画的下方是写字人的名字、印章以及最后几个字"简心勉之"。那是有一次他们去国内一个城市旅游，在一个旅游景点父亲为她和弟弟请一位通晓国学的师傅写的字画，为了勉励他们。简心把这幅字画挂在卧室的墙上，每当她觉得心累或坚持不下去的时候，这 8 个字会像一位良师益友勉励着她前行。"千里之行，始于足下"，中华传统文化多么的博大精深，意义深刻。这八个字虽然说出来写出来简单，但要真正做到是非常难的。人贵在坚持，做任何事情，如果只有三分钟热度，是不会成功的，也不会达到自己设定的很高的目标，而唯有脚踏实地，一步一个脚印往前走，坚持不懈地努力，就总有到岸的那一天。简心觉得现在的自己就如同一只蜗牛，而其他的学生如同兔子，她就仿佛是龟兔赛跑，别人可以在中途休息休息，只需要花很小的工夫，就可以到达目的地，可她却需要花很大的工夫，付出常人很多倍的努力，才有可能到达终点。而这一切主要是语言的障碍，在学习所有的功课之前，必须先解决德语的语言问题。而要学好这门语言，靠一两天的努力是没有用的，而是需要每天持续的努力，需要一个非常漫长的过程，一点点积累，经过长时间的沉淀，才能达到质的飞跃。简心看着这八个字，她暗自下定决心：我会一步一个脚印踏踏实实地过好每一天，努力勤奋。果真如此，在今后的每一天，简心按部就班地去 Herr May 那里上德语课，回到卧室后就立刻好好朗读复习。在课堂上她会积极主动地回答老师的提问，多给自己练习口语的机会，如果发音有错，Herr May 也会直接更正指出。在课堂外，她经常自己跟自己用德语说话。那个时候也没有电子词典，所以她最常用的两本字典是一本超级厚重的德语 – 中文字典以及后来 Herr May 推荐她买的朗文的德语 – 德语字典。为了更快速地掌握这门语言，她会提前预习新的课程，查阅字典查找新的词汇或者后来干脆买上德语小说，满页都是陌生的词汇，她就一个词一个词地翻阅查找字典，小说的一页文字往往需要4到5个小时才能读完，生词实在太多了，几乎每一个词都要查阅字典。这是相当耗时而费力的事情，但也是学习语言非常有效的方法。大量的阅读，读原版小说，利用好字典，这期间会学到非常多词汇以及语句的用法。随着时间的推移，经过每一天的积累，简心慢慢领悟了如何学好德语，没有别的偷懒而又聪明的办法，最好的方法便是持续而努力的学习以及积累。在学习的过程中，她也不会去想太多了，而是完全沉浸其中，专注其中，有时她觉得安安静静地专注于每天的语言学习让她越来越有价值感，因为她能看到自己的进步，懂的词汇会越来越多。但如果午餐她和学生坐在一起吃饭，她仅能捕捉到他们谈话中最基本和简单的礼貌用语，例如 Guten Morgen（早上好）、Guten Abend（晚上好）、Wie geht es dir（你好吗）等。其他人长篇大论的聊天内容还是听不懂。但她不再焦虑或着急，她知道，这是需要时间的沉淀的，需要知识积累到一定的程度，才能有更大的突破。欲速则不达，不能太心急，她能做的，就是每一天好好努力，好好积累语言知识，时间到了，奇迹就会出现。虽然她心里也没底，不确定奇迹是不是真的会出现，但她愿意让自己做这个美梦。

第十章：半夜的警报声

有一次，她还在梦乡中，突然传来刺耳而紧急的火警声，舍友立刻从床上一跃而起，披上睡衣，然后叫简心也赶快起床。简心想整整齐齐地穿好衣服，穿上外套，但舍友叽里咕噜说什么，她也听不明白，但看她的肢体语言，貌似是让简心不要再磨蹭了，要赶快离开房间。简心也没来得及好好穿戴整齐，就随意披了件厚厚的睡衣，跑出了卧室。她也不知道究竟发生什么了，大半夜突然响起了刺耳的火警声，所有的学生，管生活的老师以及工作人员都睡眼惺忪地穿着睡袍跑了出来，大家顺着同一个方向往前走。简心心里觉得很纳闷，这到底怎么回事。不管如何，她也只能跟着大队人马朝一个方向跑。学校里的学生都跑到了大楼外面，径直朝另一栋现代化的房子走去。弯弯的月牙还挂在漆黑的天空，空气冷而清新。简心环顾了一下四周，脑子里填满了疑惑与一丝不安。不一会儿，简心就顺着汹涌的人流来到了一个很大的阶梯教室，室内灯火通明，里面塞满了各个年级的学生。已经没有任何空位了，整个学校的学生和工作人员都聚到整个阶梯教室里来了。室内暖气很足，虽然穿着睡衣，但还是很舒服，全然没有寒意。简心就和其他学生一样，呆呆地站着。过了没多久，阶梯教室前面出现了一支队伍，队员都穿着专业的火警制服。等人员都到齐了，教室里立刻鸦雀无声，有一个火警队员出来叽里咕噜说了一番话，每个人都听得懂这个演讲的人在说什么，除了简心。她实在不知道大半夜搞这么一出，是什么名堂，瞅一下手表，才凌晨4：00。平时她都可以七点起床的，怎么半夜突然会有火警的警报声，然后大家都跟训练有素的队伍一样，跑到这个教室来。后来她才清楚这个活动的意义，原来在1996年学校因为疏于防范发生过一次大的火灾，高贵典雅的宫殿般的建筑在那次火灾中没能幸免，很多地方都已经被烧毁了，现在的学校大堂是已经重新整修过的。为了防止不幸再次发生，学校就培训了专业的火警队伍以及火警演习，让学生与老师在发生突发火灾时可以训练有素地逃出大楼，逃到避难场所（就是这个阶梯教室）。简心后来了解了这次演习的前因后果，不禁感叹学校的活动还是挺意义非凡的，实用性很强。这种演习是不会告诉任何人的，都是搞得突然袭击，一般都是发生在半夜，在大家都睡得很熟很深的时候。那个人宣布完什么事情，大家就有序离场了，又回到了自己的房间，继续睡觉到天明。

第十一章：绘画课

  日子在一天天地流逝，简心已经到学校两周了，可跟父母才通过一次电话，而那次国际长途一共才聊了几分钟。她很想念父母，但无法跟他们联系。她每天的生活很简单，除了上课复习便是吃饭，学校虽然有很多兴趣课例如高尔夫、游泳、骑马、攀岩等，但她貌似都没有太多的兴趣参加，可能是因为语言不通，她不知道如何参加那些兴趣课。私立学校的所有课外活动都是需要另外付费的，简心害怕增加父母的经济负担，所以她也没想报什么兴趣课。有一次，她在学校走着走着，碰到了一个面容慈善的女老师 Lesk，估摸着 50 岁左右。老师和颜悦色地问简心"Do you like drawing（你喜欢画画吗）?"简心回答道"I like（我喜欢）。"然后，这位女老师就带着简心去了一个画画的教室，里面有几个学生刚好在画画，女老师跟简心说，她可以找一块白板，随意画画，里面有各种各样的水彩颜料。简心听懂了，礼貌而有点羞涩地谢过老师后，就随心所欲地在那个白板上画了起来，其他的学生时不时向她投来好奇的眼神。她的脑海中没有很复杂的画面，而是在正中央画了一朵鲜红的花，有 6 个花瓣，每个花瓣都大小不一，不是很一致，随后用大片的深蓝色做底色。其他的学生有画肖像的，也有画风景的，还有人就是乱涂鸦，随意用各种颜色点缀白板。老师看了简心的画后，夸赞简心画得很不错，配色很好。简心自己都搞不清楚，她画的有什么特别的，就是一副再普通不过的画，这种水准小学生都可以达到。其实简心从小就很喜欢绘画的，她喜欢一切美的事物，小学二三年级参加的课外活动就是绘画课，每次绘画作业，她都完成得很好。但后来因为学业繁重，就慢慢不再画了。但她内心是很喜欢鲜艳夺目、活力四射的事物的。天赋也是需要后天精心培养与修炼的，不然这特质会变得越来越普通，最后再也不会发掘出来了。简心觉得自己现在就是这样的处境，虽然她很喜欢绘画，但因为后天没有好好培养，所以她现在的绘画水平平淡无奇，不值一提了。但 Lesk 老师的夸赞不禁让她既开心又诧异，被别人夸奖肯定是一件值得开心的事；诧异的是，她弄不明白，老师为什么会夸赞这么普通的画。她发现，虽然这里的学生有些冷漠，对别国的学生不是很热情友好，甚至有些挑刺，但这儿的老师却是很热情礼貌。无论是教她德语的 Herr May 还是这个 Lesk 老师，都是非常礼貌有耐心，并且从来不会随便批评学生，而是鼓励夸奖学生。简心很喜欢这种被夸赞的感觉，给她信心与前进的动力，让她欣赏自己的优点与自我价值。这里的老师和蔼可亲，和学生相处起来，不是很严苛，让人心生敬畏，而是更像良师益友，亲切而友善。简心感到温暖的话语很有迷人的魅力，给她力量，给她信心，给她在这寒冷的天气无限的温暖。从此以后，如果简心有时间，都会去 Lesk 老师的画室作画，画不管好坏、美丑，老师都会给与很好的评价，艺术没有对错之分，每个人对美的定义也不同，艺术体现的是包罗万象，海纳百川。在画画的过程中，简心是彻底放松的、享受的，那是一种自由而随性的美。

第十二章：体验德国家庭的生活

复活节是欧洲最重要的宗教节日之一，是纪念耶稣在十字架受刑死后的周年纪念日。学校会在复活节放一个礼拜的假期。按规定，所有的住宿生不允许在假期中住在学校，必须回家或是去其他地方。基本上所有的学生都会在复活节回家，百分之九十的学生是德国人，坐一两个小时的火车就能回家了。国际生也主要来自欧盟国家，他们回家也非常快捷便利，火车坐几个小时或飞机飞一两个小时就能抵达。简心来自遥远的东方，如果在这一个礼拜的假期回家，显然是不可能的，长途飞机要飞十多个小时。再说她来到新学校才两三个礼拜，国际长途的机票又昂贵，所以她是不可能回家的，也不允许在假期住学校，那她究竟去哪里呢？其实这个问题不需要她自己解决，学校已经为她找到解决方案了。

复活节由学校的一位秘书 Frau Stein（Stein 女士）带她回家过节。对简心而言，学校这样人性化的安排既合理又意义非凡，它让简心可以更深入地了解德国家庭的生活方式，又可以解决假期的住宿问题。Frau Stein 家就坐落在这个山脚下的小镇上，离学校的距离很近，一栋栋典型的巴伐利亚风格小洋房错落有致地坐落在绿油油的修剪得整齐平整的草坪上，每户人家都是木制的房子，尖尖的屋顶带阁楼，房子前都有独立的花园。花园里种满了各色鲜花，郁郁葱葱的灌木与绿植，树木高大挺拔，有的花园里面还有小型的欧式雕塑与喷泉，流水声带给院子更多的活力与灵气，显得生机盎然，宁静和谐而又美好。简心回忆起父亲绘声绘色地描绘过在北美见识到的洋房花园草坪，她在这里真的是身临其境了，也是这样类似的一派情景。平时在这片小镇上，见不到几个人影，只会看到三三两两慢跑的人，或是遛狗的人，整个环境很安静，安静得不可思议，这会让简心不禁对比国内的人声鼎沸与热闹非凡，完全是两个不同的世界，截然不同的生活方式。

Frau Stein 带简心进入了她家，映入眼帘的便是一个简约而非常宽敞的客厅。简心跟在 Frau Stein 身后，不敢随便乱逛。虽然已经学了好几个礼拜的德语，但 Frau Stein 说什么，她基本还是听不懂，只能懂最基本的问候话语。Frau Stein 给她介绍什么，她也只能装装样子，点点头，至于是什么意思，完全一窍不通，就跟鸡同鸭讲差不多的感觉。房子里出奇的安静，连掉一根针的声音都能听见，偌大的房子一共有三层还有一个很大的地下室，专门用作储藏食物与一些杂物的，以及还有一个客房。Frau Stein 带简心浏览了一番整个房子，楼上有三个卧室，三楼是一个阁楼，做成了家庭办公室，布置得简约大气，打扫得一尘不染，非常干净，所有的物品都摆放得井然有序。一直听都说德国人工作严谨认真，这点简心还没有得到很明确的证实，但整理技术是非常高明的。从居家环境就能看出，德国人很讲究规则与次序感，没有随意乱放的物品，东西都放得工工整整，少而简约，整洁程度简直可以媲美五星级酒店客房的标准。Frau Stein 带简心先来到了她住的房间，房间就在地下室，在储物间的隔壁。房间内布置得简约舒适，简心把自己带的行李箱放在了房间内，然后一个人静静地坐在房里。不一会儿，Frau Stein 就带来了一摞熨烫平整的浴巾递给了简心，嘴里叽里咕噜地嘱咐了些什么，简心装懂一样地点点头，这样不至于太尴尬。Frau Stein 要去厨房准备晚餐了，简心也不知道干嘛好，然后就跟着 Frau Stein 一起去了厨房。厨房用品一应俱全，非常整洁有序。简心想帮忙，但她不知道可以做些什么。看 Frau Stein 从一个半米高的柜子里把碟子都取出来，简心也模仿着一起做。原来这是洗碗机，简心有生以来第一次见到洗碗机。这才

2002年，德国中产家庭就已经用上了洗碗机，这在当时的中国闻所未闻，也从没见识过。Frau Stein 知道这个来自中国的新学生才来了没几个礼拜，德语听不懂，所以她也不知道如何跟简心交谈，两个人默默无语，房子里静得出奇。

过了没多久，门开了，一个高大挺拔的中年男人拎着公文包进了门。Frau Stein 不紧不慢地从厨房出来，朝着那个男人径直走去，两个人相互拥抱，亲吻了对方。男人的身后还有两个少年，一男一女，男孩长得英俊潇洒，女孩长得甜美可人。男孩女孩也拥抱了 Frau Stein，显得很亲密开心的样子。简心看一眼，心里就全明白了，这是 Frau Stein 的老公 Herr Stein 和儿女，一家人打招呼的仪式感满满。Frau Stein 笑意盈盈地向她的家人介绍了简心，他们都跟简心礼貌而友好地握了握手。一家人都到齐了，Frau Stein 瞅了瞅挂在墙上的钟，立刻钻进了厨房，马不停蹄地准备晚餐，简心就傻傻地待在厨房，看着 Frau Stein 忙东忙西，她也帮不上什么大忙。过了一个多小时，晚餐准备好了，Frau Stein 呼叫着几个人名，那个男孩还噔噔噔地跑到地下室，过了一小会，手里拎着几瓶饮料以及一瓶红葡萄酒就上楼了，摆放在长形的桌子上。餐桌上摆放着一盆紫红色的兰花，还点了一些蜡烛，大家都坐在了餐桌旁。随后 Frau Stein 端出了沙拉、意大利面等。Frau Stein 也解下了围裙，坐在了餐桌前，每个人说了一句"Guten Appetite"，然后就拿起刀叉开动了。窗外下起了皑皑白雪，圣洁的雪花静静地在天空中飘落，一家人吃着晚餐聊着天，时不时看看落地窗外的风景，看着飘落的雪花。简心专心地吃饭，他们聊天的内容几乎一句话也听不懂，只知道他们讲话很斯文，压低着声音聊个没完没了，仿佛有说不完的话，孩子和大人聊得也跟朋友一样亲近而自然。简心坐在桌子前，伸长耳朵仔细听，想方设法地想听懂一些他们说话的内容，可惜真的是什么都听不懂，他们说话的语速飞快，简心感觉像一条鲇鱼似的，想抓住它，可一溜烟就跑得无影

第十二章：体验德国家庭的生活

无踪了，根本来不及反应。简心觉得食物很美味，落地窗外飘着雪花的意境很美，但她内心是有些无奈与酸楚的。她听不懂也不会说，只能用眼睛默默地观察别人的举动，偌大的房子里只有这一家人低矮的聊天声以及说笑声，显得是那样的静谧祥和。简心很纳闷，怎么学了好几个礼拜的德语还是不见效，她每天都有好好上课和复习，还额外听录音、看小说，居然还是没法听懂人们的日常交流，她需要学的实在是太多了。就这样，一家人这顿晚饭吃了将近有两个半小时，边吃边聊，对他们而言好不惬意，可对简心而言，简直是无聊至极，两个多小时的时间过得像两天一样，因为她什么都听不懂，只能这样干巴巴地坐着。

晚餐终于结束了，Frau Stein 示意简心去休息吧，时间也不早了。简心不好意思就这样离开，跑进厨房，帮忙收拾。Frau Stein 觉得简心是客人，很不好意思差使她帮忙收拾，就用带德语口音的简短英语搭配肢体语言，叫她赶紧回房间休息吧。简心也不好勉强，再说这是她第一次在一个德国人家生活，总是有些拘谨与不好意思，主人家让她干嘛，那她就干嘛，这应该是最好的方式，不要帮了倒忙，还讨人嫌。所以她就知趣地离开了厨房，来到了地下室的一个客房，今天她要在这个房间过夜。梳洗完毕后，她关掉灯，房间里显得格外安静，出奇地安静，和之前在客厅感受一样。不同的是，现在的她，显得更自在，因为是她一个人独处的空间，不需要顾及他人的表情神色，也不需要干巴巴地坐在餐厅听两个多小时令人乏味而不解的德语。她躺在床上，睁着眼睛，房间里没有一丝灯光，伸手不见五指，脑子里洞洞一片，不去想什么事情，就这样安安静静地没多久就睡着了。

一早醒来，简心感到神清气爽，房间里还是那样的安静，曾经的她不喜欢太安静，因为她习惯了国内热闹的生活，习惯了人声鼎沸，觉得那样才更有人间的烟火气，那样的生活才有意思，充满了活力。现在的她，发现在这样一个新的国度，每个地方似乎都很安静祥和，没有那般的人潮汹涌与车水马龙，一开始那种安静让她经常陷入孤独中，让她觉得特别不适应，让她会像一个哲学家一样经常思考人生。但随着时间的流逝，她也会越来越享受那份静谧，那份安静带给她平和稳定的情绪以及有更多的时间去感受那份悠闲自在，自得其乐。她洗刷完毕后，就爬上了楼，看到 Frau Stein 已经在从容不迫地准备早餐。早餐很丰盛，有各种麦片、面包、黄油、熏肉、果酱、煎鸡蛋、水果等。每个位置前，都摆放了一个用金色包装纸做的兔子形状的巧克力。简心看到 Frau Stein 忙里忙外，她腼腆而礼貌地问候 "Guten Morgen（早上好），Frau Stein"。Frau Stein 见到简心，微笑着问候道 "Guten Morgen。Hast du gut geschlafen（早上好，你睡好了吗）?" 简心听懂了这句最简单的德语，回答 "Ya。Danke（是的。谢谢）。"之后，她帮着 Frau Stein 把餐具整整齐齐地摆到餐桌上。过了没多久，Herr Stein 以及他们的儿女们也睡眼惺忪地从楼上下来了，互相打过招呼，大家就坐到了餐桌前，开始吃早饭。窗外依然下着洁白的雪花，大家有说有笑，悠然自得地吃着早餐，简心也在一旁，默默地享用着美味而营养的牛奶麦片。她和昨天晚上一样，依然是听不懂他们这一家人在说什么，只是感觉这一家人聊得很开心、很和谐，从语调与他们的神情都能感受得到，这一家人感情很好，父母和孩子之间像朋友那般交谈，仿佛坐在一起，总是有很多话题可以探讨与交流，窗外虽然寒冷，但这家人温暖的家庭氛围让简心觉得舒心。这一次她在餐桌前又坐了很久，但她已经慢慢习惯了德国人慢节奏享受生活的方式。吃完早饭后，大家都剥开金色兔子的包装纸，开始津津有味地吃巧克力。Frau Stein 指了指简心面前的金兔子，招待简心也吃。等早餐完毕，Frau Stein 的女儿 Nicole 和儿子 Alex 开始在整个客厅里搜寻着什么，简心后来才懂，他们原来是在找藏在客厅的复活节彩蛋。简心也加入了找彩蛋的行列，三个人在客厅中像五六岁的孩童一样，天真烂漫地寻找彩蛋，当其中一个人找到了一个彩蛋，如同发现了宝藏一般，兴奋地叫了起来，渐渐地所有的彩蛋都被找了出来。游戏结束了，大家还有些意犹未尽，找到彩蛋那一刹那的满足感让她久久地沉浸其中，很享受。她的拘谨感也随着这个彩蛋游戏烟消云散，慢慢地变得大方起来。游戏过后，雪也停了，户外万籁俱静，Frau Stein 的一对儿女穿上厚厚的冬衣，去院子里打羽毛球。简心看着这一幕，内心暖暖的，那样的画面是多么的美好，手足之间在一个温暖的家庭共同成长，相互陪伴，一起玩耍聊天，是人世间最治愈与温暖的事情。这个时候，她也会想起在家的弟弟。她和弟弟之间少了一份默契，他们两个从小吵到大，谁也不让着谁，貌似没有这两个兄妹那样相处得和谐。她不是很理解，可能是个性不同，总而言之，她很羡慕这样美好而又平静的兄妹关系，她和简阳之间完全是另一种相处模式。但吵归吵，她还是很挂念远在国内的弟弟，从小到大闹惯吵惯了，突然因为距离的原因，再也没法和弟弟拌嘴争执了，她也感到内心有些不舍与孤独，她想弟弟一切都好吗，好久都没见了，他读书是不是很忙？

　　Frau Stein 和她的老公在复活节还安排了其他的家庭活动，天气晴朗的时候，他们带上一双儿女以及简心一起去郊外骑脚踏车，简心骑得最慢，总是落在他们身后。但这一家人会耐心地等简心，直到她跟上他们的节奏。鸟儿叽叽喳喳地叫个不停，远处是连绵不断的阿尔卑斯山脉，简心呼吸着新鲜的空气，骑着脚踏车，跟在这一家人身后，遇到流淌的清澈的小溪，他们会停下来，绕道而行，她感到舒心而平静，这样简单而又健康的户外活动她长这么大一次都没有和家人一起玩过。她记得，小时候她的父母非常忙，没有太多的时间陪伴她，她以前的生活里更多的是读书，以及和一些小伙伴玩耍的时光。但她深深地理解，因为国情不同，经济发展水平的差异之大，所以导致父母没那么多闲情逸致和大把的时间陪伴着孩子长大，也没那么多精力安排家庭聚会与活动，这些她是非常能理解的。

德国人非常热爱和崇尚大自然，所以在节假日的时候，他们会带着自己的家人一起去爬山、远足或骑脚踏车，这样的假期既放松又健康，还能增进一家人的凝聚力与亲密关系。德国人建立了家庭后，除去工作时间以外，会把剩下的空闲时间毫不吝啬地留给家人与自己，几乎是零社交，他们会把大部分精力专注在自己的事情或家庭上，所以他们这样的生活是简单而安逸的。而国内非常注重人际关系、人际交往与人脉资源，为了发展事业或是其他因素，人们会把大部分精力放于工作与社交，而会忽略与家人相处的时间。很多父母因为工作关系分隔两地，儿女完全由母亲带大。或是因为经济所迫，父母都需要背井离乡，去外地打工，只能把孩子留给祖父母带养，这样的情况显然不利于一个孩子健康而快乐地成长，但迫于无奈，人们只能这样选择。由此可见，充裕的物质基础是最基本的保障，如果物质非常匮乏，何谈精神世界的富足。在不同的国家，因为经济水平的截然不同，发达资本主义国家的中产家庭更注重工作与家庭的平衡，他们不会为了多赚些工资牺牲和家人相处的宝贵而美好的时间。但在发展中国家，人们极度追求物质生活的改善，而不得不牺牲陪伴孩子长大的时间或是一家人其乐融融的相处时光。

他们骑了大概2个多小时，便到达了一个优美而精致的小村庄，一条小街上摆满了各种各样的摊位，有卖蜡烛的，还有卖手工艺品的，以及品种繁多的奶酪摊位等，甚至还有些摊位会向行人展示中世纪时期烤面包的流程。摊贩都穿着中世纪的服装以及配饰，漫步于这个集市，会让人感到时光仿佛倒流回古老的欧洲中世纪。简心看着眼前的集市，觉得尤为新奇，这一切对她而言都是新的体验。游人悠闲地在市集中踱步，这儿听听，那儿看看，然后还能品尝刚出炉的香喷喷的面包，好不惬意。简心跟着 Frau Stein 一家，推着自行车，也漫步其中，他们走了没多久，就来到了一座古宅旁。这座古宅一共有两层楼，空间显得有些狭小而局促。入内参观需要交2欧元的门票，Frau Stein 不假思索地付了门票后，他们一家人带着简心入内游览参观。简心进入室内，感到房顶实在太矮了，大概只有1米7左右的高度，每个游客都需要低着头、弓着背才能在室内走动。里面的摆设很简陋，几乎没有什么像样的家具与装饰品，只有很简陋的厨房或几把木制椅子等，二楼便是卧室，房顶也出奇的低矮，人在里面走动觉得有些压抑感。参观完后，简心问Frau Stein：这是什么古宅，屋顶这么低。Frau Stein用英文夹杂德文解释："这是中世纪时候普通人家的房屋，几百年前，欧洲人的身高也不高的，大概只有1米5左右，可不像现在的人，都长得这么人高马大，高大挺拔。"简心心里想原来如此，怪不得屋顶建得这么低矮，原来古代的欧洲人也矮的，不是一直长得这么高的。人种随着时间和人类文明的发展也在不断地进化中。逛完集市，简心便跟着Frau Stein一家人骑自行车回家了，整个复活节假期就在这样不紧不慢的节奏中过完了。到了开学那一天，Frau Stein开车把简心送到了学校，跟简心相互拥抱了几下，就挥手告别了。经过这次复活节，简心大致了解了德国家庭的生活方式，她觉得学校这样的安排很不错，非常人性化，不仅帮她解决了假期回不了国的难题，也让她多了和德国人生活相处以及了解德国文化的机会，她不再感到那么孤独了。

第十三章　在德语课上交到的第一个朋友

　　在学校里简心几乎没有一个朋友，不去上德语课的时候她都是一个人待着的，她持之以恒地复习德语课学的内容，不敢落下一丁点功课。随着时间的流逝，她发现积累的德语词汇与语句越来越多。从第二个月开始，Herr May 不再用英语给她上德语课，他说："从今天开始，我会用德语给你上德语课，只用德语，不用其他语言，因为这对你学习一门语言非常重要。你不能老是想着把一门语言用另一门语言翻译过来，而是要直接把德语当成母语来学。我们每个人在学母语的时候，从来不会想着用其他的语言来翻译母语，对不对。你如果想学好德语，记住，不要用别的语言翻译过来，而是直接用德语来解释德语，这样的效果是最好的。简心，现在开始朗读课文。"简心便打开课本，一字一句地读了起来，其间有些发音不是很准，老师也会帮她纠正。读完以后，Herr May 对简心说："非常好，你现在读得比刚开始好多了。继续努力，慢慢你会听懂越来越多的德语。"听了 Herr May 的话，她惊奇地发现，Herr May 刚才放慢速度用德语说的一番话，她基本上已经都听懂了。此刻，她感受到了前所未有的满足感与成就感，虽然来德国才 1 个月，从踏上这片土地的一片茫然以及对德语的一窍不通，再到现在已经大致可以听懂德语老师说的话，在不知不觉中她已经感受到了自己的进步。她相信一切都会慢慢好起来，也相信脚踏实地好好学习与积累，慢慢地她一定会很好地掌握这门深奥而难懂的语言。

　　本来简心上的德语课是一对一的，因为其他的国际生和她的学习进度不同，他们来上这所学校时都已经有德语基础。Herr May 看她在这段时间德语进步挺快的，就把她安排在了一个三人的小班制中，这样可以增强学生之间的互动与交流。有一次，简心去上德语课，看到课堂上出现一个亚洲脸孔的学生，她名叫 Rita，长得瘦瘦小小的，五官精致，皮肤是健康的浅棕色。简心见到亚洲脸孔，内心非常有亲切感，因为整个学校除了黄小丹和她来自中国，几乎全是欧洲人以及极少的非洲人与中东人。还有一个女学生来自东欧的波兰，皮肤白皙，大大的眼睛，高挺的鼻梁，长得漂亮，和学校里其他的学生长得类似。Herr May 让每个学生在课堂上用德语做了一个简短的自我介绍，然后就开始给三个学生上课。还是按他上课的习惯，每天他都会让学生高声朗读德语文章，纠正学生的发音以及解释这篇文章的意义，之后会讲一些相关的德语语法。但德语课的重心是阅读、口语与听力，语法的学习占的比重较少。大家都专心致志地听讲，当谈到一个话题时，也会活跃地讨论，而不是一言不发地只在课堂上坐着听老师上课。这让简心经常会对比以往在国内的上课方式：在国内读初中或高中的时候，学生的课堂参与度不高，多半是老师在课堂上滔滔不绝地讲个不停，学生就马不停蹄地记笔记，基本上很少会有踊跃发言的学生。老师讲的内容，没有学生会去质疑或是去热切地讨论，更多的是接受而记录下来。现在这里的教学模式截然不同，在课堂上大家会更注重口头表达能力，老师讲的内容也可以被质疑正确与否，课堂上经常会有学生们的激烈讨论，老师会把课堂的主动权交给学生，自己退居幕后。因为学生少，所以宽敞的教室里摆放的课桌椅也不是一成不变、紧凑地摆放成长方形，而是很随性，可以摆成长方形，也可以摆放成大大的圆形。总而言之，教室里课桌椅的摆放非常多样化，不拘一格。国内的教育注重的是传授知识、规矩与学生的团体意识；西方的教育把重心放于了创新力的开发以及个性化教育，强调个人优势的发展，从来不会强调需要小我服从大我（大我指的是班级团体）。东方文化教育人要学会低调、隐忍以及含蓄、不张扬，个人服从集体。但反之，西方文化崇尚自由、民主以及个人发展，注重个性教育与培养。简心之前是接受的东方思想，现在她又开始接受西方思想，她就在这两种思想的碰撞与交汇中一天天成长，她的思维方式与行为处事既不像一个传统的中国人，也不像典型的西方人，而是两者的结合体。

上完德语课，简心主动而又礼貌地跟那个印尼女孩 Rita 打招呼，Rita 也大方而礼貌地回应简心。从那以后，两个人成了无话不谈的好友，这是简心来到这片陌生而新鲜的土地上交的第一个好朋友，她非常开心与满足。因为她心心念念想找一个好友的愿望终于实现了，她不再是孤零零一个人，远离父母与亲人，最需要友谊这种情感。她们两个的德语都还不是很流利，但普通的交流没什么问题，如果要表达复杂一点的意思，找不到恰当的词汇来表述，也可以用肢体语言，并且她们俩经常一起上德语课，在一起相处久了，会有心有灵犀的感觉，彼此都知道对方想要说什么。虽然德语还是讲得磕磕巴巴的，但简心发现，自从交了 Rita 这个好友，她说德语的机会多了，她也不管说的句型语法是不是正确，想到什么就一股脑儿说出来，Rita 也是如此。简心觉得，反正她们都是外国人，外国人不需要嘲笑外国人说的德语，但如果简心和德国人交谈，会变得非常谨慎。在表达之前，会在脑海里一丝不苟地组织语言，然后再说出来，这个过程比较缓慢，这也是为什么她交不到德国好友，因为人家没有太多耐心听她断断续续的德语语句。德国人讲话的语速飞快，简心听他们说话，几乎抓不到核心内容，只能听懂少许的问候语以及惯用的词汇。而德语老师 Herr May 的德语为什么她能听懂，因为老师特意放缓了说话的语速，一字一句清晰地用简单的词句表达出来。学习德语的道路还是漫长而艰辛的，需要不懈地努力与积累，也需要非常有耐性和毅力。现在，简心貌似找到了一个志同道合，和她情况类似的好友，怎么能让她不开心呢，也许都是来自亚洲，那种磁场会相互吸引吧。

　　有一次，他们上完德语课，约好一起去小镇上唯一的一个连锁超市买东西。自从上次黄小丹带简心逛过这个超市后，她就再也没来过，因为语言不通，看不懂每件物品上写的是什么，也可能她还没发现自己需要购置什么东西，母亲在出国前已经为她周全地准备了一切的日用品。这个小镇虽然宁静而美好，但实在是小得可怜，大概只要10分钟就可以从街头走到街尾，她们两个也不知道下课后干嘛，就去超市里转悠转悠，看看有什么需要买的。超市里的顾客非常少，就那么零零星星的几个人，过一会这几个顾客也结账离开了。简心和Rita在里面逛了一圈，选了一两只牙膏以及日霜，就准备到收银台付款。收银台坐着一个金头发，长得矮矮胖胖的女人，她神情严肃而用轻蔑的口吻问："Do you have your passport? Please show me（你们有护照吗？给我看看）。"简心和Rita都感到很奇怪，然后带着诧异的眼神问："Why do you need our passport（你为什么需要我们的护照）?"原来，在他们两个采购东西的时候，简心就觉得有一双不友好且不信任的眼睛紧紧地盯着他们两个，不知道在看什么。简心被这种眼神盯着，感到莫名的不舒服与不自在，她后来就和Rita说："我们去付款吧，也不需要其他东西了。"果然到了收银台，这个胖女人刁难她们，要检查护照。简心觉得很奇怪，为什么她不检查其他客人的证件，而就问他们两个。简心义正词严地回道："I didn't bring my passport with me（我没有带我的护照）。"这个胖女人更来劲了，严肃而冷漠地说："Please open you bag, I want to check your bag, because I see you have stolen a shampoo in your shopping bag（请打开你们的包，我需要检查一下，因为我看到你们偷偷放了一瓶洗发水在包里。）。"简心和Rita都听懂了她的意思，她们俩没有反抗，什么都没说，便让那个胖女人检查她们的包，那个胖收银员在那里东找西找，找了好半天，也没找到偷的 shampoo（洗发水），最后把包还给了简心她们。简心很气愤，想和那个胖营业员好好地理论一番，但她不知道如何用精准的德语表达，最后只能吃了一个哑巴亏，和 Rita 默默地离开了。这时候，她们两个讨论说："这个女的有很深的种族歧视，看到他们两个长得是亚洲脸孔，就故意刁难她们，还以为亚洲人没有素养。这个胖女人实在太坏了，自己没有受过很高等的教育，却戴着偏见与有色眼镜看人，瞧不起亚洲人。"这是第一次让简心感受到了当地人对外来种族的排斥与心理厌恶感，她很想改变他们的这种偏见，但她知道自己的无能为力，这类人的这种偏见是由于成长环境与狭隘的认知导致的。

　　简心碰到这样的情况毕竟是少数，大多时候她觉得当地人还是很有礼貌和涵养的。小镇上仅有一家学习用品店，里面摆满了琳琅满目的文具、整理夹、贺卡等。店主是一个非常平易近人、和蔼可亲的老人。他长着花白的络腮胡子，头发也是蓬松的自来卷，每次看到简心去店里挑选文具，会十分友好而亲切地问候她："willkommen。Wie geht es dir? my Liebling（欢迎光临。你最近好吗？亲爱的孩子）。"简心看到店主笑意盈盈的面庞，听到这么温暖人心的话语，也会非常礼貌地回复："es geht mir gut。Vielen Dank（我很好。非常感谢）。"然后便开始挑选自己需要的东西。有的时候，店主会经常来看看，简心有没有找到自己想要的东西。这位店主对待顾客十分尽心与热情，简心一踏入这家文具店，就仿佛被一股温暖与友善的气流所包裹着，她的内心暖洋洋的。

　　文具店旁是一个面包房，橱窗里摆满了令人垂涎欲滴的各种蛋糕、布丁、手工巧克力以及面包等。每次简心经过这个店，都会忍不住去瞅一瞅面包房里的精致而又美味的糕点，她想把所有的品种都尝试一遍，但她不会这么做，只是这些糕点做得实在太精美了，不禁勾起她对美食的渴望。她会偶尔买一些来吃，但一次不会买太多，主要是不舍得花零花钱，因为她觉得学校里的餐食已经让她很满意了，并且也是包括在她的住宿费用中的，所以也就没有必要再花钱买外面的糕点了。

有了 Rita 这个印尼的好友，简心的生活丰富了一些，她不再总是一个人下课后待在房间里学习德语了。有时她们约着一起在学校的南花园聊天散步。南花园的景致宜人，绿油油的草坪、高大挺拔的树木、精美绝伦的宫殿式建筑、古朴坚固的中世纪古堡，还有一座小小的教堂构成了一幅唯美的画卷。她们两个会经常站在南花园正中央的一处开阔地，眺望远方连绵的阿尔卑斯山脉，山下整个小镇的全貌尽收眼底。Rita 捋了捋头发，慢条斯理地说："这个学校国际班的德语课程挺贵的，我就上一门德语课，其他的课程都不上。"简心慢条斯理地回答"我也是，本来要上 11 年级（相当于国内的高一），但由于语言基础实在太薄弱了，在 11 年级上课也听不懂，没法跟上进度，所以现在只能先上德语课，其他的课程都没法上。德语是基础。"Rita 赞同地回答："是这样的，来到了一个陌生的国度，肯定先要把语言尽快学好，才能更好地融入这里的生活，不然会觉得特别孤独。"话音刚落，Rita 继续说："我不是这里的学生，只是来学语言的，德语学费是我的雇主帮我支付的。我在这个小镇的一户人家做家政，雇主是当地的一名牙医，他们除了支付我一些工资，还帮我支付这个德语课程的费用。过了一两个月，我可能就要回家乡了。下次我请你去我工作的那个雇主家玩玩吧。"简心听了大吃一惊，她一直以为 Rita 也是这个学校的外国学生，和她一样先要补习德语课，没想到是这样的情况。听 Rita 说，过几个月准备要回国了，简心内心感到酸楚与不舍，她在这里就 Rita 这个唯一的小伙伴，两个人无话不说，相处得轻松而默契，这段友谊给她孤独的求学生涯增添了色彩，也带给了她心灵的慰藉。她们都来自遥远的东方，文化类似，又在异国他乡相识，所以彼此之间既能相互安慰与鼓励，也能感同身受异国生活的不易与孤独感。简心觉得，自从认识了 Rita，和她建立了纯粹而美好的友谊，她不再是一个人孤军奋战了，在她孤零零的阵营里有一个伙伴和她一起面对困难与未知，彼此照应，相互勉励，就算问题解决不了，这样悠闲地聊聊天也是很不错的，总好过一个人独自在房间里待着，自言自语地练习口语。简心忧伤地问："Rita，你一定要离开吗？可以想想其他的办法留下来吗？"Rita 摇摇头，坚定地回答："我的雇佣合同马上就到期了，这是我出国前和一个海外务工的中介机构签署的。对我而言，留下来是几乎不可能的。我不能像你一样，在这里读书，因为没有父母经济上支持。我们家是很普通的，没有这样的经济条件。出来这么长时间，我也很怀念家乡的一切。虽然这里环境很优美，经济也高度发达，但我始终觉得我不属于这里，可能是东西方文化差异，也可能我不知道如何和这里的人相处。上次我们在超市，那个胖营业员那样子对我们，其实我的内心也有点受伤的，他们总是带着偏见看待我们亚洲人，觉得我们国家落后，他们生在高度发达的资本主义国家，所以骨子有优越感，显得很高傲。

  当然这儿的大多数人还是很有教养和礼貌的，但我感到他们内心深处还是对亚洲人存在种族歧视。但这也不是我想离开的主要原因，根本原因还是我的合同到期了，我只能离开。一个人在这遥远的国度，远离亲人和朋友，也是一件非常难熬的事情，我想念我的家人了。虽然那里的经济条件和这里无法相提并论，但我在自己的家乡还是会感到很浓很烈的人情味。你不觉得这些德国人都很冷漠吗？很有距离感吗？"简心听 Rita 的话，也不再挽留她，因为这是无法改变的事实，Rita 自己最清楚想要什么。她回答道："我非常理解你的，我有时也有类似的想法，觉得自己不属于这里，语言又不通，虽然学校硬件环境都很不错，但心里还是很苦闷，因为没法和这里的学生正常交流，而这个学校的很多学生确实体现的优越感满满、很高傲的样子，让人很有距离感，不敢靠近。

你在这里,觉得自己仿佛是被排挤在外的,很难融入。但大部分人还是不错的,上次碰到的那件事情也是个例,不能一概而论。我们还是多想想好的方面,东西方文化差异肯定大呀。我们从小接受的东方思想,一下子要融入西方人的社会,确实不容易呢,这需要时间,上次复活节我去 Frau Stein 家小住了几天,感觉他们一家人都挺好的,虽然我听不懂他们谈论的什么,但我感觉到他们很真诚与友好,他们还带我逛了一个中世纪的集市,很有意思。在这里,我们能开阔眼界,学习不同的传统与文化,不会就局限在熟知的文化里,我觉得很不错呢。当然你因为经济原因,无法续签合同,或是因为你真的想家了,我都能理解。虽然很舍不得你过几个月就要离开,但我还是祝福你呢,也希望你自己一切都保重。我们需要记录下联系方式,以便以后能继续保持联系。"简心话音刚落,两个好友彼此相拥,对视而笑。

过了一段时间,Rita 真的约简心去她雇主家玩了。那一天天空阴沉,简心上完下午的德语课,就和 Rita 挑了最近的那条下山的路,朝小镇走去。到了小镇上,步行大概五分钟,转一个弯,就已经到了她雇主的家门口。Rita 打开门,热诚地欢迎简心进门。此刻,雇主他们还没回家,房屋内安静整洁,静得出奇。简心心里觉得有些怪怪的,不好意思来 Rita 雇主家,因为不是主人家邀请的,是 Rita 邀请的。她再次确认,问 Rita 这样做她的雇主会不会不舒服。Rita 安慰简心说:"我已经问过雇主了,可不可以带朋友到家里来玩,说你是 Schloss Neubeuern(寄宿学校的名字:新波宫)的学生。他们很欢迎,一点问题都没有。过一会他们也下班回家了,你会见到他们的。你先在这里坐一会,我去干一些家务,还要准备晚餐。"简心客气地问:"需要我帮忙吗?"Rita 干脆利落地回答:"不用客气,你是客人,我请你来玩,哪有让你做家务的道理。"然后,她就朝地下室走去,取了一些蔬菜又进了厨房间。简心到了温馨而舒服的客厅,就找了一个位置坐了下来。她望着窗外,看到有三三两两的行人来来往往，天色越来越暗，街角路灯也亮起来了。没多久，厨房飘来了阵阵香味，不是西餐那种浓郁奶酪味的香味，而是有点像亚洲菜系的香味。简心肚子咕噜噜响了起来，来德国这么长时间，她已经好久没有吃中餐了，在学校吃的都是西餐，不是牛排，就是各种意大利面，要不然就是炖牛肉，或各种派、沙拉等，虽然她很爱吃西餐，但她也想念家乡的饭菜了。Rita 做的印尼菜勾起了她对中餐的想念，印尼菜与中餐虽然不完全相通，但也有些类似之处。过了没多久，门开了，走进了两位和蔼可亲、气质高雅的老夫妇。老夫人挽着老先生的手臂，有说有笑地走了进来。他们看到客厅里坐着一个陌生的亚洲年轻女孩，一脸诧异，正要问她是谁，Rita 已经走出了厨房，然后向这两位老夫妇问候，说"您好，先生夫人，这是我的朋友简心，她在山上的那个私立学校读书，我问过你们的，可不可以邀请我的朋友来家里玩。你们允许了。"之后，老夫妇两个人，一拍脑门才想起这回事，径直朝简心走来，很有礼貌地和她握了握手，说"Guten Tag。Herzlich willkommen（你好。热烈欢迎）。"简心面带微笑，腼腆而礼貌地回应了他们。晚餐准备好了，Rita 马不停蹄地把菜肴端到了餐桌上，刀叉摆放整齐，把室内的光线调成了柔和而黯淡的暖色灯光，然后点上了餐桌上的蜡烛，跟雇主说"先生夫人，可以吃晚饭了。"雇主热情地招呼简心坐到餐桌前，和他们一起共进晚餐。起先，简心觉得有点尴尬，因为毕竟第一次见面，也不是雇主的客人，但老夫妇面慈心善，那份拘谨感缓和了一些，她就恭敬不如从命，拿起刀叉，慢慢地吃起了 Rita 做的印尼菜。印尼菜和中餐还是不同，用了比较多的香料，有点辣，简心有点吃不惯，因为她从来都不吃辣，但雇主吃得津津有味，很享受的样子。Rita 忙完了厨房里的事情，也坐到餐桌前吃起了晚餐。其间，老夫妇会问一下 Rita 一些事情，两个人也会低语闲聊，他们问简心，是否适应新学校的生活，简心大方地回答："还行，在慢慢适应中，但就是很想念家人。"老夫妇问的有些问题,简心也貌似没听懂,来了才2个月,德语确实还不流利,只会最简单基础的对话。晚饭在不紧不慢的节奏中结束了。简心觉得欧洲人太会享受生活了,老夫老妻吃饭都这么有情调,氛围那么浪漫,国内吃饭都跟打仗一样,哪有这么大段空闲的时间用在饭桌上,一家人吃饭最多20分钟搞定。欧洲人可以慢悠悠地吃上一两个小时,虽然菜品不多,但中间还要喝些葡萄酒,之后是精致美味的饭后甜点,聊聊天,慢慢品尝,好不惬意。简心看了一眼手表,已经晚上7点半了,窗外天色已经黑得伸手不见五指,晚餐也结束了,然后就跟老夫妇和Rita告别,说:"感谢你们的邀请以及美味的晚餐,我要回学校了。"老夫妇和Rita真诚地说:"很高兴认识你,简心,欢迎你下次再到家里来做客。"简心回答"谢谢。很感谢。"Rita把简心送到门口,问:"你一个人回学校没事吧,天色这么黑了。"简心回答:"当然没事,我会自己回去的。你快回家吧。我们上课时再见面。对了,我需要你的电话号码,你下次把你在印尼家的电话留给我,以后你回国了,我们还能联系。如果你有邮箱,那就最好了。我们也可以通信。"Rita回道:"好的。我下次给你。"然后,简心就离开了。沿着上山的小路,一步一步朝半山腰的宫殿般的学校走去,走了大概20分钟,就顺利到达了。之后钻进自己的卧室,开始认真地学习德语,复习功课。室友不知道在哪里逗留,还没回寝室,她一天几乎不见人影,每天要很晚才回房睡觉。简心在房间里复习功课的时候,经常听到房门外有女孩子的打闹声,或其他房间传出来的吵闹的流行歌曲。这些女孩子无法静心待在自己的房间晚自习,晚间时时刻刻都有什么让她们更感兴趣的活动,或干脆就坐在活动室的沙发上看电视,有的女孩子突然想吃蛋糕了,会在活动室的烤炉里亲手烤一个巧克力蛋糕,满足自己的味蕾。住宿生的晚自习通常是在自己的卧室进行的,时间是晚间7:00—8:30。但简心在很长一段时间都不知道学校也有晚自习,老师也不会每次都来检查,学生们是不是在房间里认真复习功课，只是偶尔抽查一下。这里学习的氛围很宽松，和国内的严格而军事化的读书课程安排完全不同。学生在这个学校里除了每天上课，下午三点半放学后，时间都是自己安排的，可以参加丰富多彩的兴趣课，也可以去小镇采购点东西，或是在房间里学习，也可以和朋友一起去小镇的小饭馆里聊聊天喝点饮料。

第十四章：勤奋学习

虽然没有严格的管束，但简心在晚间一定会进行晚自习，每天都会学习到 12 点。她清楚地知道，自己一定要付出更多的努力，更加勤奋，才能适应新学校的学习节奏。德语对这里的学生而言是母语，他们已经对母语驾轻就熟，但对简心而言，这门语言的难度很大，她需要在最短的时间内尽最大的能力掌握德语，然后才可以顺利地进入 11 年级，和其他德国学生一样上高中课程，在三年后参加德国巴伐利亚州的 Abitur（高中会考）。而每次一想到这个目标，简心会觉得压力很大，她经常会质疑自己是否真的可以顺利考上德国大学。她已经放弃了在国内考大学的机会，现在的她一切从零开始，是真的破釜沉舟了，再也没有退路可言。她虽然不知道一切是不是会真的如她所愿，也不能预见自己会不会考上德国大学，但她会时常告诉自己：既然选择了，是一定要走下去的，不论这条路多艰辛，需要付出多少努力。路是自己挑选的，没有什么好后悔的，也不是轻易可以放弃的。我一定会努力而踏实地过好每一天，不能保证未来是不是一定能顺利达成目标，但至少每天都在努力中，就不会有自责感与愧疚感。因此，她每天晚上会学习到很晚，一个劲地学德语，阅读德语文章，查阅陌生单词，做好笔记。为了掌握德语更快，也会买来厚厚的德语小说，每看一页内容，需要查阅大概 4 到 5 个小时左右的字典，才能理解其中的意思，因为陌生的词汇实在是太多太多了，多得如同天上的繁星，数都数不清。屋子外女孩子嬉笑声、吵闹声根本影响不到她的专注力，她需要全神贯注地学习，每天都需要，日复一日，年复一年，不然她是绝对不可能在很短的时间内很好地掌握德语的。她与生俱来不甘落后的性格、自律性与上进心是她持续努力的动力，而坚持与毅力是她学习最好的助力，她隔绝外界一切的干扰与嘈杂，沉浸在自己勤奋学习的世界中，这良好的学习习惯都源于她出国前严苛而竞争激烈的国内的学习环境。在她出国前读书的学校，成绩的好坏至关重要，排名次是家常便饭，再加上学生人数又多，所以竞争的激烈程度是不言而喻的。特别是后来她就读的重点高中，每个学生都那么自律上进，因为他们曾经都是各个初中部的尖子生，所有的尖子生被安排在重点高中的班集体里，可想而知，那种学习氛围有多浓厚。简心经历了这些严苛而辛苦的学习，所以即使没有外界的管束，她也已经非常适应高强度的学习节奏。人生没有白走的路，也没有白流的汗，她始终相信天道酬勤，也相信千里之行，始于足下，所以唯有努力与踏实，每一天好好地利用好课外的时间，她会一步一步靠近目标，也会越来越适应新的环境。她告诉自己，不允许一再彷徨，无助或质疑自己的能力，因为这些伤感而悲观的情绪毫无用处，只会让人犹豫不决，平添烦恼，她需要的是相信自己，认可自己，有了目标立刻付诸行动。每次当她开始怀疑自己是不是真的能顺利考上大学，她就会在笔记本上一次次地写下这样的话语："你一定可以的，相信自己；尽力而为；梅花香自苦寒来，付出了一定会有回报等名言警句来鼓励自己，安慰自己。"她暂时得不到外界的鼓励与认可，只能向内求，通过自己激励找到克服困难的力量以及战胜心理上的动摇与怯懦感。她真的是非常努力和坚持，才获得了今后的掌声，其间辛苦的过程只有她自己最清楚。

　　简心来到这个新的国度已经两三个月了，但和父母的联系少之又少。她很想念家人，但由于通讯不发达的缘故，她和父母每一个礼拜只通一次电话。父母会给学校的秘书办公室打国际长途，会问简心是不是在学校一切都好，要自己好好照顾自己。简心从来都不曾在电话中告诉父母遇到的困惑以及体会到的深深的孤独感与思乡之情，而是会安慰他们，一切都好，让他们放心。每次通话的时间都只有三到四分钟，然后父母就急切地跟简心说："电话费太贵了，我们不能聊太久，下次再聊吧。"虽然简心很想和父母多聊聊天，说说学校的情况或是她的见闻，但由于父母说了这句话，她也不好意思跟父母长聊，不想让父母承担太高昂的国际电话费用。在2002年，智能手机还未问世，简心也没有手提电脑或其他通信工具，所以只能通过每周一次简短的国际长途和父母保持联系。简心的父母也很想念她，但好在他们还有一个儿子陪伴在身边，会释然和宽慰很多。但就算这么精打细算地节约电话费，每个月的国际长途电话费高得惊人，会达到数千元人民币一个月。那个年代出国读书的学生和远在国内的亲人联系是多么的不方便，所以要忍受更多的孤独感与不适应感，学习上的压力与精神上的孤寂只能一个人承担。但简心总会对自己说："你已经很幸运了，不用考虑经济压力，也不用为学费苦恼，只需要努力把学业弄好，然后就是尽快适应这里的一切。很多出国留学的人，只能勤工俭学，他们过得更辛苦。你这点苦算得了什么。万事开头难，虽然现在不适应，觉得学习德语是多么漫长而枯燥的过程，学校里也几乎没什么好友，但这一切会慢慢好起来的。不要总是想着一定要赶紧找到好朋友，找朋友这件事也是急不来的，顺其自然吧，能找得到就找，找不到就算了。"但有的时候，简心也会有些庸人自扰，她会担忧学费的问题，她不确定父母是不是有足够的经济实力负担她这么多年的学费。父母经营公司也是承担了很大的风险的，市场有波动，每年的行情也不一样，这就会直接影响他们的收益。简心的父母从来都不会向子女透露公司的经营状况或财务状况，他们可能觉得这是大人要考虑的事情，没有必要跟自己年幼的孩子谈起。再说简心的父母勤俭节约，也教育儿女不乱花钱，钱需要花在刀刃上，这养成了简心和弟弟简阳不奢侈骄纵的好习惯。这回父母花了这么大代价送她出国读书，她暗下决心，绝对不会让父母花的钱付诸东流，她一定不能辜负父母的期望，会尽自己最大的努力好好学习，考上好的大学。

第十五章：Candle light dinner（烛光晚餐）

　　学校的课外活动名目繁多，仪式感满满。记得有一次，简心看到宫殿大厅以及餐厅布置得很有格调与高级的氛围感，仿佛有什么重大的宴会要举办。餐厅进门口坐了一排穿着学校制服的学生，他们在宣传着什么，聊着什么，大厅里聚集了越来越多的学生、老师以及一些家长。那些家长打扮得十分高贵得体，男士西装革履，女士穿着精致的套装或是优雅的晚礼服，在大厅中的一张长桌前签字报到，或是手拿香槟酒，尽兴交谈。简心看到这一幕，不知道学校举办什么重要活动，后来问过那些坐在长桌前做义工的学生，才知道这是学校半年筹办一次的烛光晚餐，邀请全校的学生与家长盛装出席晚宴。简心有些丈二和尚摸不着头脑，长这么大第一次看到这么正式的宴会以及穿得这么隆重、打扮得光鲜亮丽又气质非凡的人群。她穿得这么普通，素面朝天，跟这群穿着优雅的人、这个高雅的氛围格格不入。当她正沉浸在其中，那个熟悉的厨房老太太见到了她，关切而热心地问"Hallo，wie geht's dir? das ist unser candle light dinner。Du sollst eine Schoene Kleidung tragen（嗨，你好吗？这是学校的烛光晚餐，你需要穿一件漂亮的晚礼服）。"简心听懂了老太太说的话，说了声谢谢，然后就一路朝自己的房间奔回去。在赶回房间的沿途中，她看到很多住宿学生都已经在精心打扮自己，化妆、用卷发棒卷头发、试穿华美而优雅的长裙，每个女孩都想让自己在烛光晚餐的宴席上魅力十足，惊艳四座，所以一个个都非常投入地在打扮自己，捯饬自己，显得热情活泼而奔放。简心当然理解，每个花季少女对自己的容貌格外在意，都希望自己长得楚楚动人、倾国倾城，那时候刚好是情窦初开，对异性产生好感的年华，所以对外貌尤其关注。

简心也在意自己的容貌，尤其是脸蛋，对身材还不怎么在意，因为她自己从小到大也没有肥胖或太瘦弱等问题，总体而言还是蛮匀称的，只是在国内读高中的时候，偶尔会对自己的身高不是特别满意。她刚好长到1米6，希望自己的个子能再高那么5厘米，对她而言就完美了。但后来小学六年级发育后，个子就不再飞快地往上蹿了，整个初中就长高了2厘米，到了高中身高基本就再也没什么突破了。她对身高显得有些在意，还要从初中年代开始说起。那个时候，她有一个形影不离，十分谈得来的好友名叫勤华，在初一的时候两个人基本差不多高，但到了初三勤华的个子已经窜到了1米68，她成了班里个子最高的那几个女生之一。勤华和简心站在一起，好友有时总会开玩笑地说："简心，你怎么不长个子，你看我们两个一开始差不多高，我现在都比你高一个头了。"说者无心，听者有意，简心虽然知道好友不是讽刺她，只是随便说说而已，但听了还是有些介意，内心会有些遗憾，觉得自己还需要再高些，才显得更有气质。其实她的身高在中国不算矮，属于中等个头吧，但好友那挺拔的高个子以及调侃的语言会刺激她一点，所以她有一阵子在鞋子里还放着助长增高的鞋垫。那是她在广播节目里听到了一个关于增高的广告，然后省下零花钱买的。她不确定效果如何，但听着广告里的说明与介绍觉得应该会有用，就买来试试看。再说到脸蛋，她的五官长得不错，大大圆圆的眼睛，长长的睫毛，鼻子不是很高挺，但也还行，嘴唇稍厚，脸圆乎乎的，有婴儿肥，显得稚气未脱。但从初二开始，端正大气的五官却完全被密密麻麻的恼人的青春痘掩盖住了。痘痘的问题困扰了她很多年，直到她上高中，以至于来到德国留学还未完全解决。她很关注自己的脸蛋，但有时因为在脸部的"T"字部位痘痘太多，不太敢经常照镜子，不敢经常见到长满痘痘的脸。她只有在学习上才能找到自信与自我价值感，才能觉得自己是优秀的、出类拔萃的，因为她从小到大基本都是学霸级的人物。所以即使从初二开始，脸上突然长了很多青春痘，同班的学生也不会嘲笑她或愚弄她，因为她成绩非常优异，也是班级的团支部书记。在中国的学校里，美丽的容貌不是让一个学生获得优越感或得到他人欣赏的唯一方式，优异的学业成绩显然更胜一筹。但现在截然不同了，在这个新学校，她现在无法从学业中找到自信心与价值感，因为语言的障碍，还没有正式进入 11 年级读书，而继续在国际部跟着 Herr May 学德语，她对自己的未来也充满了一丝不安。虽然她会一遍遍鼓励自己，安慰自己，但这种不安与不确定感有时也会伴随着她，特别是她还没有很好地掌握语言，也没有在学习上体现出优势的时候。而这里的学习氛围也没有在国内的时候那么浓厚与严苛，学校经常会举办各种各样的活动，锻炼学生其他方面的能力，开阔国际化的眼界与认知，而学习成绩不是评判一个学生的唯一标准。简心觉得，这里的学生显得成熟又活泼，和国内认真读书的毕恭毕敬的学生完全是两种不同风格。这里的学生热衷各种兴趣活动，男生女生对自己的外貌都非常在意，都想尽办法让自己看起来很帅，看起来很甜美或性感。今天她在回自己房间需要经过的走廊里看到每个女孩花尽心思在打扮自己，穿着优雅的长裙，妆容精致完美，在走廊的全身镜前照来照去，她既兴奋而又茫然无助。兴奋的是长这么大头一次在现实中看到这样的场面，简直像极了欧美电影里的高级晚宴的场景；茫然而无助的便是她不知道究竟如何打扮自己，她从来不懂如何化妆，也没有像样得体的晚礼服，来参加今晚的 candle light dinner（烛光晚餐）。她走走停停，观察那些女生们兴趣十足地让自己变美，穿上华美的服装，搔首弄姿，摆着各种俏皮而又活泼的姿势，她感到自己真的很土，格格不入，她怎么没有少女那种活泼感，显得这么老成而收敛。过多的想法也没有，就这样穿过长廊，过了七八道门便回到了自己房间。看到舍友也已经在房间里捯饬自己，她和舍友打了一个招呼，然后就开始在柜子里找裙子，找了半天都没找到适合晚宴的服装，因为她的母亲根本就没有给她准备。母亲确实不清楚新学校还有这种活动，还需要给女儿添置晚礼服。实在没有办法，她只能穿一件日常场合穿的夏天的裙子，至于化妆，她真的没有任何概念。在那个年代（20世纪90年代中期到2001年），家乡的主妇或少女从来都不化妆，都是素面朝天的，非常质朴。她以前就读的国内的高中，每天都需要5：30起床，然后只有15分钟的时间用来刷牙洗脸、穿衣以及叠被子，学生哪来的时间精心打扮自己。大家就洗个脸，涂好面霜，扎个马尾辫（很多女学生为了节省早晨的时间，都剪了短头发），就匆匆地跑去教室进行早读了。回忆起这段经历，简心觉得实在是太不可思议了，半年前在国内高中的时候，她的学习生活是那么紧张，每个学生都铆足劲用功学习，天底下最重要的事情就是读书，考上国内重点大学，什么玩游戏或女孩子打扮简直是天方夜谭。而现在，在这个阿尔卑斯山脚下的学校里，学生基本全都是欧洲人，她是除黄小丹以外第二个中国人，这里的学生不再只关注学习，而是把很多的精力与时间放在了课外活动以及学校筹办的各式各样的社会活动上，可以有灵活而充裕的时间做学习以外的其他事情。她感到世界的奇妙，在世界不同的地方，不同的环境中，人的生活方式截然不同，人的重心与关注点完全不同，可以有这种活法，也有那种活法……

　　她正在琢磨到底如何化妆打扮自己，她没有任何的化妆工具，也不知道怎么用，舍友只顾着自己，全然没有在意简心此刻难堪的境地。正当她犯愁的时候，突然听到敲门声，她打开门，看到一个长得俊俏，高高瘦瘦的女孩站在她门口，她长了一双乌黑乌黑的大眼睛，鼻梁高挺，脸庞小巧而精致，乌黑发亮的头发卷曲又蓬松，看上去不像是传统的欧洲人，而更像是中东或新疆人。她甜甜的微笑顿时融化了简心一颗不知所措的心，这个女孩自报家门："hallo, mein Name ist Lily. Kann ich herein kommen（你好，我的名字是莉莉，我能进来吗）?"简心让 Lily 进入了室内，Lily 也向简心的舍友礼貌地问候，之后 Lily 就问简心："Weisst du，wie man auf das wichtige Abend vorbereitet（你知道如何为这个重要的晚宴做准备吗）?"虽然简心经过了这两三个月的时间还听不懂所有的日常对话，但她听懂了 Lily 的问题，她的语言在一天天进步中。简心摇了摇头，心里有点纳闷，怎么 Lily 会来找她，她和 Lily 根本就不熟悉。Lily 滔滔不绝地说："我来自伊朗，已经来这个学校 2 年了，现在对这里的一切都熟悉了。刚开始来的时候，差不多和你一样，也很不适应，但我挺了过来。现在在这里交到了很要好的朋友。我有两个最好的伙伴，她们都和我在同一班级上课，一个是来自新加坡的女孩名叫 Anna，另外一个就是来自中国的女孩黄小丹。我们三个差不多是同一时间来到这个学校的，因为都来自亚洲，文化类似，并且都属于外国学生，所以自然而言会有很多话题可以聊，就渐渐地成了无话不说的好朋友。我知道你来这个学校没多久，肯定会觉得孤独，因为语言的障碍以及各种文化差异，你有时可以来找我聊天呢，我随时欢迎。"简心大致听懂了 Lily 说的所有的内容，她腼腆而友好地回答："谢谢 Lily，下次一定找你聊天。"之后，Lily 继续说："你是不是不懂如何化妆，我看你脸上还有挺多青春痘的，就知道你从来都不用 make up（粉底液），一个人的外部形象也是很重要的，这里几乎没有哪个女孩不用 make up，也没有哪个女孩不化妆。化了妆脸会显得更精致。其实有些女孩也长青春痘的，但用了 make up，脸部皮肤会均匀很多，它有遮瑕的功效，你一定要用 make up，这样你的脸会显得很美。还有，下次我带你去镇上的那个超市买一个法国药妆系类的护肤品 Vichy，它特别适用于长痘痘的皮肤或油性皮肤，如果我脸上冒出几颗痘痘，我就用它的夜霜涂抹，一两天痘痘就全消了，效果非常好。你要学会爱护自己的皮肤，虽然你脸上现在痘痘不少，但是有办法改善的，也是有办法遮掩的。"简心听完后，内心非常感动，长这么大第一次有人告诉她用什么方法可以去除青春痘，改善皮肤，告诉她如何让自己的皮肤看上去细腻光滑，她觉得Lily简直是上天派给她的美容大使，她这么热心肠又专业。在她的家乡，没有一个人会像Lily一样开门见山又毫无保留地教她如何治理痘痘肌肤，如何化妆，因为她生活的那个小地方没人懂这些专业的护肤技巧，他们是最纯朴的人群，就连简心的母亲对她女儿持续几年的痘痘问题也束手无策，她总是安慰简心说："这是青春痘，过几年总会好的。"但简心等了3年，痘痘还是不见好转，后来她只能习惯自己长满痘痘的脸，这也是一种自我安慰与自我救赎吧，不然还能怎么办呢。那个年代基本没有网络，好使她上网去搜寻解决方法。总而言之，她感到自己的愚昧与无知。Lily的一番话仿佛漆黑的夜空出现了一道光，给她光明，给她指引解决这个问题的方向。她非常感激地回答："谢谢你，Lily，其实我很想改善我的皮肤，没有人喜欢满脸痘痘，总会影响美观，大打折扣。我会照着你的方法去做。"Lily莞尔一笑，递给简心一样东西，说："这是我的make up，借给你用，我教你如何化妆，过一个小时，你就会变成一个美丽可爱的女孩。"简心感动得有些热泪盈眶，Lily拉过一张椅子，开始给简心化妆。她轻柔地把make up涂抹在简心红红的长着痘痘的脸上，涂抹得细致而耐心。等涂好以后，让简心自己照镜子看看脸部，简心看到镜中的自己真的变美了很多。皮肤不再那么红肿，而是清爽细腻了很多，端正而大气的五官显露无遗。由于长青春痘的原因，她本来很抗拒照镜子，但现在她都想多看镜子中那个长着娃娃脸的可爱的自己。Lily继续给她化妆、涂眼线、眼影以及睫毛膏、腮红等，过了大概1个小时，Lily像大功告成似的，说："wir sind fertig（我们完成了）。"简心迫不及待地去照镜子。当她看到镜子中那张美丽的脸蛋，内心兴奋而惊喜，脸像换了一张皮一样，变得如此精致。她有生以来第一次感受到化妆的魔力。现在的她充满了自信，和Lily一起出了房间，

第十五章：Candle light dinner（烛光晚餐）

来到客厅的全身镜前整理一下发型与裙子。当其他的女孩看到化妆后的简心，也有点惊呆住了，她的脸蛋突然变得如此可爱与俊俏，大家纷纷夸赞："Nancy,du bist sehr schoen [南希（简心的英文名），你很美]。"简心有点腼腆地回答："Danke（谢谢）。"Lily 跟简心说："我们快下楼吧，晚宴马上开始了。"然后，她们两个就和其他学生一起往大厅走去，一群人叽叽喳喳，好不热闹。到了大厅门口，她们按顺序依次进入了如欧洲文艺复兴时期洛可可风格的金碧辉煌、奢华高雅的餐厅，找到了空位，就不紧不慢地坐了下来。餐厅里的客人主要是住宿学生、家长以及校长、老师等，每个人都穿得高贵而典雅，这样的画面像极了上流社会的社交活动，每个餐桌上都点着浪漫唯美的蜡烛，星星点点的烛光在偌大的餐厅里影影绰绰，如同天空的繁星。餐厅里的主灯是关闭的，整个空间就只剩下蜡烛柔和而暖色调的光，大家坐在餐桌前，耐心地等待餐品。餐厅响起了悠扬的圆舞曲，有的人在兴致勃勃地聊天，交头接耳，有的人就静静地欣赏着美妙而令人遐想联翩的乐曲，还有的家长环顾四周，被这餐厅的华美所深深折服。简心坐在位置上，安静地等待着。等待着什么，她也不是很清楚了。过了半个小时左右，校长走到了餐厅的演讲台上，餐厅里的各种声音像按了静止键一样，突然消失了，整个空间变得出奇的安静，校长穿着笔挺的西装，气宇轩昂地宣读："Herzlich willkommen。Unser candle light dinner findet start。Enjoy（欢迎大家的到来。我们的烛光晚宴现在正式开始了。请大家享受其中）!"话音刚落，大家都拍手鼓掌，然后餐厅里又热闹了起来。厨房的工作人员以及做义工的学生穿梭在餐厅中，为每一位客人端上了第一道餐：南瓜浓汤。简心看到自己面前从里到外摆了大大小小五到六副刀叉，都不清楚具体怎么用，就观察其他人，先用最外层的刀叉或勺子。每个人都享受其中，慢悠悠地品尝浓汤。简心觉得南瓜汤味道香浓微甜，入口即化，美味至极。Lily 没有和简心坐在一起，她坐在了自己那个生活组的一个餐桌上，紧挨着她的好友而坐。简心坐的这一桌，没有一个熟悉的好友。虽然平时来来往往也见过几次，但几乎没有说过任何话。这些女孩子都打扮得花枝招展，气质非凡，但她们的神情也显得高傲而不可一世。她们中有些人会聊天或谈论一些有的没的，而有些人也就默默地坐着，等待其他菜品或就干脆发呆。简心喝完汤后，也就毕恭毕敬地坐在那里，等待着服务员上其他的菜。她很想融入进去，但发现几乎不可能。其一主要是语言问题，很多意思她还不能用德语流利、毫无障碍地表达出来，其二她和这些女孩没有任何共同话语，她们谈论的世界，简心没法理解，就如同，她们也无法理解简心的世界一样。东西方文化的差异不是一点点，而是一条巨大的鸿沟，体现在方方面面，例如人的世界观、人生观与价值观，以及文化与信仰都不同。简心在等待菜品的过程中，觉得时间特别漫长，有点枯燥与无聊，虽然整个环境与氛围显得特别高雅，但她觉得自己不属于这样的社交圈，她是一个另类的存在，她的内心感到孤独、寂寞与无助。她很想和要好的伙伴一起分享美食，或谈论一些有意思的话题，可坐在她一桌的人，都不是她觉得可以走得近的人。那些女孩的冷傲神情让她望而却步，不敢靠近，而宁愿把自己像一个蝉一样包裹起来，躲在自己的小世界里。有些女孩不时瞅瞅她，瞄她几眼，然后就和坐在身旁的另一个女孩窃窃私语，谈论什么。简心也不清楚她们在讨论什么，有时也会疑心，这些女孩是不是在评论她。她就坐在位置上，等呀等，过了大概大半个小时，上第二道前餐。简心也搞不清是什么东西，看上去小巧精致，很美味的样子，然后她就拿起刀叉品尝了起来。味道果然很不错，但具体是什么做的，对她而言像一个谜团，反正是有生以来第一次品尝这种精致而又美味的食物。她除了坐在那里，等服务员上菜，然后一个人慢悠悠地品尝，没有其他的事情可做。吃完了一道餐，就一个人呆呆地坐在那，也没有一个女孩跟她搭一句话。这个烛光晚餐一共持续了3个小时，前前后后上了正式的五道菜，包括两道前餐，两道主餐以及一个意大利甜品（用白巧克力做的 tiramisu）。简心觉得餐品是真的精致而美味，风味独特，但这个晚餐持续的时间实在是太漫长、太难熬了，就像蜗牛爬行那样缓慢。她觉得欧洲人的生活节奏真是慢呀，慢得让人觉得不可思议。一个晚宴就五道菜可以吃上三个小时，这对一个刚从中国来的小姑娘来说非常难理解与不适应，主要一点也还是没有志同道合，聊得来的小伙伴在一个餐桌上一边享受美食，一边分享所见所闻或是自己的心得体验。不管如何，她也体验了一回学校的烛光晚宴，感受是高雅而无聊。

　　原来在餐桌上那些女孩子是真的在背后讨论了自己。简心后来从另一个学生 Maria 口里听说的，她们评论简心拿刀叉的姿势不标准，很奇怪，坐姿也不端正，吃饭的时候总是低着头等。Maria 属于另外一个生活组，和简心不在同一组里。学校把所有的住宿生分在不同的生活小组里，大概一个生活小组有 20 个左右的学生，来自不同的年级。每个生活小组有一个生活老师，简心所在的生活小组归 Frau Koenig（Koenig 夫人）管辖。Maria 非常热情善良，有一次在餐厅中，她特意找到简心，手把手地教简心使用刀叉的正确的姿势与坐姿，还跟简心说："学会了这些正确的姿势，别人就不会笑话你了。对了，你不要把沙拉以及牛排或意大利面等主食放在一个盘子里，而是用不同的盘子盛放，用专门的一个盘子放沙拉，专门的盘子放主食，之后如果还要吃蛋糕或布丁或水果，也是用单独的盘子盛放，不要混在一起。不然其他学生看到你一个盘子装了所有的菜，又要说你奇怪，取笑你了。这里的很多学生都挺傲慢的，因为都来自富裕家庭，所以显得特别有优越感。她们缺少了几分同情心，不会设身处地或换个角度去看待不同文化背景下长大的同龄人，并且因为他们的父母工作忙碌，把重心放在了事业上，所以早早地让自己的孩子来读私立的寄宿制学校，导致他们的内心是缺乏一些安全感与家庭的爱与管教的，这也是为什么这里很多学生会显得高傲而冷漠的原因。这些学生的家长给不了情感上的陪伴，就只能用物质奖励来填补他们。所以这里的学生经常讨论的话题离不开什么车，或美女等。他们的父母在孩子满18岁后，经常会送一份大礼给他们。前不久，Astasia 的父母就给她买了一辆 Audi TT，你看门口停着呢。所以在这里交到一个真心朋友是非常难的，尤其对你而言，你来自遥远的东方，和这里的学生有很大的文化差异，因为你们成长的环境非常不同，从小接受的教育也不一样。当然语言问题还是主要原因，还有就是这里的学生家庭属于德国上流社会，他们有与生俱来的优越感以及缺乏父母管教后导致性格中出现的不健全感，这也会使你觉得无法和这里的很多学生走近。不过你不要想太多，既来之则安之，既然你已经选择了这里，就要想办法适应这里。我们先从正确使用刀叉的姿势学起，你学会了，别人就不会再取笑你了。其他的困难，需要你自己慢慢克服，会越来越好的。"

这番长篇大论，简心没有完全听懂，但能够大概猜出她说的什么意思。简心回答："Maria 谢谢你教我如何正确使用刀叉，我在中国的时候从来没有吃过西餐，我们都习惯吃家乡的饭菜，所以对我而言是很陌生与不习惯的。平时我们在家乡饭店去吃自助餐，习惯把所有的菜都夹在一个盘子里，包括甜点，这个学校的餐食也主要以自助为主，我就习惯性地用一个盘子装所有的菜和甜点，没有那么讲究呢。原来这里面大有学问，前餐、主餐以及甜点需要装在不同的盘子里，怪不得有一次一个学生一直盯着我装满菜的盘子看，还说我 komisch（奇怪），当时我就不理解，不知道她为什么这样直接说我，现在我明白了。谢谢你，Maria，你是一位很善良的姑娘，和这里的高傲的学生不同。"maria 微笑地回答："不用客气，是我应该做的。这么小的忙，不值得一提。这儿的大多学生虽然有些傲慢，但心眼不坏，对了，这里的老师很友善，从来不会严厉地批评学生，老师和学生相处得如同朋友一般，你觉得呢。"简心赞同的回复："还真的是，老师都很友好。有些学生也很善良热情的，有

第十五章：Candle light dinner（烛光晚餐）

一个叫 Lily 的来自伊朗的女孩，还主动帮我化妆，她挺友好的。"Maria 回答："Lily，我认得她，前两年刚来的时候，她也和现在的你差不多，安静而腼腆，话不多，现在基本就适应了，还找了几个很要好的朋友，所以你也会适应的，只是时间问题。慢慢来，不用急。"简心非常感谢 Maria 无私地教会了她使用刀叉以及这番真诚的话语。虽然在今后的日子里，Maria 没有再主动找简心聊天，或和她成为无话不说的好友，但这已经足够了。后来，简心慢慢懂得，在德国找到一个真正的好友是非常难的，因为德国人不轻易交朋友，他们的一生中只有那么一两个或两三个真正的好友，他们喜欢非常充裕的私人空间，自己的空间不喜欢被人打扰，很多时候他们喜欢独处，或在空闲的时间一个人做自己的事情，这和中国人的相处模式截然不同。如果说中国宣扬的是频繁的社交以及错综复杂的社会关系网，而德国人崇尚的更多是自我空间、个性发展、自由与无拘无束。简心夹杂在这东西方文化之中，真切地感受到了不同文化的冲击与碰撞，让她无所适从，需要长久的时间去消化磨合。

第十六章：学校里的 disco party

学校的各类活动真的让简心大开眼界，相比以前她在国内单一的上学经历，这里的课外活动极大地颠覆了她的想象。她不能否认，在不同的国家，上学的体验感也完全不同。有一次她上完德语课，一如既往在自己的卧室里复习上课内容以及阅读德语小说。他们生活组的唯一的黑人女孩 Euginia 敲响简心卧室的门，问："亲爱的，你要不要和我们一起参加今天晚上的 party？很好玩。"简心有些疑惑地问："什么 party？我从没听说过呀，在哪里？"Euginia 摆出故作神秘的表情，热情洋溢地说："我们学校在每一个季度都会举办 disco party，你是新来的，当然不知道呢。我带你一起参加，很好玩的。不要天天念书，这多无聊。也要享受生活嘛，这里的学生都很爱玩的。我还从没见过哪个学生像你这样，整天坐在房间里念书。你们中国人真勤奋，真棒。但亲爱的，努力读书是优点，也需要劳逸结合。放学后，我们一起放松放松嘛。我带你一起去啊。今天你一定要穿得美美的，穿性感一点，不要那么保守，好吗？"说完，她还扭动她超级大的臀部，踩着均匀的节奏，跳了几步 HIP HOP 的舞。简心觉得 Euginia 的话有道理，但她第一次听说学校还举办 disco party，实在是让她觉得太不可思议了。但她有生以来从没去过这种场合，在国内认为学生去那种场合是不适宜的或不正经的，会严重影响学习，也会影响一个女孩的形象。大众会认为这种女孩是一个坏女孩，只会鬼混。但在这个私立学校，会定期开展 disco party，让学生尽情玩乐，享受他们这个年纪该享受的美好年华，简心觉得这两种不同教育体制的差异实在大得惊人。虽然她不想打破自己乖乖女的形象，但也想入乡随俗，并且她从来都是对新鲜事物有着极强探索欲望的。对于 Euginia 的邀请，她虽然想尝试，但还是回答道"Euginia，很感谢你的热情邀请，但我没有合适的衣服去参加这种 party，别人看到我穿着日常的衣服去参加这种活动，会不会觉得我很奇怪，会笑话我吗？"Euginia 摇摇头，说"Nancy（简心的英文名，因为大多数人不会她中文名的发音），不要担心那么多嘛。我有衣服可以借给你穿，但我们两个的尺寸不一样呢。你就穿你自己的衣服，不会有人笑话你的。你先去参加了再说。"简心最终还是被 Euginia 的热忱与自己强烈的好奇心驱使了，决定去一探究竟，参加今晚 7：30 学校举办的 party。

　　自从上次 Lily 教会了简心化妆，她就去小镇买了些化妆品：包括粉底液、眼线笔、腮红以及睫毛膏、唇膏等，还购置了 Lily 推荐的法国药妆 Vichy 和洗面奶。用了这些护肤品，她脸部的痘痘改善了很多。并且从此以后，她每天都会早晨起床后，用粉底液均匀地涂抹脸部，化一个淡妆，开始美好而充满希望的一天。她意识到了自己这种良性的改变。现在她已经学会了基础的化妆术，如果去参加今晚的 party，她已经可以自己化妆了，不再需要其他人的帮助。用了大概半个小时，她就化好了妆，然后在镜子里照了照稚嫩而又青春洋溢的脸，满意地笑了。她在衣柜里翻箱倒柜地找了半天，也找不到一件适合今天场合穿的衣服。实在没有办法，就穿了一件日常的深蓝色毛衣以及一条喇叭裤腿的牛仔裤。她好久不穿这条牛仔裤，发现腰部特别紧，使了好大的劲，才把拉链拉上。但她全然不会去怀疑这几个月是不是长胖了很多，因为每天在镜子中她看不到自己变胖很多的变化，周围的人也从来不会评价她是不是胖。和这些体重偏胖，个子高大的欧洲女孩或黑人女孩 Euginia 相比，她觉得自己还是很小巧玲珑的，虽然也有点自欺欺人。准备就绪，Euginia 和她的室友 Celia 就带着简心一起下山了。她们两个穿得特别性感，上衣露着很深的乳沟，非常性感，下半身也穿得是紧身的牛仔裤。Celia 的身材很不错，上突下翘，女性的曲线美被体现得淋漓尽致，如果男孩子看了，会流口水的感觉。美中不足的便是腰间被紧身的牛仔裤挤出了一些赘肉，但这不影响整体的美感。Celia 是纯正的德国女孩，身高足足有 1 米 75，她来自巴伐利亚首府慕尼黑，家里具体是什么情况，简心也不得而知，因为 Celia 不怎么喜欢聊太多自己家里的事情。Euginia 的整个体型过于臃肿肥胖，上半身还行，她也穿了一件性感紧身的露肚脐的黑色短 T，下半身臃肿得不行，屁股很翘但超级大，从头到尾，最引人注目的便是她硕大的臀部，让人看了印象深刻。但她的脸上依然充满自信，不会因为自己的体重过胖而有自卑感。简心第一次看到朝她热情微笑打招呼的黑人女孩便是 Euginia，她是整个学校唯一的黑人，来自遥远的南非，从八年级开始就读于这个私立学校，据说她是被新波宫学校（schloss neubeuern internatsschule）在南非选中的学生，提供全额奖学金，这种机遇简直是不可多得，凤毛麟角。Euginia 肯定有她的优势与独特之处，才会拥有这样幸运的机会，被学校选中，到欧洲这个闻名遐迩的巴伐利亚州私立寄宿制学校免费就读。简心猜想，她最大的优点毫无疑问是她与生俱来的热情与亲和力、强大的自信心与同理心，当然这只是从简心个人的视角去看待的。他们三个步行了大概 15 分钟左右，就到了山下的一个独立屋前。门口站着两三个学生，每个人的手背上需要盖一个印章，才可以进入 party。几个欧洲男孩，长得英俊帅气，瞅了几眼简心，觉得很面生，他们估计第一次见到这个亚洲女孩，很好奇，其中一个男孩嘴里还叼着一根香烟，看上去痞痞的。简心小心翼翼地跟在 Euginia 和 Celia 的身后，进入了室内。简心顿时被眼前的一幕惊呆了，室内已经挤满了年轻的男孩女孩，这些学生打扮得时尚又性感，在劲爆而节奏感很强的 disco 音乐的带动下，扭着身躯，跳着活力四射的舞。有的学生手里还拿着啤酒罐边喝边跳，屋顶的射光灯360度旋转照射在这满屋子跳舞的人群身上，有些年轻男女在跳舞的时候，还抱在一起，伴着舞姿热吻，沉浸其中。简心简直不敢相信自己的眼睛，这个学校居然会组织这样类似成人世界的活动，供学生尽情享受其中，让他们绽放属于这个年龄的活力与激情。Euginia与Celia看到这么热闹非凡的场面，也很兴奋，情不自禁地踏着活跃的节奏，跳起热舞来。简心就一动不动地杵在那里，显得不知所措，她不知道怎么跳。长这么大第一次来到这样的场所，她觉得这里的学生实在太奔放活泼了，和她以前在国内读书认识的学生完全是两个世界的人。她深受国内严格教育的影响，觉得做学生就要有学生的样，规规矩矩，本本分分，集中所有的精力在学业上，好学生是不应该去disco party这类场所的，那类场所被认为都是社会人或是小混混才去的。在国内的班级里，她周围同学的行为举止仿佛都是从一个模子里刻出来似的，大家都特别上进好学，一板一眼，几乎没有除了学习以外的任何娱乐，这样的party对简心曾经就读的重点高中的学生而言简直是天方夜谭，不可思议到极致。Euginia发现简心木讷地站在原地不动，就对她说："Nancy，你跳舞呀，不要一直站着，活泼一点，随便你怎么跳，别人不会笑话你的。"简心尴尬地回答："Euginia，我不会跳舞，真的不知道怎么跳disco的舞。我觉得其他人肯定会笑话我的，我不敢跳。"简心突然发现，几双眼睛正盯着她看，脸上挂着浅浅的笑容，她无法猜透其中包含的意思，是善意的笑容，还是恶意而轻蔑的笑容。但是站在这热烈而激情四射的一群花季年龄的男男女女中，她呆若木鸡，觉得这样的自己太过显眼，大家都在跳舞，就她一个人站在那里静止不动，左看右看，确实会让别人觉得很奇怪。收起自己的顾虑与尴尬，她开始跳了起来。但她跳得和其他人不一样，跳得姿势仿佛是在做广播体操，有一个身材很胖高高大大的德国男孩看到了她这奇特的跳舞姿势，不禁笑得前仰后合。Euginia和Celia看到了简心这样怪异的舞姿，也捧腹大笑，简心看到了这些人的反应，也不知道是应该立刻停下来还是继续跳下去。她只会跳像广播体操一样的舞，她似乎很放不开的样子。这时候，Euginia 说："简心，你跟我学，我来教你跳舞，很容易的，你只要踩着节奏，扭动身躯和屁股，很快就能学会了。"之后，Euginia 便放慢了舞步，友善地教简心最基础的 disco 舞步。简心发现，其实这舞步非常简单易学，只需要有音乐节奏感，可以很快便掌握，应用自如。才学了大概 10 分钟左右，她基本就会了，跳舞的样子和其他人没有太大差异了，在旁边捧腹大笑的那几个学生看到简心的改变，立刻竖起大拇指，夸耀"wunderbar"（很好）。简心也没听清他们说的什么，因为 disco 里面的音乐声太火爆了，但能心领神会。Euginia 贴着简心的耳朵窃窃私语："Martis finder eich ser suess（Martis 觉得你很可爱）。"简心听了，很不好意思地笑了。这是简心有生以来第一次参加 disco party，给她留下了非常难忘的印象。所有的第一次体验都是那么新奇而特别，像烙印一样深深地刻在她的脑海里，即使多年以后，再度回首，画面依旧那样的清晰，仿佛发生在昨天一样。但有的时候她也会问自己，这样的场景真的在她的生活中曾经出现过吗，好似和她现如今的生活完全不同，她觉得人类的记忆太奇妙了。

第十七章：柏林之行

每周星期五下午4：30，简心所在的 Frau Koenig 小组会举行一次轻松的小组会议。在会议中，Frau Koenig（管生活的老师）会清晰地宣读下周他们需要齐心协力完成的事情、小组活动计划等。简心也会按惯例参加这样的小组活动，她坐在那里，安安静静地听 Frau Koenig 条理清楚地列举活动事项，其间也有几个女孩会提问，或讨论一些细节，参与感满满。简心不是很好的参与者，但却是规矩虔诚的倾听者。经过这几个月的努力学习，持续地积累与最佳的德语环境，她在不知不觉中发现自己的德语进步了很多，而且这一次的小组会议内容让她十分兴奋与憧憬。Frau Koenig 宣布了下周的远行活动：去德国首都柏林旅行。当简心听到了这个消息，她激动地想欢呼雀跃，虽然她还是安静地坐在那里，但心里已经翻江倒海，周围其他的女生已经发出了各种各样欢叫的声音。她简直不敢相信，学校还定期带学生去欧洲闻名的城市旅行，这在她以前国内读书的学校想都不敢想，连出个校门也基本不可能，那里完全是封闭式管理的。除此之外，每周的休息时间只有周日下午半天，其他的时间基本上全都是在教室里度过的，不是上不完的课，就是永无止息地自习刷题，这样高强度的军队化的学习让曾经的她习以为常，因为在那里所有的学生都是这样统一的课表，都是需要被严格管理起来的，所以她也不会觉得尤为奇怪。可现在她来到了一个完全不同的学校，这里的教育体制十分灵活，自由与多样化。课堂的知识不是唯一，课后还有各种各样的兴趣活动以及远足，如果让她再回到以前在国内读书的环境中，她想自己是再也无法适应了。人见识了不同的生活方式与学习环境，会用更加多元的视角去看待这个世界，而不会狭隘、单一地认为这就是唯一的生活方式或行为准则。

简心长这么大都没去过自己国家的首都，唯一去过的城市就是大连，那次是父母带她和弟弟，以及另一家亲戚一起去玩的。那是一座美丽而现代化的海滨城市，有很多新鲜而性价比很高的海鲜，气候宜人，简心的父亲在大连有些生意上的合作伙伴，所以就带着一家人去外面开开眼界。他这么多年在外打拼，平时基本不会带着家人一起出差或旅行，为了节约开销，在火车上经常是买的站票，从首发站一直站到终点站，其间也会跟火车里认识的一些有缘的陌生人聊天，父亲的商业灵感有时就来自这种不咸不淡、不谋而合的出差途中和其他旅客的闲聊。他是一个有心人，也是一个思维非常敏锐灵活的人，这种看似普通的聊天会时常给他带来灵感，让他找到做生意的机会，而大多普通人基本上是捕捉不到闲聊中的有效信息的。所以机会永远只会垂青有准备的人，不是所有人都能抓住天赐良机，很多人甚至都无法识别出机会。简心的父亲出差在外，异常辛苦，他在外住的经常是廉价的招待所或地下室，因为那个时候才刚刚开始创业，手头没有多少资金，所以能省则省，不该花的绝对不乱花，特别是个人的享受方面，简心的父亲对自己真的很吝啬，但对企业的发展，他觉得需要投入或投资的是义无反顾，绝不犹豫。还有一点便是对他孩子的教育，他也真正做到了尽自己最大的努力，给孩子好的教育，更加国际化开放式的教育。简心非常感谢父亲为她创造了这样难得的机会，让她在 16 岁就可以去异国他乡求学，接受海外的教育，虽然在独自一人求学的路上，要面对很多孤独、寂寞以及学业和心理上前所未有的压力，但她真的开阔了视野与认知，让她感受到世界的丰富与多元，看到了更大的世界，接触了在不同文明下熏陶长大的人，从而变得更加自信与坚强。

柏林是一个充满故事的城市，现如今是德国最大的政治、文化与经济中心。1945年德国纳粹在第二次世界大战中惨败，由于盟军的空袭与苏联红军的进攻，柏林作为德国首都遭到了毁灭性的破坏。最终柏林被分割成两部分：由苏联控制的东柏林，以及由美国、英国与法国控制的西柏林。柏林变成了苏美冷战的聚集点，长达45年之久。由于大量东德国居民通过不设防的柏林分界线涌入西柏林和西德，因此1961年东德建起了柏林墙，完全封锁了东德与西德通行之路。柏林成了东西方意识形态交锋的最前沿。直到1989年德国柏林墙才被推倒，1990年东西德合并，德国重新统一。简心对德国的历史不是特别了解，但在国内的时候隐约听过这段东西德分裂后来又统一的历史。她对这座历史悠久的德国首都充满了无限的憧憬与向往，而现在马上要一睹它的风采，怎能不感到格外的激动呢。

经过他们生活小组商议，最终定下了柏林旅游的行程。时间在悄无声息地流逝，终于到了去柏林的这一天。在Frau Koenig的带领下，十几个女孩一起坐上了驶向柏林的快速火车。这是简心第一次搭乘快速列车，车厢内位置宽敞舒适，不是很拥挤，还留下了很多空位。她们一群女孩找到了座位就坐了下来。简心坐在位置上，看着窗外移动的连绵不断的高山、奔腾不息的河流、嫩绿嫩绿的青草地、一排排错落有致低矮的欧式风格的房屋，心情舒畅，这样悠然自得美如画的风景近在咫尺，她真心感到欧洲的安逸、自然与精致，是现代与古代，自然与人类文明的完美结合。曾经的她不懂得欣赏美景或美丽的事物，除了学校生活便是家庭生活，生活没有太多的惊喜与波澜，见识的事物也真的屈指可数。她觉得以前在国内，学校从来都不曾带他们去博物馆参观或有任何远足，所以每天的事情基本就是在学校上课，做作业或复习功课，准备考试，周而复始。现在的她能有这样的机会，去领略广阔的天地，更丰富多彩的生活，这是以前的她想都没有想过的。曾经的她愚蠢地以为生活就是这样子的，平平淡淡，规规矩矩，按部就班。什么美景美物，她没有任何概念或者也不知道如何去欣赏，但说句实话，在20世纪90年代到2000年左右，中国的经济还非常落后，基础设施陈旧，老板姓的房子也是破旧不堪，所以美与精致和当时她生活的环境是根本搭不上边的。但现在不同了，她到了一个自然环境绝美、文明与经济高度发达之地，她突然发现自己其实是拥有一双欣赏美的眼睛的，她不用刻意去寻找，便能在新的世界里随处发现美的事物，美得让人窒息，而又那样的默默不语，只供人类去慢慢欣赏。列车窗外的美景让她感受到了人世间的万般美好以及大自然的瑰丽多姿。其他的女孩在聊天，或睡觉，或和她一样静静地欣赏着窗外疾驰而过的风景，每个人都似乎找到了自己舒服放松的状态，在这个旅途过程中。

其间，Frau Koenig 给每个女孩发了午餐三明治，是学校厨房为她们专门准备的。简心接过三明治，慢慢品尝，烤鸡胸肉配生菜与奶酪的经典搭配在齿间留香，味道醇美、新鲜而浓郁，就算再来一个，她也不嫌多。来德国留学的这几个月，她的胃口似乎每天都很好，她很享受这些西式餐点。说来也奇怪，很多人到了新的环境会有水土不服的问题，可对她而言，完全没有这种感觉。每次吃各种西式餐点，她都无法抗拒这些美食的诱惑，特别是学校每周日早晨的 brunch（早午餐），从琳琅满目的各种面包到精致糕点，再到 brunch 配菜等，她取完一盘还嫌不够，会接着取第二盘，甚至第三盘。她对法式羊角包的喜爱简直可以用狂热来形容，一口气可以连吃 4 个。松松脆脆的面包皮，搭配粉末状的白糖，或是融化的巧克力酱，一口咬下去，她的胃得到了极大的满足感，然后继续第二口、第三口，吃了仿佛停不下来的样子。有时坐在一桌的学生看到她这么好胃口，简直惊讶她这个小巧玲珑的亚洲女孩像个超级大胃王，不停地吃呀吃呀，非常沉浸在美食中。简心无法理性地解释，为什么她对西餐的喜爱会那么自然而言，与生俱来。每天在学校里，她最感兴趣的事情是学校的各类餐点以及每次可以悠闲自在地吃上一个多小时，但以前在国内读书的时候她很热衷于和小伙伴在就餐时间聊天，对吃饭只是当任务完成一样，草草地扒几口就结束了。她无法理解自己的这种转变，但可以肯定一点的是，她深深地感受到自己在异国他乡的不适感、孤独寂寞感需要找到一个发泄口，那就是热衷美食。她在学校里几乎没有真正的朋友，几个热情又好的学生，例如 Lily、Euginia 或另一个教她正确使用刀叉的那个女孩还谈不上是她的好朋友，其实也只是点头之交，因为他们已经有自己熟知的朋友圈，不会太主动把简心融入他们各自的圈子里去的。自从上次 Rita 请简心在她的雇主家吃了一顿晚餐之后，没多久也离开了德国，之后也了无音信，当时简心很伤心难过，唯一的小伙伴都离她而去了。她的内心极度渴望在异国找到纯真的友情，可以让她这漫长而孤独的留学生涯多一份温情与相伴，找到心灵的共鸣。她是一个非常需要朋友的女孩，和朋友在一起，她会有自我存在感，并且可以满足她超强的表达欲和分享欲，可现在她追寻的友情始终无法得到，自从 Rita 离开后。她在学校里每次都是一个人上课下课，一个人去吃饭，所有的事基本是一个人做，她就像一个独行侠。父母亲人远在国内，虽然她很想念他们，但国际长途的昂贵费用以及通讯的不发达而无法经常联系他们，所以她只能收起这份思乡之情，一遍遍地慰藉自己，"要坚强，独立，你已经长大了。"无数个夜晚，她很怀念在国内的生活，那里虽然经济还很落后，读书生活也很辛苦，但有很多好友，她在家乡的日子鲜少会有孤独寂寞无助的感觉。可现在这样的空落落的感觉会时常浮上心头，外界的自然风光无论多优美，经济有多发达，她都觉得自己如同一个异类或有点像边缘人，很难融入进他们的主流文化圈里。这样的感受只有她自己一个人体会，周围的学生都是本地人，是无法感同身受的。她们对外国人保持了很大的距离感，如同一只只雄鹰，睁大了圆圆的眼睛，在不远处盯着异类，观察它们的一举一动，不愿靠近。简心和新学校里的学生就是这种感觉，无法靠近，熟悉的脸孔每一天从她眼前晃过，但很多人没有跟她说过一句话，有的也只是一句短短的问候，而就再也没有下文了。她没觉得自己被排挤，而只是有深深的无力感，她为自己无法融入学生的主流圈而感到无助，但却只能独自一人躲在角落里默默地承受无尽的孤独与落寞，而她自己内心精神世界的空虚需要找到恰当的事物来疗愈或填补，那便是她对西餐的喜爱。她在这个新的环境没有朋友，没有亲人，所以对美食由衷地热爱以及享受其中，味蕾的满足感也会对心灵产生连锁的正面效应。

　　列车飞驰，她看着窗外的风景，不一会儿就睡着了，眼前闪现出一幕幕小时候和小伙伴一起玩耍的场景，就像放电影一样。其他的学生没有一个人和她同坐或聊天，她们都在热火朝天、天南地北地聊天或打闹嬉戏，简心始终是一个人坐着的。过了大概5个小时，列车抵达了柏林中央火车站，大家都欢呼雀跃，Frau Koenig 叫学生们拿好自己的背包或箱子，有序下车。简心就跟在她们生活组的后面，跟着她们的步伐，下了这列她人生中第一次坐的快速列车，紧紧地跟在后面，不敢随便乱走。中央火车站古典而气派，整个建筑是新古典主义风格，车站内人头攒动，一条条火车轨道蜿蜒地伸向远方，时不时会有火车出发，又有其他火车到站，来来往往，川流不息，车站内有很多面包房、烤香肠店以及糖果店。行人在路途中为了节省用餐时间，也为了更随心便利地买到食物，一般都会选择购买三明治、面包卷等。简心没见到过这么热闹繁华而又充满活力的大都市，内心充满了无限的期待，希望在接下去的几天好好地了解柏林。Frau Koenig 带着这群女孩穿过了一阵阵人群以及气势磅礴的中央大厅，一路奔向地铁站。她在指示牌上仔细而又快速地浏览一番，就找到了需要乘坐的地铁线路，然后嘱咐大家说："带好自己的行李，我们要坐地铁了，地铁的车门关得很快，你们跟好了。"简心跟一只无头苍蝇一样，什么也不懂，也不了解，这是她长这么大第一次坐地铁这种交通工具，以前在她生活的那个小城镇，出行的公共交通只有大巴车，时间还不确定，只能傻呆呆地站在站台等。她隐约记得在家乡时坐大巴车的次数屈指可数，几乎就那么两到三次。平时她除了上下学就在她们那个小村庄待着，有点与世隔绝的感觉。现在的她来到了高度文明发达的世界，这里的一切都显得那么古典而又现代化，建筑风格还是保留了欧洲18世纪或19世纪的古典美感，但建筑物内部使用的各种设施已经非常高端与先进。过了3分钟左右，地铁就到达了，她们一群人立刻上了地铁站。地铁飞速前进，经过一个一个站台，把一群群旅客带向他们的目的站。简心觉得地铁的发明具有划时代的意义，它不仅带给人们出行的便利，也节约了出行成本，让人们不再局限于自己那个生活的小范围，而是可以很快捷而方便地去往城市的各个角落，人的日常生活也会因为高度发达的交通变得丰富而有趣很多。地铁大概行驶了20多站，Frau Koenig和女孩子们说："我们已经到达终点站了，下车吧。"之后，一群女孩子就带着自己的行李，兴高采烈地下了地铁。出了地铁口，步行了大概10分钟左右，便到达了青年旅舍。Frau Koenig安排女孩子们入住房间，每间房间有4个床铺，关系亲密的女孩子总会选择和自己的小伙伴同处一室，所以Frau Koenig会征求大家的意见。只有简心一个人，不知道和谁同住，因为平时和小组里的这群女孩关系都非常疏远，根本谈不上亲密二字。等大家选好了室友以后，就只剩下简心一个人孤零零地没被安排在内。Frau Koenig显然心知肚明，清楚地知道简心还未被这群女孩真正地接受，当然她也不好指责女孩子们，这个年纪的年轻人有自己独到的见解与想法，老师的观点也未必需要全盘被学生接受。在德国，学生可以对老师提出疑问，可以在公开场合表达自己的观点，有时甚至会产生激烈的辩论，这些都是被允许或鼓励的。老师对于学生更多的是尊重，不会有太多的指责。所以即使Frau Koenig觉得小组里的学生有排外或一些种族偏见的倾向，她都不会去指责这些学生。简心需要靠自己的努力去融入团队，但简心也不想逼迫自己，因为她清楚，很多时候，不是自己一个人努力就可以的，如果别人从心理上就抵制你或对你有偏见，你做再多努力，也是徒劳。虽然她渴望交到真正的朋友，但她绝不会太勉强，她知道，他人的意志与情感是最不可控的，她只能把关注点放在自己身上，做好自己，做好自己应该做的，才是最重要的。

Frau Koenig 看没有一个女孩子主动叫简心和她们共住一个房间，她就把简心分配到还有空余床位的最角落的客房里。进入房间后，大家稍作休息，不一会儿就小组集合了。因为到达的时间已经是傍晚了，所以第一晚也没什么特别的活动，就安排大家一起找个性价比高的餐厅吃个晚餐。女孩子们都喜欢吃意大利的 Pizza，Frau Koenig 就在附近找了一家 Pizza 店，一到餐厅，女孩子们找到室外两张未被预定的餐桌，便惬意地坐了下来。服务员为这两张餐桌点上了蜡烛，灯光昏暗而柔和，餐厅里正播着轻快而悠扬的音乐，每个人手里都捧着一本菜单，仔细地挑选菜肴。简心从头到尾看了一道道菜，很多单词都看不懂，虽然另外还有英文的注解，但她的英语也不怎么样，在国内学的那点英语在欧洲只能算是懂一点皮毛。最后她挑选了一道非常经典的 PIZZA Hawaii，主材料是熏肉与菠萝片。服务员首先为每个人端上了饮料，有苏打水、苹果汁、橙汁等。在欧洲的餐厅吃饭，是一个慢慢享受美食的过程，急性子的人肯定受不了。大家一边喝饮料一边聊天，耐心地等待，悠闲自在。简心对女孩子们谈话的内容不是都听得懂，因为毕竟才学了几个月的德语，但比刚到学校那会强了很多，至少可以隐约听懂些了。在他们的闲谈中，简心根本插不进去。她还是一个人默默地坐在位置上，慢慢地喝了几口苹果汁，看着学生们聊得眉飞色舞，有时她们笑得前仰后合，有时学生脸上又显出几分清高的神情。Frau Koenig 也跟一位慈祥的家长一样，和学生打成一片，聊得无拘无束，惬意而放松。只有简心一个人内心是孤寂的，她很喜欢这种浪漫而又惬意的氛围，但她无法融入这个团队，而她们组里没有一个人会主动而又热情地跟她搭话，询问她的情况，关切而友好地问她是不是适应新学校生活这类的话题。简心心里有些难过，她很怀念在国内曾经有那么多的好友，很怀念和小伙伴在一起畅所欲言，无所不谈，她几乎总是主角。而今天的她，只能一个人像被人遗忘一样默默地蜷缩在角落里，无人问津，无人关心。她对柏林之行是充满了何等的期待，现在终于有这种感觉，期待越大，失望越大。虽然还没有真的目睹这座举世闻名的城市的真面目，但一路以来她融入不了这个团体以及这些女孩对她态度的冷漠给第一次远行抹上了一丝凝重感，她就像一只孤独的大雁，怎么飞都不能和一群大雁飞在同一条线上，而她越挣扎越是努力，却发现和这群大雁的距离越来越远，渐渐地掉队了一样。简心感到自己挺傻的，为什么要这么执着地奢求自己能够很融洽地融入这个团队呢，她不喜欢被排挤在外的感觉，虽然没有一个人对她恶言相向，但这群女孩子对她的毫不关心以及冷漠至极的神情让她感到自己无形之中被他们否定与排挤。或许真的是她太敏感了，这群女孩子可能觉得简心不会德语，所以也就懒得花精力或耐心跟她聊天，干脆就置之不理了。大家闲聊了大概1个小时左右，服务员终于端上了一盘盘各式各样的PIZZA。等了好久，肚子都咕噜噜叫了，吃着新鲜出炉的脆脆香香的PIZZA，每个人都显得很满足。简心最喜欢的便是美食了，少了朋友与亲人，她只能把自己所有的热情与情感倾注在看看得见摸得着的令人垂涎欲滴的美食上了。美食是不容辜负的，她心里这么想着。晚餐过后，大家回到了旅社，互道晚安，就回房间休息了。简心静静地躺在床上，几秒钟后便进入了深睡眠。

一觉醒来，天空湛蓝，万里无云，新的一天开始了。在旅舍用了简单的早餐，大家便坐了地铁，开始了柏林一日游。到达的第一站是勃兰登堡门（Brandenburger Tor），典型的新古典主义风格建筑。它是柏林的象征，也是德国的国家象征标志。勃兰登堡门顶中央是一尊高约 5 米的胜利女神铜制雕像，女神张开身后的翅膀，驾着一辆四马两轮战车面向柏林城内；右手手持带有橡树花环的权杖，花环内有一枚铁十字勋章，花环上站着一只展翅飞翔的鹰，鹰戴着普鲁士的皇冠。这座雕塑象征着普鲁士战争的胜利，显得庄严肃穆，壮丽巍峨。很多游客都站在勃兰登堡门前拍照留念，为了把这美好的柏林之行永远定格下来。简心看到了这么气势恢宏，雕刻精美的建筑物，发自内心地感叹艺术家们巧夺天工的技艺。站在雄伟高大的勃兰登堡门下，人类显得那么渺小。在时间的长河中，这些建筑物经历了风风雨雨，见证了柏林这座名城的兴衰更替以及波澜壮阔的历史事件，依然屹立不倒，骑着战马斗志昂扬的胜利女神像仿佛在向世人述说着："经历了这么多坎坷与起伏，我们终于胜利了。"布兰登堡门是德国坚忍不拔、永不妥协、精益求精的精神的象征。Frau Koenig 叫大家站在一排，在这座地标性建筑前拍照留念。

  下一站是久负盛名的国会大厦，体现了古典主义、哥特式、文艺复兴和巴洛克式的多种建筑风格，是德国统一的象征。高技派风格与传统建筑风格巧妙结合：保留外墙不变，而将室内全部掏空，以钢结构重做内部空间体系。因而国会大厦这一古老庄严的外壳里包裹的是一座现代化的新建筑，堪称是古典与现代的完美结合。始建于 1884 年的国会大厦，在第二次世界大战中被严重摧毁再到东西德统一之后的大规模整修与翻新，如今的国会大厦成了欧洲最引人注目的艺术品，吸引了来自全世界的观光游客。国会大厦不仅是联邦议会的所在地，其屋顶的玻璃穹形圆顶也是最受欢迎的旅游胜地。Frau Koenig 带着这一群女孩子登上了玻璃穹顶：其内为两座交错走向的螺旋式通道，裸露的全钢结构支撑，参观者可以通过全透明玻璃窗 360 度眺望柏林的景致。玻璃穹顶里面游人如织，络绎不绝，游客们都为这样一件艺术品般的建筑深深折服，惊叹不已。简心看到如此美轮美奂的建筑群,内心激动不已,欧洲建筑的气势磅礴与精美绝伦在她脑海中留下深刻而挥之不去的印象。

  游览完国会大厦,她们一群人来到了一个露天广场的café(咖啡)馆休息。服务员拿出了酒水单,供客人浏览。简心点了她最爱的苹果汁,安安静静地欣赏着四周的风景。成群结队的白鸽在广场飞来飞去,有时站立在广场地面上,慢悠悠地踱步,游人见到了站立着的洁白而硕大的白鸽,会忍不住走近,想和白鸽一起拍照留念,或给它们喂食。这里的白鸽见到人类,不会惊慌失措地立刻飞走,而是仍然站立在原处,尽情地让游人抚摸它们洁白无瑕的羽毛,人与大自然和谐共生。白鸽、广场四周矗立的一座座巍峨壮丽的古典建筑物以及懒散而又悠闲的游客,构成一幅典型的欧洲休闲生活的画面,在简心看来,这样的生活美好而简单,这里的人们没有太多的生活压力,可以尽情地享受户外温暖和煦的太阳,在休闲的日子外出度假或和朋友聚在一起晒太阳聊天,慵懒而又惬意地度过一天。在家乡,她几乎从来没有看到过这样悠闲的画面,她从小到大看到的是大人们整日辛勤劳作,忙里忙外,鲜少有空闲时间坐下来喝喝茶,聊聊家常,更别提度假或旅游了。在那个年代(2000年之前),在简心生活的那个小地方,大部分人终其一生就去过附近的城市或小镇,有很多老一辈的人一辈子生活的核心范围就只有他们的故里,认识的人也只有村子里的左邻右舍和亲朋好友,因为交通设施的滞后以及信息的不流通,村子里的人很难走出去,很难去见识外面丰富而博大的世界。他们也习惯在这个小地方日出而作,日落而息,过简单淳朴的生活。简心感到了这两个不同世界的人们生活情景的巨大差异,内心不禁震撼,虽然在异国他乡,她举目无亲,也很难找到好朋友,因为文化的差异以及语言的匮乏,但是她看到了一个完全不同于她以往生活的世界,她对这个新奇而高度发达的世界充满了强烈的好奇心与探索欲。她很享受在café馆中悠闲地看着游人来来往往,什么都不做,静而不语，只用双眼去捕捉这个美好的万千世界。组里其他的女孩也懒洋洋地躺在椅子上悠闲地聊天，很放松的样子。这时，Frau Koenig 温和地说："你们觉得今天的行程怎么样？"有些女孩回答："可以呀，挺好的。"还有一些女孩就默认地点点头，她们都戴着太阳眼镜，显得成熟而气质，完全不像一个个青涩害羞的小女孩。Frau Koenig 喝了一口饮料，接着说："下午我们可以去游个船，然后可以早点一起吃晚餐，之后就自由活动了。"大家听了，都觉得这个行程安排很合理，都异口同声地回答："好的，Frau Koenig。"

午餐很简单，大家吃了经济实惠而又可口的三明治，就径直前往游船码头。一波一波的游客正站在码头上等着上船，Frau Koenig 让女孩们站在固定的位置等待，她需要先去买票。过了大半个小时，票买到了。女孩子们排着队，等候在码头，等待下一艘游船的到来。川流不息的运河，在太阳的高照下，微风吹来，河面上波光粼粼，银光闪闪，如同缎面的丝绸，高贵而典雅。一条条来来往往的游船行驶在运河上，悠闲自得。时间在不知不觉中流逝，一艘游船终于靠岸了。等待的游客依次按顺序踏上了游船的甲板，进入了船舱内。游客最青睐的第一层船舱在很短暂的时间内就被填满。简心和这群女孩子们顺着舱内楼梯往下走，来到了底层船舱，里面坐了三三两两几个游客，她们刚要坐下，Frau Koenig 便说："女孩们，底层船舱的视野不好，我们去露天船舱。"然后大家就顺着楼梯，爬上了游船的最顶部，刚好还有十几个空位，她们立刻坐了下来。到了出发时间，游船如同一只海龟缓慢而又沉稳地在运河上滑行，身后留下了一条发光的水迹。简心看着运河两岸移动的一座座古典与现代融合的建筑物，壮观而唯美。有的游客手拿照相机一路拍个不停，还有的游客喜欢静静地只用双眼观赏当下如此优美的风景，细细地品味运河两岸拥有上百年历史的建筑群的魅力，不愿意用过度照相去搅乱当下惬意而舒适的心境，他们觉得照相机拍到的只是某个角度的风景或建筑物,如此美丽的风景是需要360度呈现出来的,而这样的全景真的只有人身临其境才能感受到。简心也没有带照相机,她只是安静地坐在游船上,欣赏这美得让人无法用精准的语言表达出来的景色。组里的女孩子们都戴上了墨镜,显得成熟而气质高雅,虽然她们的平均年龄只有14到15岁,但几乎看不出她们只是稚气未脱的少女,因为她们的穿着打扮十分时尚而性感。6月下旬的柏林,在阳光灿烂的日子里,气温也已经略高,女孩们穿着紧身的T-Shirt,雪白的脖子露出了一大截,丰满的胸部在低领口的T-shirt的包裹下显得格外性感而充满诱惑力。在欧洲这样穿着的年轻女孩子比比皆是,根本不是什么过分而招摇的打扮。但对简心而言,这样的衣着毕竟太过暴露与成熟,她在含蓄的东方文化中成长,因而骨子里会更保守与矜持。简心对这些女孩子的打扮无从评价,这是她们个人的喜好与自由。但如果有人建议她穿这样子的T-shirt,她是怎么都不会尝试的。组里的这群女孩子坐游船最爱的事情是晒太阳,希望把自己雪白的皮肤晒成健康的荞麦色,但简心却有一点担心自己的皮肤会晒得太黑,这样会显得更土更老气。不同的文化,观点如此不同。如何了解欧洲人的审美观,还要从一件事情说起。有一次,学校那个唯一的黑人女孩Euginia刚好在简心的房间说什么事情,她看到了一个中文字包装的Crème(日霜),觉得很好奇,便问简心"Nancy, was ist das(这是什么)?"简心回复道:"这是我从中国带来的crème,是美白面霜。"Euginia听到这个Crème的功效是美白的,大吃一惊,便直爽地问"为什么需要美白?"简心回答:"因为在中国,一个女孩五官长得再美再精致,如果皮肤黑或黄,也是不漂亮的。亚洲人都喜欢皮肤雪白,所以我也买这个美白面霜呀。"Euginia听到这个解释,笑得前仰后合,然后说:"真的吗?你们中国人喜欢白皮肤,那我在你们那里岂不是长得很丑了。我的皮肤这么黑"。其实第一次见到Euginia,简心用东方人的审美思维来看,她确实长得不是一般的丑,皮肤黑如碳，嘴唇太厚，鼻子也塌得厉害，整个脸部的五官除了大大的眼睛没有可取之处。但后来简心看习惯了，觉得黑人也有黑人很独特的美，虽然黑但皮肤很细腻，牙齿也洁白整洁，尤其是她的性格非常好，热情大方，自信满满，富有同理心。简心听了 Euginia 的玩笑话，立刻礼貌地回答："没有呀，当然不丑了，每个人种的美是不一样的，这个世界拥有各种各样的美才变得那么多姿多彩，那么有趣，不是吗？"Euginia 回答："是的，简心。你知道吗，在欧洲没有一个白种人喜欢自己的皮肤雪白，他们都喜欢把自己的皮肤晒成健康的古铜色，这样的颜色代表健康与财富，因为他们觉得多晒太阳，说明你很健康，说明你有时间有钱出去度假休闲，你看，沙滩上、游泳池边几乎都是白种人，他们拿一本小说坐在泳池旁，一躺就可以躺一下午，就为了把自己的皮肤晒成古铜色。到了冬天，德国或北欧国家的日照时间很短暂，他们为了让皮肤变成深颜色，还会特意去躺在 solarium（人造日光装置）里，你说神奇不神奇。所以你在这里不需要美白，这里的人不觉得皮肤雪白是美的标准。"简心听了以后，大跌眼镜，实在是颠覆她的思维模式，原来不同的文化审美竟然有这么大的差异，在亚洲以白为美，可在西方世界，古铜色的皮肤才是美和健康的标准。可虽然如此，她骨子里还是有浓的东方思维，所以也不热衷在大太阳下暴晒。组里的其他女孩子们懒洋洋地坐在热辣辣的太阳下，觉得非常开心与享受，而简心一心躲着大太阳，就怕自己被晒成一个"黑鬼"。

晚餐过后，Frau Koenig 说："你们可以自由活动了，但不要太晚回旅舍，明天我们还要继续游玩呢。"除了简心一个人想休息了，组里其他的女孩子都还兴致正浓，还想去柏林的酒吧玩玩，过过瘾。她们正是青春年少，对酒吧、disco 这类夜生活特别着迷，在那样的氛围可以释放她们无尽的青春活力以及热情而奔放的心，可以肆无忌惮地喝酒跳舞。酒吧或 disco 播放的歌曲劲爆而激烈，一听到那样的音乐，整个人就会跟随强烈而火爆的节奏扭动起来，停都停不下来，整个人特别兴奋而激情四射。在 pub（酒吧）或 disco 里还经常会有些艳遇，两个陌生的年轻男女看对眼了，在那样充满活力的氛围下会经常搂在一起跳舞，这样的不期而遇是充满无限的刺激与新鲜感的。这群女孩子在这个花季的年龄，是那样的向往无拘无束、自由而又刺激的生活，所以她们对夜生活那样的趋之若鹜也是有迹可循的。然而简心对这样的娱乐不是特别感兴趣，上一次她在学校举办的 disco 已经体验过了，也没觉得这样的活动有什么好玩，就一群男男女女抱在一起跳舞喝酒，音乐声震天响，离开 disco 以后，还觉得耳旁依然有点嗡嗡嗡的声音，仿佛还有 disco 的余音绕耳。并且她是一个生活作息规律的人，不喜欢一整晚不睡觉，去泡这种酒吧或 disco。其实组里的女孩也没有一个问她，有没有兴趣一起去酒吧，可能她们猜想，简心不会感兴趣，也或者她们觉得简心的表象给人一种乖乖女的感觉，太规规矩矩了，不好玩不有趣，所以她们也不想带上这个中国女孩一起。既然如此，简心在晚餐过后，就和 Frau Koenig 一起回了旅舍，然后各自洗漱休息了。至于那群女孩子到底玩到几点回来的，也不得而知，总之她们应该玩得很尽兴。简心真真正正地觉得欧洲的年轻人过得潇洒自在，没有那么重的课业负担，就算是读书的年纪，重心不会只是在学业上，除此之外，她们还有很多业余活动，她们在这个美好的年纪可以尽情地享受这个年纪赋予她们的青春活力，可以体验各种活动，无论是旅行，还是爬山、滑雪，或是去酒吧或 disco 疯玩，也或者在公开场合谈恋爱，两个人毫无顾忌地卿卿我我、热情相拥、浪漫相吻。她们是幸运的，成长在这样一个高度发达与文明的国度，她们也是受到上帝眷顾的。相比较而言，在发展中国家或第三世界，很多人还挣扎在贫困的边缘，连饭都吃不饱，也不能接受高等教育，根本没有生活品质可言。简心觉得世界各地的生活差异实在太大了，每个地方的人都有不同的生活方式，在她以前生活的家乡，人的观念是保守、守旧而传统的。如果年轻的女孩子去酒吧或早恋，肯定会背负骂名，会觉得这样子的女孩子不正经，是坏女孩。由于受到这种传统思维的影响，简心的骨子里其实也是有些内敛而克制的，所以她不是那么热衷于这些夜生活，关键的原因来自从小接受的教育。虽然她现在人已经身在欧洲，但还是无法像这些女孩子一样活得那么洒脱，那么无拘无束。所以让她真正融入这样的主流文化，还是非常难的。

说到 Frau Koenig，前文已经提过无数次，她是简心她们那个组的生活老师，大概50多岁的样子。她有一头金色的齐耳短发，蓝蓝的眼睛，五官精致而立体，脸庞小巧，属于巴掌脸那种，除了皮肤有些松弛，额头也已经爬了几道皱纹，在她的脸上再也找不出什么缺点。可以想象，年轻的时候应该是个不折不扣的气质美人。简心第一次见到她，就觉得她是一位很有亲和力的老师，从来不训斥组里的女孩，说话轻声细语，总是带着温柔而友善的微笑。她和一位跟她年龄相仿的男士住在学校的一个教师公寓里，公寓恰好就在简心她们那个组所在的楼层，这样也便于 Frau Koenig 管理组里的学生。有一次，简心在活动室里和几个女孩一起看电视，透过透明的玻璃门，第一次看到 Frau Koenig 和那位气质儒雅而又憨厚的60岁左右的男子从公寓里一起走出来。简心便很好奇地问组里的女孩子那位是不是 Frau Koenig 的老公。简心觉得其实自己也有点八卦的，也好奇别人的隐私，但一般情况下，人都会拥有这种与生俱来的好奇心与猎奇心理。组里的女孩 Celia 回答："不是她的老公，是她男朋友呢，她们只是同居而已，应该说是 Lebenspartner（生活伴侣）。"简心听了，觉得特别吃惊，心里想：哇，这样也可以，他们两个有50多或60多岁的样子了，居然没有结婚住在一起，还只是生活伴侣。当然她内心的这种想法没有对 Celia 说出口，因为怕别人鄙视她大惊小怪，这种现象可能在德国很正常，但对于简心而言，真的是出乎意料。"Lebenspartner"（生活伴侣）这个词格外新潮和时髦，简心觉得，

第十七章：柏林之行

她长这么大，第一次听过，两个人不领结婚证，就这么一直住在一起，做一辈子生活伴侣。再说他们两个都50或60多岁了，居然也是这么时尚，简心无法理解，两个人既然可以很默契地生活在一起，互相需要对方，那为什么不能光明正大地结婚呢？这样在法律上更加于情于理。那时候的简心看待问题还是用传统的中国人的思维，想问题过于简单，过于单纯。其实很多成年人经历了婚姻生活，才会懂得婚姻和爱情是完全不同的，婚姻生活有太多的繁琐，几乎和浪漫搭不上边了，如果遇到夫妻两人性格不合，三观不一致，还需要磨合；磨合不了，可能婚姻生活也不会太幸福。甜蜜的恋爱比比皆是，但是浪漫而甜美的婚姻在这个世间少之甚少。欧洲的人思想开放，早就看透了婚姻的本质，可能也不愿被婚姻束缚，所以就选择一同居住在一起，做生活伴侣吧。当时的简心年龄还小，从来没有真正的恋爱过，更别谈婚姻，所以她觉得很奇怪，跟Frau Koenig同居的那位男士居然不是她老公，只是她的生活伴侣。世界之大，无奇不有。

接下去的几天，Frau Koenig带着这群女孩子们还参观了柏林大教堂。在欧洲，教堂遍布城市与乡镇，是西方人精神世界的神圣之地，风格多样化，有哥特式建筑、古典主义风格、巴洛克式等。柏林大教堂建造于1894—1905年，是德国威廉二世皇帝建造的文艺复兴时期风格的基督新教教堂，三个突出的大圆顶明显地诠释了这一特点，不同于哥特式教堂的尖顶，它的圆顶从视觉上给人一种圆润丰盈的感觉。当简心踏入教堂内，被教堂内部的金碧辉煌、奢侈华丽震撼到了，宗教题材的壁画惟妙惟肖、栩栩如生，线条复杂的柱子都是镀金的，教堂穹顶镶嵌着耶稣登山传福音的镶嵌画，所有的地面都是用昂贵稀有的大理石铺砌而成。游客们在教堂中祈祷与参观，手中拿着介绍这座教堂的历史与由来的小册子，静而不语，安安静静地漫步在古典而浮华的教堂内部。那一刻，每个人的心灵应该是那样的平和与安详。大部分的游客都信仰基督教，进入这个圣地，他们也会在教堂内的一排排座位上坐下，默默地注视着圣坛上巨大的耶稣像，然后轻声细语地默念着圣经里的章节或静思，祈求主的庇护与保佑。偌大的教堂内没有任何的嘈杂与喧哗，即使之后入内的游客越来越多，大家都很遵守礼仪，不发出任何的响声；就算说话，也是压低声音，绝不会影响到其他人。简心对德国人这种规则感与次序感非常钦佩。她发现，在德国的餐厅、博物馆、教堂、咖啡馆、火车车厢内以及公园等几乎所有的公共场合，没有嘈杂，没有喧嚣，人们都轻声细语地聊天说话，整个环境是那样的静谧。她有时坐在餐厅或坐在路边休息，会经常听到鸟儿叽叽喳喳地欢叫声，仿佛在唱着轻盈而欢快的歌。从此以后，简心在这样的环境中，也养成了用最低的分贝说话的习惯。安静的环境在一开始让她感到孤独与寂寞，但随着时间的流逝，人的喜好是会随着环境的改变而改变的，她慢慢地爱上了那份随处可寻的宁静与平和，让她的情绪平稳安定，几乎没有太多波澜。宁静似乎蕴藏着一股巨大的力量，让人可以更好地休息，更好地思考，而不会被外界的喧嚣与纷扰搅和得心神不宁，烦躁不安。为了让学生们更好地了解这座壮丽而浮华的大教堂，Frau Koenig还专门聘请了一个向导，给大家讲述这座教堂的历史。大家都听得津津有味，就只有简心没怎么听懂，向导用了太多专业而高深的德语词汇与句型表述，语速又飞快，她实在还没有那么强的理解力，毕竟才学了几个月的德语，但教堂的浮华与壮美深深地刻在了她的脑海里，挥之不去。而她也一点点被欧洲艺术的璀璨吸引住了，通过感官世界对欧洲建筑与艺术品的欣赏，她变得越来越有审美力与鉴赏力。在不知不觉中她已经不再是曾经那个懵懵懂懂的、在中国的小村庄长大的淳朴的小女孩，而是变得越来越中西合璧，越来越追求自我实现与热爱那唯美的意境，而这样的改变可能就缘由这段漫长的留学经历。

为了让学生们拥有更多的艺术情怀，Frau Koenig还带着他们参观了柏林美术馆。美术馆里展出的主要是19世纪的绘画与雕塑，有很多著名画家例如费德烈、勃克林以及法国印象派大师马奈、莫奈、塞尚的作品。站在一幅幅巨大的画作面前，简心钦佩艺术家绘画技术的炉火纯青，这些伟大的艺术家用自己的灵感、绘画天分以及卓越的艺术表现手法完成一幅幅巨作，流传百世，供世人参观欣赏，让普通人也能在艺术的殿堂里自由地遨游，想象力与浪漫主义情怀被激发。画廊里展出的画作分好几个题材，宗教题材的画作无疑是欧洲画派最重要的一个分支。巨大的画作里描述的是圣经里的一个个故事，人物与情景画得非常细致与具有立体感，色彩鲜艳，显得栩栩如生。简心不是很了解基督教，也没有阅读过圣经里的故事。但很多具有基督教信仰的欧洲人看到这些画作，就会知道是哪一个宗教故事，出于哪一个圣经的章节。他们从小长在这片土地上，耳濡目染，自然会更了解当地的文化。在简心看来，欧洲人的艺术熏陶真的是非常普及，老师会经常组织学生去游览美术馆或博物馆，不管你懂不懂，这些作品见多了，这类保留人类辉煌精神财富的圣地去多了，再没有一点艺术细胞的人，也会被逐渐感染，变得越来越有艺术修养了。普通的欧洲民众更是热衷于去这类场所，当他们外出旅游的时候。欧洲大大小小的城市也有着数量庞大的艺术馆与画廊，非常适合供游人参观。简心觉得，这里的人非常注重精神世界的丰盈与滋养，所以才会喜欢去欣赏艺术品与名家的画作。一方面是由于从小到大艺术的熏陶，另一方面还是由于经济的发达与生活的富足，人们才有充裕的时间去追求内在的精神世界。在简心的家乡，老百姓都忙着生计，忙着养家糊口，过年过节的时候，亲戚朋友聚在一起唠嗑，或打牌搓麻将，联络感情，去游览艺术馆与博物馆对他们而言是天方夜谭，有些人还会鄙视说"装高雅"。简心真心觉得，经济基础决定上层建筑，物质生活得到了保障，人才会去追求更高层次的需求，比如社会认同感、自我价值感、精神财富等。如果没有充裕的物质保障，人的关注点不会停留在这些虚无缥缈的艺术鉴赏上的。当然也跟人受教育的程度息息相关，如果一个人靠努力与运气得到了财富，但他没有接受过高等教育，也没有任何后天条件可以让他得到艺术熏陶，他也是对艺术品不会有半点兴趣的。

自然风光也是画家们很喜欢的一个主题。当简心看到印象派鼻祖莫奈的经典作品《睡莲》时，如同身临其境，仿佛自己正静静地站立在开满睡莲的池塘边，湖面波光粼粼，水面上的睡莲显得那样的温柔，沿着湖面，睡莲一片片向湖面远处扩展开来，花朵在绿树的倒影下显得十分有层次感，光与影得到了完美的融合，画面具有朦胧美以及浪漫主义情调。在莫奈的这幅作品下，花园的这个池塘如同他内心的一方净土，是他心灵深处的神秘花园，大自然是那样的美好，充满着无限的活力而又是那样的宁静而神秘。

法国著名画家保罗·塞尚十分热衷于画静物，例如洒落的水果、水果盘以及放置于桌子上的花卉等。他的静物画《静物苹果篮子》是他最典型的画作之一：一张简陋的木桌，放上一块桌布，上面陈设一些苹果、酒瓶、篮子、盘子等，每一只苹果的体和面的结构被重点强调与刻画，色彩严谨，线条浑厚浓重，真实地再现实体和表现光线与空间的表象。通过描绘自然，塞尚在他的作品里追求的已经不再是简单的复制对象，而是实现了人的感觉。

简心在这高雅的艺术殿堂里慢慢地欣赏一幅幅画作，发现每个画家的作画风格都是不一样的，有的是采用十分细腻而严谨的手法，重在表现人物或场景的立体感与真实性，而有的画家喜欢把更多的个人情感融到绘画作品中，作品里几乎无法清楚地识别物体或人物的细节，但通过色彩与特殊的笔触可以和画家的个人感受产生某个程度的链接，例如有些作品展现出来的阴郁与压抑的感觉，而有些作品的内容会让人联想到明媚或活泼的感受，而这些作品所呈现的刚好是画家们所要表达的个人情感。艺术作品是非常主观的，仁者见仁，智者见智，呈现手法也是十分多样化，而这最能体现人类的创造力，灵感以及感性思维的光芒。

在柏林旅游的这4天时间里，简心发现柏林的很多地铁口的墙壁上画满了涂鸦，她觉得有些涂鸦还是很有艺术价值的，画得很有创意。但还有些涂鸦纯属是乱涂乱画，在她主观审美中，这类涂鸦没什么美感，和柏林新古典主义的风格不是很协调。但她很费解，为什么政府会允许各种各样的涂鸦在这个德国的首都随意展示出来，难道是拥护人权和自由吗？还是想留给普通民众展示才华与自我的环境？她也不清楚具体是什么原因。总之通过这4天时间，她看到的柏林是一个古典而现代，有着浓厚历史文化底蕴而又活力满满的欧洲大城市。

谈到关于柏林的近代历史，最著名的便是引发第二次世界大战的德国纳粹。柏林是纳粹德国的中心，由于纳粹在世界大战中的惨败，柏林在战后被分割成东柏林与西柏林，直到1989年柏林墙才被推翻，此后德国才实现了真正意义上的统一。柏林见证了德国这段令人耻辱而又难忘的历史。Frau Koenig为了让学生们更加深入了解这段历史，特意带他们去参观了柏林犹太博物馆，馆内记录和展示了犹太人在德国前后约两千年的历史，以及包括德国纳粹迫害和屠杀犹太人的历史。展品以历史文物、信件与生活记录为主，让人了解到那个年代犹太人如何遭受屠杀、驱逐以及迫害的。那是一段非常血腥、残暴以及凝重的历史，充分地展现了纳粹的心狠手辣以及惨无人道的屠杀行为，从读犹太人的手稿以及当时的报纸剪图来说，他们是那样的无助而绝望，在纳粹的恐怖统治下。历史虽然已经成为过去，但需要人们不能忘记这段历史带给人类的教训。简心虽然觉得在当时那个年代德国纳粹的统治确实很残忍，没有任何人道主义，但现在德国人为了牢记这段让国人蒙羞的阴暗史，会在他们的学习过程中主动去教育后代这段历史以及带给他们的教训，这种坦然承认前人犯下的错误的诚恳态度是值得人敬佩的。

在柏林之行的最后一天，Frau Koenig 带着女孩们来到了柏林最著名的百货大楼"KaDeWe"。简心进入了这座百货大楼，被内部奢华的装潢以及琳琅满目的商品吸引住了。Frau Koenig 说："你们可以自由活动，购物时间大概是 4 个小时，之后我们在大厅集合。希望你们玩得开心。"之后，女孩子们都三三两两地逛起街来，就只剩下简心一个人，没有一起逛街的朋友。Frau Koenig 关心地问："简心，你一个人逛街没事吧？要不我叫组里的女孩带你一起逛。"简心回答："没事呢，我可以的，Frau Koenig。"听到简心这样回答得干脆利落，Frau Koenig 便礼貌地说："bis später, viel spass（待会见，玩得开心）。"随后，Frau Koenig 也一个人开始了购物活动。简心这次没那么觉得孤独了，可能是慢慢也适应了吧，一个人也有一个人的精彩，虽然没有人说话，不能分享喜悦，但可以很随性地逛街，不用顾及他人的感受，这是一种很自由的感觉。她就一个人慢悠悠地在这高贵典雅而又华美的百货大楼逛啊逛，从一层逛到二层，再到三层。商品品质卓越但也非常昂贵，她对奢侈品不崇尚也不追求，因为没有那种强烈的虚荣心，并且她本来也没多少零花钱，所以就更不会去关注这类商品。但她对衣服比较感兴趣，所以当她逛到女装那一层，她也会去留意一下衣服的款式。她很惊讶地发现，这些衣服的款式不是很适合年轻女孩，更适合年长的妇人，40 岁以上，她不是很理解，为什么女装的款式这么老成。后来她才理解原来欧洲的富裕阶层几乎都是老年人，年轻人没有雄厚的经济实力，所以这些高端衣服只有年纪大的客户才能消费得起。怪不得很多欧洲的老年人打扮得这么高雅与得体，很多老年男士穿得也很体面，不是笔挺的西装，就是气度非凡的风衣，或者是休闲的运动装。而欧洲的老妇人浓妆艳抹，穿金带银，穿着优雅的裙子或套装，戴着和衣服搭配的首饰，他们俨然活得十分有尊严而自信。这让她又联想到家乡的情况，在她的印象中，她出生的那个小地方，生活拮据以及没有经济实力的几乎更多是老年人，很多老年人为了有些养老钱，年纪一大把，还会去做苦力，例如扫马路，或是做些手工品，改善生活。因为缺乏经济基础，家乡的老年人过得是节俭而淳朴的生活，根本无法和这些德国老爷爷老太太相比。简心心里暗暗地想"希望我以后也能优雅地老去"。她逛了一圈，什么都没有买，商品的价格太高了，她买不起，或者说她不舍得乱花钱。最后她来到了地下一层，立刻被眼前品种繁多的美食吸引住了，各式各样的手工巧克力（praline）摆在玻璃橱柜里，精致小巧，看得人垂涎欲滴，真想一口气买个十几个尝个遍，但她看了一下价目表，每个这么小的巧克力需要2到3欧元（当时欧元和人民币是1比9），她舍不得买这么昂贵的巧克力。每次在买东西的时候，都会自动换算成人民币，2002年的时候，中国的物价还非常低，所以显得欧洲的物价特别高。她一想到国内的父母省吃俭用，每天辛苦工作，就不舍得乱花零用钱，不然会有心里负罪感，觉得自己很不应该，一点都不体谅父母的难处。父母从小到大教育她"在花钱之前，先想一下是不是这件东西非要不可，如果不是必需品，就不要买。赚钱不容易，不能没有控制地乱花钱。"父母教育她的这种金钱观已经在她内心深入骨髓，她不好意思乱花父母的辛苦钱，所以即使内心是那么想尝试这些精致而美味的手工巧克力，她还是忍住欲望没有买，而只是透过玻璃橱柜仔细地欣赏这些类似艺术品的mini巧克力。虽然她没有亲口尝试，但是能在现实中欣赏这些精致的巧克力，简心觉得已经是一件很美好而幸运的事情了，有时不需要得到而是静静地观察美食美物，也是一种得到与享受。好的东西成千上万，人怎么可能都能拥有，这是她母亲经常说的话。记得小时候，简心的母亲会偶尔带着她和弟弟简阳去城里逛街，那个物质贫乏的年代，对于生活在小乡村的人来说，去城里简直就像刘姥姥进入大观园，一切都是那么新奇而有趣，母亲在商场里可以转悠几个小时。虽然衣服从一家店铺试到另一家，但却不舍得买，因为她只想要挑出一件最满意的衣服，可能是预算有限，也有可能母亲平时节俭惯了，不是很舍得花这么多钱买件昂贵的衣服，犹豫来犹豫去，挑来挑去，无法下决定，等她选中一件衣服，大概要花了3到4个小时。在母亲逛街选衣服的过程中，简心和弟弟会变得无聊而不耐烦，总会嘀咕"妈妈怎么还没挑好衣服，都挑了几个小时了。"作为小孩子，想法当然和成年人不同，他们的想法是单纯的，觉得挑选一件衣服还不容易吗，有必要花那么多时间选择吗？可母亲自有母亲的道理，这取决于她一贯严谨而节约的做事风格以及思维方式。总而言之，简心的父母都是勤俭惯了的，他们挣钱不容易，所以会特别珍惜付出很多心血与努力赚来的钱，这不是吝啬而是一种非常聪明的做法。所以在简心从小生活的那个小地方，她的家庭是第一个富裕出来的，靠的不仅是父亲聪明灵活的经商头脑，以及敢于冒险和尝试的精神，还有便是他们夫妻两个的勤俭持家。俗话所得好：赚钱再多，如果不懂得克制无穷无尽的物质欲望，最终也都攒不下钱。而很多富人也不都是一开始都富有的，是靠自己的努力、勤奋、节俭以及在天时、地利与人和万事俱备的情况下抓住转瞬即逝而又千载难逢的机会，才攒下第一桶金，然后如同滚雪球一样，越滚越大。所以为什么每个家庭在中国80到90年代的时候经济条件都差不多，但到了90年代后期有些家庭富裕起来了，其一是因为国内政策的改变，改革开放使经济建设变得越来越活跃，而那么非常小的一部分人抓住了改革开放的红利以及市场经济发展的机会，再加上灵活的头脑以及卓越的商业思维，所以才赶在了很多普通的人前面，发展了起来。记得简心还在家的时候，偶尔会听到父亲说"我们幸好赶上了改革开放这趟班车，抓住了机会，不然怎么可能会有现在这样的发展，所以人的一生抓住难得的机会非常重要，但大多数人是抓不住的，这需要敏锐的洞察力以及大胆地敢想、敢做，再加上努力与勤奋"。简心父母的一言一行也影响了她，所以她是上进的，她不甘心浑浑噩噩地混日子。她清楚地知道，如果想要崭露头角，她需要有一颗上进心，

第十七章：柏林之行

还需要踏实、勤奋以及坚强的毅力。不论如何，只有付出比别人更多的努力，更多的汗水，才有可能做人上人，也才有可能实现自己设定的目标，懒惰与怀疑是帮不上任何忙的，只会削弱人的意志力以及奋斗的动力。简心就是这样一个女孩，不论在何种环境中，她内心始终保持着一颗上进的心，不甘落后的心，也始终坚持着自己的一套思维方式以及价值体系。

虽然没有买巧克力，但她心里没有一点失落，她懂得自我安慰"学校里这么多美食都尝遍了，不吃这些巧克力我又不会少块肉，等以后再说吧。这些巧克力确实不是一般的贵，没必要花这些钱"。她继续在美食那一楼层转悠，里面真的应有尽有，让人逛起来十分享受其中，光是奶酪就有几百种，考究而又富有美感地摆放在购物架上，还有品类繁多的蛋糕，面包，以及各种鱼类，意大面的半成品，酸奶等等。天底下所有的精品美食似乎都已经罗列在这个美食中心了，简心逛的是真的尽兴呀，虽然没有大包小包买很多，但看看也已经很满足了。后来，她感到肚子都咕噜噜叫了，就买了一个价格实惠的面包加香肠，在收银台付款后，在 KaDeWe 百货大楼找到了一个舒服的休息场所便津津有味地吃了起来。一边吃她一边观察来来往往的行人，脸上带着安详而平和的神情，没有眉头紧锁的感觉，脚步是缓慢而从容的，不紧不慢，她心里想"这些行人都有不一样的人生故事，来自四面八方，一会儿就消失在我的眼前了，遇到只是那么一刹那，只是那么一瞬间。人的一生中真正产生情感链接的只是很小的一部分人，这是真正的缘分。今后的我会遇到怎样的人呢，会和谁产生深度的链接呢……"她觉得自己的想法有些傻，也有些痴，但16岁的她很喜欢在心中编织美丽而浪漫的梦想。虽然不同于现实，但梦想需要有，无论实现还是没有实现，如果人不愿意做些梦，人生会少了很多情趣和意境。她情不自禁地想"在这里，会不会碰到一个令人心生仰慕之情的男孩子呢？"，这就是属于她这个年龄的浪漫与超脱现实的情怀，不需要在现实生活中——印证，但可以留存在她的想象世界中。

过了大约 4 个多小时，简心回到了 KaDeWe 的大厅，Frau Koenig 指定的集合场所。有几个学生已经在大厅等候了，有些学生也是两手空空，什么都没采购，还有些学生买了一些东西。简心除了在这个高档的百货大楼吃了一些东西，也没有采购任何东西，但她内心很充盈和开心，收获满满，收获了一段美好而又难忘的经历，也收获了开阔的眼界。等大家都到齐了，Frau Koenig 慈祥而谦逊地说："我们的购物之旅结束了，你们都玩得开心的吧，有没有买到自己中意的东西？这是我们柏林之行的最后一天了，明天我们就要坐上火车回学校了。柏林之旅圆满结束，如果大家满意，以后我们还可以组织类似的活动。"只见学生们异口同声地回答"我们满意，Frau Koenig，我们玩得很开心。谢谢。"这次短暂而又难忘的旅行就这样落下帷幕，简心虽然在旅程中感到有些孤单，因为没有好友，组里没有其他女孩和她做伴，热情地带她一起游览柏林，她会时常觉得自己被有意无意地孤立了一样。但她还是很感恩自己有这样难得的机会可以参加这样有意义的活动，让她深入了解这个世界名城，让她增长了很多见识。她内心也很感谢 Frau Koenig 对活动合理地组织与安排，老师的和蔼可亲，平易近人让简心觉得没有任何紧张感与不适感。简心默默地想："感谢生命中遇到的每一个人，让我的人生增加宽度与广度，也感谢父母的培育，让我能跨越不同的地域，经历和了解不同的文化与价值体系，让我能够在不同的文化背景中成长，视角变得更加多元化，体验这个世界的多姿多彩。感谢今天所有的一切，未来的路无论怎样，我都会努力走好，也会相信自己，一定可以。"

第十八章：与阿尔卑斯山的对话

　　柏林之行结束后，简心和往常一样，过着平静而规律的生活。除了周末，她每天都会按课程安排去德语老师 Herr May 那里上课，老师与她的互动越来越频繁。因为经过半年沉浸式的德语学习，简心已经可以流利地进行日常的德语交流。在这半年的时间里，除了刚开始到达学校时与黄小丹的认识与对话，以及与父母每周一次的电话沟通，她再也没有说过一句中文，这个得天独厚的语言环境让她以最快的速度进入了学习德语的状态，也逼迫着她只能使用这种语言。可想而知，虽然只有短短半年的时间，但她在德语上的进步是显而易见的。Herr May 是一位开明的老师，每次简心在学习上有所进步，他都会毫不吝啬地夸奖这位中国学生，并且总是不厌其烦地鼓励她一定要多用德语，不懂就大方地问周围的老师或学生。简心是一位听话的学生，老师的建议她都会真诚地采纳并且付诸实践。从刚开始不敢开口说话到半年之后口语的应用自如，她付出了超出常人的努力、勤奋以及坚持，每天都会在空闲时间复习德语内容，阅读厚达 600 多页的原版德语小说，遇到的多如繁星的德语词汇，不厌其烦地查阅翻烂了的字典，以及即使不是很懂周围人的谈话内容，还是会竖起耳朵去有意识地仔细地倾听。虽然这个学校的教风不是很严格，培养的是学生全面的素养以及自律的精神，不会给学生施加很强的外部压力，但她始终保持着很好的学习习惯，并没有被学校里各种各样的活动而彻底野了心。她内心如同明镜，知道自己想要什么，需要达到什么目标，就算外界有再多的诱惑都不会干扰到她那颗上进而好学的心。每天她都主动晚自习，吃过晚饭，她会把每个晚上宝贵的时间都用于学习德语，几乎每天都会学习到凌晨12：00。小组里面的女孩打闹嬉戏或看电视都不会真正影响到她，因为她心里很清楚，她需要加倍的努力，才可以把语言学好，然后才能在暑假过后顺利地进入11年级（相当于国内的高一）。她在一开始就已经落后于这边的学生，德语完全是从零开始的，她不能偷懒，要付出大量的时间和精力来补习德语，以后的学习之路才会平坦和顺畅很多。语言是基础，如果德语都不过关，是无法顺利学习别的功课的，也就谈不上几年以后的Abitur（大学会考，相当于国内的高考）。简心是不敢松懈的，即使外界的环境有多美，活动有多丰富，她的重心依然是学好德语，顺利进入11年级，当然最重要的一个目标是通过Abitur。以怎样的成绩毕业，现在的她还无法预测，因为感到目标是那么的遥不可及，她每次想到Abitur，心里总会有点隐隐的担忧与不安，她有些担心自己是不是真的能顺利考入德国的大学。她的基础实在太薄弱了，主要是语言的问题，她内心经常有不同的声音在打架，一个声音是乐观而向上的，会一遍遍鼓励她"简心，你要相信自己，一定可以的，脚踏实地地一步步往前走，总会到达终点。"另一个声音会带着质疑与犹豫，显得有些悲观与消极，它总是会问简心"你到底行不行，是不是真的在几年后，可以顺利通过Abitur？德语这么难学，要学的和母语一样好，这真的可能吗？还要用德语学各类功课，例如历史、地理、数学、化学、物理、德语等，全都是用德语，这到底有多难。你真的行吗？"这两种不同的想法会经常在简心的心里左右摇摆，有时是乐观的想法打败悲观的想法，而有时消极的想法会占据上风。如果简心那天状态不是很好，感到特别孤独无助与迷茫，她很想念父母与亲人，她只能一遍遍安慰与鼓励自己。简心有时会觉得自己的力量很渺小，甚至她会去怀疑，以前那个拥有强大内心的她到底去哪里了，为什么总是会去怀疑自己，为什么不能那么义无反顾地坚定自己的信念，相信自己的能力与实力。每次她感到无助和能量不足的时候，会经常抬头去看挂在她卧室房间里父亲送给她的字画"千里之行，始于足下"，然后摈除一切杂念与怀疑，凝神静气，坐在书桌前，让自己专注在学业上，有时甚至会达到一种忘我的状态。

每次她情绪低落的时候，最喜欢去的一个地方是学校的南花园。出了这座如宫殿般的学校大厅，步行3分钟，便可以进入这个风景秀丽、绿草如茵的花园，各类灌木与品种繁多的鲜花点缀其中，巴洛克式风格的石雕喷泉里流淌着迷人而动听的流水声，显得是那样的静谧而美好。站在花园的开阔处，便能看到山下小镇的全貌，一座座小洋房隐藏于茂密而又青翠欲滴的树木之中，显得是那样的和谐与唯美。远处便是层峦叠嶂，连绵不断的欧洲著名的阿尔卑斯山脉，她经常会对着阿尔卑斯山自言自语，"亲爱的阿尔卑斯山，今生有幸可以遇见你，当我内心不够强大时，便会跟你对话。我知道，你会默默地保佑我，支持我，不论未来发生什么。而我也一定会努力，乐观而内心向阳，自信而独立，世界上有各种各样的难题，但一定会有解决的办法。我每天需要做的便是努力与勤奋，坚持与相信自己，而不是去怀疑自己的能力，也不是去设想各种不好的结果。既然已经选择了这条路，我会义无反顾地勇敢地走下去。"

阿尔卑斯山是那样的巍峨、伟岸，简心站在南花园遥望远处的山脉，获得了内心的平静，获得了一股神奇而又强大的精神力量，而这股力量会帮助她披荆斩棘，勇往直前。

Encountering the Alps

Preface

Education plays a very important role in the whole life course of a person. When everyone is born, they are like little angels, so pure and flawless, simple and beautiful, and extremely elastic. However, due to the influence of acquired factors, such as the family environment and the educational environment of school, each person's growth trajectory becomes completely different. Some people through the family and school excellent education will eventually in the achieve outstanding results, become the pillars of society; On the contrary, if the family education is failed, the school education is backward, such people may give up on themselves, in the long road of life in the future bumpy and difficult, become very fragile and sensitive, and even pessimistic. However, some people will not give up themselves in the harsh and difficult external environment, and become more courageous, independent, strong and brave. Education is a very deep and complex topic, which can not be explained clearly in a few words.

Nowadays, the domestic education environment is very internal, fierce competition, due to the restrictions of social resources and the large population, many parents in order to let their children have a better future, make every effort to give their children a variety of interest classes, or buy expensive school district housing, just to create excellent conditions for children to study, not to lose at the starting line. Even when places are secured at key primary or junior high schools, parents and children can become more anxious or nervous. In order to avoid such excessive competition and let their children have a more free and comfortable study life, some parents choose to let their children study abroad at a young age to avoid thousands of troops across the single-log bridge. But is going abroad the best solution? Is it really right for every child? If no parents accompany, but rely on their own to study and live overseas, the child will really adapt to the foreign life, really can endure loneliness ? Is it really easy to study abroad? Obviously, the results are not the same for different children, depending on each child's personality, attitude, ability to withstand pressure and frustration, and adaptability to the new environment.

Education is a long process, if the long-term in this high-pressure state, is it really beneficial to the growth of children? Competition is important, but are the negative effects of excessive competition even greater? The growth of a child is a gradual process, not a process that only pursues speed and pursuit of transcendence.

This novel mainly tells the story of a girl named Jianxin, who is far away from her hometown and parents at the age of 16 and studies in a foreign country (Germany). In the new country, she needs to face not only loneliness, but also huge learning pressure and the impact of Western culture. But on her way to school, she also met different people, there are racist supermarket cashiers, or arrogant students. The activities in her new school have greatly broadened her horizons and upended her traditional perceptions. In the face of challenges and pressures, does she choose to compromise or fight? Next, please follow me into the story of Jianxin, I hope that readers after reading this novel, you can bring spiritual enlightenment and nourishment. Get more insights and ideas on the topic of education.

Thank you for everything. Thank you for your trust.

Author: Jiang Jingxian
October 10, 2022

Chapter 1: Simple childhood and youth

Jianxin is a simple ,kind and sensible south of the country girl. She grew up in a large traditional family with her grandparents, parents and younger brother. In her memory, her parents work very busy, do things diligently, and take care of her life is a female elder, mother or grandmother. From the time she could remember, she felt that her father was often away from home, because he was very busy, in order to make the family life more comfortable, or also for his own ambition - to achieve personal self-worth. But in those days (70s and 80s), her father didn't think clearly what personal value was. What he faced was working hard every day to support his family. At that time, people lived a very hard life, the material life was extremely scarce, and they would not pay attention to so many spiritual needs. If even food is a problem, people's lives are more focused on doing their best, working hard to make money, and feeding everyone in the family. Therefore, in her childhood, Jianxin saw her father very little time, because her father put most of his energy and time in work, and did not have much free time to accompany the child and accompany the family. When she was a child, every time she saw her father come home from a business trip, she did not know what to say to her father, which was a little strange, and she was afraid of saying the wrong thing. Her father looked at her in a loving, warm, accepting way, even though he didn't say much at home. Many children born in that era have this feeling, that is, they want to talk to their parents, talk about home affairs, but their parents are busy, they don't have time, so after a long time, children don't know how to open their hearts with their parents.

In the absence of high-quality companionship and communication from her parents, Jianxin will share her innermost feelings with her friends, perhaps because she and her friends live in the same era, many ideas will resonate, and each other can comfort a small soul. When she was young, there were many good friends who had nothing to say, and we played together, talked, and were very lively. In dealing with her peers, she gained confidence, generosity and fearlessness. The more important point is that she has excellent grades and is often praised by teachers, which are all due to her hard work, self-improvement, self-discipline, persistence and unwillingness to mediocrity. Of course, she also has a weak side, like to get along with everyone peacefully, do not like to tear up the face to make unhappy. When the class cadre in the school, the teacher let her discipline, she always dare not act in accordance with the principle to punish the naughty students, dare not be too imposing, because of fear of the relationship with the classmates, but like an angel of peace to maintain the discipline of the class, turned a blind eye to the troublemaking pupils, or just give them a good advice. So she got along well with her classmates, because of her "weakness" and because of her sense of balance, although at her age, she did not know what balance was or the golden mean. Her "weak" character has personal factors and family education factors, her parents are very generous, do not like to go to war with others or make them unhappy because of a little thing, so in the growth of the Jianxin, often hear parents say: people should be open-minded, can not care about every ounce, otherwise tired is their own, why? Such a growing environment will tell children how to behave and how to do things, and children will learn their parents' behavior imperceptible. Parents are the first teachers of their children, and good family education is the premise of all successful education.

  For children, the days pass slowly; But for adults, the days go by so fast. When Jianxin was young, although she was looking forward to the arrival of summer vacation, because she didn't need to go to school so hard, and she could lazily spend summer vacation for two months. But this long two months, she really do not know how to kill, because in the 1980s or 1990s in the countryside, there is no advanced and convenient infrastructure, only one or two simple facilities of the commissary, you can buy a Popsicle to eat, but also can not buy every day, because there is not so much pocket money, to save some use. Parents often teach: "to save a little, do not waste too much, if not very necessary things, do not buy, buy money all at once spent, it is not easy to make money." Therefore, Jianxin grew up in such a family environment and did not develop luxury habits, even if the family became more and more wealthy. During the summer vacation, Jianxin often plays or talks with her cousin at her aunt's house. Sometimes she watches some TV programs. At that time, there were few TV channels, and there were only a few varieties of TV programs. What they liked most was the Hong Kong drama "Legend of the New Lady White" and "Legend of the Condor Heroes", as well as the later domestic drama "Princess Huanzhu". The plots in the TV dramas were fascinating and exciting, and the characters shaped by actors had distinct personalities. They often have fun discussing the plot of the show or commenting on the relationships between the characters. At that time, the countryside was very isolated, there were not many new things, and there were always a few people who could see another different world or different dynasties in the TV series, which was of great appeal to children, so Jianxin sometimes liked to imitate the characters in the TV series to play house. At that time, although the material life was poor, the people were very simple,kind and poor, because everyone lived a similar life, there was not much difference between the rich and the poor, and this phenomenon often appeared: When the overall economic conditions are backward, the psychological distance between people will be closer, when the material level increases, people become more and more wealthy, the sense of distance between people will increase. This may be because everyone's values, worldviews and outlook on life change, in different circumstances, in different times. Jianxin sometimes miss that simple era, after she grew up. Because in that era, everyone seemed so simple and simple, there was not too much vanity and comparison, and there was not too much anxiety. In fact, a simple and peaceful life is originally a beautiful state, how to make ordinary days as picturesque and meaningful as that, the key depends on people's inner world, depends on people's perspective and way of thinking.

Jianxin is three years older than her brother, and like many siblings, the two grew up fighting and fighting. In the 1980s, China introduced unprecedented family planning, allowing families to have only one child. Perhaps the leaders at that time felt that China's population was too large, and the resources allocated to each person was very small, and the huge population would hinder economic development, so the central government began to promote family planning. However, traditional Chinese families like to have more children and grandchildren, so many families could not accept the family planning policy at that time. Family planning is more strictly enforced in government offices and cities; In the countryside, by comparison, it will be a little more relaxed. After having a daughter, Jianxin's parents wanted a boy, finding it too lonely to have a child, and they were typical of carrying on the family line. So after all the obstacles, Jianxin's younger brother Jianyang was born in another Jiangnan city. In order not to let the village people find out the fact , Jianxin can not follow her parents to hide in another city, she can only follow her grandparents to stay at home. At that time, she was only two and a half years old, and she should miss her mother very much, so every evening she would look at the door of the house, looking forward to her mother coming home. How much she wanted her parents to give her meticulous care and companionship, but obviously this is not possible, parents have more important things to deal with or solve. When she couldn't wait for her parents, she would often ask her elderly grandmother, "Where are Mom and dad? I miss them so much. Why don't they come home?"

In order to make her feel better, Grandma will kindly cajole her: "Mom and dad have work, and they will not be able to go home for a while, and when they finish the work at hand, they will come back." sweetheart, you be good. Mom and Dad really can't take you with them."

At a young age, Jianxin hopes to see her parents every day and grow up with her every day, how warm and sweet it will be. She cannot express her sadness and loneliness in words, because she has no way to change the status quo. Sometimes, people face a lot of things are helpless, the heart is willing but insufficient, especially when people are not independent enough, it sounds a little sad, but it is true. People face the vast universe is how small and insignificant, the universe, mountains and rivers can be eternal, eternal, but each person's life is short and only once.

After Jianxin's younger brother was born, the family had more laughter, children and daughters, full of happiness. Later, Jianxin's father's career became more and more successfully, and he was the envy of many people in the village. Eat bitter bitter, the master, want to be prominent in front of people, must pay double efforts and diligence, with exceptional courage, coupled with the weather, geographical and people, in order to cast a success. All of these factors are indispensable.

Jianxin's excellent grades, studying in the city's key high school, every day's school life is very tense: get up at 5:30 and wash up, the first morning class began at 5:45, the course for the whole day is full, has been night self-study until 9:30 PM, 10:00 on time lights out sleep. She and 7 girls live in a dormitory, usually in addition to study, there is not much time to chat and play, everyone is very conscious, will not disturb each other. Some roommates have to flash a flashlight to review their homework in their bed after lights out at night. Lying on a single bed in the dormitory, Jianxin often saw the light of a flashlight in the mosquito net of her studiously studying roommates. She admired such a studious roommate and seized all spare time to study hard, but she could not do it herself. Because the daily study intensity is already very high, she does not want to spend the poor free time all on studying, rest is equally important. Learning is about efficiency and method, not just by grinding out time. Such a high school life is really full and tense, everyone is carrying the dream of entering a famous university, so again hard and tired, these years are hard. Study atmosphere is very strong, everyone is not willing to lag behind, because all the top students in various junior high schools study in this key high school , you can imagine how fierce the competition is. Jianxin often discusses some topics with her best friend Wen Hua, imagining the future, the two of them are inseparable, comfort and encourage each other, and grow and progress together. Although learning is hard, but there are dreams and firm goals in her mind she feels that life is extraordinary and the future is promising. The goal is like a lighthouse, can guide the direction of people to move forward, if the life loses the goal, it will become muddled, lose the passion of life. In the bones of Jianxin there is a strong drive and ambition, she is not willing to be a frog in the bottom of the well, always stay in a small place, she wants to contact the world through their own efforts, set goals at each stage, work hard for this, perseverance to implement, when the goal is achieved, she will have a sense of achievement, will be proud of their own pay and harvest.

Chapter 2: Face the choice

In 2001, her father went to the United States and Canada as part of a local business tour group, this was the first time her father went abroad. He has been to many large and small cities in China, in order to find business opportunities,. Although he is the helm of the enterprise, but also a salesman, because the scale of the development of the enterprise is not very large, a lot of things need him to do it himself, although her father is not yet called to have a broad vision and open mind, but than many ordinary people in the village have a more forward-looking vision and dare to dare, pioneering courage. Thanks to his hard work, bravery and business acumen, his company's business continues to expand. The first time he stepped out of the country, her father was full of curiosity about everything in the outside world, he and a dozen business partners traveled to the most famous cities in the United States and Canada, and visited some modern factories.

After this business trip abroad, her father's thinking completely opened up, he found the huge economic difference between China and foreign countries, in the United States and other highly developed capitalist countries, ordinary people's life has reached a very high quality, they live leisurely, the living environment is very comfortable and beautiful. By contrast, China was still poor and backward. If he had not traveled to this country, he would never have felt the huge difference between life at home and abroad. Jianxin remembers very clearly, after his father came back from North America, he brought back a large number of photos, and then said significantly: "The difference between China and developed capitalist countries is still very large, about 100 years, assuming that the United States and other countries do not move, the economy is stagnant, China needs to fight full power, spend at least 100 years to catch up." In Vancouver, Canada, the whole city is like a giant garden. Every house, every street is full of flowers, and the lawns are perfectly manicured. It's just beautiful." Jianxin looked at the photos like the beauty of the fairyland on earth, the heart is looking forward to and yearning, but also feel very strange, feel too incredible, how can there be such a beautiful place in the world, she had never seen. Colorful and dazzling flowers, tall and straight trees and lawns such as green carpet, she has only seen in a local park at most, other places are dirt or cement, people are more concerned about filling their stomachs, food has a big harvest. The land in the village is used to grow wheat or rice, and the floor in front of every house is paved with concrete to dry the rice after the annual harvest. This was the first time that Jianxin vaguely felt the diversity and vastness of the world, and felt that her knowledge and vision at that time were very narrow, and she only stayed in this small village in the south of the Yangtze River that she was familiar with. She had a deep longing for the outside world, and she wanted to go out and see the outside world. Because she had never been there, she had a greater curiosity than most people about the unknown things.

Since Jianxin's father returned from North America, he re-established the future development plan of the enterprise, and decided to no longer buy cheap domestic second-hand machines, but ordered a German imported machine assembly line through a trade intermediary company. At the time, the imported machine was a sky-high price for his small business. He believes that the guarantee of product quality is one of the most core factors in the development of an enterprise, so he would rather spend much more moneyto buy advanced foreign machinery and equipment. After months of long transportation, the machine line finally arrived smoothly. But at the same time, companies must also hire professional technical staff from overseas to install the equipment. The arrival of two tall blue-collar German technical workers with tall noses, blue eyes, aroused the enthusiastic attention of all employees of the company, because in 2000, this was a sensational event for a small village, and actually foreigners would come to this small place. When the two German technicians appeared in the factory, the whole village was excited, and they saw foreigners for the first time in their lives.

Theywanted to communicate with these two foreign technical employees, but found that they were talking like ducksand could not understand what they were saying. In order to overcome the language barrier, Jianxin's father could only hire an interpreter for the two German technicians. At night, he lay in bed and sighed: "How can foreign skilled workers be so valuable, an hour's wage can equal the income of an ordinary employee here in a month, foreign labor is really expensive." The interpreter job is also in demand."

Jianxin's father, also a very curious person, wanted to see the instructions for the device. Looking at the thick instructions (written in German and English), he suddenly lamented that he did not understand, did not know what was written. Crooked words, dense like ants. Subconsciously, he suddenly felt the importance of knowledge, the importance of vision and pattern, and also deeply felt the limitations of his knowledge. He wanted to know the operation process in these instructions, but felt that his knowledge was limited and he could no longer learn these foreign languages. His focus is on how to run a good business and make the company better and better.

He suddenly thought of his hope, his children, his mind flashed a very adventurous and bold idea: "Yes, I can let my daughter study abroad first, let her receive western education, learn these foreign languages, learn advanced modern business management, let her broaden her vision and pattern." But on the other hand, his heart was a little uneasy, and he said to himself: "If she really went out, would she adapt to the life there?" She was so young that she had never been far away by herself. What if she gets bullied out there? At her young age, in a foreign country, she needs to face a lot of difficulties, can she overcome? Is she mentally strong?" Jianxin's father is not willing to send his daughter to such a foreign country, and will not meet several times a year later, but he is not willing to let his children stay in this small place forever, because he and all parents in the world want their children to become talented, want to create better development opportunities for them. Parents' inner desire for children is always very contradictory, on the one hand, hope that the child is a dragon, hope that the woman is a phoenix, on the other hand, also hope that the children do not stay away from their parents. Do not fly too far after growing up, because they are not at ease, hope that the children are safe, smooth, a thousand li mother worries, said this is the meaning. Parents are always worried about their children who are far away from home. Jianxin's father was so conflicted that he finally decided to ask her what she thought first.

One day, Jianxin's father asked her, "Would you like to study abroad? If you want to go abroad, you must study for at least eight years." Do you want to go out?" Jianxin thought for a moment and answered decisively, "Yes." Although her heart suddenly flashed a touch of sadness, but she did not give this answer after careful consideration, it seems a little crisp, this is her style of doing things, for the important major decisions, she will not be timid, muddled, hesitant, but rely on their own intuition and accurate judgment, immediately make a decision. Regardless of whether this decision is really right or appropriate, she believes in herself, can meet challenges, can overcome obstacles. Of course, when she makes decisions, she will never imagine or amplify the problems that will arise in the future, but will look forward to an unknown environment. She is a highly motivated girl, pushing her to move forward is the heart of not admitting defeat, not willing to muddle-headed life, her mind has been thinking of some beautiful pictures, and she feels that going out can open cognition, have a broader vision, which is particularly similar to her father's character, they all have a brave heart, before doing anything, Will not go too much to look ahead, although the plan is not careful enough, will try to do it first, the road is out of people, things are also done one by one, people only to practice, to implement, in order to know whether it is feasible, in the mind one hundred times one thousand times are on paper, because the actual situation is always not necessarily the same as envisaged, The actual situation will change from moment to moment. Action is the best way, in the unchanged should change, troops block, water cover, encounter unexpected situations can be adaptable, timely adjustment. Jianxin's mind came up with a learned wisdom: "practice is the truth." Yes, all she has to do now is answer her father that I am willing to study abroad.

Her father asked her only tentatively, and her daughter answered with unexpected crispness. Her father could not help but be a little surprised, thinking: her daughter's answer is so decisive, she is so young, not afraid of going abroad alone? Did she think it was new? Just saying. He seemed to believe something, but he didn't show it in words. Then he continued to ask Jianxin: "Do you have any country you want to go to, you tell me."

Jianxin thought for a moment and said bluntly, "I don't know. I've never been to the outside world. Help me decide, Dad, which country I should go to."

Her father thought for a moment, and said earnestly: "Originally I wanted you to go to the United States, but just happened September 11 terrorist attacks, feeling that the United States is a little unsafe, and everyone can carry a gun, which is legal in their country, and I guess, after the terrorist attack, the United States will control entry, study in the United States will be stricter than before, so it is not suitable to choose the United States. Later, I thought that Canada is also very good, the environment is beautiful, the people live and work happily, the economy is also very developed. my concern is that the people there are too lazy, lack of fighting spirit and ambition, everyone is only busy in enjoying life you will be influenced by them and lack the motivation for working hard Although I have not been to Europe, I have not been to Germany, but Germany is the world's famous industrial power, the Germans do things seriously, which is a very good character, our company's machine is imported from Germany, you see the quality of their products. In addition, I also think that if you go to the UK, the US, Canada or Australia to study, you can only learn English at most, but Germany is different, you can also learn German, Germany is not far from the UK, you can go to the UK to catch up on English during the holiday if you go to Germany to study, you can learn two foreign languages, which may be better for your future careerbecause you have more language advantages. There are more possibilities for development; I think most Chinese send their children to study in English speaking countries in the United Kingdom or the United States, we don't follow the crowd, we take a different path, although Germany is now a cold choice for Chinese people to study abroad. Second, Germany is safer than America in terms of security. Finally, studying abroad costs a lot of money, it is said that the tuition fee of public universities in Germany is very low, many are free, as long as the grades are good enough, you can apply for public universities, which can also ease our economic pressure. So going to Germany is the best choice, the above points are the results of my analysis, what do you think?"

Jianxin has no idea which country is better to study in, because she has never been there. She believed that her father would not be wrong to help her choose, so she answered readily: "OK, then I will go to Germany to study." The answer was crisp, and from that moment on Jianxin was clear. From then on, the course of her life would change drastically, and it was a major turning point, even though she was only 16 at the time, and she knew it.

  Jianxin's mother didn't approve of the decision. Her mother was a traditional housewife, kind, dignified and strict, born into a family of local cadres. Due to the strict family education, Jianxin's mother has developed a cautious and careful character. In Jianxin's childhood impression, her mother's expression is often very serious, and she does not laugh often. So when Jianxin was young, she was a little afraid of her mother, and she tried to be careful not to make her mother unhappy. After growing up, Jianxin slowly understood that it is not easy to be a mother, her husband is on a business trip for a long time, she is a woman to take care of the family, take care of two children, but also take care of work, the hard life make Jianxin's mother become a little anxious and mood swings, so her mother doesn't often smile. When she was young, Jianxin could not understand why her mother always looked serious and a little fierce. Her mother is also very careful to take care of people, she took care of the two children's life carefully, filial piety in-laws, is a typical sacrifice of self good wife and mother. Her mother has a cowardly and introverted side, she is very conservative in accepting new ideas, does not like to change easily, is afraid of the unknown, and likes to stay in the familiar environment. Jianxin did not inherit this character from her mother at all, but like her father, she likes to meet challenges and is full of infinite curiosity about unknown and unfamiliar things and environments. Therefore, when Jianxin's father proposed to send her to study abroad, her mother was very opposed and did not agree to let her go abroad, saying, "My daughter is still young, I am afraid that she will not adapt to living alone in a foreign country and be bullied; Moreover, it is also considered for economic reasons, because there are two children, I am afraid of the economic burden is too heavy, the expenseof going abroad is too high. Jianxin is a daughter, it is better to stay with her parents, Jian Yang is a boy, a boy with aspirations in all directions, if the economic conditions are limited, it is better for the boy to receive higher education." Jianxin has a little pain in the heart, know the mother's idea, on the one hand she understands the mother's concerns, worried that her daughter is not safe outside But the second reason is that Jianxin absolutely disagreed with and did not accept, she felt unfair, because in her heart, she has a strong self-esteem and not willing to lag behind the boy's ambition, and she never felt that "girls are not as good as boys ", so the traditional concept of mother can not be recognized by her. But in China at that time, many traditional parents would have this idea and this traditional idea is deeply rooted.

The decision is always in Jianxin's hands, because her father respects her decision, no matter how much her mother disagrees. Her father wants her to be successful and provides her with a better platform for development, whether it is a boy or a girl. She was grateful to her father for his openness and breadth of mind. Once the important decision was made, her father immediately consulted with the study plan abroad. He is not an expert, and there are many business that he needs to deal with, so in order to save energy and time, her father contacted a local agency to take full charge of the matter. Jianxin is still as usual, boarding in that key high school, take notes in class every day, the days are tense and full, she did not think too much about the future, but focus on the moment, focus on what should be done at the moment. She also did not tell her classmates, not even her best friends, about the idea of studying abroad that her father had talked to her, and maybe she was not sure whether it could really be done, because in 2001, studying abroad was still very rare, especially in a small place like theirs.

Life without any waves, lived a calm and peaceful, because of the high pressure from the stufy life she was lack of physical exercise, fell ill, she was received by her parents to the school near the small hospital hanging water. She was lying in bed, watching the drip of salt water in the infusion tube trickling down, watching her mother like a hard little bee busy in and out, giving her warm water, cutting fruit, and often telling her: "Don't study too hard, be sure to pay attention to the health, take care of yourself, parents can't always be around you, you must learn to take care of your health, so that your mother can rest assured."

Jianxin knows that her mother loves her very much, although she will not use words to express it, Chinese people are very subtle, do not want to express "mom and dad love you, love you very much" and so on, but Jianxin can feel the mother's meticulous, it is the performance of caring for her. The corners of her eyes were a little wet, and the wings of her nose were sour, and she wanted to say to her mother: Mom, I love you, and thank you for raising me, but she could not say it, and did not know why. She stared out of the window, listening to the sound of birds, and lay still, eyes closed.

After hanging salt water for a day or two, Jianxin felt significantly better, and she returned to school and continued to studyin the intense high school life. The days passed silently. Suddenly, one day, Jianxin's father said, "Jianxin, dad will take you to an agency that deals with studying abroad. You can choose a school."

Filled with curiosity and reverie, Jianxin followed her parents. The agency is in a high school in the city, very humble, only two rooms, there are three or five staff, although small, but inside the layout and furnishings are very delicate, the ground is also covered with a very comfortable gray carpet. After entering the room, a young man warmly received them and introduced the situation of the country where they studied. Jianxin did not listen very carefully to his introduction, but kept staring at a library with various manuals and school materials. She wanted to read it, but was too embarrassed to hold it, and listened silently to the adults talking to each other, but afterwards she could not remember any of the conversation. During that time, her mind flew to where she did not know. After about an hour or two, when the conversation was over, the man handed the parents a school brochure containing references to hundreds of private boarding schools, mainly in England, Germany and Switzerland. Jianxin flipped through it, casually looked at the brief and concise introduction of several schools inside, and was deeply attracted by the picture: the students have a variety of outdoor sports and interests, such as horse riding, football, basketball, sailing, etc., and there are many activities. It was a far cry from the traditional Chinese education she had grown up with. She also found that these schools abroad pay special attention to multilingual teaching, with each school having four or five languages to choose from, such as English, German, Spanish, French and Latin. Jianxin had heard of all the other languages, and she thought to herself, "What is this Latin, and whichcountry does this language belong to?" She said to herself and followed her parents out of the agency.

After a while, one day, like other students, Jianxin was listening attentively to the teacher's class in the classroom. Suddenly, two familiar faces appeared at the window. At first, she did not dare to look out of the window, for fear that the teacher would find out that she did not focus on her class and criticize her. It was the first time she had seen her parents at her school. The students in the classroom with surprised expressions, are wondering what will happen. The intense high school life makes students particularly interested in a little things outside the window. It is estimated that they study all day long, feel boring and have no interest in life, and yearn for the outside world very much. Jianxin asked for leave with her teacher and went to the principal's office with her parents. Parents gently knocked on the door of the principal's office, heard a "please come in", and then Jianxin followed behind the parents for the first time into the principal's office, she did not carefully observe the indoor furnishings, but listen to the adults discussing some things, only to hear the parents said straight away: "Hello, headmaster, I'm sorry, but we are going to send our child to study in Germany early next year, and we are here to check out the withdrawal procedures."

After listening, the principal thought for a moment, checked the learning archives of the Jianxin, and said politely: "Your daughter's academic performance is very good, she is in the foreign language special enrollment class, our school is the best high school here, she can go to a domestic famous university, should not be a problem." If she fails in the college entrance exam, it will not be too late to send her abroad after she finishes high school."

Jianxin's father politely said, "Thanks to the headmaster's suggestion, we have decided to let her go abroad now and start high school again in Germany and take the university entrance exam there."

This is a unanimous decision within their family, if the students want to drop out, the principal is not good against, but he feels some pity, another year and a half to participate in the domestic college entrance examination. In this way, Jianxin's parents helped her to withdraw from school. She returned to the classroom, a heart could not keep down, what the teacher said, she could not listen to it, only saw the teacher's lips moving, her mind had long ago flew out of the window, a little reverie, as for her exactly what she thought, she did not know. Jianxin feels not only has the joy of exploring the unknown and new things, but also a little sadness, because she knows that in the near future, she will have to leave the familiar environment, leave her parents, relatives and friends, go to a completely strange country, there will be no one she knows, and there will be a big communication barrier. How can she overcome all the difficulties by herself? There was no answer in her heart. She just believes in one thing: I'm going to go out and see the outside world, no matter what happens in the future, no matter how difficult it is, I won't be afraid, and I won't think too much about the problems that may arise in the future. This is her inherent courage, her mother often said that she has a bold, may refer to this aspect, Jianxin will not carefully guess the future will appear all kinds of difficulties or problems, but through their own intuition and overall judgment, choose a general direction, and then go forward, charge into the battle, as for what special situation will appear, We'll deal with them when they actually come up. Because everything in the world is constantly developing and changing, people can not accurately predict all the possibilities of the future, gain and loss, thinking ahead, it is better to determine the general direction, do it first, and then make continuous adjustments or amendments according to the specific situation, which is the most time-saving, and it will not be easy to miss a good opportunity. Because it takes too long to think about.

  In school, Jianxin's favorite class is sports free activity class, because finally she does not have to tense nerves, can relax herself. Sometimes she will talk with friends in the playground, walk around a few times, share some ideas about the future or gossip about the people and things around, and sometimes hide in the dormitory alone, cook instant noodles, although she knows that instant noodles are not nutritious. But the delicious bubble noodles can satisfy her , Q play Q play, very refreshing, saving time and effortless, high school tense study life let her understand the importance of time planning. she ate delicious instant noodles alone, feel happy and relaxed although the kind of happiness is so small, but for her,   she can get a moment's restshe is already very satisfied. In the younger age, the more material scarcity of the age, people's desires are more easily satisfied, people seem to have more happiness. When the economy develops rapidly, people get a lot of material satisfaction, but people are less and less satisfied, because the desire is difficult to fill, the more you get, the higher the requirement, the less the happiness may be. She is a young girl in the flower season, full of endless longing and hope for the future life, even if the current study life is hard and tired, she also feels worth it, because her eyes are full of hope, because she thinks that every day's efforts will make her more and more progress, to achieve a life goal set by her own, and all the efforts are worth it.

Chapter 3: Dropping out

    Winter is coming, all is quiet,outside of the window is very quiet, the class teacher as usual in the political class, the students are very quiet and carefully focused in listening, listening while taking notes, before the end of a class, the teacher announced: "Students, the final exam of the first semester of the second year of high school will be held in 3 weeks, I hope you will study well in the remaining weeks, and strive for everyone to get a satisfactory note and go home happily for the New Year. Now you are already in the second year of high school, after the final exam, the time is getting closer and closer to the third year of high school, you must seize this precious one and a half years, study hard, and lay a solid foundation for your future. In addition, before the end of class, I would like to announce a news to your classmate Jianxin will not participate in the final exam, because she will soon leave us, leave the school, and go to Germany to study. In the last few days, we would like to say goodbye to Jianxin, hoping that everything goes well in her future life in Germany and her academic success in Germany. Well, that's all for today. Class is over."

    When the director of the class teacher's voice fell, the quiet classroom suddenly exploded into a pot, everyone talked, feel that this news is really unexpected, at that time (2001), in their ordinary remote town, is a very rare event, almost no one will go abroad, let alone study abroad. Even taking a plane to travel to other cities is extremely rare things, people in that era did not have such a sufficient material basis, many people are still living on the edge of poverty, so students in that era generally study hard, because many people believe or think that the entrance to a good university can better change the fate of a person's life.

    Everyone to Jianxin cast a variety of eyes, eyes full of deep blessings, but also full of envy and incomprehension, more full of surprise. Everyone seems to be very agitated, at this time, the teacher has just announced that the final exam is approaching after throwing away, becoming not important, everyone is more concerned or concerned about the point is "our classmate Jianxin is going abroad, to Germany", which is really an unheard of big event, not only in this class is a big event, the whole school is also a "sensational event".

In 2001, almost no one studied abroad, in that small place. after listening to the head teacher's announcement, her cheeks flushed, she was a little at a loss, because of this thing, pushed her suddenly to the center of the class attention, she felt like a person on the stage, exposed to the spotlight, suddenly became shy and uncomfortable, but also a little secretly happy, No longer having to prepare for the intense final exams like other students, she suddenly became the envy of almost all her classmates, as if she had been granted a privilege or a pardon. No student likes to prepare for exams intensely. There is a student in the class who can skip the final exam and no longer prepare for the national college entrance examination. Isn't this the envy of every student?

After the evening self-study of the same day, Jianxin and other roommates returned to the dormitory on time, everyone talked, chattered, began to discuss this matter, very lively, to the calm monotonous study life added a very special color. Her roommate Xiao Hong asked Jianxin: " I never heard you mention this thing, you have done too much secret work. You are going to Germany, Germany should be a strong industrial country in the world, I only know that the capital of Germany is Berlin, are you going to Berlin?"

Jianxin answered: "I'm not sure whether I can study abroad successfully, and I don't know if my parents are joking with me, maybe it's not true, so I didn't say." If it doesn't work, it's a joke. Besides, my focus has been on learning, so nervous about learning every day, how can I care about the progress of this matter? My dad was supposed to entrust it to an agency, and they tried. It feels so far away. I don't know. Berlin? Didn't listen to my dad. I don't know where the school is."

As soon as Jianxin spoke, another roommate could not wait and was full of curiosity to inquire: "Jianxin, your family is so strong, your parents can send you to study abroad, I see you usually dress so simple, completely can not tell, ."

After listening, Jianxin answered sheepishly: "I don't know how my father suddenly asked me whether I want to go abroad, without any warning in advance, nor any thorough and detailed planning, my father went to the United States and Canada in this summer, and then asked me whether I want to go abroad." I readily agreed." In that night, they talked very late to sleep, but it can be seen that everyone sincerely wishes and envies Jianxin, can go out, seek better development, go to a broader place. That night, Jianxin lying in bed, can't fall in sleep , what she was thinking, she knows by herself most clearly, perhaps she did not think anything, but slept vaguely.

At 5:30, hearing the bell to get up early, Jianxin's heart jumped up, and like other roommates, began an ordinary but special day. Quickly folded the quilt, went to the bathroom, 10 minutes has been finished, and then all the way out of the dormitory building, and many students rushed to the classroom. At 5:40 in the winter morning, the sky is still dark, and the students have started a new day of study with the bell. On the way to the classroom, they meet acquaintances or friends, and sometimes they have to exchange small greetings or chat for a while. At 5:45, she arrived in the classroom on time, with no empty seats, and began a day of learning. Jianxin's study life in this key high school is very militarized and institutionalized, the time is tightly arranged, one class after another class, but the students have been accustomed to such a learning rhythm, so they will not feel particularly hard, because every student is so, everyone is carrying the dream of entering a famous school, think that the effort is worth it. Jianxin knows that today is her last day in this school, so she cherishes it very much, and it will not be so easy to see familiar classmates or return to this school in the future. As usual, she listened carefully and took good notes. Although she knew that what she was doing now might not be of much benefit to her later studies, she did not want to break the class discipline or affect the learning atmosphere. In this way, to the evening self-study, the head teacher suddenly appeared in the lecture hall, solemnly announced: "Students, today is the last day of Jianxin in our class to study, tomorrow she will leave the school we give her a farewell party, OK? Next, please let Jianxin speak on stage and make a farewell to everyone. "

Suddenly there was thunderous applause in the classroom, Jianxin was a little overwhelmed, but finally stepped onto the platform and made a brief and memorable farewell speech. She looked at a familiar face, a little reluctant to say: "Dear students, I am very grateful to know you, today I will leave you, but you will always kept in my memory, hope that we work together, no matter where, to bravely pursue dreams. There is always a return, efforts will not be let down in vain, we all refuel together. Thank you."

At the end of the speech, the classroom was filled with a passionate atmosphere, and the students prepared a variety of heart-warming blessing cards and correspondence books on their seats, hoping to keep in touch with Jianxin, no matter where she is in the future. At that time, advanced communication devices, such as smart phones or laptops, were not developed or widely used, and the connection between people mainly depended on the recording and writing of characters. In order to keep in touch with someone, people usually used a written address book, which contained the main information such as name, telephone number, home address and greetings. Although compared with the developed and convenient communication tools, it seems a little primitive, but it confirms the unique memory of that era, handwritten address books are more temperature, more personalized, because each person's handwriting is different, such records are the most authentic preservation of memory. Looking at the innocent and simple faces of her classmates and what they had done, Jianxin's heart was full of gratitude. She suddenly became very reluctant to leave the familiar classroom and classmates. Although her learning life was intense and hard, she was also touched and had many unforgettable and beautiful memories during this period. All the unforgettable times will come to her mind, and all the time that is about to pass will feel precious when it becomes a memory. Lost will know how to cherish, really is such a feeling. She wrote down her contact information and greetings on the address book of her classmates, and the greetings were roughly like this: "The future is promising, we work together; The moon on the sea, the end of the world at this time "" eat bitter bitter, the master" "the journey of a thousand miles, began with a single step" "forever friends" and so on, wrote later, her hands are some numb. At the last moment, the students were ready to sing a few songs for Jianxin. The lights in the classroom went out, and the candles were lit, like a prairie fire or a star in the vast dark night sky. Jianxin listened to the students' sometimes loud and sometimes deep singing voice, deeply immersed in it. She also couldn't help singing, "Let us who are weak know how to be cruel and mercilessly face the cold of life every time, the people who have loved reluctantly are often destined to have no points..." Beautiful life, kind people, you and I come and go with him, it is better to forget a light smile, nepenwort, forget it, know how much in the dream..." Yes, in fact, everyone has trouble, even teenagers. Jianxin although there is not a lot of pressure to learn, but she knows she also has personal troubles, she is an adolescent girl, especially concerned about the appearance, from the second day, her face has a lot of acne, the original good young face suddenly covered with a variety of acne, although she does not often mention, but she is still worrying about her skin. She will habituated to cover with bangs, which will make her feel more secure, she is not clear, why is the child of the same parents, the younger brother never has skin problems, even after Jianyang in adolescence, there are not as many acne as she has a large area, she is very envious of the clean skin of her brother or others. She never once wondered in her heart: "God, why do you let me have so many acne, why can't I have clear skin like other people, when the acne will disappear?" She also looked for various reasons for acne over and over again, "Is it because I often eat fried chicken legs? But other people eat it, too. It's not long. In short, she did not know how to solve this "problem of youth."

Her mother also once comforted her: "Don't worry, it will be fine in a few years, when puberty is over, the oil secretion is not so strong, it will be fine, you don't squeeze, otherwise it will leave a scar." But her mother is not always calm and steady in the face of Jianxin's skin problems, and sometimes she will casually say: "No matter whether the skin is fair or not, as long as the face is clean, it is good." With so many pimples, it has to have some negative effect."

it is also very clear that these annoying pimples really affect a girl's beauty, so she began to become unwilling to look in the mirror, unwilling to see herself covered with acne, walking with her head down, afraid of others noticing her face covered with acne, feel very uncomfortable, or have no confidence. From the beginning of the second year to high school, did not stop, at the beginning of the time she was sad, but also helpless, but then slowly accustomed to, sometimes she really feel unhappy in the heart, will write a diary to heal the heart. Diary is the record of her spiritual demands, is her spiritual territory, is completely belongs to her .she will write in the diary, so that the pain of her inner world will be released, a lot of unhappiness will be relieved. Adults always think that children don't have any worries, just study, but in fact, children and teenagers also have their own worries. At that time, parents were very busy with their work, and they had little time and energy to pay attention to the inner world of their children. As long as they were fed, everything was on the right track, they felt that there was no problem. Jianxin's inner world is diverse and sensitive, she will not tell everything. There is a territory that belongs to her alone, and she does not allow others to enter it. She will always keep this territory. When she feels tired inside, she will adjust in her own way. At this stage, the main way is to write a diary and talk to herself. Writing a diary is like telling your thoughts and troubles to a confidant you have never met, this confidant does not exist in the world, she will never have the possibility of leaking or mocking, because this is another self she imagined. By writing a diary, she found a good outlet, and sometimes to read the articles she had written, she would feel that the difficulties that felt huge at that time, or things that particularly affected her mood, had become less important. It was an oasis of her mind, a protective wall and a placebo she built for herself, often admonishing or comforting herself with beautiful, inspiring, philosophical aphorisms. So although the acne had an effect on her for several years, that effect was not enough to give her a deep sense of inferiority, because she had learned early on to self-regulate, no matter how unpleasant or difficult the problem. It may also be because of her academic excellence, so that she has more confidence and unyielding spirit. She shifted her focus on her appearance entirely to her schoolwork, and since she couldn't control her acne, it didn't help to focus too much on it. In high school, she still has acne on her face, but she doesn't care anymore, can't say she doesn't care, it should be used to this state, used to having acne. People are such creatures, once you get used to it, you won't feel so struggling.

  Jianxin sang nepenthes with empathy, and she felt that the lyrics of the song were well written and comforting. Singing and singing, looking at the stars of the candle light, watching the students immersed in the song, she felt very peaceful and calm at this moment, nepentheus, "let us hug each other, a light smile, forget all the troubles, only remember the good happy moment." She whispered such blessings in her heart. The farewell party finally came to an end in a song of lotus grass, everyone sent each other the most sincere wishes, such a special farewell party in the previous was unique, because the most concerned here is learning, and no student like Jianxin, study for a year and half to leave such a provincial key high school.

Chapter 4: Dissuasion and concern of relatives

After returning home, Jianxin felt a little strange, so interrupted the study in high school, she had discussed with her best friendwhich university she wanted to take. Her first choice is Beijing Foreign Studies University, which should be a university that many students dream of. There are a lot of talents there, and it is a top university for foreign language majors in China. It turned out that deep in her heart, there was always this idea that there was nothing wrong with mastering several foreign languages, that she would have stronger competitiveness, that she would not be afraid to travel the world in the future, that she would fly freely, that she would communicate with people who grew up in different cultures, that she would meet people from different nationalities and races, and that her life would be rich and diverse. She is naturally a person who likes to challenge new things. Now she has chosen to study abroad, which should also be an unknown and fresh road, extremely challenging.

At home, Jianxin heard a lot of opposition and worry, in addition to her father's approval and encouragement, other relatives and friends with more or less concern. Once, one of her father's business partners was invited to attend a company business party, and Jianxin was also present. The kind uncle said warmly, "Jianxin, I heard from your father that you are going to study in Germany soon, is it true" How are your parents willing to send such a small child abroad, don't you worry about it, let a child study alone in a foreign country, in case of an emergency, no family members around, Jianxin, do you really want to go? Have you considered the pros and cons carefully? After going abroad will encounter a lot of problems, everything has to start over, have you ever thought about it? How safe it is to be around your parents, the wind can't blow, the rain is not wet, and it is safe." Then he said to Jianxin's father by the way: "How cruel you are to send such a young child abroad, and she doesn't know a word of German, so suddenly decided that she is a girl, and girls are easy to suffer losses outside." Jianxin's father listened, without too much justification, firmly stood his ground, and said, "I believe in my daughter, there should be no problem." Jianxin also did not care too much about the concerns of others, once she made up her mind, she would not be easily affected by others, she would listen more to her own inner voice.

When Jianxin's cousin heard the news, she also consoled Jianxin why she wanted to go abroad? Isn't it nice to be here? If you work hard, you are sure to get into a good university. Go abroad, everything depends on their own, the difficulty factor is greater, no one can help you. Have you ever thought that you will encounter a lot of difficulties, it is not easy to be alone outside Jianxin listened to her cousin's words, very grateful for his concern, but she finally answered: "Brother, you don't have to worry, I think it should be okay, since I have chosen this road, I will not be afraid of the various difficulties to face in the future, I didn't think these difficulties in my mind everything will slowly get better, let me solve problems in the future." I've made up my mind, thanks for your kind advice." Jianxin's dearest mother, grandmother, grandmother are actually very reluctant to let her leave, gray-haired grandmother once pulled her hand, gentle and loving said: " child, you must take care of yourself, grandma actually do not want you to leave, but you have decided, grandma can not say what, you must take care of yourself." Looking at Grandma's wrinkled and kind face, Jianxin's nose turned sour and she thought of the time she spent with grandma. Since the age of two and a half, Jianxin has spent more time with her grandmother than her parents, and has a deep affection for her, all of which stems from her grandma's companionship and care for her every day. Jianxin's parents do not have enough time to accompany their children because of their busy work, and her grandmother has become the most important backing and helper for her parents. Grandma is simple ,kind and serious, and she often smiles. She gave birth to five children, in that poor era, there was no other source of income, all the income came from hard work with hands, there was not enough food, grandma often ate moldy or already spoiled food, she wanted to leave the good things to the children to eat. Grandma's love is selfless and great, without any complaints and dissatisfaction, although she sometimes recite some discontent words, often called the child is a debt collection ghost in a previous life, but her deep heart is full of endless love and dedication to their children, she left the best only things to the children, to herself forever is leftovers or metamorphic. She will not use warm and gorgeous language to express her concern for her relatives, but will use practical actions to express her full of selfless friendship. Grandma walks especially fast. she remember when she was a child, Jianxin never kept up with the pace of her grandmother, her grandmother seemed to be in a hurry to go to the market, in fact, this is her unique style, doing things or walking fast, never like to delay. Father or other uncles, aunts may have inherited grandma's serious and responsible, strong personality and extremely motivated, so grandma's children are very successful in the local, relying on keen business acumen and hard and simple character. Grandma was blessed with a real family of grandchildren. She had five children of her own, four boys and a girl, and they each had two more children, so she had ten grandchildren in total. The family is really lively, just like a big family .

In every New Year relatives gather together, full of happiness. Sometimes, her relatives and friends would play a joke on her: "Jianxin, grandma has disappeared. Today, Grandma has to take care of her other grandchildren, so she can't stay at your house." Jianxin would cry and then say in a loud voice, "No, Grandma will always be with me. She is my grandma." For Jianxin, grandma temporarily replaced her mother's position, giving her a sense of security, but it is impossible to completely replace, grandma is grandma, mother is mother. Jianxin yearns for her mother to be with her more. But her mother has a job, but also need to take care of the young brother, there is not much time to give her, and she is sensitive and fragile, the need for love and care is very strong. In the young heart of Jianxin, grandma naturally became one of the very important spiritual pillars of Jianxin. Grandma believes in Buddhism, she sits on a small stool every day, silently chanting the sutra, a sitting will sit all day, very focused. Although she is illiterate, she is very devout, and she hopes that the Buddha will bless everyone in the family in peace and health. she remember when she was a child, Jianxin looked at her grandmother chanting the sutra all the time, not understanding why she did it, what the meaning was. But now she understands how much her grandmother loves her family by doing this, and she hopes that she can bring a lifetime of peace and health to her family through faith and worship.

She was about to leave her grandmother for a faraway country, and she didn't know how long it would take her to see her again. Looking at grandma with silver hair, she knew that grandma was old, and what she wanted most was her children and grandchildren to accompany her, so that they could stay by her side in peace. But this time, Jianxin can not do, because she also has her own dream to chase, or, no matter where, grandma will always hide in her heart, silently bless her in peace.

In the eyes of the Chinese people, the Spring Festival is the most important and solemn of all the traditional festivals. This is the Reunion Festival when families get together. No matter where they are, as long as they are Chinese, they will try their best to get back home, just to get together with their families after a busy year. It should be said that at that time this affinity was particularly strong and simple. In today's era of rapid development, the atmosphere of the Spring Festival has become more and more weak, many families choose to travel to celebrate the Spring Festival, and it is no longer like the past, from the first day to the tenth day there are endless family feasts every day, now the Spring Festival has been simplified, and there is less movement between relatives and friends, everyone attaches importance to each other's private space. Of course, the taste of the New Year is not what it used to be. But in 2002, when Jianxin was about to leave her hometown, the Spring Festival was still in full swing. On New Year's Eve, every family is busy for the New Year's Eve dinner, stick couplets, set off fireworks, set off firecrackers, children happily chase and play, adults get together, unload busy work and life, talkOn ordinary days, the village is particularly quiet at night, but on New Year's Eve, the night sky is decorated by the gorgeous fireworks bloom is particularly charming, the ear sometimes comes crackling firecrackers, Jianxin heart feel this lively festival, silently in the heart for the family, pray for themselves, hope in the New Year family safe and smooth, always happy and happy, she also wish her all the best in the new life she is about to start. Life unsatisfactory things out of ten, this is a lot of people grow up or experienced a variety of hardships in society after feeling, how can people's life forever safe and smooth, no wind no waves? There will always be setbacks and difficulties, but everyone will always meditate on all peace in the heart when praying, which is the desire of people. Although the desire and the reality are very different, but this kind of spiritual comfort and psychological comfort of human beings is also precious. Jianxin is very clear in her heart that in the future life in a foreign country, she can only rely on her own, parents or relatives can not always be around her to protect her or deal with various problems encountered in life for her. But she is not timid, this is the process of growing up, everyone will grow up, have to face all the unknown and changes in the future, if you dare not bear or face it alone, this is not the real growth, nor the real sense of independence. She is not afraid, because she has confidence in herself, she will not think too much, because the future of various variables she can not predict, now think too much, is a fuss, there is no meaning.

She looked at her family sitting together, eating the steaming New Year's Eve dinner, chewing the fragrant meat bones on the pig's head, listening to the fireworks outside the house, the heart is very warm, also very warm, every New Year has brought her hope and vision, but also bring her memories of good times. She is not old, but also can not help but sigh a "time passes so fast, and the New Year, the New Year is coming, continue to work hardand lead a happy life. "

Chapter 5: Visa Trip

After the year, one day, after Jianxin's father came back from a business trip, he couldn't wait to tell her: "Get ready, these days we will go to the German embassy in Shanghai if you get a student visa , will soon leave for Germany." Jianxin listened, do not know what a visa is, because she grew up so big, has been staying in this small place, at most with her parents and brother to travel to the surrounding cities for a few days, did not step out of the country. To her, the word seemed to come from outer space, and she had no idea what she needed to do, but she listened to her father's arrangements and instructions, and she did what he said. After a short time, they waited for the reply from the embassy, and Jianxin's parents prepared to take her to the German Embassy in Shanghai for a visa. That day, she sat in the car, feel that the car drove for a long time, long so rarely sit for such a long time of the car, the buildings outside the window and rows of trees seems to have a long feet, in constant movement. Although she knows that the car is moving, but sitting in the position, she feels that the space is stationary, all the things outside of the window is moving, which is the problem of perspective. People stand at different angles and treat the same thing with different ways of thinking, and the results or choices they make are completely different. People with different personalities look at the same problem and come up with very different answers or choices. Jianxin does not understand such a profound philosophy of life, but she is clear in her heart, not to worry too much about the future, just live every day, every moment, now she is completely immersed in the current situation. Her father suddenly mentioned on the way: "Jianxin, there are two other classmates with you to the German embassy visa today, they go to school in the city and also go to high school in Germany." The two of them are going to the same boarding high school, you're going to the other one alone, and you will fly together to germany, which makes it easier for us, because mom and Dad can't take you to Germany themselves. You get along well, you can get together when you have time in Germany in the future, and there is no family member outside, and fellow countrymen are relatives." Listening to this, Jianxin nodded silently and answered cleverly: "I know, Dad." It took about three and a half hours for the car to arrive at the parking lot of the German Embassy in China. According to the scheduled interview time, Jianxin nervously lined up to enter the embassy alone, her parents were not allowed to enter the building, and had to wait patiently in the car. Jianxin went to the visa for the first time, and was not familiar with all the procedures, only to see a security guard with an electric baton at the door to check the applicant's carry-on bag and the information bag he was carrying, his tone was stern and his attitude was not very friendly. Jianxin was told that she was not allowed to bring her carry-on bag and other items into the embassy, only allowed to bring visa documents, she carefully put the bag in the storage box, and then passed the security check and smoothly entered the building. The staff inside the embassy indicated that she needed to get a number, and when it was her turn, the number she had drawn would automatically appear on the electronic screen, and if no corresponding number appeared, she would have to wait patiently. She looked around and saw a lot of people applying for visas. The whole hall was full. She thought by herself , "There are so many people who want to go abroad. I thought it was only a small number. She wanted to avoid the crowd, so she found a seat in the corner and sat down quietly and waited patiently. At that time, she did not dare to take the initiative to talk to strangers or chat, a little timid, but also a little overwhelmed, did not know how to start. All this is new and strange to her, the applicants in the ambassador are dressed in a very trendy, fashionable and decent, and she looked at her dress, not foreign at all, only a strong smell of country, always feel that their dress and this high-level place is incompatible, there is a little uncomfortable, but there is no in-depth study. She thought to herself: "Didn't dad say that there were teenagers villagers who also came for the visa, I don't know how they look like, I have never seen them, where they are, if we sit together and talk together, we won't feel that time has passed so long." Well, I don't even know them and I don't know where they are, so just sit and wait patiently." As she watched applicants linger in front of the interviewer, she wondered which important questions she had asked them. The waiting number on the electronic screen changed frequently, but it was still not Jianxin's turn. Time is ticking away quietly, this has been waiting for more than 5 hours, still did not turn her interview. By this time she became impatient, her stomach was growling, and she suddenly realized that she was hungry, but she was not allowed to eat anything in the embassy. She was confused, not sure how long she would have to wait for her turn, and it would close in an hour or so. She is a little anxious, her parents took her, drove three and a half hours to arrive, and waited in the building for such a long time, almost a day's time is spent on it, can't not turn her to handle it today? She silently prayed in her heart: "God bless, bless my visa, bless my turn today." Half an hour before closing, it was finally her turn. She adjusted her clothes, took stock of the information she needed, and strode toward the interviewer. The interviewer looks serious, no smile, Jianxin respectfully sat, waiting for the interviewer's questions. At first, she was a little worried that there would be a lot of tough questions or that she would be asked something in English, but these worries were completely unnecessary. The interviewer briefly asked basic questions in Chinese, such as "Why study in Germany?" "If you go to study in Germany, where will you live?" Without thinking, Jianxin answered the interviewer's questions directly and without any embellishments. The interviewer did not say anything, sorted out the information, and then told her: "The interview is over, go home and wait for notice, the visa will be issued in two weeks or a month or so." Jianxin is very grateful to the visa officer's tolerance, so that she successfully passed the interview. She thought that the interview might be very complicated, but the result was unexpected. The whole process of question and answer was simple and easy. After the interview, she went out of the embassy gate, her parents asked with concern: "Jianxin,are you hungry? you have waited so long." How was the visa process?" Jianxin answered with a sigh of relief: "Mom and dad, don't worry, everything is going well with the visa, although I waited a long time for my turn, the questions asked by the interviewer were very simple, and they were all asked in Chincse. At first, I was worried that my oral English was not fluent enough, or that I could not understand his questions." Everything's fine. It should be fine. The interviewer told me to wait patiently at home for the result." Parents listened to the affirmative answer, a stone finally landed, gently said: "If there is no problem with the visa, everything is on the right track, you can start to arrange the next matters."

When they were just about to leave, Jianxin suddenly saw two young people coming in their direction. Their father greeted them politely. Jianxin looked at the two young people carefully. Both were dressed up in avant-garde fashion. The man wore a black cashmere coat, which was elegant, while the woman wore a fashionable and playful woolen skirt, which was both youthful vitality and extraordinary temperament. Jianxin thought by herself: "These two young people should also be preparing to study in Germany, Father seems to have mentioned it last time." Suddenly, there was a sense of shyness mixed with a little lack of confidence in Jianxin, she felt that her dress was very old-fashioned, and not in the same level as these two bright and energetic young people. In addition, her face is covered with zits all the time, so she seems particularly unsure of herself. She was quietly talking to herself in her heart: "Ah, how can my face see people, their faces are clean." My face is covered with pimples." Another voice sounded the alarm for her: "Jianxin, you don't have to mind so much, people have no time to pay attention to the acne on your face, it's okay, don't think so much, you have to be confident, don't try to figure out how people will look at you, be yourself." Two different voices sounded in her ears, contradicting themselves and competing against each other. It turns out that everyone's personality has a different side, everyone has a different voice, the so-called "one mind goes to heaven , one mind goes to hell", in everyone's youth, when people are not calm enough, they will be more susceptible to external influences, will care more about others and the views of the world. But fortunately, in the end, Jianxin was still driven by a strong self-suggestion and adjustment ability, no longer taking into account some negative and timid ideas, she and the two young people shake hands and chat, talk about some of their own recent situation and the future of the imagination. The three of them chatted happily, and there were always plenty of topics to talk about among peers. Jianxin and the girl belong to the outgoing character, not afraid of life, it is easy to talk with strangers, there will not be too much taboo or defensive heart, they are very keen to share. A man slightly restrained and calm, not much to say, should be an honest and reliable and simple person. Adults are also in a lively exchange, they all have a common goal: send their children to study in Germany. So the whole conversation revolved around that subject, and beyond that, there was no deeper exchange. Conversations between adults are always more borderline and alert, while conversations between young people are open and interesting. Through chatting, Jianxin learned that these two young people who are similar to her age are to study in key high school in the city , of which the girl is a sport special student, her cultural performance is general, but the sports performance is particularly top, each running race is among the best. Everyone has their own unique talent and expertise. Jianxin felt that schools in the city were different from those in the countryside or districts, with more flexible teaching, more emphasis on personalized training and individualized teaching, so the two young people appeared to be very temperament and full of confidence. The rich cultural atmosphere in the city and the relaxed and flexible education system nourish their hearts. In contrast, Jianxin felt that the education she received was more traditional and rigid, with a strong local flavor. This is not an unconfident or self-deprecating view, but an objective self-analysis.

Chapter 6: The Mysterious Letter

The visa trip to Shanghai went well, and in the following days, Jianxin patiently waited for the reply at home. One day, as usual, Jianxin was staying in an office in her parents' company, spending more time at the company than at home. Parents work hard all year round, a lot of things need to worry about, so long ago the workplace as their own home, Jianxin and brother Jianyang every time home from school, will follow their parents, in the company to write homework, read books, or play. She was sitting in her mother's office, flicking through the Reader magazine, when a postman hurried into the office and called out, "Who's Jianxin Xin, please? It's from overseas. It's her letter." Jianxin heard this news, feel very surprised, their family in foreign countries have no acquaintances or relatives and friends, who will write to her, she does not have any friends abroad. She felt very puzzled and curious. "Anyway, open it first and have a look." She said thanks to the courier, and then took the letter, saw the envelope really written on the recipient's name "Jianxin", and then she quickly scanned the sender's name and message, and saw that it was crooked with two languages, Chinese "Huang Xiaodan" and a foreign language different from English. Jianxin opened the letter eagerly and began to read it with a little doubt. It said:

Dear Jianxin, welcome to SCHLOSS NEUBEUERN and start your new life in a foreign country. I have been studying in this German private boarding school for two years. I come from Beijing, and now I am in grade 11. I am familiar with everything here. As time goes on, everything will gradually get better. The study life here is completely different from that in China. If you come to this school and have any questions about life or study, please feel free to ask me, I will be happy to help you and answer them. I'm glad you're here. I hope everything goes well with you.

Huang Xiaodan
February 2002

After reading the letter, Jianxin felt warm in her heart, she felt the sincerity and kindness of this girl, and said to her mother: "Mom, look at this letter, it is written to me by a Chinese student in the German boarding school." She said that in the future, if I have difficulties, I can go to her and she will help me." After hearing this, Jianxin's mother felt very relieved. Originally, she was worried that her daughter would not know anything about going abroad for the first time, nor could she speak the local language, for fear that she would suffer losses or not adapt to the outside world. Now, when she received such a warm-hearted letter, her mother was suddenly at ease. Then to Jianxin said earnestly: "Jianxin, you go to the new school, if you get any problems, go to ask Huang Xiaodan, she will help you,there is a good saying, 'at home rely on parents, go out rely on friends', multiple friends multiple roads, a person's power is limited after all, have a friend from her home country in their own country in that school, can also be a lot better, you will not feel so lonely and helpless, Ask her if you don't understand. She wrote so sincerely in her letter, she must be a warm and kind girl. Your father and I can not send you to Germany, you go to Germany alone, I was very worried, now received such a letter, my heart at ease much more. You also write a reply, thank the other person, can not receive the letter without replying to the other person, this is impolite. By the way, I will take some time these days to go to the city to choose a gift for the girl from Beijing. You will give it to her when you go to school to express your gratitude." Jianxin listened to her mother's words, very sensible nodded, answered her mother: "I know, mother, I will write a letter to reply to her, let me think about how to write well." In this way, Jianxin thinking in the heart, how to politely and thoughtfully reply to Huang Xiaodan. In order to express gratitude, and in order to let Jianxin go smoothly in the future, Jianxin's mother went to the city after a few days to choose a gift for Huang Xiaodan, and wanted to buy a beautiful dress for her, but she had never met it in real life, so this is obviously inappropriate, because she does not know what kind of style Xiaodan likes, pick and choose. Finally they decided to buy an elegant and delicate Suzhou silk for Huang Xiaodan. Every girl will like silk, it feels so smooth, and the pattern shows the elegance of Jiangnan and the charm of literati, not so fancy. A silk scarf cost about 680 yuan, at that time, such a gift is already very expensive, which shows the sincerity and gratitude of Jianxin's parents to this Chinese girl, thank her for giving Jianxin a small reassurance, so that she can be with a good friend in the future days, not so lonely and helpless, and thank Huang Xiadan's warm heart. In fact, Jianxin also wants to have such a similar silk scarf, but she clearly knows that parents are not easy to make money, so she is ashamed to open this mouth, such a small wish can only be buried in her heart silently, she does not want to embarrass her parents, and do not want to spend the money earned by their parents. She thought: later I have the economic ability to buy, now I do not need such a silk scarf, so expensive, not worth it. In fact, many secret thoughts in Jianxin's heart have not been told to her parents, for one thing, she feels that her parents may not understand her ideas, and for another, it is a characteristic of adolescence, and children at this age like to have a private space in their hearts, and not let anyone enter, because it is the most safe and mysterious. This is the process of growing up. When she was young, she was willing to talk to my intimate friends or relatives, but with the growth of age, such a sense of sharing becomes less and less, people behave different, in different stages of growth and in different environments, the way of thinking and cognition in different changes, will not remain unchanged forever.

  Jianxin and her mother went shopping in the city and then returned home. As usual, she often goes to play and chat with her cousin in her spare time, who grew up with her and is her most trustworthy friend. There are always endless topics between them, and when there is nothing new to talk about, she will begin to comment on the plot of the TV series and various characters. The relationship between the two of them is as close as biological sisters, Jianxin and her brother do not have so many topics to talk about, a large part of the reason may be different gender, interests and hobbies are different. Comfort is often found with the Cousins, because they feel the same for each other, and because they have similar and different aspects of their personalities. Compared with Jianxin, cousin's mind is more delicate, consider things more comprehensive, but the courage is not as good as Jianxin, she will be more traditional and restrained, if things are not very secure, she will not easily take risks and challenges. So Jianxin talked to her about the choice of studying abroad, and her cousin showed that she was worried. She worried that Jianxin will adapt to the life and environment there, worried that Jianxinwill be very lonely. In fact, such a worry is completely out of concern for Jianxin later , she is not willing to let Jianxin leave,the cousin still sincerely bless Jianxin, hope that she will go smoothly in a foreign land in the future. "People have joys and sorrows, the moon has Yin and qing round, at this time the ancient difficult, I hope people for a long time, a thousand miles of the moon." Such lines have been haunting Jianxin lately, and it has become increasingly clear to her that everything in the world cannot be satisfactory, that there are gains and losses. No matter how good a friend is, no matter how close the relationship is, there is also a separate day, the most important thing is to cherish the good times together, if separated in the future, the mind can also be like a movie, looking back on an unforgettable and beautiful fragment. Jianxin is also very reluctant to leave her cousin, but in order to pursue the unknown world she yearns for, it is helpless, people can not have all the things they want. Cousin looked at Jianxin, thinking of her going far away, tears blurred her eyes, she said: "Cousin, you must pay attention to safety outside alone, I hope everything goes smoothly for you, I will bless and pray for you." In the future, we will meet less, but we can write to each other and keep in touch, no matter where we are in the future. We work hard and believe that we will have a brilliant future. All right?" Jianxin's eyes moistened when she heard her cousin's words. She was not willing to leave her dear cousin and said to her: "Don't worry about me, I will take good care of myself when I go out." You must also take care of yourself. I'll write to you often when I get there, and we'll keep in touch. Little sister, let's refuel together, believe in your potential, believe that you will not be worse than anyone, as long as you are willing to work hard, as long as you persist. We encourage each other, no matter how difficult we meet. But now I have a puzzle, that is, I do not know how my German teacher teach me German, can he speak Chinese? If not, then how can I learn, my English is not good,T can not speak English fluently. I wonder how I learned German in the first place." After listening to the cousin, she also felt that this was a problem, but in order to let Jianxin relax her heart, she comforted her: "Sister, you don't worry about this, the German teacher must have a way to teach you." There are many methods. Maybe he can teach you German in some other way without explaining it in Chinese." After listening to her cousin's words, Jianxin felt relieved and clear a lot, no longer thinking too much about future, unknown problems, etc. to solve when they appear, and now these worries or considerations are useless. The proposal was made by Jianxin's mother, who was concerned that her daughter, who did not speak a word of German and went to a new school, would have difficulty fitting in. It might be better to learn some basic German knowledge in China. But at that time in their small place, there were very few foreign language training courses for small languages like German, and everyone was only interested in learning English and dealing with various exams, and there was no opportunity learn a second foreign language. Only in cosmopolitan cities like Shanghai or Beijing there can be German training courses. Jianxin's father expressed his opinion: "I don't think it is necessary for Jianxin to learn German basic courses in China, because the German teacher here may not have a standard pronunciation, which will mislead her." Go to Germany directly to learn, now do not have basic does not matter,She can quickly adapt the language environment. I believe in my daughter's ability to learn, and such difficulties will not overwhelm her. If you work hard, you can do it." Jianxin listened to her father's words, nodded in agreement, she no longer think about these things, everything will naturally be the best arrangement.

  The days pass unconsciously, leaving no trace in the long river of time, as if everything were so natural or logical, but for everyone, the passage of time will become a memory of the past, and these memories will only remain in the depths of the mind, or become vague pictures, will not be repeated in reality. In these days at home, while waiting for the visa, Jianxin has combed past experiences or memories in her mind more than once. Sometimes she can't help but marvel at the magic of human brain. She can't explain why human brain can store so much information, whether useful or useless, she can't understand it. Why do certain events or images leave a particularly strong or lingering impression in the brain, while there are many scattered events that happen that become more and more distant over time, leaving only vague fragments, so vague that she wonders if they really happened or if she imagined them. In addition, although her character is careless, she also has an extremely sensitive and delicate side, especially for some things that she cares about, she will be presented again in her brain, and then there will be two voices fighting, one is negative, the other is positive, but through the control of her self-consciousness, most of the positive aspects will prevail over the negative aspects. When she is alone, she looks into the distance and does not know what she sees, in fact, her attention is not what is happening in the outside world, but her brain will often be free to think about some things, which only she knows, and only for her own thinking. She sometimes tried hard to imagine what had happened before she was three or four years old, because she was curious about the beginning of life, and did not know how she was born, or what she was like when she was a child, and there were only a handful of photographs from that time. One of the few pictures she has seen, when she was a year old, is cute, chubby little girl riding on a wooden horse against a plain background. There is also a photo of a mother holding a small baby in her grandmother's yard. She looked at these pictures, feeling both familiar and strange, should say more strange, she had no memory of these things in her mind. Sometimes she would question the beginning of life, she did not understand why the brain is so strange, before the age of three, all the memories are basically not left in the mind, and as the age gets older, the memories start to clear or leave images in the brain, but there will be more puzzling things, even if a lot of things can not be remembered before. But if the child is familiar with the smell of a caregiver or is often cared for by the caregiver, they will feel attached to her. She often exclaims to herself that people are really amazing and complex animals.

    After waiting for nearly a month, one day, a postman delivered a Courier from Shanghai. At that time, Jianxin is reading a novel in her parents' company, she read it with relish, immersed in the twists and turns of bizarre, ups and downs of the story plot, to see such a express, her heart excited for a moment, subconsciously has guessed who the express is. "Mom, there's a delivery from Shanghai, and I think it must be about a German visa." I hope everything goes well and the visa is not refused." Jianxin's mother comforted her, saying, "It must be no problem, just open it and see." She took the letter from the Courier, her heart was pounding, very nervous, when she opened the letter, her hands and body could not help but shake a little, although she could not understand the German meaning of the letter, but there were English notes, It clearly says "your student visa for Germany is successfully processed." Seeing such a reply, she felt inexpressibly relieved and happy. A stone in her heart fell, and the student visa had been successfully signed. Originally, she was still vaguely worried that the visa would not be so easy to pass. If she can't sign it, it will put her in a very embarrassing situation, because she has given up the domestic study road, and now it is really a desperate situation, and she can only go abroad to study, and there is no way back. Now such concerns have been completely lifted. She is grateful to her parents for her hard work, but also grateful for the encouragement and care of relatives and friends, grateful to God for her kindness, let her life go so smoothly. She said in her heart: "Thank you for everything, thank you for the Buddha's blessing, thank you, the future road, I will continue to work hard, will not live up to the expectations of parents and relatives." Jianxin's mother knew this reply, and was also very pleased, and immediately said to Jianxin: "Go and tell your father that the visa has been passed smoothly." Jianxin flew to her father's office, see his father is talking to customers about things, dont want to disturb his work, just want to export words and Jianxin swallow back. When her father finished talking about the matter, she said solemnly, "Dad, my visa to study in Germany has been successfully approved, I am so happy." After hearing this, the father also smiled with joy and kindly said to Jianxin: "Very good, everything is going well, Jianxin, Dad check the international flights, and then contact the agency responsible for your study abroad to see when you go to Germany." Listening to her father's words, Jianxin felt so incredible that she could not imagine what the next day would be like, what kind of country Germany was, everything was so unknown and new.

  Jianxin's father immediately contacted the agency to discuss the date of

Jianxin's departure to Germany, and the international flight was scheduled to depart from Shanghai Pudong International Airport two weeks later, on March 4. Because Jianxin's parents decided not to send her to school personally, for the sake of safety, the father specially contacted the parents of the two classmates whom he met at the German Embassy last time, and their child successfully received the visa to study in Germany. If you book the same flight, you can keep each other company along the way, and have a caregiver, parents will feel a lot at ease.

Jianxin's mother is particularly busy these days, she has to prepare a lot of luggage for her daughter, the journey is so far away, and it is not easy to return home later, so there are a lot of things to purchase and prepare. This is the first time for Jianxin to leave home in such a big age, and still go to such a distant country, unfamiliar with life, not an acquaintance and relatives there. Jianxin's mother is still very unable to let go, in fact, she and grandma are the most reluctant to leave Jianxin, she has too much worry about the daughter, worried about the complexity of the outside society, her daughter a person outside will eat a lot of pain. As a parent, especially a mother, is the most unwilling child to suffer a lot, but in the end she is still stubborn but simple decision. Now the mother is not willing to dissuade, it has been so, what she can do is to help Jianxin pack her bags and bring all the necessary items. She took Jianxin to the local supermarket to buy a lot of snacks, instant noodles, mustard, etc., and also added clothes for the four seasons. At that time, Jianxin's parents were still very frugal, unwilling to buy brands of clothes for themselves and their children, and bought ordinary clothes from small town clothing stores, and the family cost was very large, and the cost of operating the company was also very high, and it was not easy to save money. But parents, especially fathers, will create good education conditions for their children, no matter how expensive, he thinks it is worth it. Knowledge and vision are priceless, and clothing or material things lose value. Jianxin's parents felt that as long as the clothes were comfortable, there was no need to pay attention to the brand, and they had no such concept. Jianxin's values are also influenced by her parents, she is not very particular about clothes, as long as fit and comfortable. At the time, she was focused on personal development and trying to get good grades. Jianxin's mother bought anything for her, she felt that it was okay, nothing special. Shopping for most of the day, basically has bought the needed items, and there is still some time before the day of travel. During this time, the mother packed her bags for her, a super large box filled with almost half of the household supplies, cold medicine, scarves, gloves, etc., everything the mother wanted to use, all stuffed in this box. Looking at such a big box, Jianxin thought, it must be overweight. There is always a weighing machine at home, although the elderly grandfather is more than 70 years old, but the hand is still very good, it is said that Jianxin's grandfather when he was a child with his great-grandfather practiced martial arts, a little boxing and foot kung fu, so the physical strength and hand strength are much stronger than the average person. Grandpa carried the big box onto the weight machine, and the electronic scale immediately showed 40 kilograms, which was obviously seriously overweight. It is understood that for economy class guests on international flights, the maximum weight of luggage that can be carried free of charge is 30 kg, if it exceeds this indicator, the overweight part needs to pay unusually expensive fees. Jianxin's mother said: "The luggage is too heavy, we need to simplify, otherwise we will be fined money, valuable." But it is the first time to go out so far, and can not often go home, need to take a lot of things, how to do?" Later, after a discussion with Jianxin's father, she decided not to simplify the items in the box, because her parents felt that her daughter's first trip, in a foreign country, there will be a lot of unfamiliar places at the beginning, the language is not familiar, if there is anything missing, it is very inconvenient, international express delivery is expensive, and it is troublesome. Pay the extra money if you need to. Although Jianxin's parents usually save money, but should use the money is still willing to use, they have been adhering to the concept of money: money to spend on the edge, must spend, spend out; But don't spend money on unnecessary and unnecessary expenses. It is much harder to make money than to spend it recklessly. It is essential to education and to broaden one's horizon and improve one's knowledge. There is no need to misinvest, especially in children's education. Jianxin's parents are reluctant to let their children take less luggage this time, even if they have to pay a high baggage fee, they agreed that such money can not be saved, a 16-year-old girl studying abroad alone, there will be a lot of inconvenience at the beginning, and they can not personally send their daughter to school, full preparation is better than the lack of this and that.

Jianxin saw the mother prepare so much luggage for themselves, feel that some may not need, but it is the good intentions of parents, after a person outside have to rely on their own, can no longer contact their parents so quickly, help themselves to solve the problem, the future of the road more to rely on their own to go well, go steady. Pointing to the huge suitcase, Jianxin said to her mother, "Mom, do I need to take so many things? Why do you need to bring high school books, they are all in Chinese, no use. Why do you bring so much pickled mustard and instant noodles, where you can also buy food. And so many cold medicines." Her mother answered with concern: "These need to be brought, in case you are not used to Western food at the beginning, and it is not so easy to eat the food in your hometown, bring some instant noodles and mustard can be an emergency." Take some daily medicine, in case you catch a cold, you don't understand anything at first, and you don't speak the local language, with these daily medicine, you can also relieve the symptoms of a cold. Although you may not use the Chinese books, but perhaps the content is similar, you do not understand German, you can read the Chinese information, it will be easier to understand a little, with the total right. If you don't bring it now, you will need it later, and it will take a long time to send it, and international express is not cheap, so bring it first. You will be alone in the future, you must pay attention to safety, take care of yourself, parents are not around you, life and study completely rely on your own, Jianxin, do you remember?" After saying that, the mother of Jianxin's heart flashed tears in her eyes, and the mother worried about thousands of miles. Jianxin's mother was very reluctant to give up, and did not want her daughter to leave home so early to study in such a distant and strange place, not knowing the local language, and not having any familiar people there. In fact, her heart is uneasy, but also very insecure, but the visa to study in Germany has been successfully signed, the flight has been booked, everything is a foregone conclusion, there is no possibility of going back or going back. If Jianxin goes back on her word, she will suffer a great loss, both financially and academically. In terms of economy, visa fees, agency fees and security deposits, as well as private school tuition were sky-high for ordinary Chinese families at that time, and ordinary families could not imagine spending so much money to send their children abroad. In terms of study, Jianxin has dropped out and given up the possibility of taking the college entrance examination in China. Although she once studied in the best local high school and the class she was in was also the top class in the whole grade, all this came to an end because of her decision to study abroad, and she could no longer temporarily go back to her former campus. To choose another direction means to give up the path that we have to take. These concerns Jianxin is actually very clear, since the moment she decided, she has not regretted, the decision is her own, no matter how difficult the future, she will not waver. Wavering is a big taboo, she is still very young, full of infinite expectations for the future, she believes in her own choice. At that time, Jianxin's mother did not have the same firm belief as her daughter, because the mother always has the heart to worry about, always hope to see the child often, within the safe range, so it will feel very safe. Once the child is gone, out of sight, or often out of sight, there will be all kinds of speculation and worry, this is the mother's deep, lifelong love; In contrast, Jianxin's father did not show too much worry and worry about this, his love for the child is deep, thinking more long-term and open. He is not willing to tie the children around him forever, but within his ability, will create opportunities for children, provide opportunities, let them fly out, like birds, fly freely in the vast world, to choose their favorite life or career, broaden their horizons, because the outside world is another world, if you stay in the familiar environment forever, People's vision and way of thinking will be very narrow, which is not conducive to future development. Jianxin's father can think like this, but also because he is different from ordinary people in small places, all the years of business travel, exposure to a lot of open and fresh ideas, especially the recent North America business trip, greatly subverted his understanding of the world, saw the huge difference between domestic and foreign economy and life. He really figured it out, just willing to let go of the child's hand, let Jianxin go out. If not for that trip to North America, Jianxin's father would still be reluctant to send his child abroad at such a young age, because it is an unknown world after all, and he has never been there.

  Time flowed away quietly like this, and the day of going abroad was getting closer and closer. Jianxin has been very popular since she was a child. Many of her classmates and friends from primary school, middle school and high school have sent her cards filled with heart-warming greetings, such as "Dear partner, I wish you all the best in a foreign country, go in peace, and be happy every day." "Dear Jianxin, we will always be good friends. I wish you success in your studies and all the best." Another friend wrote, "Dear Jianxin, this is my mailing address, we will keep in touch, you go to Germany, don't forget me as a good friend." Although we will be far apart in the future, but the sea memory friend, the end of the earth if neighbors, our friendship forever green, I will miss you. The good times I had with you will remain in my mind forever. Be sure to write to me when you go to Germany. When I received your letter, I knew your address. Then we can write to each other."

Greeting cards are numerous, the heart of the heart is very moved, moved by these sincere friendship, but also by these warm words moved, the text can be so magical, even if not together, even if silently speechless, see this warm heart, simple and kind words, will feel the world is very beautiful, will feel the kindness of the heart. Jianxin took these precious cards and put them in a carry-on bag. She wanted to take the cards sent by her friends to a foreign country. When she felt lonely and helpless, when she missed her relatives and friends in China, she would read them and revisit the warm friendship, which would give her strength and courage to work hard. Jianxin is actually a girl who knows how to motivate herself and suggest herself. In school, every time she encountered difficulties, she would write down words in the notebook to encourage herself and encourage herself, such as "believe in your potential", "Don't worry about the future, don't pay too much attention to the result, just do the right thing every day, naturally there will be good results;" "Smile, every morning, every time the sun rises, from this moment on keep a micro message, you will be very close to success, not far from happiness." These words are like a good teacher and friend, always encouraging and comforting her to move forward. This may seem silly or formalistic to many people, but for the simple mind, it is really helpful. Her heart needs comfort and encouragement, so that she will face every setback and difficulty, regain confidence, continue to look forward, and move forward without hesitation.

Chapter 7: Parting

The day before she left, many relatives came to her home, which was very lively. Jianxin's parents are very particular about etiquette, and her daughter is about to leave her hometown to study in distant Europe, which is really a big event in their family. To give their daughter a farewell dinner, they invited a lot of relatives, grandma, grandpa, uncle, aunt, uncles and so on. Almost all the relatives present can not understand Jianxin's father's decision to send her daughter abroad at such a young age, also feel that her father's move is very bold and risky, but this is the family of others, relatives can not obstruct what, can only sincerely wish Jianxin everything goes well in the future, there are not too many twists and downs. Jianxin didn't eat much that day, her feeling was mixed, parting was imminent, she was reluctant to leave her family, reluctant to leave the warm home of 16 years, although her parents did not spend a lot of time with her, but she understood them, in that era, how difficult it was, material life did not have a lot of security, how to pay attention to spiritual life, they don't have time to spend all day with my kids. Parents do not spoil her, let her become independent and strong, but also become less timid, get the courage to explore new things, it is such a family environment acquired casting her character: she has a woman's emotional sensitivity and delicacy, but more is fearless, dare to challenge and strong confidence. Jianxin's father on this day, there is a little worry, because he is actually afraid of her daughter's remorse, afraid that she may not be willing to go abroad at the airport, a few days ago he just heard that a friend is also ready to send his child to study abroad, everyone has arrived at the airport, at the moment of departure, the child suddenly cried and said that he is not willing to leave home, leave his parents. So he finally gave up the road to go abroad and wasted a lot of time and energy. Jianxin's father is also worried, in case Jianxin is like this, how to do, so everything is wasted? It's like losing your wife and losing your army. At the dinner party that day, he only reserved this kind of thinking for himself, he did not ask Jianxin, whether he had thoroughly thought about his decision, nor did he say to her: "Daughter, you must not go back on your word, because you have made a decision." Jianxin will soon leave home, parents are still very reluctant. The elderly grandmother held Jianxin's hand and said earnestly: "Jianxin, you must take good care of yourself when you go out, grandma will chant sutras every day, bless you in front of the Buddha, go in peace, go smoothly, and bless your academic success." Grandma will miss you." After saying that, Jianxin looked at grandma's wrinkled face, looked at grandma's wet eyes, do not know how to comfort dear grandma, in fact, her heart is very much not give up, both sad, and looking forward to a new life. There are joys and sorrows in life, there are gathering and parting.

Time passed quietly like this, the door opened a commercial vehicle, Jianxin recognized at a glance, is her father's driver, her heart like a mirror, the time has arrived, to leave home for Shanghai International airport. The flight is 00:30 in the morning and it is now 7:00 in the evening. It takes about three and a half hours to drive to the international airport. There may be traffic jams along the way. In order to allow more time, there will be no temporary missed flight situation, Jianxin's parents decided to leave early, so as not to panic. Besides, this is Jianxin's first time abroad, and her luggage is seriously overweight, so she may need to spend a little more time in checking her luggage.

Jianxin's parents said, "Jianxin, say goodbye to your friends and relatives." Jianxin nodded and waved goodbye to the people, "Goodbye, I will see you next time, I will take good care of myself, and hope you have a good life, so that I come back from Germany next time, we will join together." Just after the talk, some relatives' eyes were also wet, they told Jianxin: "Child, you must take care of yourself outside, we bless you, goodbye." Jianxin and her grandfather, parents, uncle, aunt and brother got on the commercial bus, the driver put the luggage on the car, Jianxin's mother reminded her again: "Jianxin, have you packed all the important things?" Especially the passport, the passport is like your ID card, every time before you go out, be sure to check it. Forgetting would be a problem." Jianxin answered readily: "Mom, you can rest assured, I have checked the carry-on bag several times, did not forget, you see, yes." Although the mother nagging, but full of her care for the child and deep maternal love. When everything was ready, the car started up and suddenly sped down the road, all the way to the destination.

It was dark out of the window, so she could not see any trees clearly, and she could only see the light from some houses. Jianxin suddenly felt the wonder and inconceivable of life. Life stopped and went. At the beginning, a road stretched straight out into the distance, as if one could clearly see the lighthouse not far away, which was the goal she had been pursuing for so many years or the place she wanted to reach. But soon there is a fork in the road, if you do not turn, or continue to go, you can predict where the future will roughly reach; But if you turn in one direction, choose another path, everything will change, all the life trajectory has been completely different from the past. This is how she feels now: Originally, she wanted to do well on the road planned before, study hard, enter a good university in China, and find a job in China; Now there is a fork in the road, and a new road has been taken, and what will be, she does not know, will be completely different. Jianxin thought: This is life, life is not predetermined, but full of infinite unknowns and surprises. If stability is compared with surprise, I prefer surprise and novelty. Although I am not sure that I will get what I want in the future, at least this kind of life is more interesting and challenging. I would rather take the road less traveled than be so mediocre and conformist. You only live once. It's good to get out there. After Jianxin finished thinking, she did not want to think too much, and closed her eyes to rest, she listened to the dialogue between her parents and relatives, and she did not know what was said, at this moment, her heart could not hear many outside voices, maybe she was a little tired, maybe her brain was thinking about some things she was interested in.

After about three and a half hours, they arrived at Shanghai International Airport smoothly. Jianxin got out of the car, and for the first time she saw such a magnificent international airport, with brilliant lights inside, and passengers shuttling among them, dressed very well, very temperament, and appeared to be magnificent. Jianxin feel the world wide, in their small place, everyone is dressed very simple, even can be said to be full of rustic taste, more than 200 kilometers from home in the Shanghai metropolis, in this international airport, here travelers have a completely different temperament and talk. These are people who have seen the world, Jianxin thought to herself. She felt very different from the crowd in this airport, she looked up and down at herself, and felt a little rustic, a little out of place in such a grand place. The driver helped remove the luggage from the business car, picked up a luggage cart from the airport gate, and with great effort lifted the heavy luggage onto the airport luggage cart, and then pushed the luggage cart into the airport. Her parents and other relatives entered the airport with her. What immediately caught her eye was the itinerary of all international flights, departure and arrival times, departure and destination, scrolling across a row of electronic screens. Jianxin carefully searched for the Lufthansa flight to Munich, Germany, in the early morning, for a while, found that it did not appear, and then felt some wonder, will it be temporarily canceled? Because this kind of thing is very common, especially in emergencies or bad weather. Jianxin's father comforted him and said, "Jianxin, don't worry, the flight is going well, we may have come too early, so the flight information has not appeared on the electronic screen." Why don't we find a place to rest for a while, wait slowly, and then check our bags when the flight shows up?" Jianxin agreed and replied, "Yes, Dad." Then a group of people began to look for a seat to sit down, but for a long time, did not find, the airport space is occupied by other passengers, there is no spare seat. Finally they decided to stand near the electronic screen and wait for the flight information. Time ticked by, after about an hour, Jianxin finally saw her own to take flight MU557, she excitedly told her parents: "Mom and dad, the flight information has appeared, you look." Because the first time out, in fact, she did not know what to do after finding a flight. Her father was the best at flying, because he often traveled alone, so he knew the process best. "We see which gate it is and then we take our bags to the gate to check them," he said.

Just then, they listened to Jianxin's father's instructions and hurried to gate H. When she got to the gate, she saw that there was a long line. In this kind of international airport, you must not jump the queue, you must obey the order. Jianxin and her parents pushed the luggage cart in the queue, other relatives stood nearby waiting, the team moved forward little by little, the speed is really similar to a snail, waiting for about 1 hour, and finally it is their turn to check in (registration). Without any expression, the staff said as if performing official duties: "Please put your checked luggage on this rolling belt. The luggage limit for one person on international flights is 30 kilograms, and the excess kilograms need to make up the difference." Jianxin's parents nodded tacitly, and then the father made a great effort to lift her suitcase onto the rolling belt, and the electronic screen immediately said "42 kg." Jianxin's father said: "More than 12 kilograms, it doesn't matter, make up the difference." The mother objected, "That's more than that. Let's see what we don't have to take. Let's take some out." The staff member said: "You speed up a bit, there are passengers waiting behind, more than one kilogram, each kilogram needs to pay 300 yuan, 12 kilograms need to pay 3600." Jianxin's father said: "Forget it, don't take it out, so it is, the first time to go out, you need to bring enough, otherwise what is missing, the road is so far, it will be very inconvenient." If it's expensive, it's expensive." Jianxin's mother finally agreed. At that time, in 2002, 3,600 yuan was a large amount of money, which was more than a month's salary for an ordinary family. In this way, after making up the difference, the luggage was checked off smoothly, and then the father said to Jianxin kindly and lovingly: "Jianxin, now you are going to cross the border, mom and dad can't accompany you anymore." I'm going to teach you how to cross the border and what to look out for. The plane will take off in just over an hour. You enter and exit, and then find the gate, where you patiently wait for the plane. I hope you have a safe journey." Other relatives also sent Jianxin to the entry and exit place, Jianxin and relatives said goodbye: "Rest assured, I will take care of myself." The mother's tears could not stop rolling in her eyes. She could not bear to leave her parents at such a young age and go to such a distant place. Father told the end, in the heart of Jianxin to wave away, eyes also wet, Jianxin grow so big, the first time to see his father will shed tears, will be so emotional, usually he is always smiling. Jianxin also could not help crying, in fact, she is very reluctant to leave her parents, leave relatives, after all, she has not really left home so far, she has not fully grown up, but also very attached to the family.

Chapter 8: Arriving in a Foreign country

After waving goodbye, Jianxin went alone into the entry and exit, her parents has disappeared, her heart does not know what kind of taste, a little empty, there is a little sad. Since then, the road to go alone, she was only 16 years old, is a flower age, many girls of this age still have a sense of dependence on the home, do not want to travel, do not want to be truly independent, but from today on, she can no longer rely on their parents, but really need to be independent. She stood in a long line and moved forward step by step. After waiting for a long time, the staff asked her to take out her passport, check the front page of her passport and her visa, and then said to her: "Fill out an entry checkpoint, at that long table." Jianxin according to the instructions, walked to the long table where several people gathered, saw that everyone was filling in the entry checkpoint, she also took a blank card and began to fill it out, because it was the first time to fill in, some places were not very clear, so she would take the initiative to ask other passengers, she is not that kind of particularly introverted person, encounter the aspects that do not understand, or will be eclectic, large and square to ask, she's not embarrassed. After filling in, and then queuing in order, after checking the carry-on baggage checkpoint, she successfully arrived at the gate, she looked at her watch, about 45 minutes from the boarding time, she casually walked for a while, and then sat down to the gate position to continue to wait for boarding. By this time, Gate 205 was already full of passengers, and Jianxin thought, "So many passengers are going to Munich, about hundreds of them." It seems that the two students I met last time are also on this flight, how can I not meet them at the airport? I guess there were too many people to notice. Now I'll look for it." Jianxin looked around for a while, saw two familiar faces, and felt happy: "Finally found them." The three of them met again, this time without the beginning of the unfamiliar and introverted, parents are not around, the three of them is the same age and fellow villagers, feel very cordial to meet again, cheered and chatted. The conversation was nothing more than visions of the future and what the new school would be like. Jianxin did not feel that time passed slowly. Chatting, it was time to board, they lined up, passed the inspection, boarded the plane, found their position, put the luggage in the luggage rack, and sat in their seats. One of Jianxin's quirks is that she doesn't like to put her carry-on bags in the overhead bin. She prefers to put them under her seat at her feet, which gives her comfort because she's afraid she'll forget her carry-on bags in a hurry when she gets off the plane. So every time she flew home for the summer, or back to Germany, she would always put her carry-on luggage in front of her seat, in her field of vision, where she could see it at any time. Because outside, she can only rely on her own, no one will remind her where she needs to pay attention, she has to be careful, lost things are the most troublesome.

  The three of them did not sit near each other because there were too many passengers and the seats were not optional. But it doesn't matter, 11 hours of travel, no parents personally accompanied, but you can fly to the destination with the friends you know on the same plane, for Jianxin, it is already a great luck and peace of mind, but also less a lonely and empty feeling. With the passage of time, the plane to take off, after the various safety guidelines and preparations on the plane, such a large passenger plane gently lifted off, step by step to fly higher. Jianxin closed her eyes to rest. After a night of tossing and turning at the airport, she felt a little tired and sleepy. 12 o'clock in the night is the time to sleep, but the plane is noisy, there are many passengers talking, there is also the noise of the aircraft engine, all kinds of sounds mixed together, although she is tired, but can not sleep. The seat is surprisingly small, sitting for a long time, will feel back pain, can not comfortably stretch out the limbs, she wanted to sit to sleep, but after a while, and feel sitting can not sleep, and then take down the seat to move the board, lie on the small table to sleep, but toss a long time, how can not sleep, after a time, no sleep, but the body is really tired. The whole cabin was still lit up, the economy class was full of people, after about an hour, when the plane was stable in the air, the stewardess said something in English, the cabin lights were all turned off, and the electronic screen in front of each seat was also put away. Although Jianxin could not understand what the stewardess said specifically, because her English level was still very limited at that time, her oral English and listening were very weak, and she could not use this foreign language well in reality, but her intuition told her that the cabin lights were off and it should be time for rest. Whether she can sleep or should force herself to rest, 11 + hours is a long time to fly, and even if she can't sleep, it's good to close your eyes. She didn't have any electronics to amuse herself with, she didn't have a cell phone or a laptop, she didn't have any modern communication tools, and she couldn't really get in touch with her parents. She does not want to think of any bad or unlucky things, because it is not in line with her character, and she feels that it is completely useless or frustrating to worry about what has not happened. She likes to look forward and move forward, and is not used to studying the road she has walked in the rearview mirror, asking herself whether she has chosen the wrong road or done something wrong. This is the simple and handsome heart. Stride forward, look forward to everything. She fell asleep in a misty, light sleep, as if she could hear everything around her. Small partners in the plane is estimated to have fallen asleep, they got on the plane, did not talk again, because there are many positions, chat is not convenient, and it is already late at night, everyone is very tired, are forced to sleep as long as they can in a small space.

For the first time Jianxin feels the time passed too slowly, time passed too slowly, did not have this feeling before, suddenly look back, recall what happened in the past, or sometimes recall the past of childhood, will feel the passage of time like water, gone forever, flow away so quietly, unconsciously. But this time, more than 11 hours of flight time, like a snail slowly crawling forward, like an old cow can not move. Jianxin really feel that the long flight time is difficult, the space is small, there is no acquaintance or friend to talk, just a person sitting in a small position, can not move around, come out to walk is forced, only to go to the bathroom will leave the position, otherwise the butt seems to stick to the position, it has been sitting so, waiting for time to flow away. She really can't sleep, sleep in a daze, usually her sleep quality is very good, belongs to the kind of sleep on the head, completely belongs to the second sleep type, wake up every day time is very regular, do not use the alarm clock, always no dream late at night, overnight to dawn. Wake up in good spirits, will feel that the new day begins again, all the unhappiness or worry will disappear with the beginning of the new day. So many sleep experts believe that: high-quality sleep is the best medicine to cure people, if a person on that day can not find a solution, then have a good sleep, tomorrow will be a new day, maybe there will be new inspiration, or immediately will find a solution to the problem. But if a person is always thinking, can not sleep well at night, wake up will feel that the day is very difficult, because of low energy. So for Jianxin, sleep is indeed the best medicine, every time the sun rises, she sleeps to wake up naturally, will feel that a good day has begun, and has a new hope, what problems will be solved. There are also many sports experts who believe: Exercise is a good medicine to cure everything. If you feel that the pressure of work and study is too much, if you feel that because you eat too much, you are afraid of getting fat, you have guilt, or you often catch a cold and have a fever, you should exercise regularly, especially aerobic exercise, because exercise can improve the body's immunity, keep people fit and increase the concentration of serotonin. Make people become optimistic, have a stronger ability to resist pressure and frustration, and the most important point: regular exercise can temper people's willpower, make people become more self-discipline and more able to learn to persevere. The benefits of sports are countless, but at that time, Jianxin did not know that sports have so many benefits, because in her life circle, her parents, relatives, or classmates, have formed the habit of regular exercise, there is no sense of healthy life, because many people are busy working to make money, and there is no idea how to truly improve the quality of life. And they feel that without the guarantee of material basis, how can they have the leisure to exercise regularly? In the circle of classmates, especially in the key high school where she once studied, she had very little time for herself. In addition to the short time of jogging and morning exercises after breakfast, the key task of the day was cultural courses, with endless classes and exercises, and the cultivation of regular exercise habits was impossible at school. Therefore, Jianxin did not develop this healthy exercise habit under the circumstances at that time. But good sleep is she has been trained since childhood, her family pays attention to the sunrise and sunset, healthy lifestyle, in the countryside, without the various recreational facilities of the big city, red wine and green.

At night, the small village even has no street lights, it is dark, only the summer day is longer, so almost every family will walk a little after dinner, go upstairs to watch TV for a while, fall asleep early, there is no habit of staying up late. She remembers when she was young, she would go to bed at 9:00 p.m. on time every day, a few seconds would immediately enter a deep sleep state, and then every day at 5:30 will get up, is really according to the natural law of rest. Such a sleep habit stems from the healthy rest time of grandma and parents, so no matter how busy the father of Jianxin, how frequent the business trip, sometimes at 4:00 am to get up for business, his father will fall asleep early in the evening, no matter how early the next day, is full of confidence and energy. Recalling these, Jianxin really feel that this is the first time in life, sleep so shallow, time passed so long, almost a night did not really fall asleep, she looked at countless watches, really can not sleep, get up to look at the magazine on the plane, see a variety of advertising pictures, so wait ah wait ah, by 5:30 in the morning (equivalent to China time 12: 30, the time difference between Germany and China in winter is seven hours), and the plane will finally land safely at its destination: Munich International Airport. The cabin broadcast the imminent arrival of the information, Jianxin overjoyed, the heart has unspeakable excitement, when the plane slowly landed, and finally taxied on the runway, her heart settled a lot, a person said to himself: "finally arrived."

When she got off the plane, she said hello to two other friends who were sitting in other positions. Although it was 5:30 in the morning, she did not sleep much all night, but all three were excited and did not feel sleepy. They walked together and followed the crowd into the airport. At the airport, the main crowd is no longer Asian faces, but Europeans with tall noses and blue or brown eyes, with very few Asian faces passing through. According to the instructions, the three of them marked "luggage pick up" and found the baggage claim area. One by one, the luggage was rotated on the rolling belt. Arriving passengers held small luggage stations and checked whether their luggage was out. Jianxin also took a luggage cart and stared at the luggage passing through the rolling belt, just like a mother standing outside the campus, staring intently at whether her children had already left the school gate. After waiting for a long time, she finally saw her familiar large brown suitcase, with a lock attached to it for easy identification. She tried with all her strength to get the box off the rolling belt, but it was too heavy and she was too weak to get it off the first time. At this moment, a very tall young German beside her immediately gave her a hand, lifted the super heavy box off the rolling belt, and gave Jianxin a friendly smile. What he said, Jianxin also did not understand, but the German helpful, Jianxin has understood, she is very polite to the German said "thank you", although her oral English is not very good, but the most basic communication is still a bit good. The German politely replied, "you are welcome," and suddenly disappeared from Jianxin's sight. "The people here are friendly," she thought. "They are eager to help strangers when they see them." She felt warm in her heart and felt the kindness and warmth of human nature. The other two friends also successfully took their luggage, they pushed the luggage cart, passed the security check, and finally arrived at the airport entrance.

At the door stood a few people to meet the airport, and almost everyone held up a sign in their hand, which was not written in Chinese, but in German or English. Jianxin asked two friends: "You see, which is to pick us up, I do not know." It's in German. I don't understand. The two of them are going to the same school, and they can have a companion on the road, and they can have courage, and after a while, a person with a sign comes out, and they mumble a few words, and the two friends follow the people who pick them up. Now Jianxin was left alone, and fewer and fewer people were picking her up. After a while, she took a closer look at a sign that read "Schloss Neubeuern Internatsschule." Although she had never studied German for a day and knew nothing about it, she had a strong memory. The words seemed familiar to her, as if she had seen them in a brochure describing private schools abroad, and she thought that it must be the name of the school she was going to, of course she could not verify precisely, because she really did not know German, but her intuition told her, a vague memory told her that it was the school. Then a woman with that sign walked straight up to her, shook her hand warmly, and mumbled, in English, but Jianxin couldn't understand, because she thought it was going too fast, and before she knew it, she ran away like a rabbit. She guessed that this person should be the person who picked her up, and then regardless of the thirty-one, politely replied to her "thank you", and followed the thin woman on the small commercial vehicle without hesitation. Then the woman put the big suitcase in the trunk, got into the driver's seat, and started the car neatly. In an instant, the car hurtled down the highway.

More than 5 o'clock in the morning on the highway, there are many trucks in an endless stream, but there are few private cars. Looking out of the window, Jianxin felt that there was a small population here, there were no clusters of houses, and along the way there were large fields, which had been repaired in a strange way, and neat haystacks had rolled down into the fields. She felt a special novelty, for the first time in her life, she had seen such cylindrical haystacks, although the scale of the fields was very large. But there was hardly a single human being, and the haystacks were scattered in neat, solitary rows over large tracts of pasture or farmland. The speed of the car was surprisingly fast, and the wind whistled in my ears. The lady who picked up the airport was concentrating on driving , during which she did not chat with Jianxin, because of language restrictions and unfamiliar places, but also she embarrassed to ask anything, she silently sat in the back seat, looking at the scenery out of the window, looking at a piece of uninhabited farmland and pasture.

Chapter 9: The boarding school at the foot of the Alps

After about an hour, the car stopped at the gate of a seemingly ancient palace, the lady took Jianxin's luggage down, Jianxin carefully got off the car, and then the woman closed the door and drove away. At the door stood a short, stout woman with fair hair, who looked rather old, perhaps forty or fifty years old. She welcomed Jianxin warmly and then asked two boys in T-shirts to help carry the suitcase. It was March season, but in this part of the world, there was still white snow outside. Jianxin felt very curious, such a cold day, these two boys only wear summer T-shirt, don't they feel cold? Jianxin did not think too much, as soon as she arrived at the destination, -, after a day and night of tossing and running (about 22 hours), completely arrived in a strange country, where everything is completely different from the hometown she is familiar with, the people are completely different, almost no one looks like Chinese a glance past, Several young men with blue eyes, golden hair, and tall noses were walking outside. She sincerely exclaimed: life is amazing. Jianxin entered the old palace, attracted by the classical architectural style before her eyes, she could not say which style, she first climbed a dozen flights of stairs, and then passed a door, and was greeted by a large and elegant hall with a long wooden staircase in the middle. She followed the two young men who had helped her with her suitcase up many, many stairs, round and round, through a dozen doors, and then to the top of the building (the palace), where the two young men put the suitcase in a large and bright bedroom, and left without saying anything. Jianxin guessed that this must be her room, otherwise they would not have put her suitcase here, although she did not speak the language, but this intuition is still there. She took a closer look at the room's furnishings. It was clean and tidy, with wooden cabinets and beds, and no extra furniture. There were not many things in it. The room was quite large, and there were several flights of stairs in the middle, separating the whole room neatly into two parts. A few steps up is what appears to be a separate living space, with a bed and wardrobe and a desk; In a small section below the stairs there was a very small single bed only 90 centimetres wide, a desk and a wardrobe. It was obviously a two-person bedroom, and she was curious about what her roommate looked like and what kind of person he would be. Now that her roommate is not in her room, Jianxin thinks her roommate has gone to class. It was already about 7 o 'clock in the morning, at this time in her former high school, the students had long been in the classroom for early self-study. She thought that the part of the room under the steps should be her space, and the single bed should be for her. She put the suitcase in the room first, not in a hurry to pick up, want to understand the surrounding environment first. Out of the bedroom, sheheard the sound of a hair dryer in a room, and then several beautiful young girls walked by her side, they said a simple and friendly hello to Jianxin, and walked away, stomping down the stairs. Jianxin also noticed that this attic part has a fitness machine, the whole space looks simple and fresh, not too much decoration, more practical and neat. She saw a figure moving in one of the doors from which the sound of a hairdryer came. She wondered who was blow-drying her hair, and if someone was taking a shower in the morning, it was supposed to be the bathroom. She went to her room alone and sat down on a stool at her desk, which had a small window through which she could see a little of the outdoors. She looked out and saw a large garden outside, with a perfectly manicured lawn, a classical European fountain in the center of the lawn, and a vivid little angel carved on a stone pillar. Holding a stone pot in both hands, water is pouring down from this stone pot, round and round, endless. All kinds of shrubs and flowers are planted around the fountain. Because it is a snowy day, the lawn is covered with a natural white blanket, and the shrubs and flowers are covered with white snow. At the foot of the mountain is a piece of neatly spire houses, and the distance is continuous mountains. Jianxin deeply felt the harmony and beauty of nature and human life. Suddenly came the sound of the church bell, she counted, a total of 8 times, originally in the ancient times, the church bell is also used as a clock, has been used until now, in such a magical piece of land to achieve the perfect integration of modern and classicJianxin stayed quietly alone, the room was strangely quiet, after a day and night of long travel, she did not feel a lot of sleepiness, feel very surprised, the original person a day and a night do not sleep, will not feel particularly tired. It may be that she is still very young, physical strength and physical fitness is still very good, or it may be because this is the first time in her life to go abroad, is an important turning point in her life, she is very excited about all these experiences, but also mixed with homesickness, so temporarily forget the taste of fatigue. She looked at the mountains in the distance and thought, "Could this be the world-famous Alps, which they say borders Austria, and at the foot of which the book seems to say the school is located?" Yesterday, she was in the distant east, living in the familiar hometown of 16 years, with the protection of her parents and relatives, and the company of good friends. Today, she came to the West alone, a completely strange country, and saw the famous and famous Alps. From the window of this room, she could see clearly and she really felt that life was wonderful and incredible. Once you step outside, the world is so diverse. Everything here felt new and strange to her, like a newborn baby, which seemed ignorant and confused. Suddenly, the door opened and a girl came in wearing a white bathrobe and a white towel around her head. She gave Jianxin a faint smile, and then walked into the area a few stairs up in the room. Jianxin gave her a subtle but friendly smile back, not knowing what to say, looking blank and unfamiliar. Although she did not know how to communicate with the girl in words, she guessed that it was her roommate, who had just taken a bath in the shower. The girl did not have too much warm welcome, cast a faint smile to Jianxin, then began to blow her hair, change clothes, dress up, do their own things, she may have to go to class later. Jianxin sat in front of her desk, sitting quietly like this. Was she waiting for something? She did not know, but she suddenly felt that she had become unknown about the future life, how to arrange every day, how to begin to integrate into this new environment. All of a sudden, she began to become very homesick, missing her parents, relatives and friends thousands of miles away, in the place where she used to live and study, there are so many familiar people, so many people who care about her, love her, give her warm care, and the most important point: she can speak freely, chat and play with friends, and use language freely. But now, like a newborn baby, she can't speak a word and has no idea how to make friends or interact with the people around her. She looked helpless and sad, she really missed her home, tears could not help but roll in her eyes. For the first time in her life, she felt lonely, probably because of her roommate's very weak smile, she felt a sense of human indifference and distance, which she had never felt in her familiar hometown. People there are very warm and simple, as if everyone knows each other, get along without any embarrassment and sense of distance. But she felt that maybe she thought too much, the nerves were too sensitive and delicate, perhaps because of the language barrier, they could not communicate, so a light smile of roommates could not explain others' cold and proud. She silently comforted herself: "Jianxin, you don't want to be too complicated, maybe your roommate is not a proud person, but people can't communicate with you, and they don't know how to welcome you, so they will just smile at you very weakly." Besides, you are not related to her, why should anyone be warm to you? Everyone is different." Her inner drama began to become richer, because many of the guesses in the heart can not be expressed in the local language, can only hide a lot of words in the heart, their own dialogue with themselves. Only one day after leaving her parents, she felt more and more empty in her heart, looking at a large suitcase, she had nothing to do, and began to take out the things in the suitcaseone by one, and put them in the cabinet. Because of the limited space of the cabinet, it is not possible to take out all the things in the suitcaseand put away, and some things can only lie in the - suitcase. After a while, my roommate dressed up and left the room without saying a word. When Jianxin was busy settling himself, the door suddenly sounded a knock knock, Jianxin said "please come in". A medium height, wearing a black T-shirt and blue jeans Chinese girl appeared in front of Jianxin's heart, she is not very beautiful, but also a little elegant, her face is full of confidence and independence. Jianxin thought: This must be Huang Xiaodan, the Chinese girl who had written to her. The girl started with a brief introduction of herself, and then, like an authoritative teacher, told Jianxin what she needed to pay attention to in the future, without saying it in detail, just describing it lightly. Jianxin was very grateful to have such a senior from the same country to give her sincere help and guidance, she suddenly remembered that there was another gift for Huang Xiaodan, and then looked a little timid and shy said: "Thank you for your letter and help, I brought you a gift,

I hope you like it." After that, she handed the gift containing Suzhou silk to Huang Xiaodan. After receiving the gift, Huang Xiaodan said briefly and pithily: "Thank you." Jianxin very want to be close to Huang Xiaodan, but she found that her first impression of Huang Xiaodan and her inner imagination is completely different. In her imagination, Huang Xiaodan should be very warm and generous, with a good affinity, pure and talkative. But Huang Xiaodan in front of her, gave her a completely different feeling: she is a sense of distance, dignified, arrogant, lofty like a strict teacher. So in the process of Huang Xiaodan speaking, Jianxin did not ask her too many questions, because this sense of distance makes Jianxin feel strange and not close. She did not know why Huang Xiaodan gave her a sense of distance, it may be the way she spoke, it may be her serious expression: too serious, no smile. Jianxin quietly and patiently listen to Huang Xiaodan speak. After a while, Huang Xiaodan said to Jianxin: "Go, let's go to the mountain, our school is built in the middle of the mountain, if you want to buy something, you need to go to a small town at the mountain, the town is only a few shops, there are supermarkets, post offices, and one or two restaurants." I'll take you for a walk, and then you'll know how to shop for yourself." Jianxin answered cautiously, "OK." Then the two of them went out of the room, through a door, seven twists and turns, on the way to meet the German girls in twos and threes, tall and graceful, they looked at Jianxin with curious eyes, because there was a new Chinese girl in the school, this is the second Chinese girl, they have not seen too many Asians in this school. Some students were very polite and greeted Jianxin and Huang Xiaodan with a generous "hallo". Jianxin suddenly felt that everyone's face was similar, with a high nose, big eyes, small face, white skin, blond hair color, and dark brown, she felt that her face was blind and could not distinguish the difference between faces. If it is Chinese or Asian people, in front of her, she can tell the difference very well, but in the face of this group of European boys and girls coming and going, she really can't tell who is who, it seems that everyone looks similar, as if they are all engraved in the same mold. As she made her way downstairs, she noticed a dark-skinned girl waving to her enthusiastically. The black girl was surrounded by a group of white girls, talking and watching TV in a small activity room with clear glass doors. The black girl was especially enthusiastic, and when she saw Jianxin passing by, she waved and smiled at her. Despite the language barrier, Jianxin's intuition told her that the black girl was warm and welcoming, and body language could explain it well. The other white girls just gave Jianxin a cold look, not showing their welcome. For the first time in her life, she saw the black race, she felt that the world is really wonderful, there are people with black skin as black as charcoal, teeth are surprisingly white, this black girl and white girls formed a strong contrast between black and white, she really can not describe in words. At the moment, Jianxin's aesthetic view is still very narrow and traditional, she felt that the black people really look ugly, skin as black as charcoal, lips as thick as two thick sausages, hair like cotton, not a thread, but a round knit, like a small bump; In contrast, the white girls are all very beautiful, with delicate faces and small eyes, deep and bright. However, her aesthetic has gradually changed in her future study abroad career. Later, she also felt that black people also have own beauty, with tight and delicate skin and sexy and full lips; And white people also have the common and defects of white people: lips are too thin, body shape, rough skin and so on. However, in terms of the character of the race, Jianxin felt the warmth and friendliness of the blacks, and the pride, introversion and coolness of the whites. Though she did not yet know it well or had misunderstood it, she had sensed this subtlety in the reactions of the many students she met today as she walked through the corridors of the school palace. Of course, the school staff is extremely friendly, and when a new student from the far East comes to the school, he will be very polite and polite and greet "hallo" with a smile. Jianxin will also respond to their welcome in the same way, with the short and most practical "hallo" reply to them, but her expression is a little shy and introverted, perhaps because she is unfamiliar with the place and lacks a sense of security, so her strong, bold and generous character is completely hidden. She needs to explore this unknown world carefully.

It was not long before the two of them walked out of the school gates. Looking around, outside the gate is a wide open space covered with small stones. Around the palace-like building are located other modern buildings, whose simple and modern style is somewhat incompatible with the main body of the building, but there is not much sense of contradiction. Huang

Xiaodan took Jianxin to choose a stone path to walk down the mountain, many steps, there are dense trees on the road, are covered with silver at the moment, but you can vaguely see the fresh green leaves under the cover of snow appear extra fresh green. The road is a little wet, the two of them carefully walked on the steps, Huang Xiaodan slowly said: "This road is the fastest to the mountain, although there are many steps, but the mountain will not feel too strenuous, and there is no vehicle, the weather is good, the scenery is very breathtaking, that is the town, soon." Jianxin answered, "I can see houses" After ten minutes along the mountain road, they arrived at the town. The town houses are short, there are no skyscrapers, but these houses in this small town look very elegant and delicate, the houses have been painted several colors, there are light pink, white, green, etc., the wall is also painted with exquisite murals. The streets of the town are paved with large and small stones, which is ancient and beautiful. The streets are particularly clean and tidy, without a little dust and debris. The streets are empty and almost invisible. Jianxin thought: Maybe it is because of the snow, everyone hides indoors and does not go out. The town is really small, as far as the eye can see. Huang Xiaodan pointed to a White House not far away with a yellow sign "POST" on it. Then they came to the only supermarket in the town, the supermarket is not big or small, neatly placed a variety of daily necessities, but Jianxin found that the supermarket actually has half of the space to sell pet food and supplies, which is completely different from domestic supermarkets. In 2002, there were almost no pet products in domestic supermarkets, and all the products sold were for people to eat, but here, half were for cats and dogs. "It's amazing," Jianxin thought to herself. "Pets and humans are completely equally divided here." She wondered, do people here like small animals so much? There was no such concept at all, everyone was still living on the edge of poverty, the economy was still weak, and she remembered growing up without a toy, let alone a pet. Different countries and regions, there are still quite big differences, both in terms of economy and people's lifestyle. All the items in the supermarket were marked, and below were the names of the items annotated in German, which she could not understand at all, as if she were blind. There are very few people in the supermarket, just a salesperson and a few guests, unlike the country, there are people everywhere, almost all places are filled with people. Jianxin sighs: There are so few people here, a little cold and lonely. She is used to the bustling people in China, used to the noisy and crowded atmosphere, but here is sparsely populated, and you can quietly hear the sound of a needle dropping. This huge contrast makes her feel a strong sense of loneliness and discomfort. After visiting the supermarket, they walked to the street, Huang Xiaodan pointed to another painted pink house, said: "You see, that is a stationery store, if you want to buy school supplies in the future, you can go there." Next to the stationery store is a grocery store that sells various kinds of bacon and cheese. There is also mail service here. Down the street they came to a small central square, where an old church with a spire stood majestically. It was from this chapel that Jianxin heard the bell. Further down is a small restaurant, and then at the end of the town. Outside the town, there's a lot of farmland. In Jianxin's mind, the size of the town is really mini, 10 minutes to walk, although she found the empty streets and the surprisingly quiet atmosphere made her feel a little lonely, but the town as a whole is very beautiful, very delicate, very quiet. After she stayed for two years, she was well accustomed to that kind of quiet and peaceful life.

After visiting the town, Huang Xiaodan chose another road to take Jianxin back to school, she said while walking: "There are three roads from the school to this town, this is the second road, the general pedestrians walk less, because there are many vehicles through." Redundant words, she did not say, do not ask, Jianxin silently nodded, do not know how to talk with Huang Xiaodan. The fate between people is really mysterioussome people meet together, attract each other, there will be endless topics, will find it easy to communicate or talk. But there are also people who meet and feel awkward, nervous or overwhelmed and don't know how to talk. Jianxin and Huang Xiaodan belong to the second situation, the magnetic field between them is not right, met, there is no special kind of feeling, feel very unfamiliar. So on the way back to school along the avenue, the two of them walked silently. At the gate of the school, Huang Xiaodan pointed to the direction of the third road and said to Jianxin, "You see, that is the third way down the mountain, and at the foot of the mountain is an old house for art classes and a gymnasium, and you will know when you have the class." If you have any questions in the future, please feel free to ask me. But it's better not to ask in Chinese." Jianxin gratefully said: "Thank you, Huang Xiaodan." Huang Xiaodan said she still had things, and left in a hurry. Jianxin has a general understanding of the location here. She had nowhere else to go now, and everything was so strange to her that she just wanted to go back to her dorm. Her mind is very confused, walked several times, still can not remember where she lived in the specific room, because the architectural structure of the palace is particularly complex, not like a modern building, square, but seven twists and turns, to bypass many winding corridors and porches, in order to get back to her room. "Anyway, you have to go back, otherwise why stand here alone, others will certainly find it baffling or strange." Jianxin thought to herself. Then, by memory, she climbed the stairs and stepped on the creaky wooden floor. On the second floor, to the left, down the long corridor through a door, then up the stairs, through several doors, and finally back to her room, her room is the highest bedroom in the building, it is still a little difficult to find, she hopes not to get lost again next time. Jianxin was puzzled. She did not quite understand what was wrong with her memory. When she saw many students, she could not tell who was who, and she thought they all looked the same. Looking for her room, she almost got lost in the middle of it, walked through it several times, and didn't remember it, and she couldn't rationally explain the situation. Back to the room, she saw the roommate has been in the room, the roommate did not say a word, has been busy with their own things. Jianxin sat down in front of her desk and looked out of the window at the Alps. She looked at it and started to stay, she recalled what happened at home before, some memories are still very clear, as if it happened yesterday, there are many memories have become fuzzy images, more and more distant from reality, leaving only some traces. At this moment, she is more and more homesick, she misses her family and friends at home, and truly feels the loneliness of a person outside the heart. She pulled out the photo from the suitcase, put the family photo on the wall beside the bed, looking at the smiling parents and younger brother, grandparents, she has an indescribable sadness and loneliness, this feeling is not very strong before leaving home, then mixed with more excitement, curiosity and longing for the future life. But now really arrived at the destination, she suddenly became very homesick, very miss the past lively and warm home, here is a completely different atmosphere, without the warmth of home, everything is so strange to her and cold, the weather is cold. She wanted to contact her parents, but she didn't have any communication tools, no cell phone, no computer, communication at that time was very inconvenient, only international calls. But there was no telephone in her dormitory, and she longed to hear her parents' familiar voices, to hear their comfort, but it was hopelessly impossible for the time being. Parents want to contact her, and they don't know how. At that time, far away in different countries, the connection between relatives was like a kite with a broken line, and the kite flew farther and farther, she did not know where to fly. Jianxin's parents only knew that she had gone to Germany, and it was really unknown whether she had arrived at the school smoothly. Jianxin thought her parents might be worried about her, wondering if everything was going well for her. She had no contact with her since she left Shanghai for entry-exit. The window has been dark, Jianxin feel that this day has been particularly long, night fell, it is 9:30 p.m., she lay quietly in bed alone, long travel for dozens of hours, and now she finally can have a good sleep, after a few seconds, fell asleep. In the dream, she seemed to be in the familiar school, beside her parents and relatives, as if she had never left.

Jianxin's parents are really worried about her, especially her mother, after sending her daughter away that day, her heart is very bad, lying in bed, turning over and over is unable to sleep. The mother talked to Jianxin's father: "How about my daughter, she was only 16 years old, she left home alone, went to such a distant country, unfamiliar with life, can not speak a word of German, what if she meets crooks and bad people?" Did the plane arrive safely? Jianxin in the end was picked up by the people smoothly sent to school?" With all sorts of questions in her mind, she could hardly sleep. A mother is always the most concerned about her children, for the child broke the heart, no matter how grow up the children grown up, in the eyes of parents, it will always be a child who is not big, is the parents' concern for life. Although Jianxin's father is also a little worried about his daughter, but his self-regulation ability is very strong, he comforted Jianxin's mother: "You don't need to worry, Jianxin must have arrived safely." Go to sleep quickly, it's been a busy day." With that, he fell asleep. But her mother could not sleep, after listening to these comforting words, her heart was more stable, but more worried and insecure, she did not sleep all night. In the morning, the father woke up and saw Jianxin's mother was secretly wiping tears, she said: "I can't sleep for the whole night, how can you sleep, the daughter who has been raised, has gone to a foreign country alone, and we can't contact her now." Is it your fault that she should study abroad so early and stay with us? Why must a girl go so far away, what happens, we can not help. I'm really worried. Where is Jianxin now? I miss my daughter so much." After listening to Jianxin's father, he gently and patiently comforted her and said, "Wife, don't worry too much, don't think too much, Jianxin must have arrived smoothly lead a good life, children grow up, always fly away, how can they always be together with us, this will delay their future." They comfort each other, pray for their daughter to run smoothly in a foreign land, and also hope that my dear daughter can contact them as soon as possible, so that the parents of the hanging heart can be reassured.

After a good night's sleep, she was full of energy, no longer so sentimental, but returned to the previous confidence and determination. Her roommate was still asleep. Jianxin, listening to the chirping of the birds outside the window and the deep sound of the church bell in the distance, jumped out of bed and went to the bathroom next to her room. She brushed her teeth, washed her face, took a shower, and freshened up. She never used to take a shower in the morning, because back home, she usually took a shower at night. Domestic study time, the morning time is particularly compact, there is no time to wash up well, can only be hastily and quickly packed up, immediately ran to the classroom, began a day of morning self-study, the pace of life is almost like war. Now she is learning to start her day with a shower, just like other local students. She found that after taking a shower in the morning, everything felt fresh, full of hope, and beneficial, so in the long future study career, she maintained this habit of taking a shower in the morning. When everything was ready, she followed the route she had taken before, passing through seven or eight gates, and on the way met a number of students, some of whom greeted her politely with "HALLO, Guten Morgen." Other students, quite shy and reserved, stared at her curiously. Jianxin thought in her heart: Before you understand others, don't judge others good or bad, and do yourself well. Most people here are very polite and well-mannered. A new day begins, this is a new beginning, I will adapt to the life here. Believe in yourself, you can do it, don't doubt your potential."

Soon she was in the canteen. The dining halls here are very different from those in China before. I remember that the canteen in the past was crowded with students, the facilities were outdated and backward, and everyone had to queue up to get food and rice, and the queue was almost like a long queue every day. There was a lot of noise in the canteen, and everyone needed to speak at the top of their voice in case they could not be heard. After taking the food, shesat down casually to find an empty seat and ate with several good friends together . Jianxin belongs to the lively extroverted, every time you eat, other friends are focused on eating, she likes to chat constantly, talk about a lot of things happening in the school or some gossip, sometimes talking, the food has not moved, others have finished eating, and then friends always say: "Jianxin, take the lunchyour meal has not not eaten yet." You are the king of chatting, chatting will become addicted, and you will not eat." Jianxin to see everyone finished, immediately wolfed up to eat, and then with friends arm in arm, but also to snack shop to buy snacks, to meet her greedy desire. The dining-room, not exactly the word "dining-room" to describe the place, opened the door and saw that the whole interior was divided into three large halls, in which dozens of large round tables were artfully arranged, and the great round tables were covered with white cushions, and the walls of the hall were covered with exquisite European frescoes full of art and vivid figures, Vivid and interesting, the landscape painting infatuated, quiet and beautiful. The main color of the hall is warm yellow, and the floor is also elegant and durable dark brown wood floor. Only one of the furthest halls is dominated by a pale green color, and the frescoes on the walls are even more striking. The frescoes, scanned in sequence, appear to be the plot of a complete religious story. The green hall looks fresh and elegant, the main lights in the hall are European crystal chandeliers, luxury and exquisite, a large arc window inlaid among them, through the window, is vibrant, interesting, elegant and beautiful south garden. Jianxin exclaimed: "What a beautiful dining hall, as expected, like a palace general resplendent, exquisite." Originally, Jianxin's school was once the residence of a duke, and later after the Duke's death, it was converted into a famous private school in Bavaria, from Grade 5 to Grade 13 (equivalent to domestic education in primary school 5, junior high school to high school). It is a co-educational private school with high tuition fees that are not affordable for the average family. Legend has it that there have been many famous alumni here, and later alumni in the community to achieve career success, will return to their Alma mater, make charitable donations. Jianxin was deeply attracted by the elegant dining hall. "It's beautiful, really beautiful," she exclaimed.

While she was immersed, an old woman in her fifties walked up to her, wearing a white apron and asking her with a big smile, "WILLST DU FRUSTUCKEN?" (Would you like to have breakfast?) Jianxin wondered what she was mumbling about, and made signs to say that she was hungry and wanted breakfast. The old lady was clever enough to understand what she meant, and then she took Jianxin to the kitchen. The kitchen is well-organized and clean, very different from the dining room next door, with modern kitchen appliances of excellent quality. The old lady gently and politely gesticulated and asked Jianxin what she wanted to eat. Jianxin looked at the steaming hot bread and butter in the kitchen and pointed to the bread and butter. The old lady understood her meaning, patiently put the bread and butter in a fine dish, and then gave Jianxin a knife and fork. While speaking German, she took Jianxin to the dining room, found a seat, and let Jianxin have breakfast. At this moment, Jianxin feel very warm, the heart is not so empty, encounter kind and warm-hearted people, will bring her great comfort and encouragement, although she can not understand what the old lady said, but the warmth and friendliness of the kitchen old lady let Jianxin feel the beauty of the world, the beauty of humanity, even strangers, but the heart is kind, the distance between people is so close.

Jianxin had never eaten Western food before going abroad, so she did not know how to use a knife and fork, whether to hold a knife in her left hand or in her right hand, she was not clear. She felt a little embarrassed, afraid that people would see her laugh at her, but it was very early in the day, and no one else had come to eat in the dining hall, so she used her knife and fork in whatever way was comfortable for her, or what she thought was right. She also did not know the difference between cheese and butter, and thought that the old lady had given her cheese, which should be hard and could be eaten on its own. Then she put the whole stick of butter into her mouth as if it were cheese, and found that it had no taste at all, leaving only a greasy feeling in her mouth. The old lady came in to look at her, saw that she had eaten wrong, scraped some butter with a knife, spread it on the soft bread, and let her taste it. Jianxin tasted a bite, feel really delicious, bread coated with butter, eat fragrant and moist, like coated with light ice cream, the mouth melts. Jianxin felt the charm of Western food for the first time. It was just plain bread and butter. She fell in love after the first try. Jianxin's mother was worried that she was not used to Western food at first, and prepared a large amount of pickled mustard and instant noodles for her in her suitcase. But surprisingly, Jianxin is not at all unaccustomed to Western food, she has a great interest in new things and never tried the cuisine has a great desire to explore, and western food really suits her taste. So those pickled mustard and instant noodles did not play their emergency role at all, but in silence has been lying in the suitcase. Jianxin ate very happy and satisfied, after a while, several other students also came to the dining hall to eat. They saw a new student from the East in the dining room, stared for a moment, then said hello from a distance and went to get their breakfast. After Jianxin had finished eating, she went back to her room.

My roommate is already up, cleaning up in the bathroom next door. Jianxin was confused and did not know how to arrange the day, and no one told her what the class schedule was like every day. She is like a silly child who knows nothing about her future study and life. After a while she felt bored in her room, so she went downstairs to see if she could find any clue. Walking out of the main door, she saw a group of students walking towards a building on the left side of the main building. They are tall, everyone has a folder in his hand, some students carry schoolbags, Jianxin also want to follow them to see. Sit in the classroom, the classroom becomes very noisy because of the arrival of a new student. Everyone stared at Jianxin intently, with curious eyes, talking about something which she did not understand a word. There was a clock on the wall of the classroom, and when the clock counted 8:10, a teacher with a full beard stepped onto the platform and began to lecture in a mumbling voice. It was as if Jianxin had entered an outer space, unaware of all the people, all the things that happened, and all the things they said, and could not understand what they were saying. All she saw was a row of desks with beakers and gadgets for doing experiments, and if she was right, this was a chemistry class, and the chemistry teacher walked in. The teacher has gray hair, looks more than fifty years old, although full of beard, but very friendly, gentle tone. When he was lecturing, there were students whispering under the stage, and some naughty students kept trying to get close to Jianxin, winking at them, wondering how a new student suddenly appeared in the classroom inexplicably, or from the far east. Halfway through the class, the amiable chemistry teacher also noticed Jianxin, then walked off the lectern, straight to Jianxin's seat, and first spoke a few words in German. Jianxin kept shaking her head and finally came out with two words, "English please." Then the teacher realized that the new student did not understand German and asked in perfect English, "May I help you?" Jianxin understood the teacher's words, but then she did not know how to express what she wanted to do in English, in fact, she really did not know what she was going to do, was bored in the room alone, and no one told her the course arrangement, she went downstairs to explore the following situation by herself.

  The chemistry teacher saw that the student could not answer anything, and then said to her, "Are you searching for Herr May? Follow me, I will bring you to Herr May's office. Follow me, I will bring you to Herr May's office. Come with me and I'll show you to his office." Not sure if she was really going to find something Herr May, Jianxin nodded. Then the chemistry teacher took Jianxin back to the main building and ran all the way upstairs. On the second floor, sheasked some other people passing by where Herr May's office was. Suddenly a tall black man appeared, wearing a handsome suit. The chemistry teacher saw him, exchanged polite greetings with him, talked to him for a while, and then waved goodbye to Jianxin. The black man brought Jianxin to a spacious and modern office. There are a big whiteboard and several desks and chairs in the office. The other part is the office area, with a desk neatly arranged with a pile of papers, a computer, and a row of bookcases behind the desk. The tall black man with large eyes, a wide nose, thick lips, and close-shaven hair smiled and said, "I am your German teacher Herr May." You are the new student from China, right? You are the new student from China, right? He spoke slowly and clearly. Jianxin understood him. It was her German teacher. Jianxin was very puzzled and thought: how can a black man be his German teacher? Is he a pure German? Is he also a foreigner? Is it OK for foreigners to teach foreigners German? But she did not think too much about it, and felt that to her surprise, he would teach her German in the future and be introduced to it by a tall black teacher. It's a school arrangement. There's got to be a reason for it. Later, Jianxin learned that the German teacher also has a important professionalthough he is not a pure German, but he is very talented in language, can speak several languages, French is his mother tongue, his major in the universityis German, is a language PhD. Herr May is the director of the school's international department and German teacher, responsible for the German language classes of all international students attending the private school.

Since then, Jianxin began to learn German with Herr May, and she could not attend the normal grade classes for the time being, because first of all, she had to lay a good foundation for the language, In her first German class, she learned in a fogHerr May, of course, does not speak Chinese, so for Jianxin, a German beginner, he needs to use a little creative method to teach. Although her basic english knowledge is not very good limited to dumb English, can read English passages, but I heard that it is very weak, because at that time in China to learn English, there is no good foreign language environment, usually we almost do not need to communicate in English, purely for the purpose of taking the test. But anyway, Jianxin already has some foundation of English. Naturally, Herr May began to teach simple German through English as the medium of language. He taught and explained in the shortest and slowest way possible. During the first class, he wrote down the basic letters of the German alphabet on a whiteboard, and then taught Jianxin how to pronounce each letter one by one. The German alphabet has several more special letters than the 26 English letters. His handwriting is relatively sloppy, so when Jianxin transcribes the class content in his notebook, he often does not know what letters are in the end and how to write them, which is completely different from the foreign language written by the domestic English teacher. After teaching the writing and pronunciation of the German alphabet, Herr May began to teach the most common words, such as Lehrer (teacher) and die Frau (lady), she was listening attentively to the teacher's pronunciation and taking notes. The first class, for her, both novel and unfamiliar, although the content is the most elementary, or feel very uncomfortable, can not keep up with the rhythm of the German teacher. But the only thing that makes her feel extremely gratified is that Herr May is a friendly teacher who often encourages students, unlike many teachers in China who look very serious In this unfamiliar place, she needs other people's encouragement and patient guidance, which will smooth her study career and make up for her inner loneliness and confusion. However, the problem of missing her relatives and friends cannot be completely solved in a short time, and she is only 16 years old.

After class, Jianxin ran all the way back to her room. After going back and forth several times, she could find her bedroom with great accuracy. Although she had to share the room with a German girl, it was her little world, and she had nowhere else to go except this bedroom, or, to put it precisely, she had not been brave enough to go out and explore other places until she had mastered the local language, for fear of getting lost and of being unable to control the unknown. She felt her own small and helpless feeling, so her heart was full of infinite desire and motivation, she silently said to herself: "No matter how difficult, I must adapt here, adapt here the most important task is to master this unfamiliar and difficult German knowledge." So when she returned to her little world, she immediately plunged into reviewing the contents of her first German lesson. She was ambivalent about whether some words were correct or not, because the teacher's sloppy handwriting was really barely able to memorize them. She kept her head down, trying hard to recall the letters and words the teacher had taught her in class, but her mind was still fuzzy. For her, the first class was really a muddle. She had not yet entered the state of learning German, and she might not have adapted to Herr May's teaching method. What's more, she did not have a tape recorder, so she could listen to the words and letters she had learned over and over again. It is also really to question themselves, now review the sound is not accurate. She thought, "If it is a language school, at least there will be foreign students who learn German together, we can communicate with each other, and those who don't understand can discuss together, but all the students here are basically native speakers, German is their mother tongue, how can anyone talk to me about this pronunciation problem?" Besides, I don't even know how to ask them in German or English how to pronounce it." She read very hard, looking at the beautiful scenery outside the window and the Alpine mountains standing high, it seems so calm and quiet, she has no other way, what she wants to do is to review all the content of the class every day, whether it is correct pronunciation or not, it should be smoother and more accustomed to time. Now is just the beginning, everything is difficult at the beginning, and once you get used to the pace of learning, everything will gradually be better. Don't think too much, just work hard. Then she went on reading her class notes. At this time, her roommate returned to the room, gave her a light hello, and went to work on their own things. There is almost no dialogue between the two of them, to Jianxin, this roommate seems very distant and mysterious, although in the same room, but she is only busy with her own things, the new roommate does not care about, indifferent. She heard Jianxin reading the German letters and some simple everyday words, without any comment, right or wrong, without saying anything, and after a while left the room. Jianxin sat silently at her desk, reading and reading...

At first, Jianxin was really confused about the school's lesson plan and eating and living schedule. 1:00 in the afternoon was lunch time, she followed the other students to the noble and elegant dining room, saw a round table covered with white cushions elegantly and artistically placed in the dining room, like a blossoming white lotus. At the junction of the two halls, there is a long table almost 3 meters long, and the table is also covered with a flawless white tablecloth, and all kinds of delicious food are placed on this long table. There are green salad, main course steak, or pasta, dessert cake or pudding, and various fruits. When Jianxin saw these delicacies, her stomach was rumbling and she wanted to get the meal immediately and eat it But the school has school rules, students can not immediately pick up food at will, is to strictly abide by the dining etiquette of this private school. When each student finds his or her seat, he or she is not allowed to sit in his or her chair immediately. Instead, he or she needs to stand beside his or her seat with no noise allowed. After there is complete silence in the dining room, one of the student representatives announces "Guten Appetite" and then he or she can start eating. When everyone heard "Guten Appetite", just like the valve of the hydropower station opened, the surging water gushed out, the whole dining hall became lively. The sounds of conversation, knives and forks, and the footsteps of the Italian chef and his assistant on the wooden floor form a symphony of the most natural harmony. Jianxin also imitated other students, at first standing next to her own position, and when the student representative announced the end, she saw that everyone else could sit in their position, and she also sat in her own position. She did not dare to make mistakes, because she was afraid of making a fool of herself, and her mind was almost blank about the dining etiquette of Western food, and she could not figure out which hand was holding the knife and fork. So you can only follow the gourd, carefully observe and imitate other people's dining manners and habits. Not long after, a chef brought today's staple steak, eight or nine steaks neatly lying in a rectangular stainless steel container, everyone saw that the staple food has been served, everyone in order to put a steak on their plate, and then skilfully put the brown thick meat soup poured on the steak. At first, Jianxin had still some doubts: what is the use of this stainless steel small pot, how to look like Aladdin's magic lamp, exquisite and chic. Now it dawned on her that it was used for steak gravy. She sighed in her heart: Western food is really elegant, each kind of tableware has its unique use, and also considered so thorough and detailed, which is completely different from her previous school meals in China. There were about eight or nine students at a table, and after everyone had finished picking up the steak, Jianxin was the only one left. Although she was hungry, she was very cautious and wanted to wait until everyone had finished picking it up. There is a German girl, long fair skin, big eyes, nose particularly tall, looks like the classical beauty of the Mona Lisa, see Jianxin plate is still empty, kindly help Jianxin clip a large steak. Jianxin hurriedly said "thanks" to the girl, and learned to do the same, poured some source on the steak, used the knife and fork sparingly, and ate silently with her head down. The steak was perfectly grilled, drizzled, delicious, truly delicious. Jianxin eats carefully, not making too much chewing noise, afraid of making a fool of herself and letting others laugh. During this period, she would often observe the facial expressions of the students around her, and find that some students would cast friendly and kind eyes at her, while some students would look at her without expression, and talk to the students next to her in a mumbling manner, and they did not know whether they were talking about other topics or evaluating her. she could say was understood only by herself, and that she knew nothing of what this group of people said. She thought that she had already taken a german class, why she could not understand anything, could not catch a familiar word. They talked so much, so fast, it was like a book out of heaven for her. You might as well eat. Jianxin ate with relish, and after a while, a piece of steak was finished. Then, like the other students, she went to the long table with all kinds of food to get something else to eat. She wasn't interested in salad, it was all raw, and she didn't know if it would upset her stomach. Dessert is her favorite, and the Western dessert is very exquisite, which makes people mouth watering. She had a good appetite, and at once took several different kinds of black forest cake, apple pie, and pear pie. Then she returned to herplace and put the cake in her mouth. She doesn't care about the way other people look at her eating. At this moment, she is attracted by the food, which is the most enjoyable aspect of her first arrival at this school, because she really likes Western food, no need to adapt, as if it is an innate love. Therefore, even though the life in the new school was strange for her at the beginning, she would often feel lonely and helpless, but the school food gave her the best taste buds satisfaction and spiritual comfort. Whenever she was under great pressure from study or was very homesick, she would adjust herself through food and find happiness in life. Many students do not eat as satisfied as Jianxin, they eat a few bites and then stop eating, they seem to be more interested in chatting. These students are the children of the German upper class, whose parents are either doctors, lawyers, or have their own companies. Therefore, their mouths must be more picky, what Western dishes have been tasted, these school dishes for them is very ordinary food, not particularly outstanding. There are many students who will always have some dishes or discarded bread left on their plates, and they are used to the superior material life and do not feel that this is a waste of food. Jianxin loves these dishes so much that she is not willing to throw them away. Many Chinese parents will teach their children that "who knows the food on the plate, every grain is hard", so she does not have the habit of leaving food or throwing it away.

The lunch lasted about an hour and a half, and a handsome, tall student representative came out and mumbled for about five minutes, and then it was over. Compared with the dining environment and form of domestic schools, the dining here pays more attention to the sense of ceremony and order, which is a completely different experience. Jianxin feels very special and fresh. Although the unfamiliar environment and the language barrier bring her many difficulties, it also brings her many opportunities to explore new things and other cultures. Students and teachers began to leave the elegant, classy palace-like dining room. Some students stayed there to enjoy the food before finishing their meal. Some students were still immersed in the atmosphere of chatting. When Jianxin left the dining hall, she unconsciously found that the students here were very open, kissing or hugging each other in public, and the girlfriend would actually sit on the boyfriend's lap, arms on the boyfriend, affectionately talking or flirting, the people around would not be surprised to see, but gladly accept the student's such an open love relationship. Or at least people won't look at these couples differently, they'll just think it's normal. Jianxin at the moment feel it is too incredible, here love is actually tolerated and encouraged, young men and women can be unabashedly open to the public, without hesitation in any occasion to fall in love, this is a from grade 5 to grade 13 (across the second half of the primary school, middle school and high school years) arts and sciences boarding school. If puppy love is almost banned in Chinese schools, even if there is such a phenomenon, it can only be secretly, in public places, especially in schools, it is absolutely impossible to see male and female students who love each other, passionately kissing and so on. Jianxin is like the discovery of a new continent, shocked the jaw, in the domestic high school, every student is well-behaved, like a soldier who has been trained to strictly implement or comply with all the school curriculum arrangements, let alone love. Boarders do not apply for permission from school leaders, leaving the school gate is prohibited, it is completely closed management, and there is no free personal time arrangement, everyone is trying to concentrate on learningstudy hard day and night, admission to a famous school is the most important thing in life, and other things have nothing to do with learning are put in a secondary position. In addition to classes, homework and self-study classes, there are also early morning runs, and almost no other extracurricular activities. But the school here is a very different curriculum, although it is also a boarding school, but 3 PM: After the end of the course, students have full freedom to arrange their own spare time, they can go to the town at the foot of the mountain to buy some daily necessities, or participate in various interest classes, such as painting, badminton, rock climbing, musical instrument lessons, dance lessons, etc., or go to the cafe to chat with a few friends, or they can be alone and do what they want to do. Jianxin thinks that the free space of the new school is much larger. Although she will miss home and cannot communicate with the students around her, she likes the free atmosphere of study because she does not like to study under external pressure, and likes to arrange her study and life at her own comfortable pace. She admires the open and humane atmosphere of the new school. And with the passing of time, she became more and more aware that the new school does not just put academic performance in the first place, without considering the development of other aspects of students, the new school pays attention to personalized teaching and whole-person education, so the students here are more lively and naughty, more like to play pranks, not so follow the rules, fifteen or sixteen year old young boys and girls in love is also completely allowed. You will never be labeled as puppy love, or be pointed at by parents, teachers or people around you. Here, more attention is paid to the display of personality and the protection of self-esteem. It's amazing how different Chinese and Western cultures are. Eastern culture is reserved, conservative and traditional, while Western culture is free, open and focused on individual development and personal space. She deeply lamented: the world is so big, there are no surprises, this time I really opened my eyes, puppy love is actually encouraged or allowed, male and female friends can show sweet happiness everywhere in the school, it is incredible. Because Jianxin has been influenced by Eastern culture, so for her, such a bold love is like discovering a big news.

Because of the language, she was not yet able to follow the normal curriculum of a grade like other students, because even if she were to switch classes, it would be like listening to heaven, and it would have no effect. So her classes are mainly German in the International Department. Herr May also has many international students from other European countries, but Jianxin is the only one who has no knowledge of German. Other international students have more or less already studied elementary or intermediate courses in their summer camps or language schools, so they can already communicate easily on a daily basis. Jianxin is indeed a special existence, with no basis in German, from the distant East (in addition to Huang Xiaodan from China in the whole school, she is the second), and one thing is particularly different: Before she came to this boarding school in Germany, she had hardly been to any other country or any city in China. Instead, she studied hard in the small village where she was born. That is to say, she did not have a broad vision and international cognition, but was a rustic student with careful and disciplined behavior. In contrast, the students here (including international students) are from the upper class of well-off families, born in highly developed capitalist countries, and have traveled to many countries with their parents since childhood, and have seen a broad world and diverse civilizations, so the students here are confident, lively and full of superiority. In the face of them, Jianxin will be a little unsure, because she feels the difference from what they have experienced is too great, and she does not understand and have not seen many things, so she is like a hedgehog, likes to curl up her body together, hide and protect herself, and at the same time, in the face of other people's negative evaluation or verbal attack, she will be like a hedgehog, the whole body is covered with thorns. If an enemy harms her, be prepared to turn on the defense mechanism at any time to repel or counterattack the aggressor. After lunch, she went to the classroom of Herr May, her German teacher. Herr May greets her warmly and kindly in English: "hi, how are you? Is everything all right?" Jianxin politely replied, "I am fine, thanks." In the previous lesson, Herr May had asked her name, but this lesson, he forgot how to pronounce Jianxin's name, Herr May looked a little embarrassed and asked, "Do you have a English name?" your Chinese name is really difficult for me to remember and pronounce. Do you have an English name? Your Chinese name is hard for me to remember and pronounce)." Although Jianxin's spoken English is weak, Herr May slows down to ask a short question that she can understand. Then she said to her German teacher, "You can call me Nancy. Nancy is my English name. Herr May heard, overjoyed, finally did not have to say the simple Chinese name so awkwardly, he simply answered "Great." I will call you Nancy from now on. B: OK. From now on, I'll call you Nancy." Jianxin nodded approvingly. It seems difficult for foreigners to pronounce Chinese names (written in pinyin) accurately, because they do not know the Chinese language system. For Jianxin, the same is true, because she knows almost nothing about the German system, so when she sees German names, she feels that the names are particularly long, and at a glance, she does not know how to read them, and she is completely a layman. In fact, when she was in China, she did not use her English name at all, because people used to call her Chinese name. The place where she was born and lived and studied was still very simple and isolated, and there were not so many new ideas, no one would always use an English name. Her English name was not carefully chosen or thought of by herself, but in the second year of middle school, the fashionable English teacher gave the class a list of English names and let the students choose their own English name. There were a few English names left that no one wanted, and then Jianxin chose Nancy, either because it sounded a little catchy or because there weren't many other options. In a word, all this is out of fate, in fact, a person and their own name also have inextricably linked, the name is like a person in the society symbol, with this symbol can better identify the person, and establish a more effective connection with others. Whether a name brings good luck or bad luck is unclear.

Under normal circumstances, the elders will choose auspicious words to call their newly born children, hoping that he will live a safe, happy, healthy and smooth life. It can be seen that the good intentions of parents and relatives have given their children unlimited expectations and blessings at birth. Chinese parents are especially great, bitter themselves can not bitter children, all their lives are busy for the future of children and the future, they would rather eat more bitter, as long as the thought can give children a better future, create a higher platform, these bitter these tired are worth it. How selfless and great parents' love for their children is, regardless of return, only hoping that their children can grow up and become a moral and literate person who is useful to society. Jianxin's parents are the same, would rather tighten their belts, bear the huge pressure and risk of operating enterprises, but also hope to do their best to cultivate their children into talents and become pillars.

Jianxin knows the good intentions of her parents, and also understands the difficulties of her parents' life and work, so she is very sensible, and never needs her parents to worry about her in school and life, because she does not want to disappoint her parents and relatives, and because she is a girl who knows how to be grateful and has a warm and kind heart. She can't bear to let her parents' efforts go to waste, so no matter how hard the road is, she will go on without distractions, bravely and firmly, for her parents, but also for herself.

This afternoon's class is already the second time, Jianxin feels less overwhelmed than the first class. Herr May patiently continued to teach. He prepared a beginner German textbook for Jianxin, full of drawings, new words and dialogues. Herr May read the sentences or words by herself first, and then ask Jianxin to repeat them. If there is a pronunciation error in the middle, the teacher will correct it in time. After reading the dialogue, the teacher explained the meaning of the words in English or body language, Jianxin understood some of the words, and some were not sure what the meaning was, because the textbook did not explain Chinese or English, it was all in German. After teaching the written lessons, Herr May will play the tapes to Jianxin and let her listen to them several times to really feel the unique charm of the language. Listen more to the recordings to learn how people talk to each other in the actual scene, the intonation and pronunciation of the characters. Jianxin listened intently, very focused, the teacher said every word, she was very serious in mind. Herr May told her to use the daily words she had learned boldly in real life, not to be afraid of making mistakes, the key is to speak more and practice more, if she is wrong, others will help correct, people will not laugh at her. Be sure to practice more, the language environment is so unique, as long as you work hard, slowly will be more and more adapted to everything here. If you don't understand anything, feel free to ask. Jianxin was grateful to the German teacher for introducing her and for his patient and friendly words of encouragement and comfort. In the future, every class, even if only a small progress, Herr May will not hesitate to praise her, so that she is more and more confident that she can break through the obstacles with her own efforts and diligence. At the end of the class, Herr May will emphasize again and again that you should not always translate German into Chinese to think about problems, but directly apply German and learn German as your mother tongue. So later, he recommended to Jianxin a very practical and effective Longman dictionary (German-German dictionary), where each new word was not annotated in other languages, such as English or Chinese, but explained in a complete and accurate long German sentence.

After class, she said her usual polite goodbyes to Herr May, then ran to her room, sat down at her desk, and after looking out the window at the quiet and beautiful scenery and the Alps in the distance, she threw herself into reviewing her lessons. Her roommate often seems to be out of the room, either staying in her friend's room before returning from class, or going to town to chat with friends or participate in other interests. She doesn't know where her roommate is, and he won't talk to her about anything. The two of them met, also nodded and smiled, there was no communication. Therefore, Jianxin is almost alone in this bedroom all day, because her course is not as compact as other students, only German lessons, so in the spare time, she stays alone in the room, reviewing German lessons. She really had no one to talk to, although there were many young faces in the school, and the students were chirping and lively, but she had no friends, no peers to communicate with. She is very lonely in her heart, and she often thinks of her loved ones and many warm-hearted friends when she was in China, but here she really has no relatives and no friends. She wished that if she found a good friend, she wouldn't feel so lonely and helpless, and wouldn't feel so homesick all the time, and time in a foreign country wouldn't feel so slow. She came to the new school only three to five days, but she felt how the time suddenly became so long, as if it had been more than a month. Seeing the family photo posted on the wall, she said to herself, "Mom and Dad, grandparents, I miss you so much." How are you?" As mentioned above, it was only in 2002 when international communication was still underdeveloped and there were no smart phones. When Jianxin studied abroad, she didn't even have a mobile phone or laptop, so she couldn't contact her family. She felt completely cut off from her family, like a kite with a broken string, drifting further and further away. Thinking about it, she would feel inexplicable sadness, she felt herself and this new environment is still very incompatible, although the new school is very beautiful, the teacher is very friendly, she has never shouted at her once, but she is a little happy. She always felt that something was missing, and she could not tell exactly what it was, maybe it was the warmth and touching in her heart. Here, she always felt that the whole atmosphere was a little cold, just like most students' attitude towards her. The only thing she can do now is to try her best to master the language as quickly as possible, otherwise everything else can't be normalized. If you want to make friends, fill the inner sense of loneliness, can not speak a language, is simply impossible. However, people with no basic knowledge in German need time to master it immediately, not a problem that can be solved one or two days. Jianxin know how much think is useless, it is better to act, every day to study hard, the teacher taught German class review well, don't worry too much. Don't worry about finding friends. Just go with the flow. After thinking about it, she immediately read aloud the new words and dialogues learned in class, but she was a little vague about some German pronunciation, not sure whether it was accurate, and there was no other students nearby to ask. So she immersed herself in learning, and spent a long time in language learning every day.

After about a week, one day, a classmate told her to go to the school secretariat to answer the international call. She immediately ran to the secretary's office, and when she received the phone call, she heard her parents' familiar voices, and her father asked gently and kindly: "Jianxin, Jianxin, is that you?" How's everything going at your new school? Is everything going well?" Heard the telephone parents concerned greetings, Jianxin finally could not help crying. She did not want to cry, but the tears that she had held in for several days rushed out like the flood that burst the dike, she thought she was very strong, left her parents and friends, can quickly adapt to the new environment, adapt to everything here, but in fact it is not so. she remember that before she went abroad, her mother often nagged her, and she also hated her mother's criticism and nagging, but now she can no longer hear her mother's nagging and father's encouragement. Today, she finally heard her parents' concerned and worried words on the phone again, and she really couldn't control her emotions anymore. She cried and answered her parents, "Mom and Dad, I'm all right. You can rest assured." Then she heard hermother's familiar and concerned voice: "Jianxin, after you left home that day, I didn't sleep all night, I don't know if my daughter arrived safely, I am very worried that such a long way, a person left like this." In the morning, I sat on the edge of the bed, and the tears came down unconsciously. Parents want you to be all right there, all right at home, and you don't worry about it." After listening to Jianxin, has broken down sobbing. She really misses her parents and her hometown. Although her hometown is still very poor and many facilities are still very rough, it is, after all, the familiar hometown where she has lived for 16 years. There are many warm and beautiful memories, and there are also her family and friends who she misses. Finally, on the other end of the phone, she heard her father's voice: "Jianxin, work hard, make progress every day, dad believes that you can certainly." With tears in her heart, Jianxin firmly replied to her father: "Dad, you can rest assured that I will try my best." Now that I have chosen this path, I will follow it well." After that, Jianxin's parents said: "We don't say much, international long-distance calls are very expensive, just said a few minutes, today's first chat here, knowing that you are all right, we are also relieved." Take good care of yourself and we'll call you next time." Jianxin reluctant to say "goodbye" with her parents on the phone, but she knows that international long-distance call is too expensive, can only make a long story short, let her study in this private school, parents have paid a very high tuition, she can no longer spend money. The call was over, and the parents' voices on the other end of the line had disappeared. In this way, it was the first phone call between Jianxin and her parents a few days after she arrived at the school, and the whole call lasted just a few minutes. Jianxin's tears could not stop flowing out, a lady in the secretary's office saw Jianxin so sad and sad, wanted to comfort her, but did not know how to talk to her, suddenly another teacher appeared in the secretariat, saw Jianxin's tears, he was very rich in empathy, and could really feel a 16-year-old girl leaving her country, leaving her parents. Come to such a distant western study, the heart will have what kind of loneliness and inadaptability, and then very sincere comfort Jianxin: "Are you ok?" I understand you are very sad because you can't see your parents and you miss them very much. Come on, You will get used to the life with time. Come on, you will get used to the life with time. Are you all right? I understand that you're sad because you can't see your parents and you miss them very much. Come on, you'll get used to the life here with time. Be strong)."

Jianxin didn't understand, but the teacher patted her on the shoulder and gave her a hug. She knew the teacher was trying to comfort her, and Jianxin was very grateful. Then she thanked the kind teacher and the secretary, and left the secretary's office. As usual, she went back to her bedroom alone, wiped away her tears, looked into the distance, and heard her father's encouraging words once again: "Study hard and make progress every day." She comforted and encouraged herself again: "Jianxin, don't cry anymore, crying can't solve any problems." Dear parents, you can rest assured that I will work hard and will not let you down, nor will I let your investment in my education go to waste. I will be strong and no matter how difficult it is, I believe it is only temporary and everything will be fine gradually."

Later, Jianxin remembered that her father had given her a painting and calligraphy, which was still lying in the box. She immediately took it out of the box and opened it. It read, "A journey of a thousand miles begins with a single step." Below the calligraphy and painting were the name of the writer, the seal, and the last words, "Jianxin Mian Zhi." It was once they went to a domestic city to travel, in a tourist spot for her and her brother father asked a master who is familiar with Chinese calligraphy and painting, in order to encourage them. Jianxin hung this painting on the wall of her bedroom. Whenever she felt tired or could not go on, these eight words would encourage her to move forward like a good teacher and friend. "A journey of a thousand miles begins with a single step", how profound and profound the traditional Chinese culture is. Although these eight words are simple to say and write, it is very difficult to really do it. People insist, do anything, if only three minutes of heat, will not succeed, will not reach their own set of high goals, but only down to earth, step by step to move forward, unremitting efforts, there will always be the day. Jianxin feels that she is now like a snail, while other students are like rabbits, she is like a tortoise and hare race, others can rest in the middle of the rest, only need to spend a small amount of time, can reach the destination, but she needs to spend a lot of time, pay many times the effort of ordinary people, it is possible to reach the end. And all this is mainly the language barrier, before learning all the lessons, she must first solve the

German language problem. To learn this language well, it is not useful to rely on one or two days of hard work, but need continuous efforts every day, need a very long process, a little accumulation, after a long time of precipitation, in order to achieve a qualitative leap. Jianxin looked at these eight words, she secretly determined: I will step by step to live every day, hard work. Sure enough, every day for the rest of her life, Jianxin went to Herr May's German lessons, and when she returned to her bedroom, she immediately read and reviewed. In class, she will take the initiative to answer the teacher's questions, give herself more opportunities to practice oral English, and if there is a mistake in pronunciation, Herr May correct it directly. Outside of class, she often speaks German to herself. There were no electronic dictionaries at the time, so the two dictionaries she used most often were a super-heavy German-Chinese dictionary and a German-German dictionary from Longman, which Herr May later recommended. In order to master the language more quickly, she would preview new courses in advance, consult the dictionary to find new words, or later just buy a German novel, full of unfamiliar words, she would go through the dictionary one word at a time, it often takes four to five hours to read a page of the novel, there are so many new words, almost every word had to be looked up in the dictionary. This is quite time consuming and laborious, but it is also a very effective way to learn a language. Do a lot of reading, read original novels, make good use of the dictionary, during which you will learn a lot of vocabulary and sentence usage. With the passage of time, after the accumulation of every day, Jianxin slowly realized how to learn German well, there is no other lazy and smart way, the best way is to continue and work hard to learn and accumulate. In the process of learning, she does not think too much, but is completely immersed in it and focused on it. Sometimes she feels that quietly focusing on daily language learning makes her feel more and more valuable, because she can see her own progress and understand more and more vocabulary. But if she sits down with her students for lunch, she can capture only the most basic and simple polite phrases in their conversation, such as Guten Morgen (good morning), Guten Abend (good evening), Wie geht es dir (how are you), and so on.

The rest of the long-winded chatter still doesn't make sense. But she is no longer anxious or anxious, she knows that it takes time to precipitate, need to accumulate knowledge to a certain degree, in order to have a greater breakthrough. Haste makes waste, can not be too anxious, she can do, is to work hard every day, accumulate language knowledge, the time is up, the miracle will appear. Although she was not sure whether the miracle would really occur, she was willing to let herself make this dream.

Chapter 10: The Siren at Midnight

Once, while she was still asleep, she suddenly heard the harsh and urgent sound of the fire alarm. Her roommate immediately jumped out of bed, put on her pajamas, and asked Jianxin to get up as soon as possible. Jianxin wanted to put on her clothes and coat neatly, but she could not understand what her roommate was mumbling, but her body language seemed to let Jianxin stop dawdling and leave the room quickly. Jianxin also did not have time to dress neatly, casually put on a thick pajamas, ran out of the bedroom. She didn't know what was going on. Suddenly, in the middle of the night, there was a screechy fire alarm, and all the students, the life teachers, and the staff ran out bleary-eyed in their nightgowns, all walking in the same direction. Jianxin wondered in her heart what was going on. In any case, she could only run in one direction with the crowd. All the students in the school ran outside the building and headed straight for another modern house. The crescent moon still hung in the dark sky, and the air was cold and fresh. Jianxin looked around, her mind filled with doubts and a little anxiety. After a while, Jianxin followed the flow of people to a large lecture hall, the room was brightly lit, which was filled with students of all grades. There wasn't any space left, and the entire school was packed into the entire lecture theatre. The indoor heating is very full, although wearing pajamas, but still very comfortable, no cold at all. Jianxin just stood there like the other students. Before long, a team appeared in front of the lecture theatre, all dressed in professional fire uniforms. As soon as everyone arrived, the classroom was completely silent. A fireman came out and mumbled something. Everyone understood what the speaker was saying, except Jianxin. She didn't know what was going on in the middle of the night, but she looked at her watch and it was 4:00 in the morning. Usually she can get up at seven o 'clock, why suddenly there is a fire alarm in the middle of the night, and then everyone runs to this classroom like a trained team. Later, she realized the significance of this activity.

It turned out that in 1996, the school had a big fire due to carelessness, and the noble and elegant palace-like buildings were not spared in the fire. Many places had been burned down, and now the school lobby has been rebuilt. In order to prevent misfortune from happening again, the school trained professional fire teams and fire drills, so that students and teachers can be trained to escape from the building and flee to the shelter (this is the lecture theatre) in the event of an emergency fire. Jianxin later learned about the causes and consequences of this exercise, and could not help butthink that the school's activities were still very meaningful and practical. These exercises are not told to anyone, they are carried out by surprise, usually in the middle of the night, when everyone is fast asleep. When the man had announced something, everyone left in an orderly fashion, went back to their rooms, and went back to sleep until dawn.

Chapter 11: Painting Lesson

Day by day, Jianxin has been to school for two weeks, but only once through the phone with her parents, and that international long-distance chat takes only a few minutes. She misses her parents but can't get in touch with them. Her daily life is very simple, except for class review and meals. Although there are manyafter school activities such as golf, swimming, horse riding, rock climbing, etc., she does not seem to have much interest in participating in them, perhaps because of the language barrier, she does not know how to participate in those interest classes. All extracurricular activities in private schools are paid separately, and Jianxin is afraid of adding to her parents' financial burden, so she doesn't want to take any interest classes. Once, while walking in school, she met Lesk, a benevolent female teacher who was estimated to be about 50 years old. The teacher asked her kindly, "Do you like drawing?" Jianxin replied, "I like." Then, the female teacher took Jianxin to a painting classroom, there are a few students in the painting, the female teacher told Jianxin that she can find a white board, paint at will, there are a variety of watercolor paints. Jianxin understood, politely and a little shy to thank the teacher, then at will to draw on the whiteboard, other students from time to time to cast curious eyes to her. Instead of a very complicated picture in her mind, she drew a bright red flower in the center, with six petals, each of different sizes, not very consistent, and then used a large dark blue as the background color. Other students drew portraits, landscapes, and doodles, decorating whiteboards with random colors. After seeing Jianxin's painting, the teacher praised Jianxin's painting is very good, and the color is very good. Jianxin himself is not clear, what she painted is special, is a very ordinary painting, this level of primary school students can reach. In fact, Jianxin has been fond of painting since she was a child. She likes all beautiful things. The extracurricular activity she participated in in the second and third grade of primary school is painting class. But later because of the heavy schoolwork, she slowly stopped drawing. But inside, she loved bright, vibrant things. Talent also needs to be carefully cultivated, otherwise it will become more and more common, and eventually will not be discovered. Jianxin thinks that she is now in such a situation, although she likes painting very much, but because the day after tomorrow has not been well trained, so her current painting level is ordinary, not worth mentioning. But Lesk teacher's praise can not help but make her happy and surprised, being praised by others is certainly a happy thing; To her surprise, she could not understand why the teacher would praise such an ordinary painting. She found that although the students here are a little cold, not very warm and friendly to foreign students, and even a little picky, but the teachers here are very warm and polite. Both Herr May, who taught her painting and Lesk, who taught her German, were polite and patient, and never criticized students, but encouraged and praised them. Jianxin loves this feeling of being praised, which gives her confidence and motivation to move forward, and makes her appreciate her own advantages and self-worth. The teachers here are kind and friendly, and get along with the students, not very strict, let people be awe-inspiring, but more like a mentor, kind and friendly. Jianxin felt that the warm words were very charming, giving her strength, giving her confidence, giving her infinite warmth in this cold weather. From then on, if Jianxin had time, she would go to Lesk's studio to paint, and the teacher would give good comments on the paintings, whether good or bad, beautiful or ugly. There is no right or wrong in art, and everyone has a different definition of beauty. In the process of painting, the Jianxin is completely relaxed and enjoyed, which is a kind of free and spontaneous beauty.

Chapter 12: Experience the life of a German family

Easter is one of the most important religious festivals in Europe, commemorating the anniversary of Jesus' death on the cross. The school will have a week's holiday on Easter. As a rule, all residential students are not allowed to live on campus during the holidays and must go home or elsewhere. Almost all the students go home at Easter, ninety percent of them are German, and it's only an hour or two by train. International students are also mainly from European Union countries, and their return home is also very quick and convenient, which can be reached by train in a few hours or by plane in an hour or two. Jianxin from the far east, if in this week's holiday home, it is obviously impossible, long-distance plane to fly more than ten hours. Besides, she has only come to the new school for two or three weeks, and the international air tickets are expensive, so she cannot go home, and she is not allowed to live in school during the holidays, so where will she go? In fact, this problem does not need to be solved by herself, the school has found a solution for her.

One of the school secretaries, Frau Stein, takes her home for Easter. For Jianxin, such a humane arrangement is both reasonable and meaningful, it allows Jianxin to have a deeper understanding of the German family lifestyle, but also to solve the problem of accommodation during the holiday. Frau Stein's home in the small town at the foot of the hill, a short walk from the school, is a series of typical Bavarian bungalows, each made of wood, with a pointed roof and attic, and a separate garden in front of the house. The garden is full of flowers, lush shrubs and green plants, tall and tall trees, and some gardens have small European sculptures and fountains. The flowing sound gives the yard more vitality and aura, which is full of vitality, quiet and harmonious. Jianxin recalled her father's vivid description of the bungalows and gardens and lawns she had seen in North America, and she really experienced them here, and it was a similar scene. Usually in this small town, see not a few figures, will only see three or three two jogging people, or walking dogs, the whole environment is very quiet, quiet is incredible, this will let Jianxin can not help but compare the domestic noise and lively, is completely two different worlds, a completely different way of life.

  Frau Stein entered her home with a Jianxin, and what greeted her was a simple and very spacious living room. Jianxin followed Frau Stein behind, dare not wander casually. Despite weeks of studying German, Frau Stein could barely understand anything she said, only the most basic greetings. Frau Stein introduced her to anything, she could only pretend, nodded, and as for what it meant, she was completely clueless, just like a chicken with a duck. The house is so quiet that you can hear a needle drop. It has three floors and a large basement for food and groceries, as well as a guest room. Frau Stein took a brief tour of the entire house. There were three bedrooms upstairs and a loft on the third floor that had been turned into a home office. The layout was simple and elegant, the cleaning was spotless and very clean, and everything was in good order. It has always been said that Germans work rigorously and seriously, and this Jianxin has not been clearly confirmed, but the finishing technology is very clever. From the home environment can be seen, Germans pay attention to the sense of rules and order, there is no random items, things are put neatly, less and simple, the degree of cleanliness can be comparable to the standard of five-star hotel rooms. Frau Stein took Jianxin first to her room in the basement, next to the storage unit. The room layout is simple and comfortable, Jianxin put his suitcase in the room, and then a person quietly sitting in the room. In a moment, Frau Stein brought a pile of ironed bath towels and handed them to Jianxin, mumbling instructions, and Jianxin nodded as if she understood, so as not to be too embarrassed. Frau Stein is going to the kitchen to prepare dinner, and Jianxin does not know why, and then follows Frau Stein to the kitchen. The kitchen is well-stocked and very tidy. Jianxin wanted to help, but she didn't know what she could do. Watching Frau Stein remove all the dishes from the cabinet half a meter high, Jianxin did the same. It turned out to be a dishwasher, the first time in Jianxin's life to see a dishwasher. As recently as 2002, middle-class families in Germany had already used dishwashers, which was unheard of and never seen in China at that time. Frau Stein knew that the new student from China had only been here for a few weeks and did not understand German, so she did not know how to talk to Jianxin. The two of them were silent, and the house was strangely quiet.

After a while, the door opened and a tall, middle-aged man carrying a briefcase entered. Frau Stein walked slowly out of the kitchen and headed straight for the man. The two hugged and kissed each other. There are two teenagers behind the man, a boy and a girl, the boy is handsome, the girl is sweet. The boy and girl also hugged Frau Stein, looking very close and happy. Jianxin took a look at it and understood it all in her heart: this was Frau Stein's husband Herr Stein and her children, and the family greeting was full of ritual feeling. Frau Stein beamed as she introduced Jianxin to her family, who all shook her hands politely and kindly. When the family arrived, Frau Stein looked at the clock hanging on the wall and immediately went into the kitchen to prepare dinner without hesitation. Jianxin just stayed in the kitchen, watching Frau Stein busy, she could not help much. More than an hour later, when dinner was ready, Frau Stein called a few names, and the boy clunked down to the basement, where a few drinks and a bottle of red wine went upstairs a few moments later and placed them on the long table. A pot of fuchsia orchids was placed on the table, and some candles were lit, and everyone sat down at the table. Frau Stein then serves salads, pastas and more. Frau Stein also took off her apron and sat down at the table, where everyone said "Guten Appetite" and picked up their knives and forks. Outside the window under the white snow, the holy snow quietly falling in the sky, the family eating dinner and chatting, from time to time to look at the scenery outside the window, watching the falling snow. Jianxin concentrated on eating, they chat, almost a word can not understand, only know that they speak very gentle, low voice chat endless, as if there is no end to say, children and adults talk as close and natural as friends. Jianxin sat at the table, stretching her ears to listen carefully, trying to understand some of the content of their words, but it is a pity that they really do not understand anything, they speak very fast, Jianxin felt like a catfish, want to catch it, but quickly ran away without a trace, there is no time to react. Jianxin felt that the food was delicious, and the mood of snow floating outside the window was beautiful, but her heart was a little helpless and sour. She could not understand or speak, so she could only observe others' actions silently with her eyes. In the huge house, only the low voices of the family chatting and laughing appeared to be so quiet and peaceful. Jianxin is very wondering, how to learn German for several weeks or not effective, she has a good class and review every day, but also listen to additional recordings, read novels, actually still can not understand People's Daily communication, she needs to learn is too much. In this way, the family dinner for nearly two and a half hours, while eating and talking, for them is very comfortable, but for Jianxin, it is boring, more than two hours passed like two days, because she did not understand anything, can only sit so boring

When dinner was finally over, Frau Stein motioned to Jianxin to get some rest. It was getting late. Jianxin embarrassed to leave like this, ran into the kitchen, help clean up. Frau Stein felt that Jianxin was a guest and was embarrassed to send her to help clean up, so she matched her body language with short English with a German accent and told her to hurry to her room and rest. Jianxin is not forced, and this is her first time in a German family life, always some stiff and embarrassed, the host let her do what, then she did, this should be the best way, do not help, but also annoying. So she wisely left the kitchen and went to a guest room in the basement where she was to spend the night. When she had finished, she turned off the light, and the room was very quiet, strangely quiet, just as it had been in the living room before. The difference is that she is more comfortable now, because she is alone in the space, and does not need to pay attention to other people's expressions, and does not need to sit in the restaurant and listen to more than two hours of boring and incomprehensible German. She lay on the bed with her eyes open, there was no light in the room, she could not see her fingers, her mind was empty, she did not think about anything, and so she fell asleep quietly for a long time.

Wake up early in the morning, Jianxin feel refreshed, the room is still as quiet, she did not like too quiet, because she is used to the lively life in the country, accustomed to the noise, feel that it is more human fireworks gas, that life is interesting, full of vitality. Now she finds that in such a new country, every place seems to be very quiet and peaceful, there is no such crowds and heavy traffic, and the quiet life at the beginning makes her often fall into loneliness, makes her feel particularly inconvenient, and makes her think about life as often as a philosopher. But as time goes by, she will enjoy that quiet life more and more, and it will bring her peace and stability and more time to feel relaxed and joyful. When she finished washing, she climbed upstairs and saw that Frau Stein was already leisurely preparing breakfast. Breakfast is very rich, there are all kinds of cereal, bread, butter, bacon, jam, fried eggs, fruit and so on. In front of each position, a chocolate bunny shaped from gold wrapping paper was placed. When Jianxin sees Frau Stein busy, she greets him shyly and politely with "Guten Morgen (good morning) Frau Stein." When Frau Stein saw Jianxin, she smiled and said, "Guten Morgen." Hast du gut geschlafen (Good morning, did you sleep well)?" Jianxin understood the simplest German sentence and replied, "Ya. Danke (Yes. Thank you)." Afterward, she helped Frau Stein put the dishes neatly on the table. Not long after, Herr Stein and their children came sleepily down, greeted each other, and sat down at the table to eat breakfast. Outside the window is still under snowing, they are talking and laughing, leisurely eating breakfast, Jianxin is also beside, silently enjoying the delicious and nutritious milk cereal. Just like last night, she could not understand what the family was s talking, but she felt that the family was talking happily and harmoniously, which could be felt from the tone of voice and their expressions. The family had a good relationship, parents and children talked like friends, as if they were sitting together, and there were always many topics to discuss and exchange. But the family's warm family atmosphere makes Jianxin feel comfortable. This time she sat at the table for a long time, but she was getting used to the German way of enjoying life at a slow pace. After breakfast, everyone peeled off the wrapping paper of the golden rabbit and began to eat the chocolate with relish. Frau Stein points to the golden rabbit in front of Jianxin and treats Jianxin to eat. When breakfast is over, Frau Stein's daughter Nicole and son Alex start searching the living room for what Jianxin later realizes is an Easter egg hidden in the living room. Jianxin also joined the ranks of the hunt for eggs, three people in the living room like five or six years old children, innocent looking for eggs, when one of them found an egg, as found a treasure, excitedly called up, gradually all the eggs have been found out. The game is over, we still have some unfinished, find the egg that moment of satisfaction let her immerse in it for a long time, enjoy. Her inhibitions vanished with the Easter egg game, and she slowly became more generous. After the game, the snow has stopped and everything is quiet outside, and Frau Stein's two kids put on thick winter coats and go to the yard to play badminton. Jianxin looked at this scene, the heart is warm, that picture is how beautiful, between siblings in a warm family to grow together, accompany each other, play and chat together, is the most healing and warm things in the world. At this time, she will also think of her brother at home. There is a tacit understanding between her and her brother, the two of them quarrel from childhood to large, who does not let who, it seems that these two siblings do not get along harmoniously. She does not understand, may be the personality is different, all in all, she is very envious of such a nice sibling relationship, she and Jianyang is completely another model of getting along. But noisy back to noisy, she still very much miss her brother far away in the country, from small to big used to noisy, suddenly because of the reason of distance, no longer able to quarrel with his brother, she also felt some of the heart and lonely, she hopes that everything is OK with her brother.

Frau Stein and her husband have other family activities planned for Easter. On sunny days, they take their two children and Jianxin for a bike ride in the suburbs. Jianxin is the slowest rider and always trails behind them. But the family will patiently wait for Jianxin's heart until she catches up with them. With birds chirping and the endless Alps in the distance, Jianxin breathed in the fresh air and rode her bicycle behind the family, stopping and taking a detour when they came across the clear flowing stream, and she felt comfortable and calm, such a simple and healthy outdoor activity that she had never played with her family in her whole life. She remembers that when she was a child, her parents were very busy and did not have much time to accompany her, and her former life was more about study and playing with some friends. However, she deeply understands that because of the different national conditions and the great difference in the level of economic development, parents do not have so much leisure and time to accompany their children grow up, and they do not have so much energy to arrange family gatherings and activities.

Germans love and admire nature very much, so during the holidays, they will take their families to climb, hike or bike, such a holiday is relaxed and healthy, but also to enhance the cohesion and intimacy of the family. After the Germans have established a family, in addition to working hours, they will leave the rest of the free time to their families and themselves, almost very little social, they will focus most of their energy on their own things or families, so their life is simple and comfortable. However, China attaches great importance to interpersonal relationship, social communication and network resources, in order to develop their career or other factors, people will put most of their energy on work and social interaction, and will ignore the time to get along with their families. Many parents are separated by work, and their children are raised entirely by their mothers. Or because of economic pressures, parents need to leave their homes, go to work in other places, can only leave their children to grandparents to raise, such a situation is obviously not conducive to a child healthy and happy growth, but forced, people can only take this choice. It can be seen that abundant material basis is the most basic guarantee, if material is very scarce, how to talk about the spiritual world of abundance. In different countries, because of very different economic levels, middle-class families in developed capitalist countries pay more attention to the balance between work and family, and they will not sacrifice the precious time with their families in order to earn more wages. However, in developing countries, people are so eager to improve their material life that they have to sacrifice the time spent with their children growing up or the time spent together as a family.

  After about two hours of riding, they arrived at a beautiful and exquisite village, a small street filled with all kinds of stalls selling candles, and selling handicrafts, and a wide variety of cheese stalls, and even some stalls will show pedestrians the process of baking bread in medieval times. Strollers dressed in medieval costumes and accessories, strolling through this market will make people feel like stepping back in time to the old European Middle Ages. Jianxin looked at the market in front of her, feeling particularly new, all this is a new experience for her. Visitors leisurely pace in the market, listening here, looking there, and then you can taste freshly baked delicious bread, it is very pleasant. Janxin followed Frau Stein's family, pushing a bicycle, and strolled among them, and it wasn't long before they came to an old house. The old house has a total of two floors, the space is a little small and cramped. After Frau Stein paid the 2-euro entrance fee without a second thought, the family took Jianxin on a tour. Jianxin entered the room and felt that the roof was too low, only about 1.7m high, and every visitor needed to keep his head down and his back hunched to move around the room. Inside the decoration is very simple, almost no decent furniture and decorations, only a very simple kitchen or a few wooden chairs, the second floor is the bedroom, the roof is surprisingly low, people in the inside feel some oppression. After the tour, Jianxin asked Frau Stein: What is this old house, the roof is so low. Frau Stein explained in English and German: "This is the house of ordinary people in the Middle Ages. A few hundred years ago, the height of Europeans was not very high, only about 1.5 meters, unlike today's people, who grow so tall and tall." Jianxin thought to herself that this was so, no wonder the roof was built so low, because ancient Europeans were also short and did not always grow so tall. Human beings have evolved over time and with the development of human civilization. After visiting the market, Jianxin followed Frau Stein and his family to ride their bicycles home, and the whole Easter holiday passed in such a leisurely rhythm. On the first day of school, Frau Stein drove Jianxin to school, hugged her a few times, and waved goodbye. After this Easter, Jianxin has a general understanding of the life style of German families. She thinks that the arrangement of the school is very good and very humane. It not only helps her solve the problem that she cannot go back to China during the holiday, but also gives her more opportunities to live with local people and understand German culture, and she no longer feels so lonely.

Chapter 13: The First friend she made in German class

At school, Jianxin had almost no friends, and when she didn't go to German class, she stayed alone. She constantly reviewed the content of German class, and dared not drop a bit of homework. As time went by, she found that she had accumulated more and more German words and phrases. From the second month, Herr May stopped giving her German lessons in English, saying: "From today on, I will give you German lessons in German, only German, no other languages, because it is very important for you to learn a language." Instead of trying to translate from one language to another, you should learn German as your native language. When each of us is learning our mother tongue, we never think about translating our mother tongue into other languages, right? If you want to learn German well, remember that it is best not to translate from another language, but to explain German directly in German. Jianxin, start reading the text now." Jianxin opened the textbook and read it word by word, during which some pronunciation was not very accurate, and the teacher would help her correct. After reading, Herr May said to Jianxin, "Very well, you read much better now than when you started." Keep trying and slowly you will understand more and more German." Listening to Herr May, she was surprised to find that she understood most of what Herr May had just slowed down to say in German. At this moment, she feels an unprecedented sense of satisfaction and achievement. Although she has only been in Germany for one month, she can roughly understand the German teacher's words since she set foot on this land and knew nothing about German. Unconsciously, she already feels her own progress. She believes that everything will get better gradually, and she also believes that she will study and accumulate hard on the ground, and slowly she will master this esoteric and difficult language.

Originally, Jianxin's German lessons were one-on-one, because the other international students were not at the same pace as her, and they came to the school already had a German foundation. Herr May saw that her German was improving very quickly during this period, so she was placed in a small class of three, which could enhance the interaction and communication among the students. Once, when Jianxin went to German class, she saw a student with an Asian face in the class. Her name was Rita. She was thin and small, with delicate features and healthy light brown skin. When Jianxin saw Asian faces, she felt very close to them, because in addition to Huang Xiaodan and her coming from China, the entire school was almost all Europeans and very few Africans and Middle Easterners. There is also a female student from Poland, Eastern Europe, fair skin, big eyes, tall nose bridge, beautiful, and other students in the school look similar. Herr May asked each student to give a brief introduction in German during the class and then proceeded to teach three students. According to his class habit, every day he would ask the students to read the German article aloud, correct the students' pronunciation and explain the meaning of the article, and then talk about some relevant German grammar. However, the focus of German class is reading, speaking and listening, and the proportion of grammar learning is less. Everyone listens attentively, and when it comes to a topic, they discuss it actively, instead of sitting silently in class and listening to the teacher. This makes Jianxin often compare with the previous way of teaching in China: when she was in junior high school or high school in China, students' class participation was not high, most of them were teachers who talked incessantly in class, students took notes without stopping, and basically there were few students who spoke enthusiastically. What the teacher said, no students to question or to discuss eagerly, more is to accept and record. Now the teaching mode here is completely different, in the class, people will pay more attention to oral expression ability, the content of the teacher can also be questioned whether the correct or not, there are often fierce discussions among students in the class, the teacher will give the initiative of the class to the students, and he will step back into the background. Because there are few students, the desks and chairs placed in the spacious classroom are not unchanged and compact, but very casual, can be placed into a square, can also be placed into a large circle. All in all, the arrangement of desks and chairs in the classroom is very diverse and eclectic. Education in China focuses on imparting knowledge, discipline and students' sense of community; Western education focuses on the development of innovation and personalized education, emphasizing the development of individual advantages, and never emphasizing the need for the ego to obey the big ego (the big ego refers to the class group). Oriental culture teaches people to learn to be low-key, forbearance and implicit, not publicity, individual obedience to the collective. On the contrary, Western culture advocates freedom, democracy and personal development, and emphasizes personality education and cultivation. Jianxin used to accept Eastern ideas, and now she begins to accept Western culture. She grows up day by day in the collision and intersection of these two cultures. Her way of thinking and behavior is neither like a traditional Chinese nor like a typical Westerner, but a combination of the two. After the German class, Jianxin initiatively and politely greeted the Indonesian girl Rita, who responded generously and politely to Jianxin. Since then, the two people have become friends without talking, this is Jianxin came to this new country to make the first good friend, she is very happy and satisfied. Because her desire to find a good friend has finally come true, she is no longer alone, far from her parents and relatives, the most need for friendship. Both of them are not fluent in German, but ordinary communication is no problem, if you want to express a little complex meaning, can not find the right words to express, you can also use body language, and they often take German classes together, get along together for a long time, there will be a feeling of understanding, each other know what the other wants to say. Although she still spoke German only weakly, Jianxin found that since she made Rita a good friend, she had more opportunities to speak German, and she said whatever came to her mind regardless of whether the sentence pattern was correct or not. So did Rita. Jianxin felt that they were all foreigners anyway, and foreigners didn't need to laugh at the German spoken by foreigners, but if Jianxin talked to Germans, she would become very cautious. Before expressing, she meticulously organizes the language in her mind and then speaks it out, a process that is slow, which is why she can't make German friends, because they don't have much patience to listen to her intermittent German sentences. Germans speak very fast, listen to them easily, almost can not catch the core content, can only understand a few greetings and commonly used words. why can she understand Herr May's german ?because the teacher deliberately slowed down the speed of speaking, one word and one sentence clearly expressed in simple sentences. The road of learning German is still long and hard, which requires unremitting efforts and accumulation, but also requires very patience and perseverance. Now, Jianxin seems to have found a like-minded, and her similar situation of friends, make so happy, perhaps are from Asia, the kind of magnetic field will attract each other.

  Once, after a German class, they agreed to go shopping together at the only supermarket chain in town. Since the last time Huang Xiaodan took Jianxin to visit this supermarket, she has not come again, because of the language barrier, can not understand what is written on each item, or she may not find that she needs to buy anything, her mother has prepared all the daily necessities for her before going abroad. Although the town is quiet and beautiful, but it is very small, about 10 minutes to walk from the street to the end of the street, the two of them do not know what to do after class, they go to the supermarket to look for what need to buy. There were very few customers in the supermarket, just a few people here and there, and after a while these customers also checked out and left. Jianxin and Rita walked around and picked out a toothpaste or two and a day cream before they went to the checkout counter to pay. At the cashier's desk sat a short, chubby woman with golden hair who asked in a serious but contemptuous tone, "Do you have your passport? Do you have passports? Show me)." Rita and Jianxin were both surprised and asked, "Why do you need our passport?" It turned out that when the two of them were shopping for things, Jianxin felt that there was a pair of unfriendly and distrustful eyes staring at the two of them, not knowing what they were looking at. Feeling strangely uncomfortable and uncomfortable with this kind of staring, Jianxin later told Rita, "Let's go pay, we don't need anything else." Sure enough, when they arrived at the cashier's desk, the fat woman challenged them to check their passports. Jianxin wondered why she didn't check the other guests' credentials instead of just asking them. "I didn't bring my passport with me," Jianxin replied in a stern voice. The fat woman intensified her efforts and said solemnly and coldly: "Please open you bag, I want to check your bag, because I see you have stolen a shampoo in your shopping bag, I need to check because I saw you sneaking a bottle of shampoo in your bag. " Jianxin and Rita understood what she meant, and without a word, The fat cashier searched for the stolen shampoo for a long time, but no luck, and finally returned the bags to Jianxin. Jianxin was very angry and wanted argue with the fat salesperson, but she did not know how to use accurate German expression, and finally could only eat a dumb loss, and Rita silently left. At this time, the two of them discussed: "This woman has deep racial discrimination, and when she saw that the two of them looked Asian faces, she deliberately made it difficult for them, and thought that Asian people were not educated." This fat woman is really bad. She is not highly educated, but she looks at people with prejudice and colored glasses and looks down on Asians." This was the first time that Jianxin felt the local people's rejection and psychological aversion to foreign races. She wanted to change their prejudice, but she knew that she was powerless to do anything about it. This prejudice of such people was caused by their growing environment and narrow cognition.

After all, it is rare for Jianxin to encounter such a situation. Most of the time, she thinks the locals are very polite and friendly. There is only one school supply store in the town, which is filled with a wide range of stationery, organizer, greeting cards and so on. The owner is a very approachable and amiable old man. He has a gray beard, hair is also fluffy curls, every time to see Jianxin to the store to pick stationery, will be very friendly and cordial greeting her: "willkommen." Wie geht es dir? my Liebling Welcome. How are you these days? my dear)." Seeing the shopkeeper's smiling face and hearing such warm words, Jianxin would reply very politely: "es geht mir gut." Vielen Dank: I'm fine. Thank you very much)." Then she started to pick out what she needed. Sometimes, the owner will often come to see if Jianxin has found what she wants. The owner treats customers with great dedication and enthusiasm, a simple step into this stationery shop, as if by a warm and friendly airflow wrapped, her heart is warm.

Next to the stationery shop is a bakery with a window full of mouth-watering cakes, puddings, handmade chocolates and breads. Every time Jianxin passed this shop, she could not help but take a look at the exquisite and delicious pastries in the bakery. She wanted to try all the varieties, but she would not do that, but the pastries were so exquisite that she could not help but stimulate her desire for food. She would occasionally buy some to eat, but not too much at a time, mainly because she did not want to spend her pocket money, because she felt that the school meals were already satisfactory and included in the cost of her accommodation, so there was no need to spend money on outside pastries.

With Rita, a good friend from Indonesia, Jianxin's life has been enriched. She no longer stays alone in her room after class to learn German. Sometimes they met to chat and walk in the school's south garden. The scenery of the South garden is pleasant, with green lawns, tall and straight trees, exquisite palatial buildings, simple and solid medieval castles, and a small church forming a beautiful picture. The two of them would often stand in an open field in the middle of the South Garden, looking out over the Alps in the distance, with a panoramic view of the whole town below. Rita stroked her hair and said slowly, "The German course in the international class at this school is quite expensive. I'm taking one German course and I'm not taking any other courses." Jianxin slowly answered, "Me too, I was going to be in grade 11 (equivalent to the domestic high school), but because the language knowledgeis too weak, I can't understand the class in grade 11, and I can't keep up with the progress, so now I can only take German classes first, and other courses can't be taken." German is ." Rita agreed, "Well, when you come to a strange country, you must learn the language well as soon as possible, so that you can better integrate into the life here, otherwise you will feel very lonely." Rita continued, "I'm not a student here, I'm just here to learn the language, and my employer is paying for my german class. I work as a housekeeper in a family in this town, and my employer is a local dentist who, in addition to paying me some salary, also helps me pay for this German course. After a month or two, I may go back to my hometown. Next time I'll invite you to the house of my employer." Jianxin was surprised to hear this. She always thought Rita was also a foreign student in this school, and she had to take German lessons first. Hearing Rita say that she was going to go back to Indonesia in a few months, Jianxin felt sad and reluctant to give up. Rita was the only friend she had here. They talked about everything and got along with each other easily and tacit. They are from the distant East, similar culture, and met in a foreign country, so they can comfort and encourage each other, but also can feel the difficulty and loneliness of foreign life. Jianxin felt that since she met Rita and established a pure and beautiful friendship with her, she was no longer fighting alone. In her lonely camp, she had a partner to face difficulties and unknowns with her, to take care of each other and encourage each other. Even if the problem could not be solved, it was also very good to have a leisurely chat, which was better than staying alone in the room. Practice speaking to yourself. Jianxin asked sadly, "Rita, do you have to leave? Can you think of some other way to stay?" Rita shook her head and firmly replied, "My employment contract is about to expire. I signed it with an agency that works overseas before I left the country. It's almost impossible for me to stay. I can't study here like you, because I don't have parents to support me financially. Our family is very ordinary, there is no such economic conditions. be abroad for so long, I also miss everything back home. Although the environment here is beautiful and the economy is highly developed, I always feel that I don't belong here, maybe because of the cultural difference between the East and the West, or maybe I don't know how to get along with the people here. Last time we were in the supermarket, the fat cashier treated us like that, in fact, my heart was also a little hurt, they always look at us Asians with prejudice, thinking that our country is backward, they were born in a highly developed capitalist country, so they have a sense of superiority and appear very proud.

Of course, most people here are polite and polite, but I feel that deep down they are racist towards Asians. But that is not the main reason why I want to leave, the fundamental reason is that my contract is up and I have to leave. Being alone in this distant country, away from family and friends, is also a very difficult thing, I miss my family. Although the economic conditions there are not comparable to here, I still feel a very strong human touch in my hometown. Don't you think these Germans are cold? Is it very distant?" Jianxin listened to Rita and stopped trying to keep her, because it was a fact of life that Rita knew what she wanted best. She replied: "I understand you very much, I sometimes have similar ideas, feel that I do not belong here, the language is not good, although the hardware environment of the school is very good, but I am still very lonely , because I can not communicate with the students here normally, and many students in this school do reflect a sense of superiority full, very proud look, let people have a sense of distance, dare not approach." You feel like you're on the outside here, and it's hard to fit in. But most people are still good, the last encounter that thing is also a case, can not be generalized. Let's focus on the bright side. There must be a big cultural difference between East and West. It is really not easy for us to integrate the Oriental cultures we have been taught since childhood into the western society. It takes time. Last Easter, I went to Frau Stein's house for a few days, and I felt that their family was very nice. Although I could not understand what they talked about, I felt that they were sincere and friendly. It's very interesting. Here, we can broaden our horizons and learn different traditions and cultures, not just the familiar culture, which I think is very good. Of course, if you can't renew your contract for financial reasons, or if you're really homesick, I understand. Although I am sorry to see you leave in a few months, I still wish you well and hope you take care of yourself. We need to record our contact information so we can keep in touch later." As soon as Jianxin's voice stopped, the two friends hugged each other and smiled at each other.

After a while, Rita did invite Jianxin to go to her hired master's house. It was an overcast day. After German lessons in the afternoon, Jianxin and Rita took the shortest path down the hill and headed for town. When she reached the town, she walked about five minutes, turned a corner and reached the front door of her employer. Rita opened the door and warmly welcomed Jianxin in. At the moment, the employers and they have not gone home, the house is quiet and clean, and it is strangely quiet. Jianxin felt a little strange in her heart, embarrassed to come to Rita's hired master's home, because it was not the master's invitation, Rita invited it. She double-checked and asked Rita if it would be uncomfortable for her employer to do so. Rita comforted Jianxin by saying, "I've already asked my employer if I can bring my friends over and say you're a student at Schloss Neubeuern (the name of the boarding school: Sinbo Palace). They were very welcoming, no problem at all. They'll be home from work soon. You'll see them. please sit here for a while while I do some housework and prepare dinner." Jianxin asked politely, "Can I help you?" Rita simply replied, "You're welcome, you're a guest, I invite you to visit, there's no reason for you to do housework." Then she went down to the basement, got some vegetables and went into the kitchen. When Jianxin arrived at the warm and comfortable living room, she found a seat and sat down. She looked out of the window and saw people coming and going in twos and threes. It was getting dark and the street lamp was coming on at the corner. Before long, the kitchen wafted a smell, not the strong cheesy smell of Western food, but something like Asian food. Jianxin's stomach rumbled, come to Germany for so long, she has not eaten Chinese food for a long time, eat at school are western food, not steak, is a variety of pasta, or beef stew, or a variety of pies, salads, although she loves Western food, but she also miss the food at home. Rita's Indonesian cooking reminds her of Chinese food. Indonesian food and Chinese food are not identical, but there are some similarities. It was not long before the door opened and two amiable and elegant old couples entered. The old lady took the old man by the arm and came in, talking and laughing. They saw a strange young Asian girl sitting in the living room with a surprised look on her face and were about to ask her who she was. Rita had already walked out of the kitchen and greeted the two elderly couples, saying, "Hello, Sir And madam, this is my friend Jianxin, who goes to the private school in the mountains, and I asked you if I could invite my friend over to play." You allowed it." Then the old couple, remembering this with a pat on the head, walked straight up to Jianxin, shook her hand politely, and said, "Guten Tag." Herzlich willkommen (Hello. Warm welcome)." Jianxin answered them shyly and politely with a smile on her face. When dinner was ready, Rita carried the dishes to the table, arranged the forks and knives neatly, turned the room to a soft, dim, warm light, then lit the candles on the table and said to her employer, "Sir And Madam, dinner is ready." The employer warmly beckoned Jianxin to sit down at the table and join them for dinner. At first, Jianxin felt a little embarrassed, because after all, it was the first time to meet, and not the employer's guest, but the old couple's kind face, the sense of restraint eased a little, she respectfully obeyed, picked up a knife and fork, and slowly ate the Indonesian food cooked by Rita. Indonesian food and Chinese food is still different, with more spices, a little spicy, Jianxin a little used to eat, because she never eat spicy, but the employer ate with relish, very enjoy the look. Rita finished her work in the kitchen and sat down at the table to eat her dinner. In between, the old couple would ask Rita something, and the two would chat in whispers. They asked Jianxin if she was adjusting to life at the new school, and Jianxin answered generously, "OK, I'm adjusting, but I just miss my family." Some questions asked by the old couple, Jianxin also seems not to understand, came only 2 months, German is indeed not fluent, only the most simple basic dialogue. Dinner ended at a leisurely pace. Jianxin feel that Europeans will enjoy life too, the old husband and wife eat are so emotional, the atmosphere is so romantic, domestic meals are like war, where there is such a large period of free time to use at the table, a family dinner takes about 20 minutes. Europeans can leisurely eat for an hour or two, although the dishes are not much, but also drink some wine in the middle, after the exquisite delicious dessert, chat, slowly taste, very comfortable. Jianxin glanced at her watch. It was already 7:30 p.m., it was so dark outside the window that she could barely see her fingers, and dinner was over. She said goodbye to the old couple and Rita, saying, "Thank you for the invitation and the delicious dinner. The old couple and Rita said sincerely, "Nice to meet you, Jianxin. You are welcome to visit us again." Jianxin replied, "Thank you. Thank you very much." Rita walked Jianxin to the door and asked, "Are you okay going back to school alone? It's so dark." Jianxin answered, "Of course, I will go back by myself." You should go home. We'll see each other in class. By the way, I need your phone number. Please leave me your home number in Indonesia next time. We can contact you again when you return to China. If you have an email, that's great. We can also correspond." Rita replied, "OK. I'll give it to you next time." Then, Jianxin left. Along the path up the mountain, step by step towards the palace-like school halfway up the mountain, walked for about 20 minutes, and smoothly arrived. Then she went into her bedroom and began to study German in earnest and review her lessons. The roommate has not returned to the bedroom yet, she almost disappeared for a whole day When Jianxin was reviewing her lessons in her room, she often heard a girl's racket outside the door, or loud pop songs from other rooms. These girls can not quietly stay in their own room at night to study, there are always evening activities, or they simply sit on the sofa in the activity room to watch TV .some girls suddenly want to eat cake, will bake a chocolate cake in the oven in the activity room to meet their taste buds. Evening self-study is usually carried out in their own bedroom, the time is 7:00-8:30 PM. But Jianxin did not know for a long time that the school also had evening self-study, and the teacher did not come to check every time, and the students were not carefully reviewing their lessons in the room, only occasionally spot-checking. The atmosphere of study here is very relaxed, and it is completely different from the strict and militarized curriculum in China. In this school, in addition to classes every day, after school at 3:30 in the afternoon, the time is arranged by themselves, you can participate in a variety of interest classes, you can also go to the town to buy something, or study in the room, you can also go to the town with friends in the small restaurant to chat and drink some drinks.

Chapter 14: Study hard

Although there is no strict control, Jianxin will definitely study in the evening, and will study until 12 o 'clock every day. She knew she would have to work harder and be more diligent in order to adapt to the pace of learning at her new school. German is the mother tongue for the students here, and they are already familiar with the mother tongue, but for Jianxin, the language is very difficult, she needs to do her best to master German in the shortest time, and then she can smoothly enter the 11th grade, like other German students in the high school. After three years, take the Abitur (high school Certificate examination) in Bavaria, Germany. Every time she thinks about this goal, she feels a lot of pressure, and she often questions whether she can really get into a German university. She has given up the opportunity to take a college exam in China, and now she starts everything from scratch, is really burned out, and there is no way back. Although she does not know whether everything will really be as she wishes, nor can she predict whether she will be admitted to a German university, she will often tell herself that since she has chosen, she must go on, no matter how hard the road is and how much effort is required. The road is chosen by herself, there is nothing to regret, and it is not easy to give up. "I will work hard to live every day. There is no guarantee that I can successfully achieve my goal in the future, but at least I will work hard every day So she stayed up late every night studying German, reading German articles, looking up unfamiliar words and taking notes. In order to master German faster, will also buy thick German novels, each page of content, need to look into dictionary for 4 to 5 hours in order to understand the meaning of words, because the unfamiliar words are too many, as many as the stars in the sky, countless. The noise and laughter of the girls outside the room did not affect her concentration at all. She needed to concentrate on her study, every day, day after day, year after year, or she would never have mastered German well in a short time. Her inborn character, self-discipline and ambition are the driving force for her continuous efforts, while persistence and perseverance are the best help for her study. She isolates herself from all the interference and noise of the outside world and immeres herself in the world of hard study. Her good learning habits are all due to the strict and competitive learning environment in China before she went abroad. In the school she studied in before going abroad, the performance is very important, ranking is common, coupled with the large number of students, so the fierce competition is self-evident. Especially in the key high school she studied later, every student was so self-disciplined and motivated, because they were all the top students in the middle school, and all the top students were arranged in the class group of the key high school, you can imagine how strong the learning atmosphere was. Jianxin has experienced these harsh and hard learning, so even without outside discipline, she has been very adapted to the intense pace of learning. There is no road in life in vain, and there is no sweat in vain, she always believes that heaven rewards the diligent, but also believes that the journey of a thousand miles begins with a single step, so only hard and practical, every day to make good use of extracurricular time, she will step by step closer to the goal, but also more and more adapt to the new environment. She told herself that she did not allow repeated hesitation, helplessness or questioning her ability, because these sad and pessimistic emotions are useless, will only make people hesitate, add trouble, she needs to believe in themselves, recognize themselves, have a goal immediately put into action. Every time she began to doubt whether she could really go to college, she would write in her notebook again and again such words: "You must be able to believe in yourself; Do one's best; Plum blossom fragrance from the bitter cold, pay will be rewarded and other aphorisms to encourage themselves, comfort themselves." She can not get the encouragement and recognition of the outside world for the time being, and can only seek within, and find the strength to overcome difficulties and overcome psychological wavering and cowardice through her own encouragement. She is really very hard and persistent, only to get the applause in the future, during the hard process only she is the most clear.

  Jianxin has been in this new country for two or three months, but there is little contact with her parents. She misses her family, but because of poor communication, she and her parents only talk on the phone once a week. Parents will make international calls to the school secretary's office, will ask Jianxin if everything is OK in school, to take good care of themselves. Jianxin never told her parents about the confusion they encountered and the deep sense of loneliness and homesickness she experienced on the phone, but would comfort them and reassure them that everything was OK. Each call lasted only three to four minutes, and then the parents eagerly told Jianxin, "The phone bill is too expensive, we can't talk for too long, let's talk another time." Although Jianxin wanted to talk to her parents more about the school or what she had seen, but because her parents mentioned this , she was also embarrassed to talk to her parents for a long time, and did not want her parents to bear the high cost of international phone calls. In 2002, smartphones were not yet available, and Jianxin had no laptops or devices, so she kept in touch with her parents by making short international calls once a week. Jianxin's parents miss her, too, but they are relieved and relieved that they have a son by their side. But even with such meticulous savings in phone bills, the monthly international long-distance phone charges are surprisingly high, reaching thousands of yuan a month. At that time, students studying abroad and far away from the family contact is so inconvenient, so they have to endure more loneliness and sense of discomfort, learning pressure and mental loneliness can only be borne by a person. But Jianxin always said to herself: "You are very lucky, you don't have to consider the financial pressure, you don't have to worry about tuition, you just need to work hard to do well in your studies, and then you need to adapt to everything here as soon as possible. Many people who study abroad can only work and study, and they have a harder time. What a pain you have. Everything is difficult at the beginning, although I am not used to this new environmentnow, I feel that learning German is a long and boring process, and I have few friends at school, but it will gradually get better. Don't always think that you have to find a good friend quickly, you can't rush to find a friend, just go with the flow, if you can find it" But sometimes, Jianxin will be a little worry, she will worry about the tuition, she is not sure if her parents have enough economic support to afford her for so many years. Parents also bear a lot of risk in running the company. The market fluctuates and the market varies from year to year, which will directly affect their earnings. Jianxin's parents would never disclose the company's business or financial situation to their children, and they may feel that this is a matter for adults to consider, and there is no need to talk about it with their young children. Moreover, Jianxin's parents are diligent and thrifty, but also educate their children not to spend money in vain, and money needs to be spent on the knife edge, which has formed the good habit of Jianxin and her brother Jianyang not to be extravagant and arrogant. This time, her parents spent so much money to send her abroad to study, she secretly determined that she would never let the money spent by her parents go down the drain, she must not live up to her parents' expectations, and will do her best to study hard and be admitted to a good university.

Chapter 15: Candle light dinner

The school's extracurricular activities are varied and full of ritual. I remember that once, Jianxin saw that the palace hall and the dining hall were arranged in a very stylish and high-level atmosphere, as if there were some major banquet to be held. A row of students in school uniforms sat at the entrance of the restaurant. They were promoting something and talking about something. More and more students, teachers and some parents gathered in the hall. The parents were elegantly dressed, men in suits and ties, women in elaborate suits or elegant evening gowns, signing papers at a long table in the hall, or chatting happily with champagne in hand. When Jianxin saw this scene, she did not know what important activities were held in the school. Later, she asked the students who sat at the long table to do volunteer work. Only then did she know that this was a candlelight dinner organized by the school every six months, inviting the students and parents of the whole school to dress up and attend the dinner. it was the first time for her to see such a formal banquet and such a grand dress, dress up bright and extraordinary temperament of the crowd. She was dressed so plain and without makeup, which was incompatible with this group of elegantly dressed people and this elegant atmosphere.

While she was immersed in it, the old kitchen lady, who knew her well, saw her and asked with concern and enthusiasm, "Hallo, wie geht's dir? das ist unser candle light dinner. Du sollst eine Schoene Kleidung tragen (Hi, how are you? It's a candle light dinner at school and you need to wear a nice evening dress)."

Jianxin understood what the old lady said, said thank you, and then ran all the way back to her room. On the way back to the room, she saw that many students had been elaborately dressing themselves, making up, curling their hair with curling irons, and trying on gorgeous and elegant long dresses. Each girl wanted to make herself charming and stunning at the candlelight dinner, so they were very invested in dressing themselves, working on themselves, and appearing enthusiastic, lively and unrestrained. Jianxin understand that every young girl is particularly concerned about their appearance, hope that they look beautiful, at that time is just the beginning of love, so the appearance is particularly concerned.

Jianxin is also concerned about her appearance, especially her face, and does not care much about her body, because she has not been obese or too thin since she was a child. In general, she is quite symmetrical, but when she was in high school in China, she occasionally was not particularly satisfied with her height. She was just 6 '6 "and wished she was 5 centimetres taller. That would be perfect for her. But later, after the development of the sixth grade of primary school, the body no longer quickly jumped up, the whole junior high school grew 2 centimeters, and the height of the high school basically no breakthrough. She is somewhat concerned about height, but also from the junior high school years. At that time, she had a inseparable, very good friend named Qin Hua, in the first day of the two people are basically almost high, but by the third year Qin Hua's height has jumped to 1 meter 68, she became one of the tallest girls in the class. When Qin Hua and Jianxin stood together, her friend would sometimes jokingly say, "Jianxin, why don't you grow up? You see, we were about the same height at the beginning, and now I am a head taller than you." her friend is not intentional, the listener is sensitive , although Jianxin know friends are not sarcastic her, just casually say it, but listen to still some mind, jianxin will have some regrets, feel that she needs to be more taller .In fact, she is not short in china , belong to the average level , but the friend's teasing language will stimulate her a little, so for a while she also put in shoes to promote growth insoles. She heard an AD on a radio show about height increases and saved her pocket money to buy it. She wasn't sure how it would work, but listening to the instructions and introduction in the AD, she thought it would be useful, so she bought it and tried it. When it comes to the face, large round eyes, long eyelashes, nose is not very high, but also OK, lips are a little thick, face round, there is baby fat, it seems childish. But from the beginning of the second day, the correct and atmospheric features were completely covered by the dense and annoying acne. Acne was a problem that plagued her for many years until she reached high school and came to Germany to study. She is very concerned about her face, but sometimes because there are too many acne in the "T" part of the face, she does not dare to look in the mirror often, and does not dare to see the face full of acne often. she find confidence and a sense of self-worth in the study , in order to feel that she is excellent and outstanding, because she has been a student with excellent grades since childhood. So even from the beginning of the second year, the face suddenly grew a lot of acne, the students in the class will not laugh at her or fool her, because she has very good grades and is one of the best students in her previous school in china. In Chinese schools, good looks are not the only way to make a student feel superior or appreciated by others; excellent academic performance clearly goes a long way. In this new school, she is unable to find self-confidence and sense of value from her studies. Because of the language barrier, she has not officially entered the 11th grade, but continues to learn German from Herr May in the International Department. She is also full of a little insecurity about her future. Although she will encourage and comfort herself over and over again, this sense of unease and uncertainty will accompany her sometimes, especially when she has not mastered the language well and has not shown an advantage in learning. And the learning atmosphere here is not so strong and strict as in China. The school often holds a variety of activities to exercise students' ability in other aspects and broaden their international horizon and cognition. Academic performance is not the only criterion to judge a student. Jianxin feels that the students here are mature and lively, and the domestic students who study seriously and respectfully are completely two different styles. Students here are interested in all kinds of hobbies and activities, and both boys and girls are very concerned about their appearance and try their best to look handsome, sweet or sexy. Today, as she walked down the hallway on her way to her room, she was both excited and helpless when she saw every girl doing her best to dress up, wearing elegant dresses and perfect makeup, and looking up and down the hallway in front of the full-length mirror. Excited to see such a scene in reality for the first time, it is almost like the scene of a high-level dinner in the European and American movies; What is lost and helpless is that she does not know how to dress herself, she never knows how to put on makeup, and she does not have a decent evening dress to attend the candle light dinner tonight. She stops and starts, observing the girls who are interested in making themselves beautiful, wearing beautiful clothes, playing with their faces, posing in a variety of playful and lively postures, she feels that she is really very silly, out of place, how she does not have a girl's sense of liveliness, and appears so old and restrained. Without much thought, she walked through the long corridor and returned to her room after seven or eight doors. Seeing that her roommate had already made herself up in her room, she said hello to her roommate, and then began to look in the closet for a dress, but could not find anything suitable for the dinner party because her mother had not prepared it for her. her mother did not know that such activities were available at the new school and that she needed to buy her daughter an evening dress. There was nothing she could do but wear a summer dress for everyday occasions, and as for make-up, she really had no idea. In those days (mid-1990s to 2001), housewives or girls in their hometown never wore makeup, they were plain and very rustic. At her former high school in China, she had to get up at 5:30 every day, and then only 15 minutes to brush her teeth, wash her face, dress and make the quilt, so students didn't have time to dress up. Everyone washed their faces, applied face cream, tied their ponytails (many female students cut their hair short to save time in the morning), and hurried to the classroom for morning reading. Recalling this experience, Jianxin felt it was too incredible, half a year ago in the domestic high school, her study life is so intense, every student is riveting hard work, the most important thing in the world is to study, admitted to the domestic key university, what play games or girls dress up is simply impossible. Now, in this school at the foot of the Alps, the students are almost all Europeans. She is the second Chinese besides Huang Xiaodan. Students here no longer only pay attention to study, but put a lot of energy and time on extracurricular activities and various social activities organized by the school, so they can have flexible and ample time to do other things besides study. She felt the wonder of the world, in different places in the world, in different environments, people's lifestyles are completely different, people's focus and concerns are completely different, there can be this way of living, there is that way of living...

She was thinking about how to make up and dress up herself, she did not have any makeup tools, and did not know how to use them, and her roommates were only concerned about themselves, and did not care about Jianxin's embarrassing situation at the moment. Just as she was worrying, she heard a knock on the door. She opened the door and saw a pretty, tall, thin girl standing at her door. She had large black eyes, a high nose, a small and delicate face, and shiny black hair that was curly and fluffy, and looked more like someone from the Middle East or Xinjiang than a traditional European. Her sweet smile melted Jianxin's bewildered heart, and the girl called herself, "hallo, mein Name ist Lily." Kann ich herein kommen (Hello, my name is Lily, may I come in)?" Jianxin let Lily into the room, Lily also politely greet Jianxin's roommate, after which Lily asks Jianxin: "Weisst du, wie man auf das wichtige Abend vorbereitet (do you know how to prepare for this important dinner party)?" Although Jianxin didn't understand all the daily conversations after two or three months, she did understand Lily's questions, and her language is improving day by day. Jianxin shook her head, wondering why Lily would come to her, she and Lily are not familiar at all. Lily gushed, "I am from Iran, I have been in this school for 2 years, and now I am familiar with everything here. When I first got here, it was pretty much like you, too, but I got through it. Now I have made some very good friends here. I have two best friends, they are in the same class with me, one is a girl from Singapore named Anna, and the other is a girl from China named Huang Xiaodan. The three of us came to this school at about the same time, because we are all from Asia, have similar culture, and are foreign students, so naturally there are many topics to talk about, and gradually become good friends who have nothing to talk about. I know you must feel lonely when you first come to this school, because of the language barrier and various cultural differences, you can sometimes come to talk to me, you am always welcome." Jianxin understood roughly everything Lily said, and she replied shyly but kindly, "Thank you Lily, I will talk to you next time." After that, Lily continued: "Do you not know how to make up, I see that you have a lot of acne on your face, I know that you never need to make up (liquid foundation), a person's external image is also very important, there is almost no girl here who does not make up." Makeup makes the face look more delicate. In fact, some girls also have acne, but with make up, the face skin will be a lot of uniformity, it has the effect of concealer, you must use make up, so that your face will appear very beautiful. Also, next time I will take you to the supermarket in town to buy a French cosmeceutical skin care product Vichy, which is especially suitable for acne or oily skin, if I have a few acne on my face, I apply it with its night cream, and it will disappear in a day or two, the effect is very good. You have to learn to take care of your skin, although there are a lot of acne on your face, but there are ways to improve, and there are ways to hide it." After hearing this, Jianxin was deeply moved. For the first time in her life, someone told her how to get rid of acne and improve her skin, and how to make her skin look delicate and smooth. She felt that Lily was simply a beauty ambassador sent by God, and she was so warm-hearted and professional. In her hometown, no one can teach her how to treat acne skin and make up without reservation like Lily, because no one in the small place where she lives knows these professional skin care skills, they are the most simple people. Even Jianxin's mother can't do anything about her daughter's acne problem for several years, she always comforts Jianxin by saying: "It's a pimple. It'll get better in a few years." But Jianxin waited for 3 years, the pimple still did not get better, and then she could only get used to her face covered with pimple, which is also a kind of self-comfort and self-redemption, otherwise what can be done?

There was little Internet in those days, so she went online to search for solutions. All in all, she felt foolish and ignorant. What Lily said seemed like a light appearing in the dark night sky, which gave her light and guided her to solve this problem. She replied very gratefully, "Thank you Lily, I really want to improve my skin, no one likes acne, it always affects the appearance of the beauty." I'll do it your way." Lily smiled and handed Jianxin something, saying, "This is my make up, I lend it to you, I will teach you how to make up, after an hour, you will become a beautiful and lovely girl." Jianxin was moved to tears. Lily pulled up a chair and began to make up Jianxin. She gently applied the make up to Jianxin's red, acne-prone face, carefully and patiently. After painting, let Jianxin look in the mirror to see her face, Jianxin see in the mirror herself really become a lot of beauty. The skin is no longer so red and swollen, but refreshing and delicate a lot, and the correct and atmospheric features are revealed. Because of her acne, she had been very resistant to looking in the mirror, but now she wanted to see more of her cute baby face in the mirror. Lily continued to apply makeup, eyeliner, eyeshadow, mascara, blush, etc., and after about an hour, Lily said, "wir sind fertig (we're done)." Jianxin can't wait to look in the mirror. When she saw that beautiful face in the mirror, her heart was excited and surprised, and her face became so delicate as if it had changed a skin. She felt the magic of makeup for the first time in her life. Now she was full of confidence and went out of the room with Lily to fix her hair and dress in front of the full-length mirror in the living room. When the other girls saw Jianxin in makeup, they were a little surprised, her face suddenly became so cute and beautiful, everyone praised: "Nancy,du bist sehr schoen[Nancy (Jianxin's English name), you are beautiful]." "Danke (thank you)," Jianxin replied shyly. Lily said to Jianxin, "Let's go downstairs. The dinner party will begin soon." Then, the two of them and the other students went to the hall, a group of people chattering, very lively. At the entrance of the hall, they entered in turn into the European Renaissance Rococo style of the splendid, luxurious and elegant dining room, found the vacancy, and took their time to sit down. The guests in the dining hall are mainly students, parents, principals, teachers, etc., everyone is dressed in noble and elegant, such a picture like the social activities of the upper class, each table is lit with romantic candles, the candlelight in the large dining hall , like the stars in the sky. The main light in the dining room is turned off, and the whole space is only left with the soft and warm light of the candles, and everyone sits at the table, patiently waiting for the food. The dining hall sounded a melodious waltz, some people were chatting excitedly, whispering to each other, some people quietly enjoying the wonderful and imaginative music, and parents looked around, was deeply impressed by the beauty of the restaurant. Jianxin sat in her seat and waited quietly. Waiting for what, she was not quite sure. After half an hour or so, the principal walked to the lecture platform in the dining room. The voices in the dining room suddenly disappeared like pressing the rest button, and the whole space became strangely quiet. The principal, wearing a sharp suit, read out: "Herzlich willkommen." Unser candle light dinner findet start. Welcome to Enjoy. Our candlelight dinner is now officially underway. Please enjoy it)!" As soon as he finished, everyone clapped, and then the dining hall became busy again. Kitchen staff and volunteer students make their way through the dining room to serve each guest their first meal: pumpkin puree. Jianxin saw in front of herself from inside to outside five to six large and small knives and forks, are not clear how to use the specific, observe others, first use the outermost knife and fork or spoon. Everyone enjoyed it, enjoying the thick soup. Jianxin felt that the pumpkin soup was fragrant and slightly sweet, melting in the mouth, and delicious. Instead of sitting with Jianxin, Lily sat at a dining table in her life group, next to her best friend. Jianxin sat at this table alone has no familiar friends The girls were all beautifully dressed and had an extraordinary temperament, but their expressions were also proud and arrogant. Some of them chatted or talked about something else, while others sat in silence, waiting for other dishes or just staring into space. After she finished her soup, Jianxin sat there respectfully and waited for the waiter to serve her other dishes. She wanted to fit in, but found it almost impossible. One was mainly a language problem, many of the meanings she could not yet express in German fluently and without difficulty, and the other was that she had nothing in common with these girls, and the world they talked about was as incomprehensible to Jianxin as it was to them. The difference between Eastern and Western cultures is not a little, but a huge gap, reflected in all aspects, such as people's world outlook, life outlook and values, as well as culture and belief are different. In the process of waiting for the dishes, Jianxin felt that the time was particularly long, a little boring, although the whole environment and atmosphere were particularly elegant, but she felt that she did not belong to such a social circle, she was an alternative existence, her heart felt lonely, lonely and helpless. She wanted to share food with good friends or talk about interesting topics, but the people at her table were not people she felt she could get close to. The cool look of those girls made her flinch and dare not approach, but would rather wrap herself up like a cicada and hide in her own little world. Some of the girls looked at her from time to time, glanced at her a few times, and then whispered something to another girl sitting next to them. Jianxin did not know what they were discussing, and sometimes wondered if the girls were commenting on her. She sat in her seat and waited and after about half an hour, served the second first meal. Jianxin did not know what it was, it looked small and delicate and delicious, and then she picked up a knife and fork and tasted it. The taste was indeed very good, but what exactly was made was a mystery to her, anyway, it was the first time in her life to taste this exquisite and delicious food. She had nothing to do but sit there, wait for the waiter to serve her food, and then slowly taste it by herself. After takinga meal, she sat there alone, and no girl spoke to her. The candlelight dinner lasted three hours and consisted of five formal courses, including two starters, two main courses and an Italian dessert (tiramisu made with white chocolate). Jianxin felt that the food was really exquisite and delicious, with a unique flavor, but the dinner lasted too long just like a snail crawling slowly. She thinks that the pace of life in Europe is really slow, so slow that people feel incredible. A dinner party can takes five courses for three hours, which is very difficult for a young girl who just came from China to understand and adapt to. The main thing is that there is still no like-minded friends to share what they see and hear or their own experiences at the same table while enjoying the food. In any case, she also experienced a school candlelight dinner, the feeling is elegant and boring.

Turns out the girls at the dinner table were really talking about themselves behind their backs. Jianxin later heard from another student Maria, they commented that Jianxin's posture with a knife and fork is not standard, very strange, sitting posture is not correct, and always low when eating. Maria belongs to a different group, not the same one as Janxin. The school divides all the residential students into different living groups. There are about 20 students in one living group, from different grades. Each group has a teacher, and the group that Jianxin is a part of is run by Frau Koenig (Mrs. Koenig). Maria is very warm and kind, once in the restaurant, she deliberately found Jianxin, hand by hand to teach Jianxin to use the knife and fork of the correct posture and sitting posture, and said to Jianxin: "Learn these correct posture, others will not laugh at you." Oh, and instead of putting salads and staples like steaks or pasta on one plate, you have separate plates, a separate plate for salads, a separate plate for main dishes, and then if you have cake or pudding or fruit, you have separate plates, don't mix them together. Or the other students will see you with all the dishes on one plate and say you're weird and make fun of you. Many of the students here are arrogant, because they come from rich families, so they seem to have a special sense of superiority. They lack some sympathy and do not put themselves in the shoes of their peers who grow up in different cultural backgrounds. Moreover, because their parents are busy with work and focus on their careers, they send their children to private boarding schools early, resulting in a lack of security and family love and discipline in their hearts. That's why so many students here seem arrogant and aloof. Parents of these students, unable to provide emotional companionship, have to fill them with material rewards. So students here often talk about things like cars or beautiful women. Their parents often give their children a big gift when they turn 18. Not long ago, Astasia's parents bought her an Audi TT. Look at the car parked out front. So it is very difficult to make a true friend here, especially for you, who are from the far East and have a very different culture from the students here, because you grew up in a very different environment and received a different education. Of course, the language problem is still the main reason, and the students here belong to the German upper class, they have an innate sense of superiority and lack of parental discipline led to a sense of unsoundness in character, which will make you feel unable to get close to many students here. But don't think about it too much, just take it as it comes, and since you have chosen this place, you have to find a way to adapt here. Let's start by learning how to use the knife and fork properly. If you learn, people won't make fun of you anymore. you need to overcome other difficulties slowly, will get better and better." Jianxin did not fully understand this long talk , but can probably guess what she said. Jianxin replied, "Maria, thank you for teaching me how to use a knife and fork correctly. When I was in China, I had never tried Western food. We were all used to eating the food from my hometown, so it was strange and unaccustomed to me. Usually, we go to the buffet in our hometown restaurant, and it is customary to put all the dishes in one plate, including desserts. The meals in this school are mainly self-help, so I habitually use one plate to pack all the dishes and desserts, and I am not so particular about it. It turns out that there is a lot of knowledge in this, the starters, the main meal and the dessert need to be placed in different plates, no wonder one time a student kept staring at my plate full of dishes, and also called me komisch (strange), I did not understand at the time, I do not know why she said so directly to me, now I understand. Thank you, Maria. You are a very kind girl, unlike the proud students here." maria replied with a smile, "You're welcome, I should do it." Such a small favor is not worth mentioning. Most of the students here, though a little arrogant, are not unkind. By the way, the teachers here are friendly and never criticize them harshly. They get along with their students like friends, don't you think?" Jianxin agreed with the reply: "It is true, the teachers are very friendly and kind." Some students are also very kind and warm. One girl from Iran, Lily, offered to help me with my makeup. She was very kind." Maria replied: "Lily, I know her, when I first came here two years ago, she was just like you now, quiet and shy, not talking much, and now basically adapt to it, and found some good friends, so you will adapt to it, it is only a matter of time." Take your time, no rush." Jianxin is very grateful to Maria for selflessly teaching her how to use a knife and fork and for these sincere words. Although in the future days, Maria did not take the initiative to chat with Jianxin, or become friends with her, but it was enough. Later, Jianxin gradually learned that it is very difficult to find a real friend in Germany, because Germans do not make friends easily, they only have one or two or three real friends in their life, they like a very abundant private space, their own space does not like to be disturbed, most of the time they like to be alone, or do their own things in their free time. This is very different from the Chinese way of getting along. If China advocates frequent socializing and intricate social networks, Germans advocate more self-space, personality development, freedom and unfettered. Jianxin's heart is mixed with the eastern and Western cultures, and she really feels the impact and collision of different cultures, which makes her confused and needs a long time to digest and adjust.

Chapter 16: disco party at School

The various activities at the school really opened Jianxin's eyes. Compared with her previous school experience in China, the extra-curricular activities here greatly subverted her imagination. She can't deny that the experience of going to school is completely different in different countries. Once, after a German class, she went over the lessons and read German novels in her bedroom as usual. Euginia, the only black girl in their life group, knocked on Jianxin's bedroom door and asked, "Honey, would you like to come to the party with us tonight?" It was fun." Jianxin asked somewhat puzzled, " which party? I've never heard of it. Where is it?" Euginia put on a mysterious expression and enthusiastically said, "Our school holds disco parties every quarter, you are new, of course you don't know." I'll take you along. It'll be fun. Don't study every day, it's boring. You have to enjoy life. The students here love to have fun. I've never seen a student sit in his room all day learning like you. You Chinese are so hardworking and good. But, my dear, studying hard is a good thing, and it also requires a combination of work and rest. Let's relax together after school. I'll take you with me. You've got to look good today, dress sexy, don't be conservative, okay?" With that, she wiggled her super-large hips and danced a few HIP HOP moves to an even rhythm. Jianxin thought Euginia's words made sense, but the first time she heard that the school held a disco party, she thought it was too amazing. But she has never been to such an occasion in her life, and it is considered inappropriate or improper for students to go to such occasions in China, which will seriously affect study and affect a girl's image. The public will think that this kind of girl is a bad girl, only fooling around. But at this private school, where disco parties are held regularly to allow students to have fun and enjoy the wonderful years of their age, Jianxin felt that the differences between the two different education systems were surprisingly large. Although she does not want to break her image as a good girl, she also wants to do as the

Romans do, and she has always had a strong desire to explore new things. To Euginia's invitation, although she wanted to try, she still replied, "Euginia, thank you very much for your warm invitation, but I don't have suitable clothes to attend this kind of party. When people see me wearing everyday clothes to attend this kind of activity, will they think I am strange and will they laugh at me?" Euginia shook her head and said, "Nancy, don't worry so much." I have some clothes you can borrow, but we're not the same size. Just wear your own clothes, and no one will laugh at you. You have to attend first." Jianxin was finally driven by Euginia's enthusiasm and her own strong curiosity, and decided to find out and attend the party held by the school at 7:30 tonight.

Since Lily taught Jianxin to make up last time, she went to the town to buy some cosmetics, including liquid foundation, eyeliner, blush, mascara, lip balm, etc., and also bought the French cosmeceuticals Vichy and facial cleanser recommended by Lily. With these skin care products, the acne on her face has improved a lot. And from then on, she would get up every morning, apply the foundation evenly on the face, put on a light makeup, and start a beautiful and hopeful day. She was aware of this benign change in herself. Now that she has learned the basics of makeup, if she goes to tonight's party, she can do it herself and no longer needs help from others. In about half an hour, she finished her makeup, looked at her young face in the mirror, and smiled with satisfaction. She rummaged in the closet for a long time, but couldn't find anything suitable for the occasion. she had no choice but to wear her dark blue sweater daily and a pair of jeans with flared legs. She had not worn these jeans for a long time, and found that the waist was particularly tight, so it took a lot of effort to zip them up. But she will not doubt whether she has gained a lot of weight in the past few months, because every day in the mirror she can not see a lot of changes in her weight, and the people around her will never evaluate whether she is fat. Compared with these fat, tall European or black girls, Euginia, she thought she was still very small, although she was also a little self-deceiving. When they were ready, Euginia and her roommate Celia took Jianxin down the mountain. The two of them were dressed very sexy, the top showed deep cleavage, very sexy, and the lower body was also wearing tight jeans. Celia's figure is very good, protruding at the top and bending at the bottom, and the curvy beauty of women is reflected incisive and vividly, if the boys see it, they will drool. The only drawback is that the waist is squeezed out by tight jeans, but this does not affect the overall beauty. Celia is a pure German girl, the height of 1 meter 75, she comes from Munich, the capital of Bavaria Jianxin also do not know, because Celia does not like to talk too much about her family. Euginia's whole body is too fat, the upper body is OK, she also wore a sexy tight belly button bare black short T, the lower body is not bloated, the butt is very upturned but super big, from beginning to end, the most striking is her huge buttocks, let people see impressive. But her face is still full of confidence, not because of her weight and inferiority complex. The first black girl Jianxin saw greet her with a warm smile was Euginia, the only black in her entire school. She was from South Africa and had been attending the private school since eighth grade. It is said that she was selected by the schloss neubeuern internatsschule in South Africa and offered a full scholarship, which is a rare opportunity. Euginia must have her advantages and uniqueness to have such a lucky opportunity to be selected by the school to attend this famous private boarding school in Bavaria for free. Jianxin guess, her greatest strength is undoubtedly her innate enthusiasm and affinity, strong self-confidence and empathy, of course, this is only from Jianxin's personal perspective. The three of them walked for about 15 minutes until they reached a detached house down the hill. two or three students stood at the entrance , each of whom needed a stamp on the back of his hand to enter the party. Several handsome european boys glanced at Jianxin for a few secondes, feel very curious, they estimate that the first time to see this Asian girl, very curious, one of the boys is still holding a cigarette in his mouth, looking luffian. Jianxin carefully followed Euginia and Celia into the room. Jianxin was immediately stunned by the scene in front of the room has been packed with young boys and girls, these students dressed fashionable and sexy, driven by a strong and rhythmic disco music, twisting the body, dancing energetic. Some students are still holding beer cans in their hands while drinking and dancing, and the rooftop light is rotating 360 degrees to shine on the crowd of dancers in the room. Some teenagers are still hugging each other while dancing, kissing with the dance, immersed in it. Jianxin could not believe her eyes, this school would organize such an adult activity, for students to enjoy it, let them bloom belong to this age of vitality and passion. Euginia and Celia were so excited to see such a lively scene that they couldn't help dancing to the lively rhythm. Jianxin just stood there, confused. She didn't know how to dance. This is the first time to come to such a place, she felt that the students here are too bold and lively, and she used to study in the country to know the students are completely two worlds of people. She is deeply affected by the domestic strict education, feel that students should behave like students and concentrate all energy on study, good students should not go to disco party such places, that kind of places are considered to be social people or small gangbangers to go. In the domestic class, the behavior of the classmates around her seems to be engraved from the same mold, everyone is particularly eager to learn, a straight line, almost no entertainment except study, such a party for the students of the key high school that Jianxin once studied is simply impossible, incredible to the extreme. When Euginia found Jianxin standing still, she said to her, "Nancy, dance. Don't stand still all the time. Be lively. Jianxin replied awkwardly, "Euginia, I can't dance and really don't know how to dance at disco. I thought the others would laugh at me. I didn't dare." Jianxin suddenly found that several pairs of eyes were staring at her, with a shallow smile on her face, she could not guess the meaning contained in it, whether it was a kind smile, or a malicious and contemptuous smile. But standing in this warm and passionate group of teenagers, she was dumbfounded, feeling that she was too conspicuous, everyone was dancing, and she stood still alone, looking left and right, would really make others feel very strange. Swallowing her doubts and embarrassment, she began to jump. But she danced differently from the others, dancing as if she were doing radio gymnastics, and a very fat tall German boy saw her dancing in this strange position and couldn't help laughing. Euginia and Celia also laughed when they saw Jianxin's weird dance. Jianxin saw the reaction of these people and did not know whether to stop immediately or continue to dance. She can only dance like radio gymnastics, and she seems to have a hard time letting go. At this moment, Euginia said: "Jianxin, you learn from me, I will teach you to dance, it is very easy, you just step on the rhythm, wiggle your body and buttocks, you will soon learn." After that, Euginia slowed down and kindly taught Jianxin the most basic disco moves. Jianxin found that in fact, this dance step is very simple and easy to learn, only need to have a sense of musical rhythm, can be quickly mastered and applied freely. After only about 10 minutes of learning, she basically could dance, and there was not much difference between the way she danced and others. The students who laughed in their belly beside her saw the change of Jianxin's heart, and immediately gave a thumbs up and boasted of "wunderbar" (very good). Jianxin also did not hear what they said, because the music in disco is too noisybut can understand. Euginia whispered in Jianxin's ear, "Martis findet dich sehr suess.(Martis thinks you're cute)." Jianxin smiled shamefully when she heard this. This was Jianxin's first time to attend a disco party, which left a very memorable impression on her. All the first experiences were so new and special that they were imprinted on her mind, and even after many years, when she looked back, the images were still as clear as if they had happened yesterday. But sometimes she will also ask herself, such a scene really appeared in her life, as if and her life is completely different, she felt that human memory is too mysterious.

Chapter 17: The Journey to Berlin

Every Friday at 4:30 p.m., the Frau Koenig group of which Jianxin is a member holds a relaxed group meeting. During the meeting, Frau Koenig (living group Teacher) will clearly read out the group activities plan, etc. Jianxin would also participate in such group activities as usual. She sat there quietly listening to Frau Koenig list the activities in a clear way. During the process, several girls would ask questions or discuss some details. Jianxin was not a good participant, but she was a faithful listener. After several months of hard study, continuous accumulation and the best German environment, she unconsciously found that her German has improved a lot, and the content of this group meeting made her very excited. Frau Koenig has announced a trip to the German capital city Berlin for next week. When Jianxin heard the news, she excitedly wanted to cheer, although she was still sitting there quietly, but the heart has been overturned, the other girls around have issued a variety of sounds of joy. She could not believe that the school also regularly took students to travel to famous cities in Europe, which was unthinkable in her former school in China, and it was almost impossible to even leave the school gate, where it was completely strict school control. In addition, she only has half a day of rest on Sunday afternoon every week, and spends the rest of her time in the classroom, either taking endless classes or studying by herself endlessly. Such high-intensity military-style learning has made her accustomed to it, because all the students there have such a unified class schedule and need to be strictly managed. So she won't find it particularly strange. But now she is in a completely different school, where the education system is flexible, free and diverse. Classroom knowledge is not the only thing, after class there are a variety of interest activities and excursions, if let her go back to the previous domestic study environment, she thinks she will not be able to adapt. When people see different lifestyles and learning environments, they will look at the world from a more diversified perspective, rather than thinking that this is the only lifestyle or code of conduct.

Jianxin has never been to the capital of her own country, and the only city she has been to is Dalian, where her parents took her to play with her brother and another relative. It was a beautiful and modern coastal city with plenty of fresh and cost-effective seafood and a pleasant climate. Jianxin's father had some business partners in Dalian, so he took the family outside to broaden their horizons. He struggled for so many years outside, usually will not take his family to travel or travel, in order to save costs, often buy a standing ticket on the train, from the first station to the final station, during which he will also chat with some predestined strangers in the train, the father's business inspiration sometimes comes from this kind of coincidental business trip and other passengers on the small talk. He is a thoughtful person with a keen and flexible mind. This seemingly ordinary chat often gives him inspiration and enables him to find business opportunities, while most ordinary people are basically unable to capture effective information in small talk. Therefore, opportunities will always favor those who are prepared, not all of us can seize the God-given opportunity, and many of us can't even recognize the opportunity. Jianxin's father is on a business trip, extremely hard, he often lives in the cheap guest house or basement, because at that time he just started a business, there is not much money in hand, especially in terms of personal enjoyment, Jianxin's father is really stingy to himself, but for the development of the enterprise, He feels the need to invest Another point is the education of his children, he has really done his best to give children a good education, a more international and open education. Jianxin is very grateful to her father for creating such a rare opportunity for her to study in a foreign country and receive overseas education at the age of 16. Although on the road of studying alone, she has to face a lot of loneliness and unprecedented academic and psychological pressure, she really broadens her vision and cognition, and makes her feel the richness and diversity of the world. Seeing the bigger world and getting in touch with people who have grown up under different civilizations, she became more confident and strong.

Berlin is a city full of stories and today it is Germany's largest political, cultural and economic center. In 1945, Nazi Germany suffered a crushing defeat in World War II, and Berlin as the capital of Germany was destroyed by Allied air raids and the offensive of the Soviet Red Army. Berlin was eventually divided into two parts: East Berlin, controlled by the Soviet Union, and West Berlin, controlled by the United States, Britain, and France. Berlin became the rallying point of the Cold War between the Soviet Union and the United States for 45 years. Due to the influx of East Germans into West Berlin and West Germany through the undefended Berlin dividing line, the Berlin Wall was built in 1961 to completely block the access between East and West Germany. Berlin was at the forefront of the ideological battle between East and West. It was not until 1989 that the Berlin Wall was torn down, and in 1990 Germany was reunited with East and West Germany. Jianxin is not particularly familiar with German history, but when she was in China, she had vaguely heard about the history of the division and later reunification of East and West Germany. She is full of longing and longing for this historic capital of Germany, and it is very exciting to see it soon.

After the discussion of their group, they finally decided on the itinerary of Berlin travel. Time passed silently, and finally it was the day to go to Berlin. Led by Frau Koenig, a dozen girls boarded a fast train to Berlin. It was Jianxin's first time on a fast train, and the compartment was spacious and comfortable, not too crowded, and left many empty seats. A group of girls found their seats and sat down. Jianxin sat on the position, looking at the continuous mountains moving outside the window, the rushing river, the verdant green grass, rows of scattered and low European-style houses, feeling comfortable, so leisurely and picturesque scenery is close at hand, she really felt the ease of Europe, nature and exquisite, is the perfect combination of modern and ancient, nature and human civilization. Once she did not know how to appreciate beautiful scenery or beautiful things, in addition to school life is family life, life does not have too many surprises and waves, and the things she has seen are really countable. She felt that before in China, school never took them to visit museums or have any excursions, so everyday things are basically in school, do homework or review lessons, prepare for exams, repeat. Now she can have such an opportunity to enjoy the vast world, a more colorful life, which is she never thought of before. Once she foolishly thought that life was like this, plain, regular, orderly. What beautiful things, she did not have any concept or did not know how to appreciate, but to be honest, in the 1990s to 2000, China's economy is still very backward, the infrastructure is old, the house is also dilapidated, so beauty and refinement and the environment she lived in at that time is not on the side. But now it is different, she arrived at a beautiful natural environment, civilization and highly developed economy, she suddenly found that she actually has a pair of eyes to appreciate beauty, she does not have to deliberately look for, they can find beautiful things everywhere in the new world, beautiful people suffocate, and so silent, only for human beings to slowly appreciate. The beautiful scenery outside the train window made her feel the beauty of the human world and the magnificence of nature. The other girls were chatting, or sleeping, or quietly enjoying the scenery rushing by the window as she did, and each seemed to find their own state of comfort and relaxation in the course of this journey.

In the meantime, Frau Koenig hands out lunch sandwiches to each girl, specially prepared for them in the school kitchen. Jianxin took the sandwich and tasted it slowly, the classic combination of grilled chicken breast with lettuce and cheese lingering in her teeth, delicious, fresh and rich, even if she had another one, she could not get enough. In the months since she came to Germany to study, her appetite seems to be good every day, and she enjoys the Western-style meals. Strange to say, many people have problems with acclimation to a new environment, but for her, there is no such feeling. Every time she eats a variety of Western-style meals, she can't resist the temptation of these delicious foods, especially the school brunch every Sunday morning. From various kinds of bread to exquisite pastries, brunch and other side dishes, when she finishes one plate, it is not enough, and then she will pick up the second or even the third plate. Her love of French croissants can be described as fanatical, and she can eat four of them in a row. One bite of the crunchy crust, with powdered sugar or melted chocolate sauce, gave her a great stomach satisfaction, and then went on for a second, and a third, as if she could not stop eating. Sometimes the students sitting at a table to see her such a good appetite, simply surprised that she is a small Asian girl who has a super big stomach, eat and eat and eat, very immersed in food. Jianxin could not rationally explain why her love of Western food was so natural and innate. Every day at school, she is most interested in all kinds of school meals and can eat leisurely for more than an hour each time, but when she was studying in China, she was very keen on chatting with her friends during the meal time, and she only grilled a few bites when the task was completed. She can't understand her transformation, but one thing is certain that she deeply felt her discomfort and loneliness in a foreign country and needed to find an balance, that is, love food. She hardly has any real friends at school. Several enthusiastic and nice students, such as Lily, Euginia or another girl who taught her how to use knives and forks correctly, are not real friends, in fact, they are only nodding friends, because they already have their own familiar circle of friends, and they will not take the initiative to integrate Jianxin into their respective circles. Not long after Rita invited Jianxin to a dinner at her employer's house, she left Germany, too, and never heard from her again. At that time, Jianxin was very sad, and her only friends had left her. she is desperate to find pure friendship in a foreign country, which can give her more warmth and companionship during her long study abroad and find a resonance in her heart. She is a girl who needs friends very much, and with friends, she will have a sense of self-existence, and can satisfy her strong desire to express and share, but now the friendship she seeks has not been able to get, since Rita left. In school, every time she goes to class alone, she goes to dinner alone, and everything is basically done by herself. She is like a lone ranger. Although her parents and relatives are far away in China, she misses them very much, but the high cost of international long-distance and underdeveloped communication can not often contact them, so she can only put away this homesickness, and comfort herself over and over again, "Be strong, independent, you have grown up."

Countless nights, she missed the life in China, although the economy is still very backward, study life is also very hard, but there are many friends, in the hometown she rarely had a feeling of loneliness and helplessness. But now such a feeling of emptiness will often float in her mind, no matter how beautiful the natural scenery of the outside world is, how developed the economy is, she feels like an alien or a little like a marginal person, it is difficult to integrate into their mainstream cultural circle. Such a feeling is only her own experience, the students around are local, can not feel the same. They maintain a great sense of distance from foreigners, like an eagle, with wide round eyes, staring at aliens not far away, observing their every move, and unwilling to get close. Jianxin and the students in the new school are like this feeling, unable to get close, familiar faces pass by her eyes every day, but many of them have not said a word to her, and some are just a short greeting, and there is no further. She does not feel excluded, but only has a deep sense of powerlessness. She feels helpless for her inability to integrate into the mainstream circle of students, but she can only hide alone in the corner silently enduring endless loneliness and the emptiness of her own inner spiritual world needs to find appropriate things to heal or fill, that is, her love for Western food. She has no friends and no relatives in this new environment, so she sincerely loves and enjoys food, and the satisfaction of taste buds will also have a chain positive effect on the soul.

The train was flying, she looked at the scenery outside the window, and soon fell asleep, and her eyes flashed scenes of playing with her friends when she was a child, just like showing a movie. None of the other students sat or chatted with her, they were all in the heat, chatting or playing all over the country, Jianxin was always sitting alone. After about five hours, the train arrived at Berlin Hauptbahnhof station to great cheers, and Frau Koenig told the students to grab their backpacks or suitcases and get off in an orderly manner. Jianxin followed the back of their life group, followed their pace, and got off the fast train that she took for the first time in her life, closely following behind, not daring to go randomly. The central station is classical and magnificent, the whole building is neoclassical style, the station is crowded, a train track winding into the distance, from time to time there will be trains, and other trains arrive, coming and going, there are many bakeries, sausage shops and candy shops in the station. In order to save meal time on the road, pedestrians generally choose to buy sandwiches, bread rolls, etc., in order to buy food more easily. Jianxin has never seen such a bustling and vibrant metropolis, she is full of infinite expectations, hoping to get to know Berlin well in the next few days. Frau Koenig leads the girls through the crowds and the mighty Central lobby, all the way to the subway station. After careful but quick scanning of the signs, she found the subway line she needed to take, and then told everyone, "Pack your bags, we are going to take the subway, the subway doors close quickly, you stay with us." Jianxin is like a headless bird, do not know anything, do not understand, this is her first time to take the subway this means of transportation, before she lived in the small town, the public transportation is only the bus, she can only stand dumb on the platform and so on. She usually stays in their small village except for going to and from school, which makes her feel a little isolated. Now she has come to a highly civilized and developed world, where everything is so classical and modern, the architectural style still retains the classical beauty of the 18th or 19th century in Europe, but the various facilities used in the interior of the building have been very high-end and advanced. After about 3 minutes, the subway arrived, and a group of them immediately boarded the subway station. The subway sped along, passing one platform after another, bringing groups of passengers to their destination stations. Jianxin believes that the invention of subway has epoch-making significance. It not only brings convenience to people's travel, but also saves travel costs. People are no longer limited to their own small circle of life, but can quickly and conveniently go to every corner of the city. After about 20 stops on the train, Frau Koenig and the girls said, "We've reached the terminal. Let's get off." After that, a group of girls with their own luggage, step down the subway. Exit the subway, walk about 10 minutes, then arrived at the youth hostel. Frau Koenig arranges the girls to stay in the rooms, each room has 4 beds, and the girls who are close to each other will always choose to share the room with their friends, so Frau Koenig will ask everyone's opinion. Only Jianxin a person, do not know who to live with, because she has a distant relationship with girls in the group. After everyone chose a roommate, Jianxin was left alone and was not arranged. Frau Koenig clearly knows that Jianxin has not been truly accepted by this group of girls, of course, she is not easy to blame the girls, young people at this age have their own unique opinions and ideas, the teacher's point of view may not be accepted by the students. In Germany, students can question their teachers, express their opinions in public, and sometimes even have heated debates, which are all allowed or encouraged. Teachers treat students with more respect and don't criticize them too much. So even if Frau Koenig thinks the students in her group are xenophobic or racist, she doesn't accuse them. Jianxin needs to rely on her own efforts to integrate into the team, but Jianxin also does not want to force herself, because she knows that many times, it is not possible to work hard alone, if others psychologically resist you or have prejudice against you, you do more efforts, it is useless. Although she is eager to make real friends, but she will not be too reluctant, she knows that the will and emotions of others are the most uncontrollable, she can only focus on herself, do what she should do, is the most important.

When Frau Koenig saw that none of the girls offered to ask Jianxin to share a room with them, she assigned her to the corner room with a spare bed. After entering the room, everyone took a short rest, and soon the group was assembled. Because the time of arrival is already in the evening, so at the first night there is no special activities, they arranged to find a cost-effective restaurant for dinner. The girls love Italian Pizza, Frau Koenig found a Pizza restaurant nearby, once in the restaurant, the girls found two outdoor tables that were not reserved, and sat down comfortably. The waiter lit candles for the two tables. The lights were dim and soft. The dining room was playing light and melodious music. Everyone held a menu in her hand and carefully selected dishes. Jianxin read a dish from beginning to end, she doesn't know many words, although there are also English words, but her English is not good, the point of English learned in China can only be regarded as a little understanding in Europe. Finally, she chose a classic PIZZA Hawaii, which is made with bacon and pineapple slices. The waiter first brought drinks for everyone, including soda, apple juice, orange juice, etc. dinner in a european restaurant is a slow process of enjoying the food, and the impatient can't stand it. Everyone drinks while chatting, patiently waiting, relaxed. Jianxin did not understand everything the girls were talking about, because after all, her german knowledge was much stronger than when she first arrived at school, and could at least vaguely understand some of it. Jianxin could not get into their small talk. She was still sitting alone in her position, slowly drinking a few sips of apple juice, watching the students talking excitedly, sometimes they laughed, and sometimes the students' faces showed a kind of lofty expression. Like a kind parent, Frau Koenig mingled with the students, talking freelyandrelaxed .Jianxin is the only one who is lonely, and she likes this romantic and cozy atmosphere, but she can't fit in with the group, and no one in her group will actively and warmly talk to her, ask her how she is doing, and ask her kindly whether she is adjusting to the new school life. Jianxin was a little sad in her heart, she missed having so many friends in China, and she missed talking freely with her little friends, and she was almost always the protagonist. And today, she can only be a person like being forgotten silently huddled in the corner, no one cares about her. She had been full of expectations for the trip to Berlin, and now she finally had this feeling, and the greater the expectations, the greater the disappointment. Although she has not really seen the real face of this world-famous city, her inability to integrate into the group and the apathy of these girls towards her all the way gave the first trip a sense of sadness.She is like a lonely goose, unable to fly in the same line as a group of geese, and the more she struggles, the harder she tries. Only to find that the distance from this group of geese is getting further and further, and gradually falling behind. Jianxin feel very silly, why should she persistent think that they can be very harmonious into the team, she does not like the feeling of being excluded, although no one to her unkind, but this group of girls do not care about her and the expression of extreme indifference let her feel that they are invisible negation and exclusion. Perhaps she is really too sensitive, the girls may feel that Jianxin does not know German, so they are too lazy to spend energy or patience to chat with her, simply ignore it. After chatting for about an hour, the waiter finally brought trays of different kinds of PIZZA. After waiting for a long time, the stomach is rumbling, eating the fresh baked crispness of the PIZZA, everyone seems very satisfied. Jianxin's favorite is the food, no friends and relatives, she can only pour all of her passion and emotion into the sight and touch of the mouthwatering food. delicious food is worth living up to, she thought. After dinner, everyone went back to the youth hotel, said good night to each other, and went to their rooms to rest. Jianxin lay quietly on the bed and after a few seconds fell into a deep sleep.

  She wakes up, the sky is blue, cloudless, a new day began. After a simple breakfast at the hostel, they took the metro and started their day trip to Berlin. The first stop is the Brandenburg Gate (Brandenburger Tor), a typical neoclassical architecture. It is the symbol of Berlin and the national symbol of Germany. In the center of the top of the Brandenburg Gate is a bronze statue of the Goddess of Victory about 5 meters high. The goddess spreads her wings behind her and drives a four-horse two-wheeled chariot toward

Berlin. In her right hand she held a scepter with a wreath of oak trees, an iron Cross within the wreath, and on the wreath stood an eagle flying with wings, and the eagle wore the Prussian crown. This sculpture symbolizes the victory of the Prussian war, which is solemn and magnificent. Many tourists stand in front of the Brandenburg Gate to take pictures, in order to make this wonderful visit to Berlin forever. Jianxin saw such a magnificent and beautifully carved building, and sighed from the heart that the artists were skilled in nature. Standing under the mighty Brandenburg Gate, human being looks so small. In the long river of time, these buildings have experienced ups and downs, witnessed the rise and fall of the famous city of Berlin and magnificent historical events, and still standing, riding on the war horse, the statue of Victory, as if to tell the world: "After so many ups and downs, we have finally won." Brandenburg Gate is a symbol of the German spirit of perseverance, uncompromising and excellence. Frau Koenig asked everyone to stand in a line and take pictures in front of the landmark building.

The next stop is the prestigious Reichstag Building, which embodies the various architectural styles of classicism, Gothic, Renaissance and Baroque and is a symbol of German unification. The high-tech style is cleverly combined with the traditional architectural style: the exterior wall is left unchanged, but the interior is completely hollowed out, and the internal space system is rebuilt with a steel structure. So inside the stately old shell of the Capitol is a modern new building, a perfect combination of classic and modern. Originally built in 1884, the Reichstag was severely destroyed during World War II and underwent extensive renovations and renovations after the reunification of East and West Germany. Today, the Reichstag has become one of Europe's most striking works of art, attracting tourists from all over the world. The Reichstag is not only the building of the Federal Parliament, but the glass dome on its roof is also a popular tourist attraction. Frau Koenig took the girls to the top of the glass dome: inside, two spiral-shaped passageways crisscrothed and supported by an exposed all-steel structure, visitors can enjoy 360-degree views of Berlin through transparent glass Windows. Inside the glass dome visitors are woven, an endless stream, visitors are deeply impressed by such a work of art like architecture Jianxin saw such a wonderful building group, she was excited, the European architecture of the majestic and exquisite left a deep and lingering impression in her mind.

After touring the capital, the group took a break at a cafe in a piazza. The waiter brought out the wine list for the guests to browse. Jianxin ordered her favorite apple juice and quietly enjoyed the scenery around her. Flocks of pigeons flying around in the square, sometimes standing on the ground of the square, slowly pacing, visitors see standing white and huge pigeons, can not help but approach, want to take photos with the pigeons, or to feed them. When the pigeons here see humans, they will not panic and fly away immediately, but they still stand in their place, and enjoy letting visitors touch their flawless white feathers, which is a harmonious coexistence between people and nature. White doves, towering classical buildings around the square and lazy and leisurely tourists constitute a typical picture of European leisure life. In the eyes of Jianxin, this life is beautiful and has a high quality. People here do not have too much pressure in life and can enjoy the warm sunshine outdoors. Go on vacation or get together with friends in the sun and chat. Spend a lazy and relaxing day, In her hometown, she almost never saw such a leisurely picture, she grew up seeing adults working hard all day, busy, rarely have free time to sit down to drink tea, talk about the family, let alone vacation or travel. At that time (before 2000), in the small place where Jianxin lived, most people had been to the nearby city or town all their life, and many of the older generation only had their hometown as the core area of their life, and only knew their neighbors and relatives and friends in the village, because of the lagging transportation facilities and the lack of information circulation. It is difficult for people in the village to go out and see the rich and diverse world outside. They are also used to work in this small place at sunrise and ending at sunset, living a simple and simple life. Jianxin felt the huge difference in the lives of people in these two different worlds, and her heart could not help but be shocked. Although she had no relatives in a foreign country, it was difficult for her to find good friends because of cultural differences and the lack of german language, she saw a world completely different from her previous life, and she was full of strong curiosity and desire to explore this novel and highly developed world. She enjoyed leisurely watching visitors come and go in the cafe, doing nothing, quiet and silent, just using her eyes to capture this wonderful world. The other girls in the group are also lounging on chairs and chatting leisurely, very relaxed. Then Frau Koenig said gently, "What do you think of today's trip?" Some of the girls said, "Yes, it's fine." There are some girls on the default nod, they are wearing sunglasses, look mature and temperament, not like a shy little girl. Frau Koenig takes a sip of her drink and adds, "We can go for a boat ride in the afternoon, then we can have an early dinner, and afterwards you can enjoy your free time." When they heard this, they all agreed that the schedule made sense, and they all answered with one voice: "Yes, Frau Koenig."

Lunch was simple, everyone ate affordable and delicious sandwiches and headed straight to the boat pier. Waves of tourists were standing at the dock waiting to get on the boat, and Frau Koenig had the girls stand in a fixed position to wait while she went to buy tickets first. After the better part of an hour, the tickets were bought. The girls lined up at the dock, waiting for the next boat to arrive. Flowing canal, in the sun's high light, the breeze blowing, the river surface shimmering, silver sparkling, like satin silk, noble and elegant. A line of cruise ships come and go on the canal, leisurely. Time passed imperceptibly, and a cruise ship finally landed. The waiting tourists stepped on the deck of the cruise ship in turn and entered the cabin. The first tier of cabins, the most popular among tourists, was filled in a very short time. Jianxin and the girls went down the cabin stairs to the bottom cabin, where there were a few tourists in pairs.Just as they were about to sit down, Frau Koenig said, "Girls, the view from the bottom cabin is not good, let's go to the open cabin." Then they climbed up the stairs to the top of the boat, and there were just a dozen empty seats, and they sat down at once. When it was time to leave, the boat glided slowly and steadily along the canal like a turtle, leaving behind a glowing trail of water. Jianxin looked at the moving classical and modern buildings on both sides of the canal, spectacular and beautiful. Some tourists take pictures all the way with the camera in hand, while others like to enjoy the beautiful scenery with their eyes and taste the charm of the buildings with hundreds of years of history on both sides of the canal. They do not want to disturb the good mood with excessive photography. They think that the scenery or buildings captured by the camera are only from a certain Angle. Such a beautiful landscape needs to be presented in 360 degrees, and such a panorama can really only be felt by people. Jianxin did not bring a camera, she just sat quietly on the cruise, enjoying the beautiful scenery that people can not use accurate words to express. The girls in the group are wearing sunglasses, looking mature and elegant, although their average age is only 14 to 15 years old, but you can hardly tell that they are just young girls, because they dress very fashionable and sexy. In Berlin in late June, on a sunny day, the temperature has been slightly higher, the girls are wearing tight T-shirts, their white necks are exposed to a large section, and their full breasts are particularly sexy and seductive under the wrap of low-neckline T-shirts. There are many young girls in Europe wearing this kind of dress, and it is not an excessive and ostentatious dress at all. But for Jianxin, such clothes are too revealing and mature, after all, she grew up in the reserved Eastern culture, so she will be more conservative and reserved. Jianxin has no comment on the dress of these girls, this is their personal preference and freedom. But if someone suggested that she wear a T-shirt like this, she would never try it. The favorite thing of this group of girls on the cruise is to bask in the sun, hoping to tan their white skin into a healthy buckwheat color, but Jianxin is a little worried that her skin will be too dark, which will appear more primitive and old. Different cultures, so different views. How to understand the European aesthetic, but also start with one thing. Once, Euginia, the only black girl in the school, was just talking in Jianxin's room. She saw a Creme (day cream) wrapped in Chinese words and felt very curious, so she asked Jianxin, "Nancy, was ist das?" Jianxin replied: "This is creme I brought from China, it is a whitening cream." Euginia was shocked to hear that Creme is whitening and asked, "Why do I need to whiten?" Jianxin replied: "Because in China, if the skin is black or yellow, it is not beautiful." Asians like white skin, so I'll buy this cream." Euginia laughed her head off at this explanation and said, "Really? You Chinese like white skin, so I look very ugly in your place. My skin is so dark." In fact, the first time she saw Euginia, Jianxin used the Oriental aesthetic thinking to see that she was indeed not generally ugly, her skin was as black as carbon, her lips were too thick, her nose was also badly collapsed, and the features of the whole face had no redeemable features except big eyes. But later, Jianxin got used to it, and felt that black people also had unique beauty. Although euginia is black, her skin was delicate, and her teeth were white and clean. Especially, her personality was very good, enthusiastic and generous, confident and full of empathy. Listening to Euginia's joke, Jianxin immediately politely replied: "No, of course you are not ugly, the beauty of each race is different, the world has a variety of beautyso interesting, isn't it?" Euginia replied, "Yes, Jianxin. Do you know that in Europe, white people don't like their white skin, they want to tan their skin into a healthy tan, which represents health and wealth, because they think that more sun, you are very healthy, that you have time and money to go out for vacation leisure, you see, onthe beach, swimming pool side almost all white people, They sit by the pool with a novel and lie down all afternoon just to get a tan. In the winter, the sun in Germany or Northern European countries is very short, and in order to make their skin dark, they will deliberately go to lie in the solarium (artificial sunlight device). So you don't need whitening here, people don't think that white skin is the standard of beauty." jianxin was surprised, it is subvert her thinking mode, the original different cultural aesthetic has such a big difference, in Asia to white beauty, but in the Western world, tan skin is the standard of beauty. But even so, she still has a strong Oriental thinking in her bones, so she is not keen on exposure to the sun. The other girls in the group were sitting lazily in the hot sun, feeling very happy and enjoying, while Jianxin was hiding from the sun, afraid of being tanned as a "nigger".

After dinner, Frau Koenig said, "You are free to do as you please, but don't go back to the hostel too late, we will continue the tour tomorrow." to she wants to rest, the other girls in the group are still interested in vibrant night lifes, but also want to go to the Berlin bar to play, have fun. They are young and young, especially obsessed with nightlife such as bars and disco, in such an atmosphere can release their endless youthful vitality and enthusiasm and unrestrained heart, you can drink and dance recklessly. The songs played in bars or discos are hot and fierce, and when you hear that music, people will follow the strong and hot rhythm and twist up, and they feel particularly excited and passionate. In the pub (bar) or disco there are often some encounters, two strange young men and women look at each other, in such a vibrant atmosphere will often hug together to dance, such an unexpected encounter is full of unlimited stimulation and freshness. This group of girls at the age of this flower season, is so yearning for unrestrained, free and exciting life, so their pursuit of nightlife is also tracable. However, Jianxin is not particularly interested in such entertainment, she has experienced the disco held in the school, and she did not feel that such activities have any fun, a group of men and women dancing together to drink, the music is loud, after leaving disco, still feel that the ear has still a little buzzing sound, as if there is disco aftersound around the ear. And she has a regular and healthy life style and does not like to stay up all night and go to this kind of bar or disco. In fact, none of the girls in the group asked her if she was interested in going to the bar together, maybe they guessed that Jianxin would not be interested, or they felt that Jianxin's appearance gave people a kind of good girl feeling, too regular, boring ,so they did not want to bring this Chinese girl together. In this case, after dinner, Jianxin and Frau Koenig went back to the hostel, and then each washed and rested. As for the group of girls in the end to play to come back, it is not known, in short, they should have a good time. Jianxin really thinks that young people in Europe live a cool and comfortable life without such a heavy burden of schoolwork. Even at the age of studying, the focus will not only be on study. In addition, they have many spare time activities. Or climbing, skiing, or going to a bar or disco crazy, or falling in love in a public place, two people have no qualms about touching each other, passionately embracing, romantic kissing. They are lucky to grow up in such a highly developed and civilized country, and they are also blessed by God. In contrast, in developing countries or the third world, many people are still struggling to live on the edge of poverty, with little to eat, no access to higher education, and no quality of life at all. Jianxin felt that the difference in life around the world is too great, each place has a different way of life, in her former hometown, people's ideas are conservative and traditional. If young girls go to bars or puppy love, they will certainly bear the name, and they will think that such girls are bad girls. Due to the influence of this traditional thinking, so she is not so keen on these nightlife, the key reason comes from the education received from a young age. Although she is now in Europe, she still cannot live as freely as these girls. So it is very difficult for her to really integrate into this mainstream culture.

  Frau Koenig has been mentioned countless times before, she is the teacher of Jianxin's living group and she is about 50 years old. She had short blond hair, blue eyes, delicate and three-dimensional features, a small face of the kind of slap face, except for the skin is a little loose, forehead has crept a few wrinkles, in her face can not find any faults. As you can imagine, when she was young, she should be a real beauty. The first time Jianxin met Frau Konig, she felt that she was a very friendly teacher, never reprimanded the girls in the group, spoke softly, always with a gentle and friendly smile. She lives with a man in her age in a faculty apartment on the campus, which happens to be on the same floor as Ms. Koenig's group, making it easier for Frau Koenig to manage her girls. Once, in the activity room with several girls watching TV, through the transparent glass door, Jianxin saw Frau Koenig and the temperament of the elegant man about 60 years old out of the apartment together. Jianxin was curious and asked the girls in the group if that was Frau Koenig's husband. Jianxin think that in fact they are a little gossip, also curious about other people's privacy, but in general, people will have this innate curiosity. Celia, the girl in the group, replied: "Not her husband, her boyfriend, they just live together, Lebenspartner (life partner)." Jianxin listened to the heart, feel particularly surprised, thought:, the two of them have more than 50 or 60 years old, not married to live together, but also just a life partner. Of course, she did not open her thoughts, she was afraidthat others would despise her and make a fuss, this phenomenon may be very normal in Germany, but for Jianxin, it is really unexpected. The word "Lebenspartner" (life partner) is particularly new and fashionable, Jianxin feels that she has grown so big, the first time to hearthat two people do not get a marriage license, so have been living together, become a lifetime partner. Besides, both of them are 50 or 60 years old, they are also so fashionable, and the Jianxin cannot understand that since two people can live together , why can't they get married honestly? In this way, the law is more reasonable. At that time, the Jianxin looked at the problem with the traditional way of Chinese thinking In fact, many adults have experienced the marriage life, will understand that marriage and love are completely different, there arc too many cumbersome marriage life, almost not romantic, if you encounter two husband and wife personality, three views are inconsistent, but also need to run; If it doesn't work out, maybe married life won't be too happy. Sweet love is everywhere, but romantic and sweet marriage is rare in this world. People in Europe are open-minded, have seen through the nature of marriage, and may not want to be bound by marriage, so they choose to live together and be life partners. At that time, Jianxin was young and had never really been in love, let alone married, so she found it strange that the man who lived with Frau Koenig was not her husband, but her life partner. The world is so big that there are no surprises.

Over the next few days, Frau Koenig took the girls on a tour of the Berlin Cathedral. In Europe, churches are all over cities and towns and are sacred places in the spiritual world of Westerners, with diversified styles, such as Gothic architecture, classical style, Baroque style and so on. Berlin Cathedral was built in 1894-1905, is the German Kaiser Wilhelm II built the Renaissance style of Protestant Christian church, three prominent dome obviously interpretation of this feature, different from the Gothic church spire, its dome from the visual give a sense of round and rich. When Jianxin stepped into the church, she was shocked by the magnificent and luxurious interior of the church. The religious murals were vivid and lifelike, the columns with complex lines were gold-plated, the church dome was inlaid with the Mosaic of Jesus' Gospel preaching on the mountain, and all the ground was paved with expensive and rare marble. Tourists pray and visit in the church, holding pamphlets introducing the history and origin of the church, quiet and silent, quietly walking in the classical and flashy church interior. At that moment, everyone's mind should be so peaceful and serene. Most of the tourists are Christian, entering this holy place, they will also sit in the rows of seats in the church, silently staring at the huge statue of Jesus on the altar, and then quietly recite the Bible chapters or meditation, praying for the Lord's protection and blessing. There is no noise in the huge church, even after more and more tourists enter, everyone is very abide by the etiquette, do not make any noise; If you talk, you talk in a low voice, so that no one else is affected. Jianxin admired the Germans for their sense of order discipline. She found that in German restaurants, museums, churches, cafes, train cars and parks and almost all public places, there is no noise, no noise, people are talking quietly, the whole environment is so quiet. Sometimes sitting in the restaurant or sitting on the roadside to rest, she would often hear birds chirping merrily, as if they were singing light and cheerful songs. Since then, Jianxin has developed the habit of speaking at the lowest decibel level in such an environment. The quiet environment made her feel lonely at the beginning, but with the passage of time, people's preferences will change with the change of the environment, she slowly fell in love with the tranquility and peace that can be found everywhere, so that her mood is stable There seems to be a great power in tranquility, allowing people to rest better, to think better, and not to be disturbed by the noise and distractions of the outside world. In order to give students a better understanding of this magnificent and flashy cathedral, Frau Koenig also hired a special guide to tell them about the history of the church. Everyone listened with relish, only the Jianxin did not understand, the guide used too many professional and profound German words and sentence patterns, and the speed of speech was very fast, she really did not have such a strong understanding, after all, only to learn German for a few months, but the glitz and magnificence of the church was deeply engraved in her mind, lingering. Moreover, she was gradually attracted by the brilliance of European art, and through the appreciation of European architecture and artworks in the sensory world, she became more and more aesthetic and appreciative. Unconsciously, she is no longer the naive little girl who grew up in a small village in China, but has become more and moreinternational, pursuit of self-realization and love for the aesthetic aspect. such a change may be due to this long study abroad experience.

  In order to let the students have more artistic feelings, Frau Koenig also took them to visit the Berlin Art Museum. The museum exhibits paintings and sculptures from the 19th century, including works by famous painters such as Frederick, Brooklin and the French Impressionists Manet, Monet and Cezanne. Standing in front of a huge painting, Jianxin admires the artist's painting technique, these great artists with their own inspiration, painting talent and excellent artistic expression techniques to complete a masterpiece, passed down through the centuries, for the world to visit and appreciate, so that ordinary people can also roam freely in the palace of art, imagination and romantic feelings are stimulated. The paintings on display in the gallery are divided into several themes, and religious paintings are undoubtedly the most important branch of the European school of painting. The huge paintings depict stories from the Bible. The characters and scenes are very detailed and three-dimensional, and the colors are vivid. Jianxin did not know much about Christianity and had not read the stories in the Bible. But many Europeans of the Christian faith looked at these paintings and knew which religious story they were from, which Bible verse. Having grown up on this land, they will naturally understand the local culture better. In Jianxin's view, the artistic influence of Europeans is really very popular, teachers will often organize students to visit art galleries or museums, whether you understand or not, this kind of holy land to retain the brilliant spiritual wealth of human beings to go to more, people will be gradually infected, get more and more artistic cultivation. Ordinary Europeans are especially keen to visit such places when they travel. European large or small cities also have a large number of art galleries and galleries, which are ideal for tourists to visit. Jianxin thinks that people here pay great attention to the richness and nourishment of the spiritual world, so they like to appreciate artworks and paintings of famous artists. On the one hand, because of the influence of art from childhood to adulthood, on the other hand, because of the developed economy and rich life, people have enough time to pursue the inner spiritual world. In Jianxin's hometown, people are busy making a living, busy supporting their families, during the New Year, relatives and friends gather together to chat, or play cards and mahjong, contact feelings, to visit the art gallery and museum for them is a fantasy, some people will despise that "elegant". Jianxin sincerely believes that the economic level determines the superstructure, the material life is guaranteed, and the talent will pursue higher levels of needs, such as social identity, self-worth, spiritual wealth and so on. If there is no abundant material security, people's attention will not stay in these illusory art appreciation. Of course, it is also closely related to people's level of education. If a person gets wealth by hard work and luck, but he has not received higher education, and there is no acquired condition for him to be influenced by art, he will not have any interest in art.

  Natural scenery is also a popular subject for painters. When Jianxin saw the classic work "Water Lilies" by Monet, the founder of Impressionism, she felt as if she were standing quietly beside a pond full of water lilies. The water lilies on the water surface appeared gentle. Along the lake, water lilies spread to the far side of the lake one by one, and the flowers appeared very layered under the reflection of green trees. Light and shadow are perfectly integrated, and the picture has a hazy beauty and romantic atmosphere. In this work of Monet, the pond in the garden is like a pure land in his heart, a mysterious garden in the depths of his heart, the nature is so beautiful, full of infinite vitality and so quiet and mysterious.

Paul Cezanne, the famous French painter, was passionate about painting still life objects, such as spilled fruit, fruit trays and flowers placed on tables. His still life painting "Still Life Apple Basket" is one of his most typical paintings: a simple wooden table with a tablecloth, on which some apples, wine bottles, baskets, plates, etc., are displayed. The structure of the body and surface of each apple are emphasized and depicted, with rigorous colors and thick lines, to truly represent the entity and the representation of light and space. By depicting nature, Cezanne's pursuit in his works is no longer a simple copy of the object, but the realization of human feeling.

In this elegant art palace, Jianxin slowly appreciated one painting after another, and found that each painter's painting style was different. Some used very delicate and rigorous techniques, focusing on the three-dimensional sense and authenticity of characters or scenes, while some painters liked to integrate more personal emotions into their paintings, and it was almost impossible to clearly identify the details of objects or figures in their works. However, through color and special brushstrokes, there can be a certain degree of link with the personal feelings of the painter. For example, some works show a feeling of gloom and depression, while the content of some works may remind people of bright or lively feelings, and these works just show the personal feelings that the painters want to express. Works of art are very subjective, different people have different opinions, and the presentation methods are also very diverse, which can best reflect the creativity, inspiration and the light of emotional thinking.

During the four days of travel in Berlin, Jianxin found that the walls of many subway gates in Berlin were covered with graffiti, and she felt that some graffiti was still very artistic and creative. But some of the doodles were mere doodles, which in her subjective opinion were not aesthetically pleasing and did not fit in well with Berlin's neoclassical style. But she wondered why the government would allow all kinds of graffiti to be displayed in the German capital in support of human rights and freedoms. Or do you want an environment where ordinary people can show their talents and themselves? She doesn't know exactly why. In short, through these four days, she saw that Berlin is a classical and modern European city with a strong historical and cultural heritage and full of vitality.

When it comes to the recent history of Berlin, the most famous is the German Nazis who triggered the Second World War. Berlin, the heart of Nazi Germany, was divided into East Berlin and West Berlin after the war due to the Nazis' defeat in World War II, until the Berlin Wall was toppled in 1989, after which Germany was truly unified. Berlin bears witness to this humiliating and unforgettable part of Germany's history. In order to give students a deeper understanding of this history, Frau Koenig took them to visit the Jewish Museum in Berlin, which records and displays about 2,000 years of Jewish history before and after Germany, as well as the history of the persecution and slaughter of Jews by the Nazis in Germany. The exhibits, dominated by historical artifacts, letters and life records, shed light on how Jews were massacred, deported and persecuted during that time. It is a very bloody, brutal and dignified history, which fully shows the merciless and inhuman slaughter of the Nazis, from reading the manuscripts of the Jews and the newspaper clippings of the time, they were so hopeless under the Nazi terror. Although history has passed, it is necessary that people should not forget the lessons that this history has brought to mankind. Although Jianxin felt that at that time, the German Nazi rule was indeed cruel and without any humanitarianism, but now Germans in order to remember this dark history that humiliated the people, will take the initiative in their learning process to educate future generations about this history and the lessons brought to them, and this sincere attitude of frankly admitting the mistakes made by predecessors is worthy of admiration.

On the last day of her visit to Berlin, Frau Koenig took the girls to KaDeWe, Berlin's most famous department store. Jianxin entered the department store and was attracted by the luxurious interior decoration and the dazzling array of goods. Frau Koenig said: "You are free to move around, the shopping time is about four hours, and then we will meet in the lobby. I hope you have fun." After that, the girls went to the street in twos and threes, leaving only Jianxin alone, no friends shopping together. Frau Koenig asked with concern, "Jianxin, are you okay shopping alone?" Maybe I'll ask one of the girls in the group to show you around." Jianxin replied, "It's okay, I can do it, Frau Koenig." Hearing Jianxin's crisp answer, Frau Koenig politely said: "bis spater, viel spass (see you later, have fun)." Later, Frau Koenig also started shopping alone. Jianxin didn'tfeel so lonely, may be slowly adapted to it, a person also has a person's wonderful, although she has no one to speak, can not share the joy, but can beher free time. She does not take into account the feelings of others, this is a very free feeling. She walked slowly alone in this noble and elegant and gorgeous department store building, from the first floor to the second floor, and then to the third floor. The quality of the goods is excellent but also very expensive. She does not advocate or pursue luxury goods, because she does not have that strong vanity, and she does not have much pocket money, so she will not pay attention to such goods. But she is more interested in clothes, so when she walks down to the women's floor, she also pays attention to the style of the clothes. She was surprised to find that the style of these clothes is not very suitable for young girls, more suitable for older women, over 40 years old, she did not understand why the style of women's clothing is so old fasioned

Only later she understand that the rich class in Europe is almost all old people, and young people do not have strong economic strength, so these high-end clothes can only be affordable for older customers. No wonder many elderly people in Europe dress up so elegant and decent, many elderly men wear very decent, a straight suit, is extraordinary windbreaker, or casual sportswear. On the other hand, the old ladies of Europe wore heavy makeup, wore expensive jewelry, elegant dresses or suits, and matching jewelry, and they seemed to live with dignity and confidence. This reminds her of the situation in her hometown. In her impression, in the small place where she was born, most of the people who live in poverty and have no economic strength are elderly people. Many elderly people will do hard work in order to have some pension money, such as sweeping the road or doing some handmade goods to improve their lives. Because of the lack of economic foundation, the elderly people in their hometown live a frugal life, which is simply not comparable to these German old people. Jianxin secretly thought in her heart, "I hope I can grow old gracefully in the future." She shopped around, I didn't buy anything, the price of goods is too high, she can't afford to buy, or she is not willing to spend money. Finally, she reached the basement floor and was immediately attracted by the variety of food in front of her. All kinds of handmade chocolates (praline) were placed in glass cabinets, delicate and small, and people wanted to taste them all at once, but she looked at the price list. Each such small chocolate cost 2 to 3 euros (at that time, the euro and the yuan were 1 to 9), and she could not bear to buy such an expensive chocolate. Every time she bought something, it is automatically converted into RMB. In 2002, the price of goods in China was still very low, so the price of goods in Europe is particularly high. When she thought of her parents in China scrimping and saving and working hard every day, she would not be willing to spend her pocket money in a disorderly way, otherwise she would have a sense of guilt and feel that she should not be at all considerate of her parents' difficulties. From childhood, her parents taught her that "before spending money, think about whether it is necessary, If it is not necessary, don't buy it." It's not easy to make money and you can't spend it without control." The concept of consumption that her parents taught her has been deeply rooted in her heart, and she is embarrassed to waste her parents' money, so even though she wants to try these exquisite and delicious handmade chocolates, she still refuses the desire not to buy them, but just carefully appreciates these mini chocolates like artworks through the glass cabinet.

  Although she did not personally try, but can enjoy these exquisite chocolate in reality, Jianxin feels that it is a very beautiful sometimes do not need to get but quietly observe the beauty of food, is also a kind of genjoyment. There are thousands of good things, how can people own all of them, her mother often said. she remembers when she was a child, Jianxin's mother would occasionally take her and her brother Jianyang to the city shopping, that material poverty era, for people living in a small village, going to the city is just like Grandma Liu into the Grand View Garden, everything is so new and interesting, mother can wander around in the mall for a few hours. Although she chose the clothes from one shop to another, but not willing to buy, because she just want to pick out the most satisfactory dress, maybe the budget is limited, or maybe the mother is usually thrifty, not willing to spend so much money to buy expensive clothes, hesitate to make a decision. it took about 3 to 4 hours for her to choose a dress. In the process of her mother shopping to choose clothes, Jianxin and her brother would become bored and impatient, always mutting "Mom hasn't picked out the clothes yet, it has been hours." As a child, of course, the idea is different from adults, their idea is simple is it necessary to spend so much time to choose? But the mother has her own truth, which depends on her consistent rigorous and economical work style and way of thinking. All in all, Jianxin's parents are industrious and thrifty. It is not easy for them to make money, so they will cherish the money they earn with a lot of effort. This is not stingy but a very smart approach. Therefore, in the small place where Jianxin lived from childhood, her family was the first to become rich, relying not only on her father's smart and flexible business mind, as well as the spirit of daring to take risks and try, but also on their husband and wife's diligence and thrift. As the saying goes: no matter how much money you make, if you do not know how to restrain your endless material desires, you will eventually not be able to save money. And many rich people are not all rich at the beginning, relying on their own efforts, diligence, frugality and seize the fleeting and once-in-a-lifetime opportunity in the case of the right time, geographical location and people and everything, to save the first bucket of gold, and then like a snowball, rolling bigger and bigger. Therefore, the reason why every family in China had similar economic conditions in the 1980s and 1990s, but some families became rich in the late 1990s is that domestic policy changes, reform and opening up made economic construction more and more active, and so a very small part of the people seized the opportunity of market economy development. Coupled with a flexible mind and excellent business thinking, so it caught up with many ordinary people in front of the development. Jianxin remember when she was still at home, she occasionally heard her father say, "Fortunately, we caught up with the bus of reform and opening up and seized the opportunity, otherwise how could there be such a development now, so it is very important to seize rare opportunities in one's life, but most people cannot grasp it, which requires greatinsight and courage to think, dare to do, coupled with efforts and diligence." Jianxin's parents' words and deeds also affected her, so she is motivated, she is not willing to muddle along. She clearly knows that if she wants to be excellent, she needs to have a self-motivated, but also need to be practical, hard work and strong perseverance. In any case, only by paying more effort than others, it is possible to besuccessful and it is possible to achieve the goals they set. Laziness and doubt can not help, and will only weaken people's willpower and motivation to struggle. Jianxin is such a girl, no matter what kind of environment, she always maintains a heart of progress, unwilling to lag behind the heart, but also always adhere to their own way of thinking and value system.

Although she did not buy chocolate, but she did not lose a little in her heart, she knew how to comfort herself, " I have already tried so many food in my school, I won't lose anything if I don't try these chocolates here. " These chocolates are really expensive, there is no need to spend this money." She continued to wander around the food floor, where there was really everything to enjoy, hundreds of cheeses alone, elegantly and aesthetically placed on the shopping shelves, as well as a wide variety of cakes, breads, fish, pasta semi-finished products, yogurt, and so on. All the fine food under the world seems to have been listed in this food center, Jianxin enjoyed shopping in KadeWe, although there is no big bag to buy a lot, but she hasbeen very satisfied. Later, she felt hungry and bought an affordable bread and sausage, paid at the register, found a comfortable resting place at the KaDeWe department store and ate it with gusto. While eating, she observed the pedestrians coming and going, with a serene and peaceful expression on her face, without the feeling of frowning, the pace is slow and calm, she thought to herself, "These pedestrians have different life stories, from all directions, and disappear in front of my eyes for a moment, just for a moment." Only a small number of people in a person's life really have emotional links, which is the real fate. What kind of people will I meet in the future......" She felt that her idea was a little silly and a little crazy, but at 16 years old, she liked to weave beautiful and romantic dreams. Although different from reality, but the dream needs to have, whether realized or not realized, if people are not willing to dream, life will be less interesting and boring. She could not help thinking, "Will I meet a boy here whom you admire?" This is the romantic and surreal feelings of her age, which do not need to be confirmed in real life, but can remain in her imaginary world.

After about four more hours, Janxin returned to KaDeWe's hall, Frau Koenig's designated meeting point. A few students were already waiting in the hall, some were empty-handed and didn't buy anything, and some had bought something. In addition to eating something in this high-end department store, Jianxin did not purchase anything, but she felt satisfied and happy, and she gained a good and unforgettable experience, and also gained a broad horizon. When everyone arrived, Frau Koenig kindly and humbly said, "Our shopping trip is over, have you all enjoyed yourselves? did you find anything you like?" This is the last day of our trip to Berlin, and tomorrow we will take the train back to school. The trip to Berlin was a success, and if everyone is happy, we can organize similar events in the future." The students answered in unison, "We are satisfied, Frau Koenig, we had a good time." Thank you." This short and unforgettable trip came to an end, although Jianxin felt a little lonely in the journey, because no friends, no other girls in the group and her company, enthusiasm to take her to visit Berlin, she will often feel that they are intentionally or unintentionally isolated. However, she is still very grateful that she has such a rare opportunity to participate in such a meaningful activity, which allows her to deeply understand this world city and increase her knowledge. She is also very grateful to Frau Koenig for her reasonable organization and arrangement of activities. The teacher's affability and approachability make Jianxin feel no tension and discomfort. Jianxin silently thought: "I thank everyone I meet in my life, so that my life can increase the width and breadth, and I also thank my parents for their cultivation, I can experience and understand different cultures and value systems and grow up in different cultural backgrounds, get more diversified perspectives, and experience the colorful world." Thank you for everything today, no matter what the future road will be , I will work hard to go well, and I will believe in myself, I will be able to."

Chapter 18: Dialogue with the Alps

After the Berlin trip, Jianxin led a quiet and regular life as usual. Every day except weekends, she attends classes with her German teacher Herr May, who interacts with her more and more frequently. Because after half a year of immersion in German learning, Jianxin has been able to fluently carry out daily German communication. During this half-year period, she never spoke a word of Chinese except for the understanding and dialogue with Huang Xiaoda when she first arrived at the school, and the weekly telephone communication with her parents. This unique language environment allowed her to enter the state of learning German at the fastest speed, and forced her to use this language. It can be imagined that although only in a short time of half a year, her progress in German is obvious. Herr May is an open-minded teacher. Every time Jianxin makes progress in her study, he praises her Chinese student ungrudgingly, and always encourages her to use German more and ask the teachers or students around her if she doesn't understand it. Jianxin is an obedient student, she will sincerely adopt the teacher's advice and put it into practice. From the beginning when she was afraid to speak, she has made extraordinary efforts, diligence and persistence. Every day, she reviews German in her spare time, reads more than 600 pages of original German novels, encounters as many German words as stars, takes pains to consult the dictionary, and even though she does not understand the conversation content of people around her. Or will she keep her ears open and consciously listen carefully. Although the teaching style of this school is not very strict, cultivating students' comprehensive quality and self-discipline spirit, and will not exert strong external pressure on students, she has always maintained good learning habits, and has not been completely wild by various activities in the school. Her heart is like a mirror, she knows what she wants, what she needs to achieve, even if there are many temptations outside will not interfere with her heart to learn. Every day, she took the initiative to study at night. After dinner, she would spend her precious time in learning German every night, almost every day until 12:00 in the morning. The girls in the group playing or watching TV didn't really bother her, because she knew she needed to work extra hard to learn the language so she could enter 11th grade after the summer break. She has lagged behind the students here at the beginning, German is completely from scratch, she can not be lazy, to pay a lot of time and energy to catch up on German, the future learning road will be smooth. Language is the basic , if the German language is not passed, it is not able to learn other subjects, there is no Abitur (college entrance examination, equivalent to the domestic college entrance examination) a few years later. No matter how beautiful the external environment is and how rich the activities are, Jianxin's focus is still to learn German well and successfully enter the 11th grade. Of course, the most important goal is to pass Abitur. At present, she can't predict how she will graduate, because she feels that the goal is so far away. Every time she thinks of Abitur, she always has a little faint worry and unease in her heart, and she is worried about whether she can really successfully enter the German university. Her german knowledge is too weak, mainly the language problem, she often has different voices in the heart of the fight, a voice is optimistic and upward, will encourage her over and over again, "Jianxin, you have to believe in yourself, must be able to, step by step down to earth, always reach the end." The other voice will be somewhat pessimistic and negative with doubt and hesitation, and it will always ask Jianxin, "Can you do it in the end, is it really in a few years, can I successfully pass Abitur?" Is it really possible that German is so difficult to learn that you have to learn it as well as your native language? How hard is it to learn all kinds of subjects in German, such as history, geography, mathematics, chemistry, physics, German, all in German. Can you really do it?" These two different thoughts will often swing back and forth in Jianxin's mind, sometimes the optimistic thoughts will defeat the pessimistic thoughts, and sometimes the negative thoughts will take the upper hand. If Jianxin is not in a good state, feeling particularly lonely and helpless and confused, she misses her parents and friends very much, and she can only comfort and encourage herself over and over again. Jianxin sometimes feels that her strength is very small, and even she will doubt where she has gone before with a strong heart, why she always doubts herself, why she can't be so resolute in her belief and believe in her own ability and strength. Every time she felt helpless and lacking in energy, she would often look up to see the calligraphy and painting "a journey of a thousand miles begins with a single step" given to her by her father in her bedroom room, and then get rid of all distractions and doubts, calm down, sit in front of the desk, and let herself focus on her studies, and sometimes even reach a flow state.

One of her favorite places to go when she was feeling down was the school's South Garden. Out of this palace-like school hall, you can walk for 3 minutes to enter this beautiful and grassy garden, which is decorated with various shrubs and flowers, and the charming and beautiful sound of water flowing in the Baroque stone fountain, which is so quiet and beautiful. Standing in the open part of the garden, you can see the whole picture of the town below the mountain, and the small bungalows hidden in the dense and verdant trees appear to be so harmonious and beautiful. In the distance is the mountains, continuous Europe's famous Alps, she often said to the Alps, "Dear Alps, I am so lucky to meet you, when I am not strong enough, I will talk to you." I know that you will bless me and support me, no matter what happens in the future. And I will also work hard, optimistic confident and independent, there are all kinds of problems in the world, but there will be solutions. What I need to do every day is to work hard and be diligent, persist and believe in myself, instead of doubting my ability and imagining all kinds of bad results. Now that I have chosen this path, I will continue it bravely and without hesitation."

The Alps are so lofty and magnificent, Jianxin stood in the south garden looking at the distant mountains, gained inner peace, gained a magical and powerful spiritual power, and this power will help her to break through the thorns and go forward.

www.ingramcontent.com/pod-product-compliance
Lightning Source LLC
Chambersburg PA
CBHW080322080526
44585CB00021B/2438